C0-AWT-131

GROWTH, INDUSTRIAL ORGANIZATION AND ECONOMIC GENERALITIES

Growth, Industrial Organization and Economic Generalities

William J. Baumol

Professor of Economics at New York University, and Senior Research Economist and Professor Emeritus at Princeton University, USA

Edward Elgar

Cheltenham, UK • Northampton, MA, USA

Published by
Edward Elgar Publishing Limited
Glensanda House
Montpellier Parade
Cheltenham
Glos GL50 1UA
UK

Edward Elgar Publishing, Inc.
136 West Street
Suite 202
Northampton
Massachusetts 01060
USA

Printed and bound in Great Britain by
Antony Rowe Ltd, Chippenham, Wiltshire

A catalogue record for this book
is available from the British Library

ISBN 1 84376 350 8

Contents

PART III GENERALITIES ON THE ECONOMIC LITERATURE

Acknowledgements

The publishers wish to thank the following who have kindly given permission for the use of copyright material.

American Economic Association for article: 'Productivity Growth, Convergence, and Welfare: What the Long-Run Data Show', *American Economic Review*, **76** (5), December 1986, 1072–85; 'Unbalanced Growth Revisited: Asymptotic Stagnancy and New Evidence', with Sue Anne Batey Blackman and Edward N. Wolff, *American Economic Review*, **75** (4), September 1985, 806–17; 'Contestable Markets: An Uprising in the Theory of Industry Structure', *American Economic Review*, **72** (1), March 1982, 1–15; 'Communication. The Optimal Cash Balance Proposition: Maurice Allais' Priority', with James Tobin, *Journal of Economic Literature*, **XXVII**, September 1989, 1160–62.

American Philosophical Society for article: 'Social Wants and Dismal Science: The Curious Case of the Climbing Costs of Health and Teaching', *Proceedings of the American Philosophical Society*, **137** (4), 1993, 612–37; 'A Millennium of Economics in Twenty Minutes: In Pursuit of Useful Knowledge', in *Useful Knowledge*, Alexander G. Bearn (ed.), **234**, Philadelphia, Pennsylvania: American Philosophical Society, 1999, 161–70.

Blackwell Publishing Ltd for article: 'On the Possibility of Continuing Expansion of Finite Resources', *Kyklos*, **39** (2), 1986, 167–79; 'Inefficient and Locally Stable Trade Equilibria Under Scale Economies: Comparative Advantage Revisited', with Ralph E. Gomory, *Kyklos*, **49** (4), 1996, 509–40.

Eastern Economic Association for article: 'On the Perils of Privatization', *Eastern Economic Journal*, **19** (4), Fall 1993, 419–40.

International Atlantic Economic Society for article: 'Towards Microeconomics of Innovation: Growth Engine Hallmark of Market Economics', *Atlantic Economic Journal*, **30** (1), March 2002, 1–12.

MIT Press Journals for article: 'What Marshall *Didn't* Know: On the Twentieth Century's Contributions to Economics', *Quarterly Journal of Economics*, **CXV** (1), February 2000, 1–44.

University of Chicago Press for article: 'Entrepreneurship: Productive, Unproductive, and Destructive', *Journal of Political Economy*, **98** (5), October 1990, 893–921; 'Use of Antitrust to Subvert Competition', with Janusz A. Ordover, *Journal of Law and Economics*, **XXVIII** (2), May 1985, 247–65; 'Predation and the Logic of the Average Variable Cost Test', *Journal of Law and Economics*, **XXXIX** (1), April 1996, 49–72.

Yale Law School for article: 'Having Your Cake: How to Preserve Universal-Service Cross Subsidies While Facilitating Competitive Entry', *Yale Journal on Regulation*, **16** (1), Winter 1999, 1–17.

Every effort has been made to trace all the copyright holders but if any have been inadvertently overlooked the publishers will be pleased to make the necessary arrangements at the first opportunity.

Preface

Many years ago I attended a lecture in London by the venerable A.C. Pigou. 'Like an ancient squid,' he began (as I remember it), 'I find myself compelled to continue ejecting streams of ink.' This book is testimony to the fact that in this he was not alone.

Nothing in the remainder of this volume is meant to entail any matters personal, but recent experience has suggested that some exceptional and isolated material of this sort is not entirely unwelcome to the reader. Accordingly, this preface, which the publisher has invited me to prepare, is deliberately and primarily subjective.

An attribute of this assembled group of articles that seems likely to strike the reader at once is their heterogeneity. Indeed, had it not been for the wise admonition of my editor, Luke Adams, this compendium would probably be even more chaotic, with little, if any, discernable relation among the included items. As it is, I have managed only with some difficulty to find enough that I have written on any one topic in the last 16 years,[1] and consider sufficiently valuable, to reduce the table of contents to three disparate areas. This is no accident but is, rather, the hallmark of my research: its enthusiastic but relatively short-lived ventures into one arena after another, in each case well aware that I was no master of the pertinent literature, and that my knowledge of the relevant facts, analytic tools and previous discoveries was at best fragmentary. In those instances when I was able to seduce a better-informed partner to join my enterprise, this was not a serious handicap. But where I went at it alone, it clearly was a weakness that I could only attempt to transform, somehow, into a virtue.

The hoped-for virtue is akin to that of the little boy and the emperor's new clothes. Not that the writings in the fields I invaded were without substance – I do not mean to imply that the emperors were naked. But my ignorance did seem to have the benefit of relieving me of some older baggage, giving the advantage of innocence for my travels through the unfamiliar area. I flatter myself that this sometimes permitted me to make some obvious but significant observations that the much more competent and knowledgeable researchers in the field had overlooked, enmeshed as they were in detail and the commendable search for rigor.

I will not comment on the contents of the book, item by item. Several of the pieces, as I will note, have achieved some degree of notoriety and, like any author, I am grateful for the attention. But there are those that I feel have suffered undeserved neglect or misunderstanding, and I will begin with a few words on them.

In my view, the one arena of work in which I have participated in which my professional colleagues have most severely short-changed themselves is the series of writings on international trade by Ralph Gomory, with myself as contributing assistant.[2] With this work, Gomory – mathematician, inventor of integer programming, successful business person and much more – has contributed a breakthrough complete with powerful new analytic tools, illuminating theoretical results and significant policy implications. His model entails trade between two (or more) countries in n commodities, with the traded items subject to differential productivity growth or, alternatively, to scale economies. While it has long been known that scale economies lead to multiple equilibria, the new analysis shows that the equilibria rapidly grow astronomical in number with rising n, increasing in the two-country case as 2^n. Further, the analysis shows that these equilibria fall into an orderly pattern, one of considerable analytic interest in itself. That pattern also tells us, for example, under what circumstances one of a pair of trading partners benefits from increased prosperity of the other partner, and when it does not, surely no unimportant matter.

The work by my colleagues and myself on the theory of contestable markets is quite another matter. Hardly neglected, our work has been widely misinterpreted (*mea culpa*) to its undeserved discredit. It has repeatedly been asserted that our work claims that most markets are, if not perfectly contestable, then very nearly so. But I defy anyone to find such a contention in any of our published works. On the contrary, I am convinced by experience that many if not most markets are *not* contestable. I am also convinced that where a market is claimed to be obviously contestable, most often by an overzealous defense lawyer in the course of some antitrust litigation, that assertion should be discounted in the absence of careful and adequate evidence. What I do believe is that the theory of contestable markets has provided a number of very different insights, about the economics of multi-product firms and about the economic determinants of industry structure. As a purely theoretical concept, *perfect* contestability has also provided far more usable guidance to regulators and antitrust authorities than the concept of perfect competition, which precludes both the large firms and the scale economies so important in the arena. What can a court do with the guidance of the older competitive concept that is pertinent to defendants and plaintiffs who both appear to benefit from scale economies and who could not conceivably operate, much less survive, as atomistic firms of negligible size?

Among the articles that have been well-received and have proven influential, I will mention only 'Productivity Growth, Convergence and Welfare' and 'Social Wants and Dismal Science: The Curious Case of the Climbing Costs of Health Care and Teaching'. The first seems to have induced the birth of an extensive literature. I was, of course, far from the first to enunciate the convergence hypothesis. But I do seem to have begun systematic empirical work on the subject, drawing attention to the data sources and the testing criteria that, in modified and superior form, continue to be used today. The second article (which was first delivered as a talk before that marvelous institution, the American Philosophical Society) quickly migrated, as it were, from Philadelphia to Washington and embroiled me in the battles over President Clinton's health care program, working along with my friend, Daniel Patrick Moynihan. That article's 'cost-disease' story – which posits that relatively lagging productivity growth (in the sense of difficulty of labor-saving improvement) condemns health care, education and the live performing arts to ever-rising costs, relative to the overall inflation rate – continues to surface in political and academic discussions in various parts of the globe. Yet politicians and the public continue to search for villains – greed, waste or inefficiency – as the witches that must be burnt at the stake to bring these burgeoning costs under control. More important, perhaps, is the failure to recognize that this 'problem' is, in an important sense, illusory. With productivity rising in almost every sector of the economy, it is patent nonsense to say that the economy cannot afford ever-better health care and education. It is only a kind of fiscal illusion that leads to underfinancing of these socially critical activities, to the severe detriment of the public welfare.

This compendium reproduces an article that can serve as an introduction to my latest book.[3] The article, 'Toward Microeconomics of Innovation: Growth Engine Hallmark of Market Economies', speaks for itself, and I will comment only that I still do not comprehend why, with all the superb research and analysis that has gone into the large literature on economic growth, so little has been written about what seems to me to be the most striking and significant attribute of our type of economy: its totally unparalleled achievement in terms of growth of per-capita income and its outpouring of rapidly applied invention. With all its shortcomings and its market failures, the capitalist economy has achieved this one thing that was undreamt of previously and has made it the envy of the world. It has carried out a growth revolution whose magnitude makes it virtually impossible to describe adequately. Why, then, is the economic literature so silent on the subject?

A final note. Jacob Viner used to remind me that whenever some historian of economic thought discovered an earlier and previously unknown source of an economic idea, it was only a matter of time before some still-earlier predecessor would be discovered. Jim Tobin and I were for many years given shared credit for our inventory-theoretic model of the demand for cash, until he, with his clear discernment, discovered that Maurice Allais had beaten us out by a considerable margin. It became our pleasure to translate the Allais discussion and to arrange for its publication. I reprint it here and dedicate it to Jim's memory.

Will Baumol
Monmouth Beach, New Jersey
November 2002

Notes

1. Compendia of earlier articles appeared in 1976 and 1986 (see Elizabeth E. Bailey (ed.), *Selected Economic Writings of William J. Baumol*, New York: New York University Press, 1976; and William J. Baumol, *Microtheory: Applications and Origins*, Cambridge, Massachusetts: MIT Press, and Brighton, United Kingdom: Wheatsheaf Press, 1986). A more recent book contains my articles on the cost disease (see Ruth Towse, (ed.), *Baumol's Cost Disease: The Arts and Other Victims*, Cheltenham, United Kingdom and Northampton, Massachusetts: Edward Elgar, 1997).
2. The item included here is the one exception, in which I took the lead. It should be noted that Gomory generously and emphatically protests when I describe my role in the work as that of junior partner, but the truth of the matter gives me no choice.
3. *The Free-Market Innovation Machine: Analyzing the Growth Miracle of Capitalism*, Princeton, New Jersey: Princeton University Press, 2002.

PART I

ON PRODUCTIVITY, GROWTH, THE COST DISEASE AND SCALE ECONOMIES

[1]

Productivity Growth, Convergence, and Welfare: What the Long-Run Data Show

By WILLIAM J. BAUMOL*

Maddison's 1870–1979 data are analyzed, showing the historically unprecedented growth in productivity, gross domestic product per capita and exports and the remarkable convergence of productivities of industrialized market economies, with convergence apparently shared by planned economies but not less developed countries. Productivity lag's relation to "deindustrialization," unemployment, and balance of payments is examined. The data are shown to suggest a tempered view of the slowdown in U.S. productivity growth and its lag behind other countries.

No matter how refined and how elaborate the analysis, if it rests solely on the short view it will still be... a structure built on shifting sands.
Jacob Viner [1958, pp. 112–13]

Recent years have witnessed a reemergence of interest on the part of economists and the general public in issues relating to long-run economic growth. There has been a recurrence of doubts and fears for the future —aroused in this case by the protracted slowdown in productivity growth since the late 1960's, the seeming erosion of the competitiveness of U.S. industries in world markets, and the spectre of "deindustrialization" and massive structural unemployment. These anxieties have succeeded in redirecting attention to long-run supply-side phenomena that formerly were a central preoccupation of economists in the industrializing West, before being pushed aside in the crisis of the Great Depression and the ensuing triumph of Keynesian ideas.

Anxiety may compel attention, but it is not necessarily an aid to clear thinking. For all the interest now expressed in the subject of long-run economic growth and policies ostensibly directed to its stimulation, it does not seem to be widely recognized that adequate economic analysis of such issues calls for the careful study of economic history—if only because it is there that the pertinent evidence is to be found. Economic historians have provided the necessary materials, in the form of brilliant insights, powerful analysis, as well as a surprising profusion of long-period data. Yet none of these has received the full measure of attention they deserve from members of the economics profession at large.

To dramatize the sort of reorientation long-term information can suggest, imagine a convincing prediction that over the next century, U.S. productivity growth will permit a trebling of per capita GNP while cutting nearly by half the number of hours in the average work year, and that this will be accompanied by a sevenfold increase in exports. One might well consider this a very rosy forecast. But none of these figures is fictitious. For these developments in fact lay before the United Kingdom in 1870, just as its economic leadership began to erode.

* Princeton University, Princeton, NJ 08544, and New York University. I express my deep gratitude to the Division of Information Science and Technology of the National Science Foundation, the Exxon Education Foundation, the Joint Council on Economic Education, the Fishman–Davidson Center for the Study of the Service Sector, and the C. V. Starr Center for Applied Economics for their generous support of the research underlying this paper. I am also heavily indebted to Edward Wolff, Wayne Farel, Robert Dorfman, Sidney Ratner, and Mariza Stipec for help in various parts of the work. Valuable suggestions from several anonymous reviewers helped to limit the errors of this amateur economic historian. I also learned a great deal from the excellent Abramovitz paper (1985) on the subject. Above all, I owe an enormous debt to Paul David for his encouragement, and for perceptive and helpful comments which guided the final revision of this paper. Entire paragraphs come from his pen.

This paper outlines some implications of the available long-period data on productivity and related variables—some tentative, some previously noted by economic historians, and some throwing a somewhat surprising light on developments among industrialized nations since World War II. Among the main observations that will emerge here is the remarkable convergence of output per labor hour among industrialized nations. Almost all of the leading free enterprise economies have moved closer to the leader, and there is a strong inverse correlation between a country's productivity standing in 1870 and its average rate of productivity growth since then. Postwar data suggest that the convergence phenomenon also extends to both "intermediate" and centrally planned economies. Only the poorer less developed countries show no such trend.

It will also emerge that over the century, the U.S. productivity growth rate has been surprisingly steady, and despite frequently expressed fears, there is no sign recently of any *long-term* slowdown in growth of either total factor productivity or labor productivity in the United States. And while, except in wartime, *for the better part of a century*, U.S. productivity growth rates have been low relative to those of Germany, Japan, and a number of other countries, this may be no more than a manifestation of the convergence phenomenon, which requires countries that were previously behind to grow more rapidly. Thus, the paper will seek to dispel these and a number of other misapprehensions apparently widespread among those who have not studied economic history.

Nonspecialists may well be surprised at the remarkably long periods spanned in time-series contributed by Beveridge, Deane, Kuznets, Gallman, Kendrick, Abramovitz, David, and others. The Phelps Brown-Hopkins indices of prices and real wages extend over seven centuries. Maddison, Feinstein (and his colleagues), and Kendrick cover productivity, investment, and a number of other crucial variables for more than 100 years. Obviously, the magnitudes of the earlier figures are more than a little questionable, as their compilers never cease to warn us. Yet the general qualitative character of the time paths are persuasive, given the broad consistency of the statistics, their apparent internal logic and the care exercised in collecting them. In this paper, the period used will vary with topic and data availability. In most cases, something near a century will be examined, using primarily data provided by Angus Maddison (1982) and R. C. O. Matthews, C. H. Feinstein, and J. C. Odling-Smee (1982—henceforth, M-F-O).[1]

I. The Magnitude of the Accomplishment

The magnitude of the productivity achievement of the past 150 years resists intuitive grasp, and contrasts sharply with the preceding centuries. As the *Communist Manifesto* put the matter in 1848, with remarkable foresight, "The bourgeoisie, during its rule of scarce one hundred years, has created more massive and more colossal productive forces than have all preceding generations together." There obviously are no reliable measures of productivity in antiquity, but available descriptions of living standards in Ancient Rome suggest that they were in many respects higher than in eighteenth-century England (see Colin Clark, 1957, p. 677). This is probably true even for the lower classes—certainly for the free urban proletariat, and perhaps even with the inclusion of slaves. An upper-class household was served by sophisticated devices for heating and bathing not found in eighteenth-century homes of the rich. A wealthy Roman magically transported into an eighteenth-century English home would probably have been puzzled by the technology of only a few products—clocks, window panes, printed books and newspapers, and the musket over the fireplace.

[1] The Maddison absolute productivity figures will be used in preference to the M-F-O data, since the former include more years and more countries. However, the M-F-O series has one advantage. They report productivity statistics only for years which can be considered to contain peaks of business cycles, so that the calculations are not distorted by the well-known effects of the business cycle on labor productivity. Yet over the long period in question here, no remarkable differences in patterns seem to emerge from the two sets of figures.

It is true that even during the Middle Ages (see, for example, Carlo Cipolla, 1976), there was substantial technological change in the workplace and elsewhere. Ship design improved greatly. Lenses and, with them, the telescope and microscope appeared in the sixteenth century, and the eighteenth century brought the ship's chronometer which revolutionalized water transport by permitting calculation of longitude. Yet, none of this led to rates of productivity growth anywhere near those of the nineteenth and twentieth centuries.

Nonhistorians do not usually recognize that initially the Industrial Revolution was a fairly minor affair for the economy as a whole. At first, much of the new equipment was confined to textile production (though some progress in fields such as iron making had also occurred). And, as David Landes (1969) indicates,[2] an entrepreneur could undertake the new types of textile operations with little capital, perhaps only a few hundred pounds, which (using the Phelps Brown-Hopkins data) translates into some 100,000 1980 dollars. Jeffrey Williamson (1983) tells us that in England during the first half-century of the Industrial Revolution, real per capita income grew only about 0.3 percent per annum,[3] in contrast with the nearly 3 percent achieved in the Third World in the 1970's (despite the decade's economic crises).

TABLE 1—TOTAL GROWTH FROM 1870 TO 1979[a] PRODUCTIVITY, *GDP* PER CAPITA, AND EXPORTS SIXTEEN INDUSTRIALIZED COUNTRIES[b]

	Real *GDP* per Work-Hour	Real *GDP* per Capita	Volume of Exports
Australia	398	221	–
United Kingdom	585	310	930
Switzerland	830	471	4,400
Belgium	887	439	6,250
Netherlands	910	429	8,040
Canada	1,050	766	9,860
United States	1,080	693	9,240
Denmark	1,098	684	6,750
Italy	1,225	503	6,210
Austria	1,270	643	4,740
Germany	1,510	824	3,730
Norway	1,560	873	7,740
France	1,590	694	4,140
Finland	1,710	1,016	6,240
Sweden	2,060	1,083	5,070
Japan	2,480	1,661	293,060

Source: Angus Maddison (1982, pp. 8, 212, 248–53).
[a] In 1970 U.S. dollars.
[b] Shown in percent.

Table 1 shows the remarkable contrast of developments since 1870 for Maddison's 16 countries. We see (col. 1) that growth in output per work-hour ranged for the next 110 years from approximately 400 percent for Australia all the way to 2500 percent (in the case of Japan). The 1100 percent increase of labor productivity in the United States placed it somewhat below the middle of the group, and even the United Kingdom managed a 600 percent rise. Thus, after not manifesting any substantial long-period increase for at least 15 centuries, in the course of 11 decades the median increase in productivity among the 16 industrialized leaders in Maddison's sample was about 1150 percent. The rise in productivity was sufficient to permit output per capita (col. 2) to increase more than 300 percent in the United Kingdom, 800 percent in West Germany, 1700 percent in Japan, and nearly 700 percent in France and the United States. Using Robert Summers and Alan Heston's sophisticated international comparison data (1984), this implies that in 1870, U.S. output per capita was comparable to 1980 output per capita in Honduras and the Philippines, and slightly below that of China, Bolivia, and Egypt!

[2] "The early machines, complicated though they were to contemporaries, were nevertheless modest, rudimentary, wooden contrivances which could be built for surprisingly small sums. A forty-spindle jenny cost perhaps £6 in 1772; scrubbing and carding machines cost £1 for each inch of roller width; a clubbing billy with thirty spindles cost £10.10s" (Landes, pp. 64–65). This suggests at least the possibility (pointed out by Landes) that part of the reason investment was low is that not very much capital may have been required.

[3] This observation does not quite seem to square with Charles Feinstein's estimates (1972, pp. 82–94) which indicate that while output per worker in the United Kingdom increased 0.2 percent per year between 1761 and 1800, between 1801 and 1830 the growth rate leaped up to 1.4 percent per annum. He estimates that total factor productivity behaved similarly. However, between 1801 and 1810, total annual investment fell to 10 percent of gross domestic product, in comparison with its 14 percent rate in the immediately preceding and succeeding periods.

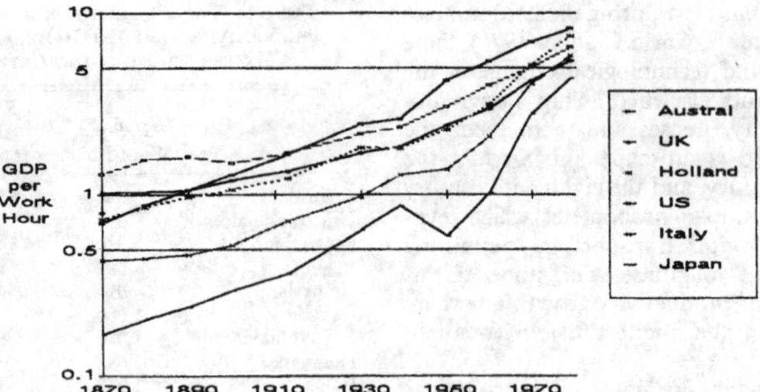

FIGURE 1. GROSS DOMESTIC PRODUCT PER WORK-HOUR, 1870–1979

Source: Maddison (p. 212)

The growth rates of other pertinent variables were also remarkable. One more example will suffice to show this. Table 1, which also shows the rise in volume of exports from 1870 to 1979 (col. 3) indicates that the median increase was over 6000 percent.

II. The Convergence of National Productivity Levels

There is a long and reasonably illustrious tradition among economic historians centered on the phenomenon of convergence. While the literature devoted to the subject is complex and multifaceted, as revealed by the recent reconsideration of these ideas by Moses Abramovitz (1985), one central theme is that forces accelerating the growth of nations who were latecomers to industrialization and economic development give rise to a long-run tendency towards convergence of levels of per capita product or, alternatively, of per worker product. Such ideas found expression in the works of Alexander Gerschenkron (see, for example, 1952), who saw his own views on the advantages of "relative backwardness" as having been anticipated in important respects by Thorstein Veblen's writings on the penalties of being the industrial leader (1915). Although such propositions also have been challenged and qualified (for example, Edward Ames and Nathan Rosenberg, 1963), it is difficult to dismiss the idea of convergence on the basis of the historical experience of the industrialized world. (For more recent discussions, see also the paper by Robin Marris, with comments by Feinstein and Matthews in Matthews, 1982, pp. 12–13, 128–147; as well as Dennis Mueller, 1983.)

Using 1870–1973 data on gross domestic product (*GDP*) per work-year for 7 industrialized countries, M-F-O have shown graphically that those nations' productivity levels have tended to approach ever closer to one another. The same phenomenon for 6 countries is illustrated in Figure 1 in a semilog representation based on Maddison's data for 1870–1979, which provide estimates of output per work-hour for 16 countries.[4]

The convergence toward the vanguard (led in the first decades by Australia—see Richard Caves and Laurence Krause, 1984—and the United Kingdom and, approximately since World War I, by the United

[4]Space prevents extensive consideration of Paul Romer's (1985) objection to the evidence offered for the convergence hypothesis provided here and elsewhere, i.e., that the sample of countries studied is an *ex post* selection of successful economies. Successes, by definition, are those which have done best relative to the leader. However, the Summers-Heston 1950–80 data for 72 countries represented in Figure 3 do permit an *ex ante* selection. Tests ranking countries both by 1950 and by 1960 *GDP* levels confirm that even an *ex ante* sample of the wealthiest countries yields a pattern of convergence which, while less pronounced than that calculated from an *ex post* group, is still unambiguous.

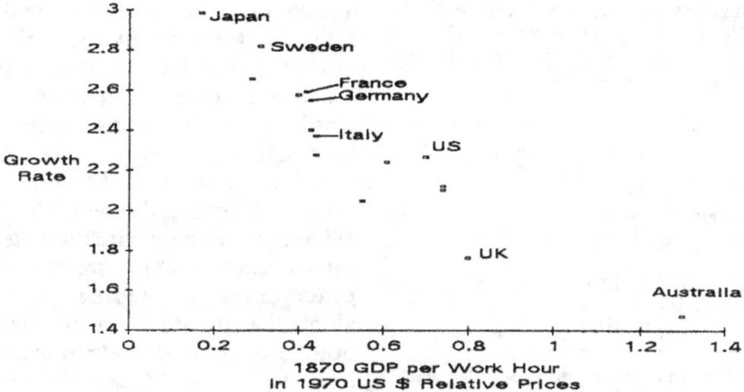

FIGURE 2. PRODUCTIVITY GROWTH RATE, 1870–1979 VS. 1870 LEVEL

Source: Maddison (p. 212)

States) is sharper than it may appear to the naked eye. In 1870, the ratio of output per work-hour in Australia, then the leader in Maddison's sample, was about eight times as great as Japan's (the laggard). By 1979, that ratio for the leader (the United States) to the laggard (still Japan) had fallen to about 2. The ratio of the standard deviation from the mean of *GDP* per work-hour for the 16 countries has also fallen quite steadily, except for a brief but sharp rise during World War II.

The convergence phenomenon and its pervasiveness is confirmed by Figure 2, on which my discussion will focus. The horizontal axis indicates each Maddison country's absolute level of *GDP* per work-hour in 1870. The vertical axis represents the growth rate of *GDP* per work-hour in the 110 years since 1870. The high inverse correlation between the two is evident. Indeed, we obtain an equation (subject to all sorts of statistical reservations)[5]

$$\textit{Growth Rate}\ (1870\text{–}1979) = 5.25 - 0.75\ln\left(\textit{GDP}\ \text{per}\ \textit{WorkHr}, 1870\right), \quad R^2 = 0.88.$$

That is, with a very high correlation coefficient, the higher a country's productivity level in 1870 the more slowly that level grew in the following century.

[5]The high correlation should not be taken too seriously. Aside from the reasons why its explanation may be misunderstood that are presently discussed in the text, the tight fit of the data points is undoubtedly ascribable in good part to several biassing features of the underlying calculation. First, the 1870 figures were calculated by Maddison using backward extrapolation of growth rates, and hence their correlation is hardly surprising. Second, since growth rate, r, is calculated by solving $y_t = e^{rt}y_0$ for r, to obtain $r = (\ln y_t - \ln y_0)/t$, where $y_t = GDP$ per capita in period t, a regression equation $r = f(y_0)$ contains the same variable, y_0 on both sides of the equation, thus tending to produce a spurious appearance of close relationship. Indeed, if the convergence process were perfect, so that we would have $y_t = k$ with k the same for every country in the sample, every dot in the diagram would necessarily perfectly fit the curve $r = lnk/t - lny_0/t$, and the r^2 would be unity, identically. As we will see, however, the 72-country data depicted in Figure 3 hardly constitute a close fit (the R^2 is virtually zero), and do not even yield a negatively sloping regression line. Thus, a relationship such as that in Figure 2 is no tautology, nor even a foregone conclusion.

In addition, if the 1870 productivity levels are measured with considerable error, this must result in some significant downward bias in the regression coefficient on $ln(GDP$ per $WorkHr$, 1870). This is a point distinct from the one concerning the size of the correlation coefficient, although the latter is affected by the fact that relatively large measurement errors in the 1870 productivity levels enter as inversely correlated measurement errors in the 1870–1979 growth rate. The argument that this bias is not sufficient to induce a negative correlation in the 72-country sample may not be wholly germane, as the relative seriousness of the measurement errors in the initial and terminal observations may be much the same for observations confined to the period 1950–80.

TABLE 2—RELATIVE GROWTH IN REAL WAGES, *GDP* PER WORK-HOUR AND CAPITAL STOCK, UNITED KINGDOM AND GERMANY, 1860–1980

	Period	Ratio: German Increase to U.K. Increase[b]
Real Wages	1860–1980	4.25
GDP per Labor Hour	1870–1979	2.35
Capital Stock[a]	1870–1979	6.26
Capital Stock per Worker	1870–1979	3.8
Capital Stock per Capita	1870–1979	5.4

Sources: Real wages, same as in fn. 6; all other data from Maddison.

[a]Net nonresidential fixed tangible capital stock.

[b](German 1979 figure/German 1870 figure)/(U.K. 1979 figure/U.K. 1870 figure) with appropriate modification of the dates for the wage figures.

III. Implications of the Inverse Correlation: Public Goods Property of Productivity Policy

The strong inverse correlation between the 1870 productivity levels of the 16 nations and their subsequent productivity growth record seems to have a startling implication. Of course, hindsight always permits "forecasts" of great accuracy—that itself is not surprising. Rather, what is striking is the apparent implication that *only one variable*, a country's 1870 *GDP* per work-hour, or its relation to that of the productivity leader, matters to any substantial degree, and that other variables have only a peripheral influence. It seems not to have mattered much whether or not a particular country had free markets, a high propensity to invest, or used policy to stimulate growth. Whatever its behavior, that nation was apparently fated to land close to its predestined position in Figure 2.

However, a plausible alternative interpretation is that while national policies and behavior patterns do substantially affect productivity growth, the spillovers from leader economies to followers are large—at least among the group of industrial nations. If country *A*'s extraordinary investment level and superior record of innovation enhances its own productivity, it will almost automatically do the same in the long run for industrialized country *B*, though perhaps to a somewhat more limited extent. In other words, for such nations a successful productivity-enhancing measure has the nature of a public good. And because the fruits of each industrialized country's productivity-enhancement efforts are ultimately shared by others, each country remains in what appears to be its predestined *relative* place along the growth curve of Figure 2. I will note later some considerations which might lead one to doubt that the less developed countries will benefit comparably from this sharing process.

This sharing of productivity growth benefits by industrialized countries involves both innovation and investment. The innovation-sharing process is straightforward. If industry in country *A* benefits from a significant innovation, those industries in other countries which produce competing products will find themselves under pressure to obtain access to the innovation, or to an imitation or to some other substitute. Industrialized countries, whose product lines overlap substantially and which sell a good deal in markets where foreign producers of similar items are also present, will find themselves constantly running in this Schumpeterian race, while those less developed countries which supply few products competing with those of the industrialized economies will not participate to the same degree.

There is reason to suspect that the pressures for rapidity in imitation of innovation in industrial countries have been growing. The explosion in exports reported in Table 1 has given them a considerably larger share of gross national product than they had in 1870. This suggests that more of each nation's output faces the direct competition of foreign rivals. Thus, the penalties for failure to keep abreast of innovations *in other countries* and to imitate them where appropriate have grown.

Second, the means required for successful imitations have improved and expanded enormously. World communications are now practically instantaneous, but required weeks and even months at the birth of the Industrial Revolution. While today meetings of scientists and technicians are widely encouraged, earlier mercantilistic practices entailed measures by each country to prevent other nations from learning its industrial techniques, and the emigration of specialized workers was often forbidden. Though figures in this arena are difficult to interpret, much less substantiate, one estimate claims that employment in "information activities" in the United States has grown from less than 1 percent of the labor force in 1830 to some 45 percent today (James Beniger, forthcoming, p. 364, leaning heavily on Marc Porat, 1977). Presumably, growth of the information sector in other industrialized nations has been similar. This must surely facilitate and speed the innovative, counterinnovative, and imitative tasks of the entrepreneur. The combination of direct U.S. manufacturing investment in Europe, and the technology transfer activities of multinational corporations in the postwar era were also of great significance (see, for example, David Teece, 1976). All of this, incidentally, suggests that as the forces making for convergence were stronger in the postwar era than previously, the rate of convergence should have been higher. The evidence assembled by Abramovitz (1985) on the basis of Maddison's data indicates that this is in fact what has happened.

The process that has just been described, then, provides mutual benefits, but it inherently helps productivity laggards more than leaders. For the laggards have more to learn from the leaders, and that is why the process makes for convergence.

Like innovation, investment, generally considered the second main source of growth in labor productivity, may also exhibit international public good properties. Suppose two industrialized countries, A and B, each produce two traded products: say automobiles and shoes, with the former more capital intensive. If A's investment rate is greater than B's then, with time, A's output mix will shift toward the cars while B's will move toward shoes. The increased demand for auto workers in A will raise their real wages, while A's increased demand for imports of B's shoes will raise real wages in B, and will raise the *value* of gross domestic product per labor hour in that country. Thus, even investment in country A automatically tends to have a spillover effect on value productivity and real wages *in those other countries that produce and trade in a similar array of goods*.

While, strictly speaking, the factor-price equalization theorem is not applicable to my discussion because it assumes, among other things, that technology is identical in all the countries involved, it does suggest why (for the reasons just discussed) a high investment rate may fail to bring a relative wage advantage to the investing country. In practice, the conditions of the theorem are not satisfied precisely, so countries in which investment rates are relatively high do seem to obtain increased relative real wages.[6] Yet the analysis suggests that the absolute benefits are contagious—that one country's successful investment policy will also raise productivity and living standards in other industrialized countries.[7]

[6] The case of Germany and Britain is a suggestive illustration. From 1870 to 1979, according to Maddison (pp. 227, 231) German net nonresidential fixed tangible capital stock grew thirtyfold while that of the United Kingdom grew only sixfold. Landes (p. 124) reports (with the appropriate warning, "*caveat lector*") that real U.K. wages in about 1860 have been estimated to be some 2.5 times those in Germany, while according to the U.S. Bureau of Labor Statistics (unpublished figures), in 1980 German real wages were 1.7 times those in the United Kingdom. Of course, I am not suggesting that correlation implies causation, or that one such case even provides a usable correlation. Still, the orders of magnitude of the figures are probably right and it is hard to believe that superior German investment rates had nothing to do with the relative lag in British wages.

[7] It must be conceded that the longer-run data do not seem to offer impressive support for the hypothesis that the forces of factor-price equalization have, albeit imperfectly, extended the benefits of exceptional rates of investment from those economies that carried out the successful investment programs to other industrialized economies. Since we have estimates of relative real wages, capital stock, and other pertinent variables for the United Kingdom and Germany, these have been compared in Table 2. If the public goods attribute hypothesis about the effects of investment in one country were valid and if factor-price equalization were an effective force, we would expect the relative rise in

Thus, effective growth policy does contribute to a nation's living standards, but it may also help other industrialized countries and to almost the same degree; meaning that relative deviations from the patterns indicated in Figure 2 will be fairly small, just as the diagram shows. (However, see Abramovitz, 1985, for a discussion of the counter-hypothesis, that growth of a leader creates "backwash" effects inhibiting growth of the followers.)

All this raises an obvious policy issue. If productivity growth does indeed have such public good properties, what will induce each country to invest the socially optimal effort and other resources in productivity growth, when it can instead hope to be a free rider? In part, the answer is that in Western capitalistic economies, investment is decentralized and individual firms can gain little by free riding on the actions of investors in other economies, so that the problem does not appear to be a serious one at the national policy level.

IV. Is Convergence Ubiquitous?

Does convergence of productivity levels extend beyond the free-market industrialized countries? Or is the convergence "club" a very exclusive organization? While century-long data are not available for any large number of countries, Summers and Heston provide pertinent figures for the 30-year period 1950–80 (data for more countries are available for briefer periods).[8] Instead of labor productivity figures, they give output per capita, whose trends can with considerable reservations be used as a rough proxy for those in productivity, as Maddison's figures confirm.

Figure 3 tells the story. Constructed just like Figure 2, it plots the 1950–80 real growth rates of *GDP* per capita for all 72 Summers-Heston countries against the initial (1950) level of this variable. The points form no tight relationship, and unlike those for the industrial countries, the dots show no negatively sloping pattern. Indeed, a regression yields a slightly positive slope. Thus, rather than sharing in convergence, some of the poorest countries have also been growing most slowly.

Figure 3 brings out the patterns more clearly by surrounding the set of points representing Maddison's 16 countries with a thin boundary and the centrally planned economy points[9] with a heavier boundary. We see that the Maddison country points lie near a sort of upper-right-hand boundary, meaning that most of them had the high incomes in 1950 (as was to be expected) and, for any given per capita income, the highest growth rates between 1950 and 1980. This region is very long, narrow, and negatively sloped, with the absolute slope declining toward the right. As in the Figure 2 productivity data for a 110-year period, this is exactly the shape one expects with convergence. Second, we see that the centrally planned economies are members of a convergence club of their own, forming a negatively sloping region lying below and to the left of the Maddison countries. The relationship is less tight, so convergence within the group is less pronounced, but it is clearly there.

German real wages and in productivity to be small (on some criterion) in comparison with the relative increase in its capital stock. However, the figures do not seem to exhibit such a pattern.

[8]There are at least two sources of such data: the World Bank and the University of Pennsylvania group. Here I report only data drawn from the latter, since their international comparisons have been carried out with unique sophistication and insight. Instead of translating the different currencies into one another using inadequate exchange rate comparisons, they use carefully constructed indices of relative purchasing power. I have also replicated my calculations using World Bank data and obtained exactly the same qualitative results.

[9]The centrally planned economies are Bulgaria, China, Czechoslovakia, East Germany, Hungary, Poland, Romania, USSR, and Yugoslavia. The 5 countries with relatively high 1950 incomes included neither in Maddison's sample nor in the planned group are, in descending order of *GDP* per capita, Luxemburg, New Zealand, Iceland, Venezuela, and Argentina. The countries with negative growth rates are Uganda and Nigeria.

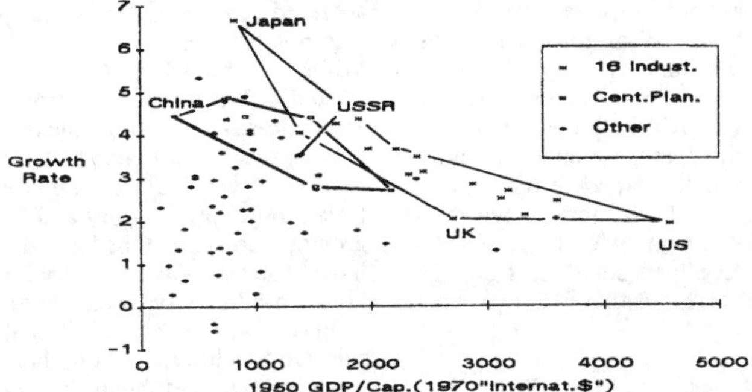

FIGURE 3. GROWTH RATE, 1950–80, GROSS DOMESTIC PRODUCT PER CAPITA VS. 1950 LEVEL, 72 COUNTRIES

Source: Summers and Heston

Finally, there is the region of remaining points (aside from the rightmost non-Maddison points in the graph) which lies close to the origin of the graph and occupies something like a distorted circle without any apparent slope. The points closest to the origin are less developed countries which were poor in 1950, and have grown relatively slowly since. They show no convergence among themselves, much less with other groups.

A few numbers suggest the difference in performance of various subgroups of the 72 countries. Using a four-set classification Summers, I. B. Kravis and Heston (1984, p. 254) provide Gini coefficients by decade from 1950 to 1980. For their set of industrialized countries, this coefficient falls precipitously from 0.302 in 1950 to 0.129 in 1980—a sharp drop in inequality. For the centrally planned economies the drop is much smaller—from 0.381 to 0.301. The middle-income group exhibits an even smaller decline, from 0.269 to 0.258. But the low-income countries underwent a small *rise* over the period, from 0.103 to 0.112, and the world as a whole experienced a tiny rise from 0.493 to 0.498.

There has also been little convergence among the groups. For the entire period, Summers et al. report (p. 245) an average annual growth rate in per capita real *GDP* of 3.1 percent for industrialized countries, 3.6 percent for centrally planned economies, 3.0 percent for middle-income market economies, and only 1.5 percent for the low-income group, with a world average growth rate of 2.7 percent.

This suggests that there is more than one convergence club. Rather, there are perhaps three, with the centrally planned and the intermediate groups somewhat inferior in performance to that of the free-market industrialized countries. It is also clear that the poorer less developed countries are still largely barred from the homogenization processes. Since any search for "the causes" of a complex economic phenomenon of reality is likely to prove fruitless, no attempt will be made here to explain systematically why poorer less developed countries have benefited to a relatively small degree from the public good properties of the innovations and investments of other nations. But part of the explanation may well be related to product mix and education. A less developed country that produces no cars cannot benefit from the invention and adoption of a better car-producing robot in Japan (though it does benefit to a lesser degree from new textile and rice-growing technology), nor can it benefit from the factor-price equalization effect of the accompanying Japanese investments, since it cannot shift labor force out of its (nonexistent) auto industry as the theorem's logic requires. Lack of education and the associated skills prevent both the presence of high-tech industries and the effective imitation (adoption) of the Japanese innovation. Obviously, there is much more to any reasonably fuller explanation of the exclusion of many less developed countries from the convergence process, but that is not my purpose here.

V. The Record of the United States

The long-run data call for a revaluation of the past productivity performance of the United States, which is rather different from what is widely believed. Figure 4 plots for 4 countries growth rates of *GDP* per work-hour derived from Maddison. It confirms, of course, that U.S. labor productivity growth has been lower than that of several other countries in recent decades. But it also indicates that this U.S. growth rate has just been middling for the better part of a century, not only in the past 15 or 20 years. This is confirmed by M-F-O (p. 31) whose data show that between 1899 and 1913, in terms of *GDP* per work year, the U.S. growth rate was already lower than that of Sweden, France, Germany, Italy, and Japan. Its growth rate was also below theirs (except for France) in 1924–37. While U.S. labor productivity grew rapidly relative to other nations during both world wars, this is attributable in good part to a slowdown in the growth of other countries. Thus, the mediocre U.S. relative performance in growth in labor productivity is an old story, not just a postwar phenomenon.

Figure 2—the graph with the inverse correlation between initial productivity level and its subsequent growth in Maddison's countries— suggests an explanation of the relatively undistinguished U.S. performance. The convergence of productivity levels in industrialized countries inevitably condemned those with high 1870 productivity levels to relatively slow growth since then. This attributes much of the modesty of the U.S. productivity growth to the high level it had achieved earlier. Indeed, U.S. performance was notably better than this view suggests. While in 1870, U.S. *GDP* per work-hour ranked fifth from the top among Maddison's 16 countries, its subsequent productivity growth was seventh, not fifth, from the bottom. And while my regression equation between initial productivity and its subsequent growth predicts that the United States should have achieved about a tenfold growth in its labor productivity since 1870, its actual achievement was some 20 percent higher than this. On this interpretation, then, rather than a manifestation of failure, the growth rate of the United States over the course of the 110 years represents a mild achievement in comparison with what might have been expected from the convergence relationship.

Next let us consider the slowdown hypothesis—the assertion that U.S. productivity has fallen sharply below its past. The U.S. figures provided by John Kendrick (see U.S. Bureau of Census, 1973), like the Maddison data, exhibit no major break in the *long-run* U.S. trend and no sign of a long-run slowdown (similar conclusions were reached by Michael Darby, 1984). In Figure 1, the time-series (semilog) representation of Maddison's figures on levels of labor productivity, the curve for the United States is remarkably close to a straight line, except for the dip in the 1930's. A graph of Kendrick's data is almost identical in pattern. In Figure 4, a century of U.S. growth rate in labor productivity clearly exhibits neither a downward long-term trend nor a marked recent dip below its historical level. The mild shortfall shown for the past few years must also be revaluated because the last year in the graph was a period of recession, which usually depresses productivity. More recent data may well wipe out much of the small fall below historical levels.

True, there has undoubtedly been a protracted fall off from the early postwar peak, and it certainly was pronounced. But it is that peak which looks like the aberration, and the decline from it may well prove to be a return to historical growth rates in labor productivity. In this connection, it is noteworthy (Figure 4) that the duration and amplitude of the great leap above historical

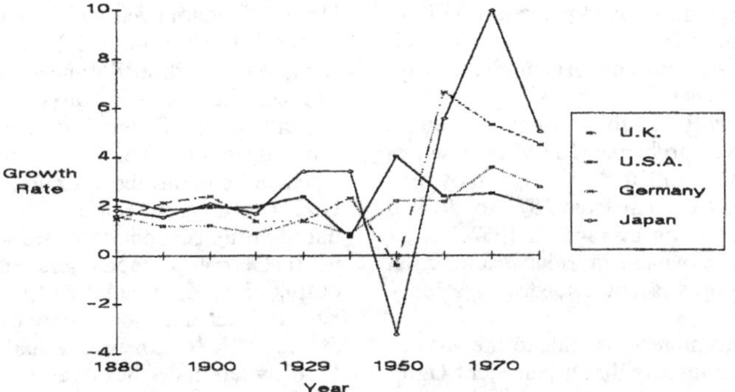

FIGURE 4. GROWTH RATES, GROSS DOMESTIC PRODUCT PER WORK-HOUR, 1870–1979

Source: Maddison (p. 212)

U.S. productivity growth in the war and early postwar years were just about as great as the previous shortfalls during the Great Depression. This encourages reinterpretation of the postwar growth period as one of temporary catch-up, merely making up for opportunities previously foregone. Perhaps the accumulated innovative ideas, unused because of the depression, as well as frustrated savings goals, fueled an outburst of innovation and investment when business conditions permitted. With time, as the backlog of ideas and investable funds was depleted, productivity growth rates declined to their normal levels. (On all this, see Abramovitz, 1979.)

VI. Productivity, Unemployment, and Deindustrialization

The long-term data also permit us to dispose of some other popular views, several of which economic theory has long ago shown to be myths. It is widely feared that rapid labor productivity growth will destroy jobs, even in the long run. Second, somewhat inconsistently, it is feared that if an economy's productivity growth lags behind that of other countries, it will lose jobs to foreign workers, its industry will suffer, and its balance of payments will face chronic deficits (these last alleged consequences are sometimes called "deindustrialization"). Economists will not be surprised that the data do not support any of these conclusions.[10]

The long-run unemployment allegation implies that the twelvefold increase in U.S. output per work-hour and the sevenfold and sixteenfold increases in the United Kingdom and Germany, respectively, must have had a devastating effect on their labor demands. Even with a 50 percent cut in annual work-hours, employment could have fallen by 5/6, relative to population, without a decline in gross domestic product per capita.

The data confirm that nothing of the sort actually occurred. M-F-O's figures for unemployment rates for the United Kingdom, the United States, and Germany from 1874 to 1973 indicate that, while unemployment rates averaged about 4 percent before World War II, they had, if anything, fallen somewhat below that level in the period 1952–73. This is so despite the substantial rise in the ratio of number of persons in the labor force to total population which, according to Maddison's figures, went up in all 3 countries from

[10] For a systematic study that rejects the deindustrialization theses for postwar United States, see Robert Lawrence (1984).

an unweighted mean of 34 percent in 1870 to 45 percent in 1979.

The same data also undermine the (nearly) opposite apprehension—that a laggard in productivity growth is subject to extraordinary unemployment problems. The M-F-O figures (p. 94) show a fall in U.K. unemployment rates from 4.7 percent from 1873 to 1913 to some 3 percent, on average, in 1952–73. Of course, unemployment rates have since risen sharply, but this is not evidence of a long-term trend.

There is no more substance to the view of many noneconomists that a persistent lag in a nation's productivity growth will place it at a competitive disadvantage in international trade, excluding it increasingly from export markets, with devastating effects upon its export industries and its balance of payments. Economic analysis denies much of this. Balance of payments will ultimately be brought into equilibrium whatever a nation's productivity performance and, since trade depends heavily on comparative rather than absolute advantage, it need have little effect on exports. Instead, the exchange rate *and the standard of living* of the country with lagging productivity will bear the brunt of the burden as it is forced, increasingly, to compete by means of relatively low wages. It is true that the United Kingdom's share of world manufacturing exports has fallen sharply from 43 percent of the world's total in 1880 all the way down to 9 percent of the total in 1973 (M-F-O, p. 425). But Britain's net exports of goods and services (the balance of visible trade) has moved fairly steadily in its favor since the 1870's (M-F-O, p. 443).

In addition, the absolute volume of U.K. exports rose spectacularly. As Table 1 reports, between 1870 and 1979 British exports increased about tenfold, and from 1855 to 1973 U.K. exports of *goods* increased 13 times (M-F-O, p. 427).

Nor has the United Kingdom been forced to deindustrialize internally. Maddison's figures (p. 205) on the share of the labor force in industry do show that Britain declined from first place among his 16 countries in 1870 to fourth place (behind Germany, Austria, and Switzerland) in 1979. But industry's share of employment in the United Kingdom was still 88 percent of that of the leader's (Germany), and the United Kingdom continued ahead of Sweden, France, the United States, Belgium, and Japan.[11] If this is deindustrialization, it certainly is not extreme.

There remains the question whether the U.K.'s decreased share of world exports damaged its economic welfare severely. That is, if Germany, Japan and Italy had not outpaced U.K. productivity growth and so had not increased their share of world trade at the U.K.'s expense, would an average Englishman have been far better off? The easy conclusion that he would is disputed by D. N. McCloskey (at least for the period 1870–1913) in a thoughtful paper (1981, pp. 173–83). First, whatever portion of Britain's output was not exported as a result must have added to domestic consumption or investment. The *net* loss on this score (the net producer's surplus on the exports) may have been negligible. In addition, growing productivity in Japan, Germany and elsewhere enables a British subject to import cameras, TV sets, and many other items far more cheaply than if the productivity of other countries had stagnated. There must also have been an upward shift in the demand curves for British goods by those countries because of their rising incomes. McCloskey concludes that reports of the detrimental effect on the U.K. living standard of the productivity record of its industrialized rivals have been greatly exaggerated.

VII. Concluding Comment

This paper is an exercise in interpretation of data supplied by others. I have examined no primary sources and have not attempted to supply, or even to revise, sets of statistics (though I have undertaken to cross check my results where several parallel data sets were available). Yet the data were able to provide

[11] Here, too, there has been a considerable narrowing of range. In 1870, with data for 4 countries missing, the share of workers in industry extended from 9.7 percent (Finland) to 42.3 (United Kingdom), with several countries near 20 percent and several in the high 30's. By 1979, that range ran only from a low of 28.7 percent (Canada) to a high of 44 percent (Germany).

some suggestive conclusions which need not be repeated here.

Above all, it seems to me the paper has reaffirmed that the study of economic history is not simply a manifestation of "idle curiosity" (to use Veblen's characterization of the motive for academic research). The long run does matter. It matters in several ways, at least one of them confirmed by the preceding discussion.

First, important current issues are, I believe, the product of path-dependent processes whose mathematical expression must take the form of functionals rather than mere functions, meaning that we cannot understand current phenomena such as the relative productive capacities of different economies without systematic examination of earlier events which affect the present and will continue to exercise profound effects tomorrow. (This, in my view of the matter, is a major element in the Hegelian and Marxian view of the importance of history.)

Second, the long run matters, because policies designed with only short-run problems and consequences in mind are all too likely to backfire once the immediate crisis is past. (This and the next point were, I believe, the main sources of Viner's preoccupation with the long run.)

Third, focus upon short-run phenomena such as recessions may lead an investigator to ignore more powerful and persistent forces such as those that were the primary concern of the classical economists.

Finally, and most pertinent to the discussion here, the long run is important because it is not sensible for economists and policymakers to attempt to discern long-run trends and their outcomes from the flow of short-run developments, which may be dominated by transient conditions. The validity of this view is surely confirmed at several points in this article, perhaps most dramatically by the way history places in perspective the recent developments in U.S. productivity which have been the focus of so much alarm.

REFERENCES

Abramovitz, Moses, "Rapid Growth Potential and its Realization: The Experience of the Capitalist Economies in the Postwar Period," in Edmond Malinvaud, ed., *Economic Growth and Resources, Proceedings of the Fifth World Congress of the International Economic Association*, Vol. I, London: Macmillan, 1979.

______, "Catching Up and Falling Behind," delivered at the Economic History Association, September 20, 1985.

Ames, Edward and Rosenberg, Nathan, "Changing Technological Leadership and Industrial Growth," *Economic Journal*, March 1963, *73*, 13–31.

Beniger, James R., *The Control Revolution: Technological and Economic Origins of the Information Society*, Cambridge: Harvard University Press, forthcoming.

Caves, Richard E. and Krause, Lawrence B., *The Australian Economy: A View From the North*, Washington: The Brookings Institution, 1984.

Cipolla, Carlo M., *Before the Industrial Revolution: European Society and Economy, 1000–1700*, New York: W. W. Norton, 1976.

Clark, Colin, *The Conditions of Economic Progress*, 3rd ed., London: Macmillian, 1957.

Darby, Michael, "The U.S. Productivity Slowdown: A Case of Statistical Myopia," *American Economic Review*, June 1984, *74*, 301–322.

David, Paul A., "Invention and Accumulation in America's Economic Growth: A Nineteenth-Century Parable," in K. Brunner and A. H. Meltzer, eds., *International Organization, National Policies and Economic Development*, Amsterdam: North-Holland, 1977, 179–228.

Deane, Phyllis and Cole, W. A., *British Economic Growth 1688–1959*, Cambridge: Cambridge University Press, 1962.

Feinstein, Charles, *National Income, Expenditure and Output of the United Kingdom, 1855–1965*, Cambridge: Cambridge University Press, 1972.

Gerschenkron, Alexander, "Economic Backwardness in Historical Perspective," in Bert F. Hoselitz, ed., *The Progress of Underdeveloped Areas*, Chicago: University of Chicago Press, 1952.

Landes, David S., *The Unbound Prometheus*, Cambridge: Cambridge University Press, 1969.

Lawrence, Robert Z., *Can America Compete?*,

Washington: The Brookings Institution, 1984.

McCloskey, D. N., *Enterprise and Trade in Victorian Britain*, London: Allen & Unwin, 1981.

Maddison, Angus, *Phases of Capitalist Development*, New York: Oxford University Press, 1982.

Marx, Karl and Engels, Friedrich, *Manifesto of the Communist Party* (1848), London: Lawrence and Wishart, 1946.

Matthews, R. C. O., *Slower Growth in the Western World*, London: Heinemann, 1982.

______**, Feinstein, C. H. and Odling-Smee, J. C.,** *British Economic Growth, 1856–1973*, Stanford: Stanford University Press, 1982.

Mueller, Dennis C., *The Political Economy of Growth*, New Haven: Yale University Press, 1983.

Phelps Brown, E. H. and Hopkins, S. V., "Seven Centuries of Building Wages," *Economica*, August 1955, *22*, 195–206.

______**, and** ______**.,** "Seven Centuries of the Prices of Consumables," *Economica*, November 1956, *23*, 296–314.

Porat, Marc Uri, "The Information Economy, Definitions and Measurement," Office of Telecommunications, Special Publication 77-12(1), U.S. Department of Commerce, Washington, 1977.

Romer, Paul M., "Increasing Returns and Long Run Growth," Working Paper No. 27, University of Rochester, October 1985.

Summers, Robert and Heston, Alan, "Improved International Comparisons of Real Product and its Composition, 1950–1980," *Review of Income and Wealth*, June 1984, *30*, 207–262.

______**, Kravis, I. B and Heston, Alan,** "Changes in World Income Distribution," *Journal of Policy Modeling*, May 1986, *6*, 237–269.

Teece, David J., *The Multinational Corporation and the Resources Cost of International Technology Transfer*, Cambridge: Ballinger, 1976.

Veblen, Thorstein, *Imperial Germany and the Industrial Revolution*, New York: Macmillan, 1915.

Viner, Jacob, *The Long View and the Short*, Glencoe: Free Press, 1958.

Williamson, Jeffrey G., "Why was British Growth So Slow During the Industrial Revolution?," unpublished, Harvard Institute of Economic Research, 1983.

U.S. Bureau of Census, *Long Term Economic Growth* 1860–1970, Washington, June 1973.

[2]

Entrepreneurship: Productive, Unproductive, and Destructive

William J. Baumol

New York University and Princeton University

The basic hypothesis is that, while the total supply of entrepreneurs varies among societies, the productive contribution of the society's entrepreneurial activities varies much more because of their allocation between productive activities such as innovation and largely unproductive activities such as rent seeking or organized crime. This allocation is heavily influenced by the relative payoffs society offers to such activities. This implies that policy can influence the allocation of entrepreneurship more effectively than it can influence its supply. Historical evidence from ancient Rome, early China, and the Middle Ages and Renaissance in Europe is used to investigate the hypotheses.

> It is often assumed that an economy of private enterprise has an automatic bias towards innovation, but this is not so. It has a bias only towards profit. [HOBSBAWM 1969, p. 40]

When conjectures are offered to explain historic slowdowns or great leaps in economic growth, there is the group of usual suspects that is

I am very grateful for the generous support of the research underlying this paper from the Division of Information Science and Technology of the National Science Foundation, the Price Institute for Entrepreneurial Studies, the Center for Entrepreneurial Studies of the Graduate School of Business Administration, New York University, and the C. V. Starr Center for Applied Economics. I am also very much indebted to Vacharee Devakula for her assistance in the research. I owe much to Joel Mokyr, Stefano Fenoaltea, Lawrence Stone, Constance Berman, and Claudia Goldin for help with the substance of the paper and to William Jordan and Theodore Rabb for guidance on references.

[*Journal of Political Economy*, 1990, vol. 98, no. 5, pt. 1]

regularly rounded up—prominent among them, the entrepreneur. Where growth has slowed, it is implied that a decline in entrepreneurship was partly to blame (perhaps because the culture's "need for achievement" has atrophied). At another time and place, it is said, the flowering of entrepreneurship accounts for unprecedented expansion.

This paper proposes a rather different set of hypotheses, holding that entrepreneurs are always with us and always play *some* substantial role. But there are a variety of roles among which the entrepreneur's efforts can be reallocated, and some of those roles do not follow the constructive and innovative script that is conventionally attributed to that person. Indeed, at times the entrepreneur may even lead a parasitical existence that is actually damaging to the economy. How the entrepreneur acts at a given time and place depends heavily on the rules of the game—the reward structure in the economy—that happen to prevail. Thus the central hypothesis here is that it is the set of rules and not the supply of entrepreneurs *or the nature of their objectives* that undergoes significant changes from one period to another and helps to dictate the ultimate effect on the economy via the *allocation* of entrepreneurial resources. Changes in the rules and other attendant circumstances can, of course, modify the composition of the class of entrepreneurs and can also alter its size. Without denying this or claiming that it has no significance, in this paper I shall seek to focus attention on the allocation of the changing class of entrepreneurs rather than its magnitude and makeup. (For an excellent analysis of the basic hypothesis, independently derived, see Murphy, Shleifer, and Vishny [1990].)

The basic proposition, if sustained by the evidence, has an important implication for growth policy. The notion that our productivity problems reside in "the spirit of entrepreneurship" that waxes and wanes for unexplained reasons is a counsel of despair, for it gives no guidance on how to reawaken that spirit once it has lagged. If that is the task assigned to policymakers, they are destitute: they have no means of knowing how to carry it out. But if what is required is the adjustment of rules of the game to induce a more felicitous allocation of entrepreneurial resources, then the policymaker's task is less formidable, and it is certainly not hopeless. The prevailing rules that affect the allocation of entrepreneurial activity can be observed, described, and, with luck, modified and improved, as will be illustrated here.

Here, extensive historical illustrations will be cited to impart plausibility to the contentions that have just been described. Then a short discussion of some current issues involving the allocation of entrepreneurship between productive and unproductive activities will be offered. Finally, I shall consider very briefly the means that can be used to change the rules of the game, and to do so in a manner that stimulates the productive contribution of the entrepreneur.

I. On the Historical Character of the Evidence

Given the inescapable problems for empirical as well as theoretical study of entrepreneurship, what sort of evidence can one hope to provide? Since the rules of the game usually change very slowly, a case study approach to investigation of my hypotheses drives me unavoidably to examples spanning considerable periods of history and encompassing widely different cultures and geographic locations. Here I shall proceed on the basis of historical illustrations encompassing all the main economic periods and places (ancient Rome, medieval China, Dark Age Europe, the Later Middle Ages, etc.) that the economic historians almost universally single out for the light they shed on the process of innovation and its diffusion. These will be used to show that the relative rewards to different types of entrepreneurial activity have in fact varied dramatically from one time and place to another and that this seems to have had profound effects on patterns of entrepreneurial behavior. Finally, evidence will be offered *suggesting* that such reallocations can have a considerable influence on the prosperity and growth of an economy, though other variables undoubtedly also play substantial roles.

None of this can, of course, be considered conclusive. Yet, it is surely a standard tenet of scientific method that tentative confirmation of a hypothesis is provided by observation of phenomena that the hypothesis helps to explain and that could not easily be accounted for if that hypothesis were invalid. It is on this sort of reasoning that I hope to rest my case. Historians have long been puzzled, for example, by the failure of the society of ancient Rome to disseminate and put into widespread practical use some of the sophisticated technological developments that we know to have been in its possession, while in the "High Middle Ages," a period in which progress and change were hardly popular notions, inventions that languished in Rome seem to have spread like wildfire. It will be argued that the hypothesis about the allocability of entrepreneurial effort between productive and unproductive activity helps considerably to account for this phenomenon, though it certainly will *not* be claimed that this is all there was to the matter.

Before I get to the substance of the discussion, it is important to emphasize that nothing that follows in this article makes any pretense of constituting a contribution to economic history. Certainly it is not intended here to try to explain any particular historical event. Moreover, the analysis relies entirely on secondary sources, and all the historical developments described are well known to historians, as the citations will indicate. Whatever the contribution that may be offered by the following pages, then, it is confined to enhanced understanding and extension of the (nonmathematical) theory of entrepreneurship in general, and not to an improved analysis of the historical events that are cited.

II. The Schumpeterian Model Extended: Allocation of Entrepreneurship

The analysis of this paper rests on what seems to be the one theoretical model that effectively encompasses the role of the entrepreneur and that really "works," in the sense that it constitutes the basis for a number of substantive inferences.[1] This is, of course, the well-known Schumpeterian analysis, whose main shortcoming, for our purposes, is the paucity of insights on policy that emerge from it. It will be suggested here that only a minor extension of that model to encompass the *allocation* of entrepreneurship is required to enhance its power substantially in this direction.

Schumpeter tells us that innovations (he calls them "the carrying out of new combinations") take various forms besides mere improvements in technology:

> This concept covers the following five cases: (1) the introduction of a new good—that is one with which consumers are not yet familiar—or of a new quality of a good. (2) The introduction of a new method of production, that is one not yet tested by experience in the branch of manufacture concerned, which need by no means be founded upon a discovery scientifically new, and can also exist in a new way of handling a commodity commercially. (3) The opening of a new market, that is a market into which the particular branch of manufacture of the country in question has not previously entered, whether or not this market has existed before. (4) The conquest of a new source of supply of raw materials or half-manufactured goods, again irrespective of whether this source already exists or whether it has first to be

[1] There has, however, recently been an outburst of illuminating writings on the theory of the innovation process, analyzing it in such terms as *races* for patents in which the winner takes everything, with no consolation prize for a close second, or treating the process, alternatively, as a "waiting game," in which the patient second entrant may outperform and even survive the first one in the innovative arena, who incurs the bulk of the risk. For an overview of these discussions as well as some substantial added insights, see Dasgupta (1988).

> created. (5) The carrying out of the new organization of any industry, like the creation of a monopoly position (for example through trustification) or the breaking up of a monopoly position. [(1912) 1934, p. 66]

The obvious fact that entrepreneurs undertake such a variety of tasks all at once suggests that theory can usefully undertake to consider what determines the *allocation* of entrepreneurial inputs among those tasks. Just as the literature traditionally studies the allocation of other inputs, for example, capital resources, among the various industries that compete for them, it seems natural to ask what influences the flow of entrepreneurial talent among the various activities in Schumpeter's list.

Presumably the reason no such line of inquiry was pursued by Schumpeter or his successors is that any analysis of the allocation of entrepreneurial resources among the five items in the preceding list (with the exception of the last—the creation or destruction of a monopoly) does not promise to yield any profound conclusions. There is no obvious reason to make much of a shift of entrepreneurial activity away from, say, improvement in the production process and toward the introduction of new products. The general implications, if any, for the public welfare, for productivity growth, and for other related matters are hardly obvious.

To derive more substantive results from an analysis of the allocation of entrepreneurial resources, it is necessary to expand Schumpeter's list, whose main deficiency seems to be that it does not go far enough. For example, it does not explicitly encompass innovative acts of technology transfer that take advantage of opportunities to introduce already-available technology (usually with some modification to adapt it to local conditions) to geographic locales whose suitability for the purpose had previously gone unrecognized or at least unused.

Most important for the discussion here, Schumpeter's list of entrepreneurial activities can usefully be expanded to include such items as innovations in rent-seeking procedures, for example, discovery of a previously unused legal gambit that is effective in diverting rents to those who are first in exploiting it. It may seem strange at first blush to propose inclusion of activities of such questionable value to society (I shall call them acts of "unproductive entrepreneurship") in the list of Schumpeterian innovations (though the creation of a monopoly, which Schumpeter does include as an innovation, is surely as questionable), but, as will soon be seen, this is a crucial step for the analysis that follows. If entrepreneurs are defined, simply, to be persons who are ingenious and creative in finding ways that add to their own wealth, power, and prestige, then it is to be expected that not all of them will be overly concerned with whether an activity that achieves these goals adds much or little to the social product or, for that matter, even whether it is an actual impediment to production (this notion goes back, at least, to Veblen [1904]). Suppose that it turns out, in addition, that at any time and place the magnitude of the benefit the economy derives from its entrepreneurial talents depends *substantially,* among other variables, on the allocation of this resource between productive and unproductive entrepreneurial activities of the sorts just described. Then the reasons for including acts of the latter type in the list of entrepreneurial activities become clear.

Here no exhaustive analysis of the process of allocation of entrepreneurial activity among the set of available options will be attempted. Rather, it will be argued only that at least *one* of the prime determinants of entrepreneurial behavior at any particular time and place is the prevailing rules of the game that govern the payoff of one entrepreneurial activity relative to another. If the rules are such as to impede the earning of much wealth via activity A, or are such as to impose social disgrace on those who engage in it, then, other things being equal, entrepreneurs' efforts will tend to be channeled to other activities, call them B. But if B contributes less to production or welfare than A, the consequences for society may be considerable.[2]

As a last preliminary note, it should be emphasized that the set of active entrepreneurs may be subject to change. Thus if the rules of the game begin to favor B over A, it may not be just the same individuals who switch their activities from entrepreneurship of type A to that of type B. Rather, some persons with talents suited for A may simply drop out of the picture, and individuals with abilities adapted to B may for the first time become entrepreneurs. Thus the allocation of entrepreneurs among activities is perhaps best described in the way Joan Robinson (following Shove's suggestion) analyzed the allocation of heterogeneous land resources (1933, chap. 8): as the solution of a jigsaw puzzle in which the pieces are each fitted into the places selected for them by the concatenation of pertinent circumstances.

III. Entrepreneurship, Productive and Unproductive: The Rules Do Change

Let us now turn to the central hypothesis of this paper: that the exercise of entrepreneurship can sometimes be unproductive or even

[2] There is a substantial literature, following the work of Jacob Schmookler, providing strong empirical evidence for the proposition that even the allocation of inventive effort, i.e., the directions pursued by inventive activities, is itself heavily influenced by relative payoff prospects. However, it is now agreed that some of these authors go too far when they appear to imply that almost nothing but the demand for the product of invention influences to any great extent which inventions will occur. For a good summary and references, see Abramovitz (1989, p. 33).

destructive, and that whether it takes one of these directions or one that is more benign depends heavily on the structure of payoffs in the economy—the rules of the game. The rather dramatic illustrations provided by world history seem to confirm quite emphatically the following proposition.

PROPOSITION 1. The rules of the game that determine the relative payoffs to different entrepreneurial activities *do* change dramatically from one time and place to another.

These examples also suggest strongly (but hardly "prove") the following proposition.

PROPOSITION 2. Entrepreneurial behavior changes direction from one economy to another in a manner that corresponds to the variations in the rules of the game.

A. *Ancient Rome*

The avenues open to those Romans who sought power, prestige, and wealth are instructive. First, it may be noted that they had no reservations about the desirability of wealth or about its pursuit (e.g., Finley 1985, pp. 53–57). *As long as it did not involve participation in industry or commerce,* there was nothing degrading about the wealth acquisition process. Persons of honorable status had three primary and acceptable sources of income: landholding (not infrequently as absentee landlords), "usury," and what may be described as "political payments":

> The opportunity for "political moneymaking" can hardly be over-estimated. Money poured in from booty, indemnities, provincial taxes, loans and miscellaneous extractions in quantities without precedent in Graeco-Roman history, and at an accelerating rate. The public treasury benefited, but probably more remained in private hands, among the nobles in the first instance; then, in appropriately decreasing proportions, among the *equites,* the soldiers and even the plebs of the city of Rome. . . . Nevertheless, the whole phenomenon is misunderstood when it is classified under the headings of "corruption" and "malpractice", as historians still persist in doing. Cicero was an honest governor of Cilicia in 51 and 50 B.C., so that at the end of his term he had earned only the legitimate profits of office. They amounted to 2,200,000 sesterces, more than treble the figure of 600,000 he himself once mentioned (*Stoic Paradoxes* 49) to illustrate an annual income that could permit a life of luxury. We are faced with something structural in the society. [Finley 1985, p. 55]

Who, then, operated commerce and industry? According to Veyne (1961), it was an occupation heavily undertaken by freedmen—former slaves who, incidentally, bore a social stigma for life. Indeed, according to this writer, slavery may have represented the one avenue for advancement for someone from the lower classes. A clever (and handsome) member of the lower orders might deliberately arrange to be sold into slavery to a wealthy and powerful master.[3] Then, with luck, skill, and drive, he would grow close to his owner, perhaps managing his financial affairs (and sometimes engaging in some homosexual activity with him). The master then gained cachet, after a suitable period, by granting freedom to the slave, setting him up with a fortune of his own. The freedmen, apparently not atypically, invested their financial stakes in commerce, hoping to multiply them sufficiently to enable them to retire in style to the countryside, thereafter investing primarily in land and loans in imitation of the upper classes.

Finally, regarding the Romans' attitude to the promotion of technology and productivity, Finley makes much of the "clear, almost total, divorce between science and practice" (1965, p. 32). He goes on to cite Vitruvius's monumental work on architecture and technology, in whose 10 books he finds only a single and trivial reference to means of saving effort and increasing productivity. Finley then reports the following story:

> There is a story, repeated by a number of Roman writers, that a man—characteristically unnamed—invented unbreakable glass and demonstrated it to Tiberius in anticipation of a great reward. The emperor asked the inventor whether anyone shared his secret and was assured that there was no one else; whereupon his head was promptly removed, lest, said Tiberius, gold be reduced to the value of mud. I have no opinion about the truth of this story, and it is only a story. But is it not interesting that neither the elder Pliny nor Petronius nor the historian Dio Cassius was troubled by the point that the inventor turned to the emperor for a reward, instead of turning to an investor for capital with which to put his invention into production?[4] . . . We must

[3] Stefano Fenoaltea comments that he knows no documented cases in which this occurred and that it was undoubtedly more common to seek advancement through adoption into an upper-class family.

[4] To be fair to Finley, note that he concludes that it is *not* really interesting. North and Thomas (1973, p. 3) make a similar point about Harrison's invention of the ship's chronometer in the eighteenth century (as an instrument indispensable for the determination of longitude). They point out that the incentive for this invention was a large governmental prize rather than the prospect of commercial profit, presumably because of the absence of effective patent protection.

> remind ourselves time and again that the European experience since the late Middle Ages in technology, in the economy, and in the value systems that accompanied them, was unique in human history until the recent export trend commenced. Technical progress, economic growth, productivity, even efficiency have not been significant goals since the beginning of time. So long as an acceptable life-style could be maintained, however that was defined, other values held the stage. [1985, p. 147]

The bottom line, for our purposes, is that the Roman reward system, although it offered wealth to those who engaged in commerce and industry, offset this gain through the attendant loss in prestige. Economic effort "was neither the way to wealth nor its purpose. Cato's gods showed him a number of ways to get more; but they were all political and parasitical, the ways of conquest and booty and usury; labour was not one of them, not even the labour of the entrepreneur" (Finley 1965, p. 39).

B. Medieval China

In China, as in many kingdoms of Europe before the guarantees of the Magna Carta and the revival of towns and their acquisition of privileges, the monarch commonly claimed possession of all property in his territories. As a result, particularly in China, when the sovereign was in financial straits, confiscation of the property of wealthy subjects was entirely in order. It has been claimed that this led those who had resources to avoid investing them in any sort of visible capital stocks, and that this, in turn, was a substantial impediment to economic expansion (see Balazs 1964, p. 53; Landes 1969, pp. 46–47; Rosenberg and Birdzell 1986, pp. 119–20; Jones 1987, chap. 5).

In addition, imperial China reserved its most substantial rewards in wealth and prestige for those who climbed the ladder of imperial examinations, which were heavily devoted to subjects such as Confucian philosophy and calligraphy. Successful candidates were often awarded high rank in the bureaucracy, high social standing denied to anyone engaged in commerce or industry, even to those who gained great wealth in the process (and who often used their resources to prepare their descendants to contend via the examinations for a position in the scholar bureaucracy). In other words, the rules of the game seem to have been heavily biased against the acquisition of wealth *and position* through Schumpeterian behavior. The avenue to success lay elsewhere.

Because of the difficulty of the examinations, the mandarins (scholar-officials) rarely succeeded in keeping such positions in their own families for more than two or three generations (see Marsh 1961, p. 159; Ho 1962, chap. 4 and appendix). The scholar families devoted enormous effort and considerable resources to preparing their children through years of laborious study for the imperial examinations, which, during the Sung dynasty, were held every 3 years, and only several hundred persons in all of China succeeded in passing them each time (E. A. Kracke, Jr. in Liu and Golas [1969, p. 14]). Yet, regularly, some persons not from mandarin families also attained success through this avenue (see, e.g., Marsh [1961] and Ho [1962] for evidence on social mobility in imperial China).

Wealth was in prospect for those who passed the examination and who were subsequently appointed to government positions. But the sources of their earnings had something in common with those of the Romans:

> Corruption, which is widespread in all impoverished and backward countries (or, more exactly, throughout the preindustrial world), was endemic in a country where the servants of the state often had nothing to live on but their very meager salaries. The required attitude of obedience to superiors made it impossible for officials to demand higher salaries, and in the absence of any control over their activities from below it was inevitable that they should purloin from society what the state failed to provide. According to the usual pattern, a Chinese official entered upon his duties only after spending long years in study and passing many examinations; he then established relations with protectors, incurred debts to get himself appointed, and then proceeded to extract the amount he had spent on preparing himself for his career from the people he administered—and extracted both principal and interest. The degree of his rapacity would be dictated not only by the length of time he had had to wait for his appointment and the number of relations he had to support and of kin to satisfy or repay, but also by the precariousness of his position. [Balazs 1964, p. 10]

Enterprise, on the other hand, was not only frowned on, but may have been subjected to impediments deliberately imposed by the officials, at least after the fourteenth century A.D.; and some historians claim that it was true much earlier. Balazs tells us of

> the state's tendency to clamp down immediately on any form of private enterprise (and this in the long run kills not only initiative but even the slightest attempts at innovation), or, if it did not succeed in putting a stop to it in time, to take over

> and nationalize it. Did it not frequently happen during the course of Chinese history that the scholar-officials, although hostile to all inventions, nevertheless gathered in the fruits of other people's ingenuity? I need mention only three examples of inventions that met this fate: paper, invented by a eunuch; printing, used by the Buddhists as a medium for religious propaganda; and the bill of exchange, an expedient of private businessmen. [P. 18]

As a result of recurrent intervention by the state to curtail the liberty and take over any accumulated advantages the merchant class had managed to gain for itself, "the merchant's ambition turned to becoming a scholar-official and investing his profits in land" (p. 32).

C. *The Earlier Middle Ages*

Before the rise of the cities and before monarchs were able to subdue the bellicose activities of the nobility, wealth and power were pursued primarily through military activity. Since land and castles were the medieval forms of wealth most highly valued and most avidly sought after, it seems reasonable to interpret the warring of the barons in good part as the pursuit of an economic objective. For example, during the reign of William the Conqueror (see, e.g., Douglas 1964), there were frequent attempts by the barons in Normandy and neighboring portions of France to take over each other's lands and castles. A prime incentive for William's supporters in his conquest of England was their obvious aspiration for lands.[5] More than that, violent means also served to provide more liquid forms of income (captured treasure), which the nobility used to support both private consumption and investment in military plant and equipment, where such items could not easily be produced on their own lands and therefore had to be purchased from others. In England, with its institution of primogeniture (the exclusive right of the eldest son to inherit his father's estate), younger sons who chose not to enter the clergy often had no socially acceptable choice other than warfare as a means to make their fortunes, and in some cases they succeeded spectacularly. Thus note the case of William Marshal, fourth son of a minor noble, who rose

[5] The conquest has at least two noteworthy entrepreneurial sides. First, it involved an innovation, the use of the stirrup by the Normans at Hastings that enabled William's warriors to use the same spear to impale a series of victims with the force of the horse's charge, rather than just tossing the spear at the enemy, much as an infantryman could. Second, the invasion was an impressive act of organization, with William having to convince his untrustworthy allies that they had more to gain by joining him in England than by staying behind to profit from his absence by trying to grab away his lands as they had tried to do many times before.

through his military accomplishments to be one of the most powerful and trusted officials under Henry II and Richard I, and became one of the wealthiest men in England (see Painter 1933).

Of course, the medieval nobles were not purely economic men. Many of the turbulent barons undoubtedly enjoyed fighting for its own sake, and success in combat was an important avenue to prestige in their society. But no modern capitalist is a purely economic man either. What I am saying here is that warfare, which was of course pursued for a variety of reasons, was *also* undertaken as a primary source of economic gain. This is clearly all the more true of the mercenary armies that were the scourge of fourteenth-century France and Italy.

Such violent economic activity, moreover, inspired frequent and profound innovation. The introduction of the stirrup was a requisite for effective cavalry tactics. Castle building evolved from wooden to stone structures and from rectangular to round towers (which could not be made to collapse by undermining their corners). Armor and weaponry became much more sophisticated with the introduction of the crossbow, the longbow, and, ultimately, artillery based on gunpowder. Military tactics and strategy also grew in sophistication. These innovations can be interpreted as contributions of military entrepreneurs undertaken at least partly in pursuit of private economic gains.

This type of entrepreneurial undertaking obviously differs vastly from the introduction of a cost-saving industrial process or a valuable new consumer product. An individual who pursues wealth through the forcible appropriation of the possessions of others surely does not add to the national product. Its net effect may be not merely a transfer but a net reduction in social income and wealth.[6]

[6] In saying all this, I must not be interpreted as taking the conventional view that warfare is an unmitigated source of impoverishment of any economy that unquestionably never contributes to its prosperity. Careful recent studies have indicated that matters are more complicated (see, e.g., Milward 1970; Olson 1982). Certainly the unprecedented prosperity enjoyed afterward by the countries on the losing side of the Second World War suggests that warfare need not always preclude economic expansion, and it is easy to provide earlier examples. The three great economic leaders of the Western world preceding the United States—Italy in the thirteenth–sixteenth centuries, the Dutch Republic in the seventeenth and eighteenth, and Great Britain in the eighteenth and nineteenth—each attained the height of their prosperity after periods of enormously costly and sometimes destructive warfare. Nevertheless, the wealth gained by a medieval baron from the adoption of a novel bellicose technique can hardly have contributed to economic growth in the way that resulted from adoption of a new steelmaking process in the nineteenth century or the introduction of a product such as the motor vehicle in the twentieth.

D. *The Later Middle Ages*

By the end of the eleventh century the rules of the game had changed from those of the Dark Ages. The revival of the towns was well under way. They had acquired a number of privileges, among them protection from arbitrary taxation and confiscation and the creation of a labor force by granting freedom to runaway serfs after a relatively brief residence (a year and a day) in the towns. The free-enterprise turbulence of the barons had at least been impeded by the church's pacification efforts: the peace and the (later) truce of God in France, Spain, and elsewhere; similar changes were taking place in England (see, e.g., Cowdrey [1970]; but Jones [1987, p. 94] suggests that some free-enterprise military activity by the barons continued in England through the reigns of the earlier Tudors in the sixteenth century). All this subsequently "gave way to more developed efforts to enforce peace by the more organized governments of the twelfth century" (Brooke 1964, p. 350; also p. 127). A number of activities that were neither agricultural nor military began to yield handsome returns. For example, the small group of architect-engineers who were in charge of the building of cathedrals, palaces, bridges, and fortresses could live in great luxury in the service of their kings.

But, apparently, a far more common source of earnings was the water-driven mills that were strikingly common in France and southern England by the eleventh century, a technological innovation about which more will be said presently. An incentive for such technical advances may have been the monopoly they conferred on their owners rather than any resulting improvement in efficiency. Such monopoly rights were alike sought and enforced by private parties (Bloch 1935, pp. 554–57; Brooke 1964, p. 84) and by religious organizations (see below).

The economic role of the monks in this is somewhat puzzling—the least clear-cut part of our story.[7] The Cistercian abbeys are generally assigned a critical role in the promotion of such technological advances. In some cases they simply took over mills that had been constructed by others (Berman 1986, p. 89). But the Cistercians improved them, built many others, and vastly expanded their use; at

[7] Bloch (1935) notes that the monasteries had both the capital and the large number of consumers of flour necessary to make the mills profitable. In addition, they were less likely than lay communities to undergo military siege, which, Bloch notes, was (besides drought and freezing of the waterways) one of the main impediments to adoption of the water mill, since blocking of the waterway that drove the mill could threaten the besieged population with starvation (pp. 550–53).

least some writers (e.g., Gimpel 1976, pp. 3–6) seem to suggest that the Cistercians were the spearhead of technological advance.

Historians tell us that they have no ready explanation for the entrepreneurial propensities of this monastic order. (See, e.g., Brooke [1964, p. 69] and also a personal communication to me from Constance Berman. Ovitt [1987, esp. pp. 142–47] suggests that this may all have been part of the twelfth-century monastic drive to reduce or eliminate manual labor in order to maximize the time available for the less onerous religious labors—a conclusion with which Bloch [1935, p. 553] concurs.) But the evidence suggests strongly that avid entrepreneurs they were. They accumulated vast tracts of land; the sizes of their domesticated animal flocks were enormous by the standards of the time; their investment rates were remarkable; they sought to exercise monopoly power, being known, after the erection of a water mill, to seek legal intervention to prevent nearby residents from continuing to use their animal-powered facilities (Gimpel 1976, pp. 15–16); they were fierce in their rivalrous behavior and drive for expansion, in the process not sparing other religious bodies—not even other Cistercian houses. There is a "record of pastoral expansionism and monopolies over access established by the wealthiest Cistercian houses . . . at the expense of smaller abbeys and convents . . . effectively pushing out all other religious houses as competitors" (Berman 1986, p. 112).

As with early capitalists, the asceticism of the monks, by keeping down the proportion of the monastery's output that was consumed, helped to provide the resources for levels of investment extraordinary for the period (pp. 40, 83). The rules of the game appear to have offered substantial economic rewards to exercise of Cistercian entrepreneurship. The order obtained relatively few large gifts, but instead frequently received support from the laity and from the church establishment in the form of exemptions from road and river tolls and from payment of the tithe. This obviously increased the *marginal* yield of investment, innovation, and expenditure of effort, and the evidence suggests the diligence of the order in pursuing the resulting opportunities. Their mills, their extensive lands, and their large flocks are reported to have brought scale economies and extraordinary financial returns (chap. 4). Puritanical, at least in earlier years, in their self-proclaimed adherence to simplicity in personal lifestyle while engaged in dedicated pursuit of wealth, they may perhaps represent an early manifestation of elements of "the Protestant ethic." But whatever their motive, the reported Cistercian record of promotion of technological progress is in diametric contrast to that of the Roman empire.

E. *Fourteenth Century*

The fourteenth century brought with it a considerable increase in military activity, notably the Hundred Years' War between France and England. Payoffs, surely, must have tilted to favor more than before inventions designed for military purposes. Cannons appeared as siege devices and armor was made heavier. More imaginative war devices were proposed: a windmill-propelled war wagon, a multibarreled machine gun, and a diving suit to permit underwater attacks on ships. A pervasive business enterprise of this unhappy century of war was the company of mercenary troops—the *condottiere*—who roamed Europe, supported the side that could offer the most attractive terms, and in lulls between fighting, when unemployment threatened, wandered about thinking up military enterprises of their own, at the expense of the general public (Gimpel 1976, chap. 9; see also McNeill 1969, pp. 33–39). Clearly, the rules of the game—the system of entrepreneurial rewards—had changed, to the disadvantage of productive entrepreneurship.

F. *Early Rent Seeking*

Unproductive entrepreneurship can also take less violent forms, usually involving various types of rent seeking, the type of (possibly) unproductive entrepreneurship that seems most relevant today. Enterprising use of the legal system for rent-seeking purposes has a long history. There are, for example, records of the use of litigation in the twelfth century in which the proprietor of a water-driven mill sought and won a prohibition of use in the vicinity of mills driven by animal or human power (Gimpel 1976, pp. 25–26). In another case, the operators of two dams, one upstream of the other, sued one another repeatedly at least from the second half of the thirteenth century until the beginning of the fifteenth, when the downstream dam finally succeeded in driving the other out of business as the latter ran out of money to pay the court fees (pp. 17–20).

In the upper strata of society, rent seeking also gradually replaced military activity as a prime source of wealth and power. This transition can perhaps be ascribed to the triumph of the monarchies and the consequent imposition of law and order. Rent-seeking entrepreneurship then took a variety of forms, notably the quest for grants of land and patents of monopoly from the monarch. Such activities can, of course, sometimes prove to contribute to production, as when the recipient of land given by the monarch uses it more efficiently than the previous owner did. But there seems to have been nothing in the structure of the land-granting process that ensured even a tendency toward transfer to more productive proprietors, nor was the individual who sought such grants likely to use as an argument in favor of his suit the claim that he was likely to be the more productive user (in terms of, say, the expected net value of its agricultural output).

Military forms of entrepreneurship may have experienced a renaissance in England in the seventeenth century with the revolt against Charles I. How that may have changed the structure of rewards to entrepreneurial activity is suggested by Hobsbawm (1969), who claims that at the end of the seventeenth century the most affluent merchants earned perhaps three times as much as the richest "master manufacturers."[8] But, he reports, the wealthiest noble families probably had incomes more than 10 times as large as those of the rich merchants. The point in this is that those noble families, according to Hobsbawm, were no holdovers from an ancient feudal aristocracy; they were, rather, the heirs of the Roundheads (the supporters of the parliamentary, or puritan, party) in the then-recent Civil War (pp. 30–32). On this view, once again, military activity would seem to have become the entrepreneur's most promising recourse.

But other historians take a rather different view of the matter. Studies reported in Thirsk (1954) indicate that ultimately there was little redistribution of property as the result of the Civil War and the restoration. Rather it is noted that in this period the "patrician élites depended for their political power and economic prosperity on royal charters and monopolies rather than on talent and entrepreneurial initiative" (Stone 1985, p. 45). In this interpretation of the matter, it was rent seeking, not military activity, that remained the prime source of wealth under the restoration.

By the time the eighteenth-century industrial revolution ("the" industrial revolution) arrived, matters had changed once again. According to Ashton (1948, pp. 9–10), grants of monopoly were in good part "swept away" by the Monopolies Act of 1624, and, we are told by Adam Smith (1776), by the end of the eighteenth century they were rarer in England than in any other country. Though industrial activity continued to be considered somewhat degrading in places in which industry flourished, notably in England during the industrial revolution there was probably a difference in degree. Thus Lefebvre (1947, p. 14) reports that "at its upper level the [French] nobility . . . were envious of the English lords who enriched themselves in bourgeois

[8] The evidence indicates that the wealth of affluent families in Great Britain continues to be derived preponderantly from commerce rather than from industry. This contrasts with the record for the United States, where the reverse appears to be true (see Rubinstein 1980, pp. 22–23, 59–60).

ways," while in France "the noble 'derogated' or fell into the common mass if [like Mirabeau] he followed a business or profession" (p. 11). (See, however, Schama [1989], who tells us that "even a cursory examination of the eighteenth-century French economy . . . reveals the nobility deeply involved in finance, business and industry—certainly as much as their British counterparts. . . . In 1765 a royal edict officially removed the last formal obstacles to their participation in trade and industry" [p. 118].) In England, primogeniture, by forcing younger sons of noble families to resort to commerce and industry, apparently was imparting respectability to these activities to a degree that, while rather limited, may have rarely been paralleled before.

The central point of all the preceding discussion seems clear—perhaps, in retrospect, self-evident. If entrepreneurship is the imaginative pursuit of position, with limited concern about the means used to achieve the purpose, then we can expect changes in the structure of rewards to modify the nature of the entrepreneur's activities, sometimes drastically. The rules of the game can then be a critical influence helping to determine whether entrepreneurship will be allocated predominantly to activities that are productive or unproductive and even destructive.

IV. Does the Allocation between Productive and Unproductive Entrepreneurship Matter Much?

We come now to the third proposition of this article.

PROPOSITION 3. The allocation of entrepreneurship between productive and unproductive activities, though by no means the only pertinent influence, can have a profound effect on the innovativeness of the economy and the degree of dissemination of its technological discoveries.

It is hard to believe that a system of payoffs that moves entrepreneurship in unproductive directions is not a substantial impediment to industrial innovation and growth in productivity. Still, history permits no test of this proposition through a set of anything resembling controlled experiments, since other influences *did*, undoubtedly, also play important roles, as the proposition recognizes. One can only note what appears to be a remarkable correlation between the degree to which an economy rewarded productive entrepreneurship and the vigor shown in that economy's innovation record.

Historians tell us of several industrial "near revolutions" that occurred before *the* industrial revolution of the eighteenth century that are highly suggestive for our purposes (Braudel [1986, 3:542–56]; for a more skeptical view, see Coleman [1956]). We are told that two of the incipient revolutions never went anywhere, while two of them were rather successful in their fashion. I shall report conclusions of some leading historians on these episodes, but it should be recognized by the reader that many of the views summarized here have been disputed in the historical literature, at least to some degree.

A. *Rome and Hellenistic Egypt*

My earlier discussion cited ancient Rome and its empire as a case in which the rules did not favor productive entrepreneurship. Let us compare this with the evidence on the vigor of innovative activity in that society. The museum at Alexandria was the center of technological innovation in the Roman empire. By the first century B.C., that city knew of virtually every form of machine gearing that is used today, including a working steam engine. But these seem to have been used only to make what amounted to elaborate toys. The steam engine was used only to open and close the doors of a temple.

The Romans also had the water mill. This may well have been the most critical pre-eighteenth-century industrial invention because (outside the use of sails in transportation by water) it provided the first significant source of power other than human and animal labor: "it was able to produce an amount of concentrated energy beyond any other resource of antiquity" (Forbes 1955, 2:90). As steam did in more recent centuries, it offered the prospect of providing the basis for a leap in productivity in the Roman economy, as apparently it actually did during the eleventh, twelfth, and thirteenth centuries in Europe. Yet Finley (1965, pp. 35–36), citing White (1962), reports that "though it was invented in the first century B.C., is was not until the third century A.D. that we find evidence of much use, and not until the fifth and sixth of general use. It is also a fact that we have no evidence at all of its application to other industries [i.e., other than grinding of grain] until the very end of the fourth century, and then no more than one solitary and possibly suspect reference . . . to a marble-slicing machine near Trier."

Unfortunately, evidence of Roman technical stagnation is only spotty, and, further, some historians suggest that the historical reports give inadequate weight to the Roman preoccupation with agricultural improvement relative to improvement in commerce or manufacture. Still, the following quotation seems to summarize the weight of opinion: "Historians have long been puzzled as to why the landlords of the Middle Ages proved so much more enterprising than the landlords of the Roman Empire, although the latter, by and large, were much better educated, had much better opportunities for making technical and scientific discoveries if they had wished to do so"

(Brooke 1964, p. 88). It seems at least plausible that some part of the explanation is to be found in the ancient world's rules of the game, which encouraged the pursuit of wealth but severely discouraged its pursuit through the exercise of productive entrepreneurship.[9]

B. *Medieval China*

The spate of inventions that occurred in ancient China (before it was conquered by the barbarian Yuan dynasty in 1280) constituted one of the earliest potential revolutions in industry. Among the many Chinese technological contributions, one can list paper, (perhaps) the compass, waterwheels, sophisticated water clocks, and, of course, gunpowder. Yet despite the apparent prosperity of the Sung period (960–1270) (see, e.g., Liu and Golas 1969), at least some historians suggest that none of this spate of inventions led to a flowering of *industry*[10] as distinguished from commerce and some degree of general prosperity. And in China too, as we have seen, the rules did not favor productive entrepreneurship. Balazs (1964, p. 53) concludes that

> what was chiefly lacking in China for the further development of capitalism was not mechanical skill or scientific aptitude, nor a sufficient accumulation of wealth, but scope for individual enterprise. There was no individual freedom and no security for private enterprise, no legal foundation for rights other than those of the state, no alternative investment other than landed property, no guarantee against being penalized by arbitrary exactions from officials or against intervention by the state. But perhaps the supreme inhibiting

[9] It has been suggested by historians (see, e.g., Bloch 1935, p. 547) that an abundance of slaves played a key role in Roman failure to use the water mill widely. However, this must imply that the Romans were not efficient wealth seekers. As the cliometric literature has made clear, the cost of maintaining a slave is not low and certainly is not zero, and slaves are apt not to be efficient and dedicated workers. Thus if it had been efficient to replace human or animal power by the inanimate power of the waterways, failure to do so would have cut into the wealth of the slaveholder, in effect saddling him with the feeding of unproductive persons or keeping the slaves who turned the mills from other, more lucrative, occupations. Perhaps Roman landowners *were* fairly unsophisticated in the management of their estates, as Finley (1985, pp. 108–16) suggests, and, if so, there may be some substance to the hypothesis that slavery goes far to account for the failure of water mills to spread in the Roman economy.

[10] Also, as in Rome, none of this was associated with the emergence of a systematic body of science involving coherent theoretical structure and the systematic testing of hypotheses on the basis of experiment or empirical observation. Here, too, the thirteenth-century work of Bishop Grosseteste, William of Henley, and Roger Bacon was an early step toward that unique historical phenomenon—the emergence of a systematic body of science in the West in, say, the sixteenth century (see Needham 1956).

> factor was the overwhelming prestige of the state bureaucracy, which maimed from the start any attempt of the bourgeoisie to be different, to become aware of themselves as a class and fight for an autonomous position in society. Free enterprise, ready and proud to take risks, is therefore quite exceptional and abnormal in Chinese economic history.

C. *Slow Growth in the "Dark Ages"*

An era noted for its slow growth occurred between the death of Charlemagne (814) and the end of the tenth century. Even this period was not without its economic advances, which developed slowly, including the beginnings of the agricultural improvements that attended the introduction of the horseshoe, harness, and stirrup, the heavy plow, and the substitution of horsepower for oxen, which may have played a role in enabling peasants to move to more populous villages further from their fields (see White 1962, p. 39 ff.). But, still, it was probably a period of significantly slower growth than the industrial revolution of the eleventh–thirteenth centuries (Gimpel 1976), about which more will be said presently. We have already seen that this was a period in which military violence was a prime outlet for entrepreneurial activity. While this can hardly pretend to be *the* explanation of the relative stagnation of the era, it is hard to believe that it was totally unimportant.

D. *The "High Middle Ages"*

A good deal has already been said about the successful industrial revolution (and the accompanying commercial revolution sparked by inventions such as double-entry bookkeeping and bills of exchange [de Roover 1953]) of the late Middle Ages, whose two-century duration makes it as long-lived as our own (see Carus-Wilson 1941; White 1962; Gimpel 1976).

Perhaps the hallmark of this industrial revolution was that remarkable source of productive power, the water mills, that covered the countryside in the south of England and crowded the banks of the Seine in Paris (see, e.g., Gimpel 1976, pp. 3–6; Berman 1986, pp. 81–89). The mills were not only simple grain-grinding devices but accomplished an astonishing variety of tasks and involved an impressive variety of mechanical devices and sophisticated gear arrangements. They crushed olives, ground mash for beer production, crushed cloth for papermaking, sawed lumber, hammered metal and woolens (as part of the "fulling" process—the cleansing, scouring, and pressing of woven woolen goods to make them stronger and to bring the threads closer together), milled coins, polished armor, and operated the bellows of blast furnaces. Their mechanisms entailed many forms of ingenuity. Gears were used to translate the vertical circular motion of the efficient form of the waterwheel into the horizontal circular motion of the millstone. The cam (a piece attached, say, to the axle of the waterwheel, protruding from the axle at right angles to its axis of rotation) served to lift a hammer and to drop it repeatedly and automatically (it was apparently known in antiquity, but may not have been used with waterwheels). A crank handle extending from the end of the axle transformed the circular motion of the wheel into the back and forth (reciprocating) motion required for sawing or the operation of bellows. The most sophisticated product of all this mechanical skill and knowledge was the mechanical clock, which appeared toward the end of the thirteenth century. As White (1962, p. 129) sums up the matter, "the four centuries following Leonardo, that is, until electrical energy demanded a supplementary set of devices, were less technologically engaged in discovering basic principles than in elaborating and refining those established during the four centuries before Leonardo."[11]

In a period in which agriculture probably occupied some 90 percent of the population, the expansion of industry in the twelfth and thirteenth centuries could not by itself have created a major upheaval in living standards.[12] Moreover, it has been deduced from what little we know of European gross domestic product per capita at the beginning of the eighteenth century that its average growth in the preceding six or seven centuries must have been very modest, since if the poverty of that later time had represented substantial growth from

[11] As was already noted, science and scientific method also began to make an appearance with contributions such as those of Bishop Grosseteste and Roger Bacon. Walter of Henley championed controlled experiments and observation over recourse to the opinions of ancient authorities and made a clear distinction between economic and engineering efficiency in discussing the advisability of substituting horses for oxen. Bacon displayed remarkable foresight when he wrote, circa 1260, that "machines may be made by which the largest ships, with only one man steering them, will be moved faster than if they were filled with rowers; wagons may be built which will move with incredible speed and without the aid of beasts; flying machines can be constructed in which a man . . . may beat the air with wings like a bird . . . machines will make it possible to go to the bottom of seas and rivers" (as quoted in White [1962, p. 134]).

[12] But then, much the same was true of the first half century of "our" industrial revolution, which, until the coming of the railways, was centered on the production of cotton that perhaps constituted only some 7–8 percent of national output (Hobsbawm 1969, p. 68). Initially, the eighteenth-century industrial revolution was a very minor affair, at least in terms of investment levels and contributions to output and to growth in productivity (perhaps 0.3 percent per year) (see Landes 1969, pp. 64–65; Feinstein 1978, pp. 40–41; Williamson 1984).

eleventh-century living standards, much of the earlier population would surely have been condemned to starvation.

Still, the industrial activity of the twelfth and thirteenth centuries was very substantial. By the beginning of the fourteenth century, according to Gimpel (1976), 68 mills were in operation on less than one mile of the banks of the Seine in Paris, and these were supplemented by floating mills anchored to the Grand Pont. The activity in metallurgy was also considerable—sufficient to denude much of Europe of its forests and to produce a rise in the price of wood that forced recourse to coal (Nef [1934]; other historians assert that this did not occur to any substantial degree until the fifteenth or sixteenth century, with some question even about those dates; see, e.g., Coleman [1975, pp. 42–43]). In sum, the industrial revolution of the twelfth and thirteenth centuries was a surprisingly robust affair, and it is surely plausible that improved rewards to industrial activity had something to do with its vigor.

E. The Fourteenth-Century Retreat

The end of all this period of buoyant activity in the fourteenth century (see the classic revisionist piece by Lopez [1969] as well as Gimpel [1976, chap. 9]) has a variety of explanations, many of them having no connection with entrepreneurship. For one thing, it has been deduced by study of the glaciers that average temperatures dropped, possibly reducing the yield of crops (though recent studies indicate that the historical relation between climatic changes and crop yields is at best ambiguous) and creating other hardships. The plague returned and decimated much of the population. In addition to these disasters of nature, there were at least two pertinent developments of human origin. First, the church clamped down on new ideas and other manifestations of freedom. Roger Bacon himself was put under constraint.[13] The period during which new ways of thinking brought rewards and status was apparently ended. Second, the fourteenth century included the first half of the devastating Hundred Years' War. It is implausible that the associated renewal of rewards to military enterprise played no part in the economic slowdown.

F. Remark on "Our" Industrial Revolution

It need hardly be added, in conclusion, that *the* industrial revolution that began in the eighteenth century and continues today has brought

[13] The restraints imposed by the church had another curious effect: they apparently made bathing unfashionable for centuries. Before then, bathhouses had been popular as centers for social and, perhaps, sexual activity; but by requiring separation of the sexes and otherwise limiting the pleasures of cleanliness, the church undermined the inducements for such sanitary activities (see Gimpel 1976, pp. 87–92).

to the industrialist and the businessperson generally a degree of wealth and a respect probably unprecedented in human history. The fact that this period yielded an explosion of output at least equally unprecedented is undoubtedly attributable to a myriad of causes that can probably never be discovered fully and whose roles can never be disentangled. Yet the continued association of output growth with high financial and respectability rewards to productive entrepreneurship is surely suggestive, even if it can hardly be taken to be conclusive evidence for proposition 3, which asserts that the allocation of entrepreneurship *does* really matter for the vigor and innovativeness of an economy.

V. On Unproductive Avenues for Today's Entrepreneur: A Delicate Balance

Today, unproductive entrepreneurship takes many forms. Rent seeking, often via activities such as litigation and takeovers, and tax evasion and avoidance efforts seem now to constitute the prime threat to productive entrepreneurship. The spectacular fortunes amassed by the "arbitrageurs" revealed by the scandals of the mid-1980s were *sometimes,* surely, the reward of unproductive, occasionally illegal but entrepreneurial acts. Corporate executives devote much of their time and energy to legal suit and countersuit, and litigation is used to blunt or prevent excessive vigor in competition by rivals. Huge awards by the courts, sometimes amounting to billions of dollars, can bring prosperity to the victor and threaten the loser with insolvency. When this happens, it must become tempting for the entrepreneur to select his closest advisers from the lawyers rather than the engineers. It induces the entrepreneur to spend literally hundreds of millions of dollars for a single legal battle. It tempts that entrepreneur to be the first to sue others before those others can sue him. (For an illuminating quantification of some of the social costs of one widely publicized legal battle between two firms, see Summers and Cutler [1988].)

Similarly, taxes can serve to redirect entrepreneurial effort. As Lindbeck (1987, p. 15) has observed, "the problem with high-tax societies is not that it is impossible to become rich there, but that it is difficult to do so by way of productive effort in the ordinary production system." He cites as examples of the resulting reallocation of entrepreneurship " 'smart' speculative financial transactions without much (if any) contribution to the productive capacity of the economy" (p. 15) as well as "illegal 'business areas' such as drug dealing" (p. 25).

In citing such activities, I do not mean to imply either that rent-seeking activity has been expanding in recent decades or that takeover bids or private antitrust suits are always or even preponderantly unproductive. Rather, I am only suggesting where current rent-seeking activities are likely to be found, that is, where policy designers should look if they intend to divert entrepreneurial talents into more productive channels.

The main point here is to note that threats of takeovers are sometimes used as a means to extract "greenmail" and that recourse to the courts as a means to seek to preserve rents through legally imposed impediments to competition does indeed occur, and to suggest that it is no rare phenomenon. This does, then, become an attraction for entrepreneurial talent whose efforts are thereby channeled into unproductive directions. Yet, to the extent that takeovers discipline inefficient managements and that antitrust intervention sometimes is legitimate and sometimes contributes to productivity, it would seem that it will not be easy to change the rules in a way that discourages allocation of entrepreneurial effort into such activities, without at the same time undermining the legitimate role of these institutions. Some promising proposals have been offered, but this is not a suitable place for their systematic examination. However, a few examples will be reported in the following section.

VI. Changes in the Rules and Changes in Entrepreneurial Goals

A central point in this discussion is the contention that if reallocation of entrepreneurial effort is adopted as an objective of society, it is far more easily achieved through changes in the rules that determine relative rewards than via modification of the goals of the entrepreneurs and prospective entrepreneurs themselves. I have even gone so far as to use the same terms to characterize those goals in the very different eras and cultures referred to in the discussion. But it would be ridiculous to imply that the attitudes of a wealth-seeking senator in Rome, a Sung dynasty mandarin, and an American industrialist of the late nineteenth century were all virtually identical. Still, the evidence suggests that they had more in common than might have been expected by the casual observer. However, even if it were to transpire that they really diverged very substantially, that would be of little use to the designer of policy who does not have centuries at his or her disposal and who is notoriously ineffective in engendering profound changes in cultural influences or in the structure of preferences. It is for this reason that I have chosen to take entrepreneurial goals as given and to emphasize modification in the structure of the rewards to different activities as the more promising line of investigation.

This suggests that it is necessary to consider the process by which those rules are modified in practice, but I believe that answers to even this more restricted question are largely beyond the powers of the historians, the sociologists, and the anthropologists into whose domains it falls. One need only review the disputatious literature on the influences that led to the revival of trade toward the end of the early Middle Ages to see how far we still are from anything resembling firm answers. Exogenous influences such as foreign invasions or unexpected climatic changes can clearly play a part, as can developments within the economy. But the more interesting observation for our purposes is the fact that it is easy to think of measures that *can* change these rules quickly and profoundly.[14]

For example, the restrictions on royal grants of monopolies imposed by Parliament in the Statute of Monopolies are said to have reduced substantially the opportunities for rent seeking in seventeenth- and eighteenth-century England and may have moved reluctant entrepreneurs to redirect their efforts toward agricultural improvement and industry. Even if it did not succeed to any substantial extent in reallocation of the efforts of an unchanged body of entrepreneurs from one of those types of activity to the other, if it increased failure rates among the rent seekers while not impeding others who happened to prefer productive pursuits, the result might have been the same. Similarly, tax rules can be used to rechannel entrepreneurial effort. It has, for instance, been proposed that takeover activity would be reoriented substantially in directions that contribute to productivity rather than impeding it by a "revenue-neutral" modification in capital gains taxes that increases rates sharply on assets held for short periods and decreases them considerably for assets held, say, for 2 years or more. A change in the rules that requires a plaintiff firm in a private antitrust suit to bear both parties' legal costs if the defendants are found not to be guilty (as is done in other countries) promises to reduce the frequency with which such lawsuits are used in an attempt to hamper effective competition.

As has already been said, this is hardly the place for an extensive discussion of the design of rational policy in the arena under consideration. The objective of the preceding brief discussion, rather, has been to suggest that there are identifiable means by which the rules of the game can be changed effectively and to illustrate these means concretely, though hardly attempting to offer any generalizations about their character. Certainly, the few illustrations that have just been offered should serve to confirm that there exist (in principle)

[14] Of course, that still leaves open the critical metaquestion, How does one go about changing the society's value system so that it will *want* to change the rules? But that is not the issue with which I am grappling here, since I see no basis on which the economist can argue that society *ought* to change its values. Rather, I am positing a society whose values lead it to favor productivity growth and am examining which instruments promise to be most effective in helping it to pursue this goal.

testable means that promise to induce entrepreneurs to shift their attentions in productive directions, *without any major change in their ultimate goals*. The testability of such hypotheses indicates that the discussion is no tissue of tautologies, and the absence of references to the allocability of entrepreneurship turned up in extensive search of the literature on the entrepreneur suggests that it was not entirely self-evident.

VII. Concluding Comment

There is obviously a good deal more to be said about the subject; however, enough material has been presented to indicate that a minor expansion of Schumpeter's theoretical model to encompass the determinants of the *allocation* of entrepreneurship among its competing uses can enrich the model considerably and that the hypotheses that have been associated with the model's extension here are not without substance, even if none of the material approaches anything that constitutes a formal test of a hypothesis, much less a rigorous "proof." It is also easy to confirm that each of the hypotheses that have been discussed clearly yields some policy implications.

Thus clear guidance for policy is provided by the main hypothesis (propositions 1–3) that the rules of the game that specify the relative payoffs to different entrepreneurial activities play a key role in determining whether entrepreneurship will be allocated in productive or unproductive directions and that this can significantly affect the vigor of the economy's productivity growth. After all, the prevailing laws and legal procedures of an economy are prime determinants of the profitability of activities such as rent seeking via the litigative process. Steps such as deregulation of the airlines or more rational antitrust rules can do a good deal here.

A last example can, perhaps, nail down the point. The fact that Japan has far fewer lawyers relative to population and far fewer lawsuits on economic issues is often cited as a distinct advantage to the Japanese economy, since it reduces at least in part the quantity of resources devoted to rent seeking. The difference is often ascribed to national character that is said to have a cultural aversion to litigiousness. This may all be very true. But closer inspection reveals that there are also other influences. While in the United States legal institutions such as trebled damages provide a rich incentive for one firm to sue another on the claim that the latter violated the antitrust laws, in Japan the arrangements are very different. In that country any firm undertaking to sue another on antitrust grounds must first apply for permission from the Japan Fair Trade Commission. But such permission is rarely given, and, once denied, there is no legal avenue for appeal.

The overall moral, then, is that we do not have to wait patiently for slow cultural change in order to find measures to redirect the flow of entrepreneurial activity toward more productive goals. As in the illustration of the Japanese just cited, it may be possible to change the rules in ways that help to offset undesired institutional influences or that supplement other influences that are taken to work in beneficial directions.

References

Abramovitz, Moses. *Thinking about Growth, and Other Essays of Economic Growth and Welfare.* New York: Cambridge Univ. Press, 1989.

Ashton, Thomas S. *The Industrial Revolution, 1760–1830.* London: Oxford Univ. Press, 1948.

Balazs, Etienne. *Chinese Civilization and Bureaucracy: Variations on a Theme.* New Haven, Conn.: Yale Univ. Press, 1964.

Berman, Constance H. "Medieval Agriculture, the Southern French Countryside, and the Early Cistercians: A Study of Forty-three Monasteries." *Trans. American Philosophical Soc.* 76, pt. 5 (1986).

Bloch, Marc. "Avènement et conquêtes du moulin a eau." *Annales d'Histoire Économique et Sociale* 7 (November 1935): 538–63.

Braudel, Fernand. *Civilization and Capitalism, 15th–18th Century.* Vols. 2, 3. New York: Harper and Row, 1986.

Brooke, Christopher N. L. *Europe in the Central Middle Ages, 962–1154.* London: Longman, 1964.

Carus-Wilson, Eleanora M. "An Industrial Revolution of the Thirteenth Century." *Econ. Hist. Rev.* 11, no. 1 (1941): 39–60.

Coleman, Donald C. "Industrial Growth and Industrial Revolutions." *Economica* 23 (February 1956): 1–22.

———. *Industry in Tudor and Stuart England.* London: Macmillan (for Econ. Hist. Soc.), 1975.

Cowdrey, H. E. J. "The Peace and the Truce of God in the Eleventh Century." *Past and Present,* no. 46 (February 1970), pp. 42–67.

Dasgupta, Partha. "Patents, Priority and Imitation or, the Economics of Races and Waiting Games." *Econ. J.* 98 (March 1988): 66–80.

de Roover, Raymond. "The Commercial Revolution of the 13th Century." In *Enterprise and Secular Change: Readings in Economic History,* edited by Frederic C. Lane and Jelle C. Riemersma. London: Allen and Unwin, 1953.

Douglas, David C. *William the Conqueror: The Norman Impact upon England.* Berkeley: Univ. California Press, 1964.

Feinstein, C. H. "Capital Formation in Great Britain." In *The Cambridge Economic History of Europe,* vol. 8, pt. 1, edited by Peter Mathias and M. M. Postan. Cambridge: Cambridge Univ. Press, 1978.

Finley, Moses I. "Technical Innovation and Economic Progress in the Ancient World." *Econ. Hist. Rev.* 18 (August 1965): 29–45.

———. *The Ancient Economy.* 2d ed. London: Hogarth, 1985.

Forbes, Robert J. *Studies in Ancient Technology.* Leiden: Brill, 1955.

Gimpel, Jean. *The Medieval Machine: The Industrial Revolution of the Middle Ages.* New York: Holt, Reinhart and Winston, 1976.

Ho, Ping-Ti. *The Ladder of Success in Imperial China, 1368–1911.* New York: Columbia Univ. Press, 1962.

Hobsbawm, Eric J. *Industry and Empire from 1750 to the Present Day.* Harmondsworth: Penguin, 1969.

Jones, Eric L. *The European Miracle: Environments, Economies, and Geopolitics in the History of Europe and Asia.* Cambridge: Cambridge Univ. Press, 1987.

Landes, David S. *The Unbound Prometheus: Technological Change and Industrial Development in Western Europe from 1750 to the Present.* New York: Cambridge Univ. Press, 1969.

Lefebvre, Georges. *The Coming of the French Revolution, 1789.* Princeton, N.J.: Princeton Univ. Press, 1947.

Lindbeck, Assar. "The Advanced Welfare State." Manuscript. Stockholm: Univ. Stockholm, 1987.

Liu, James T. C., and Golas, Peter J., eds. *Change in Sung China: Innovation or Renovation?* Lexington, Mass.: Heath, 1969.

Lopez, Robert S. "Hard Times and Investment in Culture." In *The Renaissance: A Symposium.* New York: Oxford Univ. Press (for Metropolitan Museum of Art), 1969.

McNeill, William H. *History of Western Civilization.* Rev. ed. Chicago: Univ. Chicago Press, 1969.

Marsh, Robert M. *The Mandarins: The Circulation of Elites in China, 1600–1900.* Glencoe, Ill.: Free Press, 1961.

Milward, Alan S. *The Economic Effects of the Two World Wars on Britain.* London: Macmillan (for Econ. Hist. Soc.), 1970.

Murphy, Kevin M.; Shleifer, Andrei; and Vishny, Robert. "The Allocation of Talent: Implications for Growth." Manuscript. Chicago: Univ. Chicago, 1990.

Needham, Joseph. "Mathematics and Science in China and the West." *Science and Society* 20 (Fall 1956): 320–43.

Nef, John U. "The Progress of Technology and the Growth of Large-Scale Industry in Great Britain, 1540–1640." *Econ. Hist. Rev.* 5 (October 1934): 3–24.

North, Douglass C., and Thomas, Robert Paul. *The Rise of the Western World: A New Economic History.* Cambridge: Cambridge Univ. Press, 1973.

Olson, Mancur. *The Rise and Decline of Nations: Economic Growth, Stagflation, and Social Rigidities.* New Haven, Conn.: Yale Univ. Press, 1982.

Ovitt, George, Jr. *The Restoration of Perfection: Labor and Technology in Medieval Culture.* New Brunswick, N.J.: Rutgers Univ. Press, 1987.

Painter, Sidney. *William Marshal: Knight-Errant, Baron, and Regent of England.* Baltimore: Johns Hopkins Press, 1933.

Robinson, Joan. *The Economics of Imperfect Competition.* London: Macmillan, 1933.

Rosenberg, Nathan, and Birdzell, L. E., Jr. *How the West Grew Rich: The Economic Transformation of the Industrial World.* New York: Basic Books, 1986.

Rubinstein, W. D., ed. *Wealth and the Wealthy in the Modern World.* London: Croom Helm, 1980.

Schama, Simon. *Citizens: A Chronicle of the French Revolution.* New York: Knopf, 1989.

Schumpeter, Joseph A. *The Theory of Economic Development.* Leipzig: Duncker and Humblot, 1912. English ed. Cambridge, Mass.: Harvard Univ. Press, 1934.

Smith, Adam. *An Inquiry into the Nature and Causes of the Wealth of Nations.* 1776. Reprint. New York: Random House (Modern Library), 1937.
Stone, Lawrence. "The Bourgeois Revolution of Seventeenth-Century England Revisited." *Past and Present,* no. 109 (November 1985), pp. 44–54.
Summers, Lawrence, and Cutler, David. "Texaco and Pennzoil Both Lost Big." *New York Times* (February 14, 1988).
Thirsk, Joan. "The Restoration Land Settlement." *J. Modern Hist.* 26 (December 1954): 315–28.
Veblen, Thorstein. *The Theory of Business Enterprise.* New York: Scribner, 1904.
Veyne, Paul. "Vie de trimalcion." *Annales: Économies, Societés, Civilisations* 16 (March/April 1961): 213–47.
White, Lynn T., Jr. *Medieval Technology and Social Change.* Oxford: Clarendon, 1962.
Williamson, Jeffrey G. "Why Was British Growth So Slow during the Industrial Revolution?" *J. Econ. Hist.* 44 (September 1984): 687–712.

[3]

Towards Microeconomics of Innovation: Growth Engine Hallmark of Market Economics

WILLIAM J. BAUMOL*

Abstract

The Bourgeoisie (i.e., capitalism) cannot exist without constantly revolutionizing the instruments of production. Conservation of the old modes of production in unaltered form was, on the contrary, the first condition of existence for all earlier industrial classes. The bourgeoisie, during its rule of scarce one hundred years has created more massive and more colossal productive forces than have all preceding generations together. It has accomplished wonders far surpassing Egyptian pyramids, Roman aqueducts and Gothic cathedrals...[Marx and Engels, 1847].

Baumol's Second Tautology: Innovation is a heterogeneous product.

The Big Puzzle: Why Do all Rival Systems Trail so Far Behind Free-Market Growth?

Per-capita income in the leading capitalist economies is growing at a rate that apparently permits something like an eight-fold multiplication in a century, as Keynes predicted in 1932.[1] I suggest this number is so large that it defies comprehension. What would our lives be like if we were recipients of an average family income today, and then seven eighths of that amount were suddenly removed? In contrast, it is estimated (very crudely, of course) that in wealthy eighteenth century England real per-capita income had just about re-attained its level in third-century Rome, some 15 centuries earlier. Words do, indeed, fail in an attempt to convey the incredible growth record of the free-market economies. Undoubtedly, the spectacular and unmatched growth rates of the industrialized free-market economies are what distinguish them most from all other economic systems. In no other system, current or in the past, has the average income of the general public risen anywhere nearly as much or as quickly as it has in North America, Western Europe and Japan. Though the Soviet Union planned its economy and forced its population to invest heavily in factories and hydroelectric dams, its failure to produce enough to raise the standard of living of its population to that of the free-market economies undoubtedly played a major role in its downfall. There have been great civilizations with extraordinary records of invention and engineering—medieval China and ancient Rome are clear examples. But none has approached the growth record of modern free-market economies. What is the secret of their extraordinary success? That is the economic puzzle that undoubtedly is critical to the degree of prosperity our future is able to achieve. Its answer is what the world's poorer countries are anxious to learn. Yet in

*New York University and Princeton University—U.S.A. Distinguished Address presented at the Fifty-Second International Atlantic Economic Conference, Philadelphia, Pennsylvania, October 11-14, 2001. The author is grateful to the Russell Sage Foundation and the C.V. Starr Center for their support of this work. This article is based on the author's forthcoming book [Baumol, 2002].

the theoretical growth literature there is hardly anything said about the differences between the economics of capitalism and all rival economic systems that can account for the totally unprecedented performance of the former.

In informal attempts to explain the miracle, the terms innovation and entrepreneur frequently recur. Yet in the main body of our writings on microeconomic theory these two words are also scarcely to be found.

The explanation of this miracle must surely be sought in the activities of industries and the business firms of which they are constituted. For they are the producers of the increasing outpouring of goods and services that constitutes the growth record of capitalism. It must be something about business firms and the decisions they make that plays a vital part in the this prime accomplishment of our economy. But the standard microeconomics of firms and industries, while it has included some outstanding contributions on the theory of innovation, has provided little suggesting what features of business behavior and decision making can account for all this growth. Indeed, as we know, standard welfare theory offers reasons to expect the contrary—that the capitalist economy will be characterized by levels of innovation activity that are far from optimal.

Here, I will describe some features of competitive markets to which the growth performance of business firms can be attributed, features that literally force businesses to do all they can to contribute to the growth miracle. I will then provide some hints of a microeconomic model using the most elementary of microeconomic tools, to analyze this process.

Microeconomic Models of the Firm: Where is the Entrepreneur?

The Schumpeterian entrepreneur is a widely respected concept, but in formal theory he is an invisible man. Virtually all theoretical firms are entrepreneurless.[2] It is not difficult to explain the absence. There are at least two reasons. The first is the extreme lack of standardization in innovation, the product of the entrepreneur's activity. The second is the use of maximization and minimization as the theorist's central descriptive tool.

Economic theorists have always found it difficult to deal mathematically with heterogeneous products, though there has recently been considerable progress here. But innovation is perhaps the product that attains the ultimate in lack of uniformity. If two products or processes are very similar they will not both be considered innovative. Innovative activity, by definition, is the attempt to introduce something that did not exist before. The result is that it becomes virtually impossible to say anything at all that characterizes the features of every innovation. That already is an enormous handicap for the theorist, even for one who acknowledges a key role in the growth process for the entrepreneur as innovator.

The second obstacle to incorporation of the entrepreneur into the standard theory is the nature of the generic model of the firm. In its simplest form (and in this respect the more complex and more sophisticated models are no better), the theoretical firm must choose among alternative values for a small number of rather well-defined variables: price, output, investment, perhaps advertising outlay and, occasionally, a few others. In making this choice management is taken to consider the costs and revenues associated with each candidate set of values, as described by the relevant functional relationships, equations, and inequalities. Explicitly or implicitly, the firm is then taken to perform a mathematical calculation which yields optimal (i.e., profit-maximizing) values for all of its decision variables and it is these values that the theory assumes to be chosen—that are declared by the theory to constitute the company's vector of decisions. There matters rest, forever or until exogenous forces lead to an autonomous change in the environment. Until there is such a shift in one of the relationships that define the problem, the firm is taken to replicate precisely its previous decisions, day after day, year after year.

Clearly, the entrepreneur has been read out of the model. There is no room for enterprise or initiative. The management group is left in control and yet becomes a passive calculator that reacts mechanically to changes imposed on it by fortuitous external developments over which it does not exert, and may not even attempt to exert, any influence.

What has just been said constitutes no criticism, not even an attempt to reprove mildly the neoclassical model of the firm. That model does what it was designed to do and does it well. Like any respectable analysis, one hopes that it will be modified, amended, and improved with time, but not because it is incapable of handling an issue for which it was not designed. The model is essentially an instrument of optimality analysis of well-defined business decision problems, and it is precisely such (very real and important) problems that need no entrepreneur for their solution. Rather, he is needed for assistance in accounting for the free-market's growth performance. I will return presently to the connection between the two.

Macroeconomic Endogenous Growth Models: Where is the Prince of Denmark?

None of what follows is to be interpreted as criticism, much less denigration, of the current or earlier macroeconomic growth writings. However, since it is my hope to carry study of the subject a step beyond what that work has been able to achieve, I must begin by indicating what this literature has not yet succeeded in doing. In particular, I believe that the macro analysis, like the microeconomic growth literature, has failed, indeed, it has not even tried, to grapple with the extraordinary growth record of the capitalist economies, as distinguished from economies of other sorts.

The earlier discussions took innovation to be an autonomous contribution of the passage of time—as a sort of manna dropped in a steady stream from some unspecified source, that could just as well emerge from a capitalistic economy or from any other. Later model builders recognized that this formulation was inadequate, and that there were features inherent in the economic processes that account for innovation and growth. Yet the endogenous features cited, notably the externalities of innovation, and the acquisition of human capital, in part through learning by doing, apply to many forms of economic organization and not only to the free-market economies.

In my view, like that of Schumpeter, this leaves these very valuable contributions as performances of Shakespeare's *Hamlet* that include the King, Ophelia, Gertrude, and many other of the crucial characters, but omit the Prince of Denmark. They tell us much about innovation and growth, but they fail to account for the most salient and extraordinary feature of the growth record, the entirely unparalleled success of the free-market economies. I will suggest that they fail to do so in part because they are macromodels, something patently unobjectionable in itself. But I will argue that it is a major handicap for study of the issue before us, which, I believe, is explainable primarily in terms of microeconomic behavior.

Recent growth analysis had its beginnings in the 1950s with the work of Solow and Swan, who deservedly elicited renewed interest in models of growth and in approaches compatible with statistical estimation. The models themselves represented no drastic break with the past, and clearly have their roots in the work of the classical economists, notably that of David Ricardo. The Ricardian model is sufficiently familiar and needs little review here. In short, it postulates that innovation results in a shifting of the production function and postponement of the stationary state, something that can occur repeatedly and can keep the economy expanding indefinitely. What is missing in the Ricardian story is any explanation of the innovation mechanism, and certainly any endogenous innovation model. So the innovation process in the Ricardian model must be represented simply as a (stochastic) function of time and nothing else, and with no distinguishing features that differentiate the process in a capitalist economy from that in any other form of economic organization. Thus, Ricardo's story emphatically contains no role for the Prince of Denmark. The original Solow model, the prototype neoclassical model, contains a representation of innovation not much different from Ricardo's, with invention also autonomous, and undifferentiated as between free-market economies and other economic forms. The model assumes that there are diminishing returns to capital, an attribute that predicts convergence of productivities and per-capita incomes in different economies, because wealthier economies have relatively large capital stocks whose productivities, relative to those of poorer countries, are severely reduced by diminishing returns.

Romer recognized that this neoclassical model could profit from some modification. He observed that the facts do not support the model's prediction of universal convergence—the catch-up of all economies to approximately the same levels of productivity and per-capita income. The many statistical studies of the convergence hypothesis generally conclude that while the wealthiest economies have, indeed, been converging, most of the impecunious nations are falling further behind. Second, he reminded us that the innovation process is neither largely autonomous nor largely fortuitous. The amount of activity devoted to innovation, and the output of that activity, is influenced substantially by what is going on in the economy. This led to a series of constructs referred to as the endogenous growth models (see, e.g., Romer or Lucas or Grossman and Helpman).

However, what is significant for this discussion is that none of these formulations attempts to distinguish the free-market economy from other economic forms. Thus, whatever their virtues, none of them assigns a part in the scenario to the Prince of Denmark. Nor should this be surprising. Other economies, both historical and modern, have stressed education, have innovated, have experienced spillovers from education; and other sources. In short, they have exhibited all the endogenous innovation features of the newer models. But to get at the main special distinguishing features of the capitalist economy, I believe, it is necessary to turn to microeconomics.

Innovation and the Growth Process

In discussing the growth performance of the capitalist economies, I will focus on innovation rather than other contributory sources such as human capital. A primary source of the growth miracle of the past two centuries, undoubtedly, is the surge of innovation that probably first reached a substantial pace in the first third of the nineteenth century. Improved education and the construction of factories, roads and other influences undoubtedly also made substantial contributions to growth, as the literature recognizes.

Yet, a very large proportion of the economic growth since the eighteenth century that is directly attributable to investment in human and physical capital probably is nevertheless ultimately attributable to innovation. For the incredible poverty of nations in earlier centuries meant that it was only the inventions of the industrial revolution that could provide society with the resources necessary to permit any substantial expansion of education or construction of plant and machinery. Only the growing outputs from innovation, first in agriculture and mining and then in manufacturing and transportation, made feasible the enormous increases in productive plant and equipment and in education (and other forms of investment in human capital) that are widely judged to have contributed greatly to economic growth. In other words, without innovation the expansion of education and the economy's capital stock would have been negligible. Thus, it can be argued not only that innovation has facilitated the growth process, but that without it the process would have been reduced to insignificance.

What is Different About Free-Market Economies?

It is in innovation, and not in invention alone, where we find answers to the great puzzle—the explanation of the free-market's unmatched growth performance. Earlier societies have had a spectacular invention record. The Chinese are the outstanding example. Centuries before Columbus they had invented printing, the compass, complex (water) clockwork, gunpowder, spinning machinery, a cotton gin, porcelain, matches, toothbrushes, playing cards and much more. There have been other countries in history with a considerable record of new products and new technology. Moreover, education was highly valued in the Chinese culture and others, though, it is true, much of the population was uneducated. Yet these inventions and this education never produced economic growth anything like that in the modern market economies.

It should be added that markets of substantial importance exist in virtually every economy of the world and have existed throughout recorded history. What, then, is different about modern markets that not only gives them the capacity to produce growth miracles but seems to get those miracles to happen very frequently? There can be no simple answer; indeed, any proposed answer is bound to leave out key features, ranging from political changes, evolution of religious beliefs and even historical accident. However, here it will be argued that two features of our economy have played a crucial role. The first such feature is free competition, that is, competition not handicapped by severe government regulations or tightly enforced customary rules, like those of the medieval guilds, that prevented gloves-off combat among rival firms. Of particular significance here is rivalry among oligopolistic firms. The second crucial development is the fact that in today's economy many rival oligopolistic firms use innovation as the main battle weapon with which they protect themselves from competitors and with which they seek to beat those competitors out. The result is precisely analogous to an arm's race – to the case of two countries, each of which fears that the other will attack it militarily and therefore feels it necessary always at least to match the other country's military spending. Similarly, either of two competing firms will feel it to be foolhardy to let its competitor outspend it on the development and acquisition of its battle weapons. Each is driven to conclude that at least matching effort and spending on the innovation process is a matter of life and death. Naturally, in an economy in which this is so, a constant stream of innovations can be expected to appear, because firms do not dare to relax their innovation activities.

Routine vs. Independent Endogenous Innovation

A fuller description of my analysis focuses primarily on routinized innovation processes – those on which the amount of spending is determined routinely by business firms as part of their regular competitive strategic planning. The routine character of those processes is important because it permits their incorporation into standard models of investment and other parts of microeconomic analysis. Routine innovation processes—those guided by standard business-decision principles—are, indeed, of great and probably of growing importance, with 70 percent of U.S. research and development expenditure channeled through business firms.

However, this does not mean that the entrepreneurial independent innovator no longer plays a significant role. Nelson even concludes that "...Schumpeter's prognostication that as science grew stronger technical innovation would become more predictable and routine has turned out to be a bad call." [Nelson, 1996, p. 81].

And Scherer provides a long list of major technical inventions introduced by entrant firms and consequently not subject to the pressures for routinization in established enterprises. His examples include the incandescent lamp, alternating current, radio telegraph and telephony, the dial telephone, the synchronous orbit communications satellite, the turbojet engine, the sound motion picture, self-developing photography, the electronic calculator, among many others [Scherer, 1980, p. 438].

Indeed, one can offer the plausible conjecture that most of the revolutionary new ideas are, and are likely to continue to be, provided more heavily by independent innovators. In turn, these innovators, once successful, often establish firms of their own, joining the large enterprises that engage preponderantly in routine innovation. This type of innovation is primarily devoted to product improvement, increased reliability and enhanced user friendliness of products and the finding of new uses for those products. Both the independent and the routinized innovation activities undoubtedly contribute significantly to economic growth, as Rosenberg has emphasized [Rosenberg, 1976, p. 66]. These two types of activities appear to be complementary. Together they seem to contribute more to growth than either could by itself. There is also some reason to conclude that the incremental contribution of the routine activity adds more to growth than do the more revolutionary prototype innovations. Thus, consider how little computing power the first clumsy and enormously expensive computers provided, and how much more such power has been added by the many subsequent incremental improvements.

There is no reason to expect the independent inventor or the entrepreneurial innovator to become obsolete any time in the foreseeable future. Still, at least measured in terms of spending, the bulk of research and development activity seems to have become routine and this makes it far easier to analyze, and to spell out its role in the free-market economy.

Toward a Microeconomic Model of the Firm's Spending on Innovation

One conclusion that can be drawn from a competitive model of the innovation process, characterized by ease of entry into this activity, is that one can expect its profits to be driven toward competitive levels. And in fact, there is empirical evidence suggesting that in innovative arenas such as computer hardware and software, aggregating cases of success and failure, economic profits have been remarkably close to zero. But since innovation takes much effort and money, is very risky, and if the economic profits to be expected from innovation activity are held down by fierce competition of rival innovators, why do firms do it? The answer, at least in part, is that the competitive market mechanism gives them no choice. If they do not keep up with their competitors in terms of attractiveness of their products and efficiency improvements that permit them to keep their costs low, they will lose out to their rivals, and end up losing market share and losing money. Low economic profits, that is, profits that yield little more than normal competitive returns to investors, surely are better than negative profits.

The result is like an arms race between two countries, each of which fears invasion by the other. Each is driven to keep up with the other's military expenditure. Raising its armaments expenditure will probably get it nowhere, because it can expect the other nation to match any such increase, raising expenditure without improving the nation's military security. But at the same time, neither nation will dare to cut its arms spending unilaterally, since that will simply invite invasion by the other.[3]

Consider an industry with, say, five firms of roughly equal size, and suppose that the firm with whose decision we will be concerned, Company X, sees that each of the other firms spends about $20 million a year on research and development. X will not dare to spend much less than $20 million on research and development itself, because if it does so its next year's product will probably not be nearly as good as those of some or all of its rivals. On the other hand, it sees little point in raising the ante, say, to $30 million, because it knows that if it does so the others will feel themselves forced to raise their research and development budgets correspondingly. So it will pay Company X to follow industry practice, investing $20 million a year in research and development, and it may even go on doing so, year after year.

But that is not the end of the story. All five firms in the industry will continue to invest the same amount, until some year one of them has a research breakthrough and comes up with a wonderful new product (as happens in most high-tech industries from time to time). Then, for that firm it will pay to expand its investment in the breakthrough product, because that will pay off even if the other firms in the industry match the increase. Other companies in the industry will feel forced to follow, and now the industry norm will no longer be a $20 million investment per year, but will instead be raised to $25 million per firm.

The story, then, is that competition forces firms in the industry to keep up with one another in their research and development investment. But once they have caught up, the investment expenditure remains fairly level until, from time to time, something induces one firm to break ranks and increase its spending, with all the other firms following behind. Such a ratchet arrangement holds matters steady, permits investment in innovation under certain circumstances to move forward, but generally does not allow it to retreat. Research and development spending can then be expected to expand from time to time, but once the new level is reached, the ratchet—the competitive market forces—prevent a retreat to the previous lower level.

This, then, is a critical part of the mechanism that accounts for the extraordinary growth record of free-enterprise economies and differentiates them from all other known economic arrangements. It is the competitive pressure that forces firms to run as fast as they can in the innovation race just in order to keep up with the others.

Risk Reduction Through Technology Sharing

A reason why it is sometimes suspected that free-markets will perform poorly in terms of growth is the alleged unwillingness of firms with proprietary technology to let others make use of it. The plausible story, which turns out not to be universally supported by the facts, is that the firms will always use secrecy, patents or any other means to retain the competitive advantage their technology gives them. As a result other firms are forced to use inefficient technology and to supply obsolete products, and the growth of the economy is thereby handicapped.

But it is not difficult to show, on the contrary, that if the license prices are sufficient, it will (and does) become attractive for firms to let others use their proprietary technical knowledge. Thus suppose the innovator firm can earn $10 per widget that it produces itself, using its own technology to the exclusion of others. Then if a rival offers a license fee of $12 per widget that this competitor produces it clearly will pay the proprietor of the innovation to accept the offer. And it will pay the rival to make such an offer if it is the more efficient producer of widgets (but the less efficient innovator). This is just as it pays firms to become suppliers of any other proprietary input, even to rivals, if the price is right. As a consequence, there exist profitable markets for licensed proprietary technology, of which Thomas Edison's laboratories were an early example.

Many firms also try to reduce their innovation risks by systematic technology trading. Each of two firms can be expected to fear that its labs may come up only with failures in some year, while its competitor may possibly have better luck in that period. The two enterprises will then have reason to seek an agreement for each to share with the other all of its successful future innovations, say, for the next five years.

This can also help the two technology-sharing firms to compete with a third firm, if their innovations are complements rather than substitutes. In portable computers, for example, one manufacturer may introduce an improved memory, another a more durable battery, and a third may invent a way to make the machine lighter and more compact. Each of these three firms has the choice of keeping its invention to itself. But if two of them get together and agree to produce computers combining the features each of them has contributed, they will be able to market a product that is clearly superior to what each could have produced alone. They are then likely to be in a far better position to meet the competition of the third manufacturer, which has no external sources.

Voluntary participation in the process of dissemination of technology is beneficial not only to the licenser, but generally also to the licensee, who obviously will not agree to pay a compensatory price unless it is profitable to her. As already noted, this will be so if the licensee is the more efficient user of the technology. But also relevant is the fact that such " friendly" technology transfer is both faster and cheaper than hostile transfer by means such as industrial espionage and reverse engineering. And in an industry in which technical progress is rapid, delay in access to a product can be tantamount to obtaining a product that is obsolete.

There are many firms and industries that engage in this sharing practice. They range from spectroscope manufacturers to steel producers. Firms exchange technology informally or enter into detailed contracts for the systematic exchange of technical information. The agreements often even require each firm to train technical experts from the other in the use of the new technology. The activity of business firms in providing their technology to others for profit, has become so commonplace that MIT has run a seminar for business firms, teaching how they can be more effective in the technology-provision business.

The process of technology dissemination for profit contributes to growth in free-market economies in at least two very significant ways. First, when innovations are disseminated widely, rapidly and voluntarily, they clearly hasten the retirement of obsolete technology. Second, the payments to the innovators can help substantially to internalize the externalities of innovation—the much-discussed spillovers that can constitute a major disincentive for the economically efficient amount of investment in innovation.

The Rule of Law and Productive Incentives for Entrepreneurs and Capitalists

So far, I have focussed on the mechanism of free-markets that elicits a substantial growth contribution from business firms and their routinized innovation activity. I turn next to the independent inventors and innovators, and discuss the interactions between their activities and the workings of the free-market economies.

Despite the evident continuation on substantial scales of rent seeking and other forms of wasteful entrepreneurship under capitalism, never before has productive activity been so effective and prestigious as a method for the attainment of wealth, power and prestige. It seems evident that these three goals are the primary objectives of most entrepreneurs, and history indicates that many entrepreneurs are not particularly choosy about the means they utilize to achieve these ends. They, like those engaged in any other occupation, span the range of morality and dedication to virtue. So one can expect that there will be many entrepreneurs who will choose whatever activities offer the greatest promise of attaining those objectives, whatever the social consequences of those most rewarding activities may be.

More than that—moral standards surely are not immutable. They tend to adapt themselves to current opportunities and practices, so that activities that today would be considered beyond the pale in terms of their ethics may in an earlier time have been accepted as normal and even commendable in a free-market economy.

In ancient Rome and medieval China, with their abundance of military and nonmilitary inventions, pursuit of wealth and power was considered acceptable, and even as desirable, as they are in the most greed-driven of capitalist societies. But the ideas about the means that were proper for attainment of these goals were very different from today's. Methods of wealth accumulation that were considered laudable in one or both of these societies included military aggression, ransom, bribery and usury. Some of the great figures of Roman history, for example, were respected for having acquired vast riches by these means. The Chinese mandarins, having been appointed to powerful positions, were expected to recoup in the form of bribes the heavy expenses they incurred in preparing for the difficult Imperial examinations that were requisites for such positions. No hint of scandal or disapproval attached to these means of accumulation.

But in both societies there were two types of activity that incurred unambiguous disgrace – participation in commerce or in productive activity (with the possible exception of some gentlemanly agricultural undertakings). In Rome, for example, such disgraceful endeavors were left to freedmen—to manumitted slaves and their sons. And these individuals, too, strove to accumulate sufficient means so that they could afford to leave their degrading occupations, or at least make it possible for later generations in their families to achieve respectability.

It is little wonder, then, that there was not much productive entrepreneurship in these societies. Even though, particularly, the Chinese produced an astonishing abundance of inventions, there was little innovation, in the sense of productive application and distribution of the inventions. Most such inventions were put to little productive use and often soon disappeared and were completely forgotten.

Destructive wars and rent-seeking activities as means to enhance wealth and power of course continued through the Renaissance and, indeed, they manifestly continue today. The idea that productive activity is disgraceful continued to guide continental European nobility well into the nineteenth century. But at least in Italy, the Low Countries and in England, things began to change, perhaps in the thirteenth to fifteenth centuries. As capitalistic activity rose in these countries, the relative ease of wealth attainment through banking, commerce and production may well have become irresistible. The attractiveness of such pursuits also grew as the constant and urgent need of funds by the royal houses expanded. As armies grew in size and arms and ammunition became more expensive, the kings found themselves repeatedly threatened with inability to finance their wars and with bankruptcy when they could not repay their vast loans. Phillip II of Spain—he of the Armada—underwent bankruptcy many times because the Cortes—the bodies of nobles whose assent for additional taxes was required—proved reluctant to levy additional tax payments on themselves.

The same was true of Parliament in England, where there was instituted, perhaps a century after Magna Carta, the principle of no taxation without representation (of the nobles and the gentry), an issue finally settled in the seventeenth century, in the battles between Parliament and the Stuarts. Edward IV, the Yorkist king, used many devices to get out of his financial difficulties. For us, it is most noteworthy that among the means he employed was entry into commerce. Equally important, a number of his nobles quickly followed his example.

Productive entrepreneurship in the free-market economies, then, has been encouraged materially by contraction of the opportunities for financial gain through rent seeking and destructive activities, and by the simultaneous explosion of ways of wealth-gathering in productive occupations. Productive entrepreneurship has also been stimulated by the growing power of the rule of law and the concomitant constraints upon arbitrary exercise of government power. A strong case can be made for the conclusion that without the rule of law, including the rights of property and the enforceability of contracts, the growth miracle of capitalism, indeed, capitalism itself, might not have been possible.

History also tells us about the advances in the economically crucial rule of law that occurred in the periods I have been discussing. In many earlier societies there was no such thing as the right of private property. At least in theory, all property belonged to the monarch, who was entitled to requisition any of it whenever it suited his purposes. This was notably true in ancient China, where not only money and physical property was subject to expropriation, but even innovations themselves were likely to be taken over by the state. For example, it is reported that "...frequently...during the course of Chinese history...the scholar officials...gathered in the fruits of other people's ingenuity...three examples of innovations that met that fate [are] paper, invented by a eunuch; printing, used by Buddhists as a medium for religious propaganda; and the bill of exchange, an expedient of private businessmen." [Balaszs, p. 18]. Even religion did not prevent royal takings, sometimes on a massive scale, as in the expropriation of the Templars[4] by Phillip IV of France (Phillip the Fair) in 1307 or that of the monasteries by Henry VIII of England, more than two centuries later.

The resulting uncertainty was surely a major discouragement to saving and to innovative activity alike. Wealth was best rapidly consumed, lest it serve as a temptation to government acquisitiveness, and it may be conjectured that this contributed to the propensity of the nobility in a number of societies to be perpetually in debt. Productive innovation, aside from receiving little recognition, much less admiration, was rarely worth the required effort. Without the rule of law, clearly, enormous obstacles prevented economic growth of any substantial magnitude.

Capitalism itself, even more clearly, was precluded by absence of the rule of law. Capitalism requires markets in which the participants can have confidence in any agreements arrived at. It is driven by pursuit of accumulated and retainable wealth, and opportunities to expand that wealth by devoting it to the production process. Sanctity of property and contract, as well as institutions that can be relied upon to enforce them both, are necessary conditions for the creation of the capitalist and for effective execution of his role. That is why, without the contribution of the lawyers, the free-market economies might never have evolved. And even if they had, it is unlikely that their unprecedented growth could have occurred. It is on these grounds that I base my evaluation of the enormous total contribution of the lawyers to the performance of the industrial economies (while questioning their marginal contribution).

But how was the rule of law introduced? The key to the answer arguably lies in economic forces, together with the limited power of the Kings. At various times these rulers were forced to grant (and reconfirm) privileges and protections to their subjects either under direct compulsion (as at Runnymede in the case of Magna Carta) or in exchange for needed favors. For it must be understood that the term, absolute monarchy, was always a misrepresentation of the facts. Even the most powerful kings and emperors held absolute sway only over limited geographic areas and over subjects who were not too remote in location or in station. Primitive means of transportation, absence of standing armies rather than mercenaries or troops provided by powerful subjects under traditional arrangements, perpetual shortage of funds, and tiny administrative bodies, meant that the medieval and Renaissance kings possessed only very limited power. They had no effective tax collection agencies, a gap, as we know, that prevailed in France until the Revolution. The kings also found it difficult to borrow, and had to pay higher interest rates than many other borrowers because there was no way they could make an enforceable commitment to repay. After all, there existed no court in which a debtor could sue the ruler.

The consequence, as we have seen, was that kings were frequently driven to beg for funds from the Parliament, the Cortes or the other bodies that held the power to tax, and those bodies frequently demanded and often received concessions in return. Under such pressures, and with their nobility often itself aggressive and unruly, the kings were forced, time after time, to agree to grant protections to various groups of subjects against certain arbitrary royal actions. The beneficiaries included not only the nobles but also the towns, which early began to acquire their traditional liberties. As these protections evolved and accumulated, they grew into a body of law. Driven by economic forces, the low medieval productivity and the resulting royal poverty, they became the legal foundation for a free-market economy in which entrepreneurship could flourish and production could explode.

Concluding Comment

I have stressed several features of the capitalist economy that, together, arguably contribute most heavily to its unequaled growth record. The first is the routinization of innovation that transforms much of the enterprise from a sequence of chance occurrences into a businesslike activity that can be relied upon and is reasonably predictable. The second and, perhaps, most fundamental is the role of innovation as a primary competitive weapon, and the resulting innovation arms race. The third is the profit offered by voluntary dissemination of proprietary technology and its adoption as a normal business activity. Finally, I have stressed the incentive that capitalism provides to entrepreneurs to channel their activities into productive directions, rather than, as in many other forms of economic organization, in directions that contribute little to output growth or even impede it.

As I have said, perhaps the most important of these is the competitive innovation arms race in much of oligopolistic industry in the modern free-enterprise economies. Here, I take the liberty of mis-reporting somewhat Dr. Johnson's mot to the effect that "the prospect of hanging concentrates the mind wonderfully." The prospect of insolvency concentrates management's mind on the innovation race. No other economy has ever had anything near so powerful a driving mechanism, one that makes not only for a vast stream of invention, but for its rapid harnessing in productive uses.

The results of this paper may, perhaps, also be a step toward bringing the intertemporal welfare theory closer to reality. It can help to explain some of what is left out when the theory focuses on the spillovers of innovation, thereby leading to the expectation that the innovation performance of our economy may well be seriously inefficient. In may enable us to adapt the theory to the historically unprecedented growth and innovation performance of the free-market economies, the feature of those economies that has surely (and deservedly) been their most attractive attribute to nonspecialists.

Footnotes

[1][Keynes, 1932]. I must thank Senator D. P. Moynihan for calling this passage to my attention.

[2]It should be emphasized that there is a growing and very promising theoretical literature dealing with analytical tools that seem useful for the study of entrepreneurship. But they have not found their way into the core of mainstream micro analysis.

[3]The reader will recognize the direct analogy with the Sweezy kinked demand curve model of price stickiness in oligopoly pricing. There is also a touch of the prisoner's dilemma or, rather, the red queen paradox (see Khalil [1997]).

[4]The fact that the bulk of what Philip obtained from the Templars went to the Order of the Hospitalers rather than the royal treasury does not matter here. Philip seems quite clearly to have been seeking a new source of funds, having run out of such conventional sources as the Jews, who had just been expelled from France [Strayer, 1980].

References

Arrow, K. J., "The Economic Implications of Learning by Doing," *Review of Economic Studies*, Vol. 28, June 1962, pp. 155-73.

Baumol, W. J., *The Free-Market Innovation Machine: Analyzing the Capitalist Growth Miracle*, Princeton: Princeton University Press, 2002.

Grossman, G. M. and Elthanan Helpman "Endogenous Innovation in the Theory of Growth," *Journal of Economic Perspectives*, Vol. 8, Winter, 1994, pp. 23-44.

Keynes, John Maynard, *Essays in Persuasion*, New York: Harcourt & Co., 1932.

Khalil, E. L., "The Red Queen Paradox: A Proper Name for a Popular Game," *Journal of Institutional and Theoretical Economics*, Vol. 153, June 1997, pp. 411-15.

Lucas, R. E. Jr., "On the Mechanics of Economic Development," *Journal of Economic Development*, Vol 22, July 1988, pp. N.3-42.

Marx, Karl and Friedrich Engels, *Manifesto of the Communist Party*, 1847.

Nelson, R. R., *The Sources of Economic Growth*, Cambridge, Mass: Harvard University Press, 1996.

Ricardo, David, *Principles of Political Economy*, London: 1817.

Romer, P. M., "Increasing Returns and Long-Run Growth," *Journal of Political Economy*, Vol. 94, October, 1986, pp. 1002-37.

—."Endogenous Technical Change," *Journal of Political Economy*, Vol. 98, October 1990, pp. S71-S102.

Rosenberg, Nathan, *Perspectives on Technology*, Cambridge: Cambridge University Press, 1976.

Scherer, F. M., *Industrial Market Structure and Economic Performance*, Chicago: Rand McNally, second edition, 1980.

Schumpeter, J. A., *Capitalism, Socialism and Democracy*, New York: Harper & Brothers, second edition, 1947.

[4]

KYKLOS, Vol. 39 – 1986 – Fasc. 2, 167–179

On the Possibility of Continuing Expansion of Finite Resources

WILLIAM J. BAUMOL*

> Neither reduced demand nor expanded exploration can make our finite resources limitless.'
> (BAUMOL and OATES [1979], p. 107)

The received wisdom of the environmental literature gives prominence to the fact that the earth is a planet whose contents are finite and whose resources, if used continuously, must ultimately be exhausted. Taken in its obvious sense this observation is as undeniable as it is trivial. However, as will be shown in this note, there is a sense far more significant for the social welfare in which this need not be true. On the contrary, measured in terms of their prospective contribution to human welfare the available quantity of these exhaustable and unreproducable resources may rise unceasingly, year after year.

Rather than approaching exhaustion with continued use, their effective inventories may actually be growing and they may never come anywhere near disappearance. In short, our society's growing per capita output, rather than constituting a case of profligacy in which society lives off its capital, may in fact involve what amounts to net saving of unreproducable resources, so that their effective stocks are constantly expanded by the same family of developments that underlie the growth in real per capita income since the Industrial Revolution. Moreover, I will provide evidence suggesting that this is no mere abstract possibility but is, rather, something that may actually be happening now.

*Princeton and New York Universities. – I should like to express my deep gratitude the the Exxon Education Foundation, the Joint Council on Economic Education, the Division of Information Science and Technology of the National Science Foundation, and the C.V. Starr Center for Applied Economics for their generous support of the research underlying this paper. I am also deeply indebted to DIETRICH FISCHER and MICHAEL GOLDBERG for their help in the analysis.

The explanation of these paradoxes is quite straightforward. A technological change which increases output per unit of use of resources, either directly through increased efficiency in use and recycling of those resources or by a decrease in waste (inefficiency) in the extraction or production process, obviously helps to decrease current usage, all other things being equal. But, in addition, it also increases the prospective output contribution of the as yet unused stock of those resources. If a given year's technical change thereby raises the effective quantity of the unused stocks by an amount greater than the year's direct usage, then, in the only sense pertinent to economic welfare, the stock of those resources must be greater at the end of the year than it was at the beginning. And while it must remain true that with continued usage the inventory of such a resource still remaining in its natural habitat must continually decline, as I will show, it need never be exhausted completely and what we may call its *effective quantity* may continue to rise, if not forever, at least for so long as humanity survives.

It is true and perhaps equally surprising that though the effective inventory of the resource need never decline, consumption will eventually have to decline and, indeed, it must approach zero asymptotically as the length of the elapsed period approaches infinity.

I. THE EVIDENCE OF PRICES

We economists are prone to judge the abundance of a resource by the behavior of its price. So long as demand for the item is not shifting downward and market prices are not markedly distorted by interferences such as government intervention, we expect that the real price of a resource will rise as its remaining quantity declines, in accord with the classical theorem of HOTELLING [1931].

Evidence on this issue was first assembled by BARNETT and MORSE [1963], part 3, chapters 8 and 9). They found for a sample of thirteen minerals that the real cost of extraction per unit had declined for all but two (lead and zinc) over the period 1870–1957. Using more recent data on *prices* of fifteen minerals, Frisch carried out for BAUMOL and OATES a parallel calculation for the period 1900 to 1975, using all minerals for which the required price series were readily available (see BAUMOL and OATES [1979], pp. 100–104, 108–110). Despite the much publicized and sudden upsurge in mineral prices beginning toward the end of the 1960s, it transpired that the real prices of seven of the 15 minerals actually fell over the three quarters of a century encompassed in the calculation. And of those minerals whose prices rose, almost all of them increased at a real rate less than 1 percent per year. Very similar results were just obtained from data for seven minerals extending from 1900 to 1982, with three of the seven prices declining, and none of the others rising more than 0.7 percent per year on the average. This is surely below the real rates of interest during the period – the amount by which, the HOTELLING analysis tells us, the price of a fixed depletable resource should be expected to rise each year in a competitive market.

What is one to make of this? It is tempting to jump to the startling conclusion that the market is behaving as though the supplies of these minerals – aluminium, copper, lead, mercury, magnesium, liquid natural gas and natural gas (!) – were actually increasing. As we will see, there may in fact be some substance to this view; but there is more to the story[1].

There is some evidence suggesting that whatever may have happened to inventories, a significant portion of the fall in the prices of the minerals in question is attributable to technical improvements in the extraction process[2]. I have no intention of casting doubt on this conclusion, but for the purposes of this paper some interpretive discussion is essential.

1. The paradoxical conjecture that in some sense there may have been an increase in the total stock of some mineral resources (both discovered and not yet discovered) must not be confused with the more easily explainable fact that for many minerals the 'proven reserves' have been rising. Proven reserves are usually defined as the number of years usage represented by the supply already discovered, assuming continuation of current rates of consumption. (Here no effort is usually made to differentiate among reserves whose costliness and difficulty of extraction differ and the economic feasibility of whose use may, therefore, vary considerably.) Thus, for example, between 1960 and 1980 proven world reserves rose from 24 to 42 years' supply for zinc, from 43 to 71 years for nickel, from 19 to 47 years for lead and from 37 to 49 years for copper (U.S. Bureau of Mines [1983], p. 21). The explanation is straightforward. Proven reserves are a matter of the economic incentives for exploration. The 1970s was a period of generally rising real prices of minerals. The high prices encouraged exploration and discouraged consumption and both of these made for a rise in the ratio: known supply/current consumption per year = proven reserve.

2. See, e.g., BARNETT and MORSE, op. cit. Their conclusions are supported by the results of recent interviews of my associates with minerals specialists at the U.S. Bureau of Mines.

II. REDUCED EXTRACTION COSTS AND ENHANCEMENT OF EFFECTIVE STOCKS

For our purposes it is useful to divide the savings embodying the improved extraction process into two types: (i) reduced use of labor, fuel, capital, etc., per unit of resource extracted and (ii) decreased 'waste' of the resource in the extraction process. Examples of the latter are easy to cite. Normally, when an oil well is abandoned a considerable quantity of oil will remain unextracted because it does not flow out unaided, and artifical means to force the petroleum to the surface grow increasingly expensive as the proportion of unrecovered oil approaches zero. The same is true of the separation of various solid minerals from the rock formations in which they are found. Technological progress makes it feasible both absolutely and in economic terms to obtain ever increasing amounts of usable resource from a given source (such as an oil well).

In this sense, it is clear that a reduction in the cost of extraction of type (ii) (a decrease in waste) is tantamount to a rise in effective supply of a resource. Thus, suppose that in 1960, with known extraction techniques no more than half of the oil in a well could conceivably have been extracted at a cost ever likely to be acceptable, while by 1980 this figure had risen to 80 percent. If in the meantime, say 5 percent of the available petroleum had been used up, the effective supply would have risen from its initial level, call it $0.5X$ barrels, to $0.8X(1-0.05)$, yielding a net rise of effective supply equal to $100[0.8X(1-0.05-0.5X]/0.5X = 52$ percent! That is, despite the 5 percent decline in the physical quantity of the resource remaining on our planet, its availability to consumers in the current and all future generations together will have increased by more than half. A price fall in these circumstances is surely not difficult to explain.

III. THE RESOURCE OPPORTUNITY (SUBSTITUTION) COSTS OF OTHER INPUTS

It should now be obvious how the effective supply of a depletable resource can be expanded by a decrease in wastefulness of the extraction process or, for that matter, in the wastefulness of any part of the processes through which the resource is brought to the ultimate consumer. But I want to show now that even a decrease in extraction cost of type (i), i.e., a decline in the quantities of labor, capital and other inputs used up in bringing the resource forth may also add to the effective inventory of the resource, albeit indirectly.

CONTINUING EXPANSION OF FINITE RESOURCES

The point here is rather more subtle than that in the preceding section. It involves the (partial) substitutability of virtually all resources for one another. During the period of fuel crisis of the 1970s this was illustrated dramatically in a number of ways. For example, increased expenditure on insulation to save on fuel represented the substitution of insulating materials and the labor devoted to their installation for petroleum and other sources of energy. A more romantic illustration was provided by the newspaper reports that there was a partial revival of the cattle drive, with cattle more frequently being brought to market on the hoof rather than by truck, thus substituting cowboy labor for gasoline. Professor VINER used to point out that there was, both in theory and in practice, very real substitutability between labor and the quantity of gold used in producing say, a square yard of gold leaf of given thickness and refinement (i.e., number of carats). For when the price of gold increases more labor is devoted to recovery of scraps and gold dust from workers' clothing. Thus, substitutability of inputs, rather than constituting an exceptional case, must be judged, at least in the long run, to represent the normal state of affairs.

To see the relevance of this observation to the basic issue with which we are concerned here, we need only note that if there is an increase in the efficiency of the extraction process of a resource such as oil or copper which reduces the amount of labor or electricity used up in the activity, the input saved in this way can, *and to some extent will*, be substituted for oil and copper elsewhere in the economy. The end result is in substance no different qualitatively from an outright decrease in waste of the resource itself during extraction. As electricity that would formerly have been used up in mining is released from this use, either other forms of employment will be found for it and some of those uses will entail its substitution for petroleum or, instead, there will be a corresponding net reduction in electricity output, which also entails a saving of oil via reduced use of the latter to generate electricity.

I conclude, then, that the use of any input in the extraction of a resource involves an opportunity cost in terms of the extracted resource. The labor used in bringing oil to the surface could, instead, have served as a substitute for oil in other uses. As a result, any decrease in the use of labor per unit of oil brought out of the ground to some degree constitutes an indirect addition to the economy's effective oil reserves. For, to the extent that the labor released serves to replace oil in the production of final outputs, the amount of output supportable by a given quantity of oil in the ground is enhanced correspondingly.

IV. RECYCLING AND EXTENSION OF EFFECTIVE RESERVES

Finally, it is obvious that effective reserves of a resource can be extended by technological changes which facilitate recycling. If such a change increases the number of times it pays (on the average) to reuse some metal from, say, two to three, before it is finally abandoned, then the effective reserves will clearly also have been raised by fifty percent.

Here it is important to stress the role of technical change or other forms of innovation as the source of expanded recycling. Recycling adopted willy-nilly, without regard to its economics can, as we know, actually waste resources, sometimes substantially. There is undoubtedly a negative net energy yield from a number of proposed recycling processes undertaken as sources of fuel. It is well known to students of the subject that well-intentioned attempts to impose recycling where it is not justified by circumstances can, contrary to appearances, deplete resources rather than saving them.

It is for this and perfectly analogous reasons in the other areas that have just been covered that the discussion of this note focusses its attention upon innovation and technical change as sources of reduced extraction costs, increased effective reserves of unreproducible resources and secular reductions in the real prices of those resources.

V. PRICE TRENDS, EXTRACTION COSTS AND EFFECTIVE RESERVES

This is an appropriate point to generalize the preceding discussion. What has been emphasized here is the possibility that the effective supply, i.e., the effective performance capacity of an exhaustible resource can be increased by innovation which reduces the waste (inefficiencies) that occur in the process of extraction of a resource, in its processing toward a final product and even in its consumption (either directly, as in increased fuel efficiency of automobiles, or as affected by the opportunities for financially viable recycling).

All this is reflected in the trend in the price of such a resource, which is influenced both by the costs of extraction and the effective inventory of the item.

CONTINUING EXPANSION OF FINITE RESOURCES

That is straightforward enough. Only two observations have emerged which go beyond the obvious.

First, there is the conclusion that the distinction between decreased extraction cost and enhancement of the effective inventory of the resource is marginal, or rather, the former turns out to be one of the avenues through which the latter occurs.

Second, I have shown by example that inefficiency-reducing innovations not only help to offset the decrease in the physical stock of a resource that results from its consumption, but may actually lead to a net increase in its effective inventory; that is, during a given period such changes can enhance the prospective economic contribution of the current inventory by an amount more than sufficient to offset the consumption of the resource that occurs during this period.

The two questions arise naturally: whether the rate of technical change required to achieve this second result is so large as to remove it from the realm of plausibility and, second, even if it is plausible for a time, whether such developments can conceivably continue for a substantial period, or even for the indefinite future. These are the issues to which we turn next. For their resolution it will be necessary to construct a (very rudimentary) model.

VI. THE FORMAL STRUCTURE OF RESOURCE STOCK ENHANCEMENT

The formal construct needed for our purposes is little more than a restatement of the structure of our earlier numerical example. I use the following notation:

R_t = The usable quantity of a resource remaining on the planet in period t.

V_t = The quantity used up during period t.

D_t = The quantity demanded for industrial and consumption purposes in that period.

E_t = The effective stock of the resource in period t.

M_t = R_t/E_t = the ratio of total stock to effectively usable stock, i.e., $1-1/M_t$ is the proportion that will be wasted during use.

a_t = $(D_t-D_{t-1})/D_{t-1}$ = the relative increase in quantity of resource demanded during period t.

Then we have, tautologically,

$$R_{t+1} = R_t - V_t \tag{1}$$

Moreover, with current technology, consumption of our resource today may be assumed to involve inefficiency (waste) of the same order of magnitude as prevails generally, so that resource usage will exceed the quantity of resource demanded by the proportion M_t, i.e.,

$$V_t = M_t D_t \tag{2}$$

Therefore, by (1) and the definition of M_t,

$$M_{t+1}E_{t+1} = M_t E_t - M_t D_t \tag{3}$$

That is,

$$M_{t+1}/M_t = (E_t - D_t)/E_{t+1} \tag{4}$$

We also have, by the definition of a_t,

$$D_t = D_0(1 + a_0)(1 + a_t) \ldots (1 + a_t) \tag{5}$$

I will show now, as a fairly extreme example of the possibility of E_t, the effective inventory of our resource, how it may be possible through sufficient technical progress to achieve a time path E_t which maintains strict proportionality with current effective usage, D_t. Perhaps even for a protracted (though necessarily bounded) time period, then, no matter how rapidly current consumption of the finite resource rises, in this regime its effective inventory will stay strictly abreast of current effective use[3]. Here is a widow's cruse, indeed!

It is easy to determine with the aid of (4) and (5) what rate of reduction in the inefficiency coefficient m_t is required to achieve this result. Write

$$k = D_0/E_0 = D_t/E_t,\ 0 < k < 1 \tag{6}$$

(so that $V_t/R_t = M_t D_t/M_t E_t = k$ as well) as the representation of the regime of proportionality between D_t and E_t. Then by (5) and (6)

$$E_t/E_{t+1} = 1/(1 + a_{t+1}), \qquad D_t/E_{t+1} = k/(1 + a_{t+1})$$

3. Not only will E_t keep abreast of the level of current effective use, D_t, but, because M_t will be falling, it must stay ahead of current actual use (depletion) of the resource $V_t = M_t\, D_t$.

so that by (4) this requires

$$M_{t+1}/M_t = (1-k)/(1+a_{t+1}) \qquad (7)$$

This is the solution we are seeking.

VII. UNIQUENESS, FEASIBILITY AND OTHER MATTERS

It is easy to see from (4), given the values of variables D_t, E_t and M_t, for period t, that E_{t+1} decreases strictly monotonically when M_{t+1} increases, so that the correspondence between E_{t+1}/E_t and M_{t+1}/M_t given by (6) and (7) is unique, i.e., proportional growth between E_t and D_t is the only possible outcome corresponding to the value of M_{t+1}/M_t given in (7).

Unfortunately, this regime cannot go on forever, as I have already suggested, and will prove in the next section, while E_t, the effective stock of resource, can rise in perpetuity despite a consumption rate which always remains positive. It must nevertheless be true that for E_t not to fall to zero eventually, D_t must ultimately fall below any preassigned positive bound.

What is the source of the difficulty? It is clearly true that M_t, the number of units of resource input required per unit of effective use (output), can be decreased by technological progress and may even fall below unity (as when recycling of a valuable mineral permits one unit of the resource to provide a multiplicity of uses). However, the laws of physics suggest that there is a nonzero (positive) lower bound, call it m*, to the level to which M_t can decline. No matter how much we raise the fuel efficiency of cars we cannot hope to reduce to anything like zero the amount of gasoline needed to drive an automobile from New York to San Francisco.

VIII. THE BASIC PROPOSITIONS[4]

It is now possible to provide the two basic results to which I have several times alluded:

4. I am extremely grateful to DIETRICH FISCHER who pointed out propositon 2 to me and supplied the proof of proposition 1.

Proposition 1. There exist consistent time paths involving monotonic depletion of the available quantity of physical resource, R_t and monotonic reductions in the inefficiency coefficient, which lead to monotonic and perpetual increases in the effective inventory of the resource, E_t.

Proposition 2. So long as M_t possesses a positive lower bound, m*, then E_t must be constrained by a finite upper bound and D_t must ultimately fall below any preassigned lower bound.

Proof of Proposition 1. The following pair of functions satisfies the required conditions (as will be demonstrated next):

$$R_t = R^* (1 + be^{-rt}), \qquad M_t = m^* (1 + ce^{-rt}), \qquad 0 < b < c \tag{8}$$

We obtain directly

$$E_t = R_t/M_t = R^* (1 + be^{-rt})/m^* (1 + ce^{-rt}) \tag{9}$$

and writing $E^* = R^*/m^*$ it is clear that as t approaches infinity, E_t must approach E^*. To prove that E_t increases monotonically it is sufficient to show that its time derivative is positive everywhere. Direct differentiation of (9) can be shown, with a bit of manipulation to yield,

$$dE_t/dt = m^* (c - b) re^{-rt}/(1 + ce^{-rt})^2$$

which is clearly positive for $c > b$. Q.E.D.

Proof of Proposition 2. First we prove that E_t possesses an upper bound. R_t must decline monotonically, so that $R_t \leq R_0$ for all $t > 0$, and $M_t \geq m^* > 0$, where m* is the lower bound of M_t. Then we have

$$E_t = R_t/M_t \leq R_0/m^* \qquad \text{Q.E.D.}$$

Next we prove that, for some t, D_t must lie below any preassigned positive number D*. For suppose the contrary. By (1) and (2)

$$R_{t+1} = R_t - M_t D_t \leq R_t - m^* D^*$$

Thus

$$R_t \leq R_0 - tm^* D^*$$

which must become negative for $t > R_0/m^* D^*$. Q.E.D.

While Proposition 1 shows that E_t can continue to rise forever (at least in theory) there are, obviously, more moderate solutions which also involve no depletion of the effective stock of the resource. For example, by (4) one can maintain a constant effective inventory, $E_{t+1} = E_t = E$, if

$$M_{t+1}/M_t = 1 - D_t/E \tag{10}$$

IX. NUMERICAL ILLUSTRATION

A numerical example can suggest the order of magnitude of efficiency growth through technical progress needed to achieve solution (7) or (10). Suppose that at current consumption rates a 100 years' supply of the resource remains available, so that $D_t/E_t = V_t/R_t = 0.01$. Let usage, D_t, be growing at 3 percent per year. Then, for a steady effective inventory $E_t = E$ we require, by (10)

$$M_{t+1}/M_t = 1 - 0.01 = 0.99$$

On the other hand, for the effective inventory to grow like demand, by 3 percent, we require, according to (7)

$$M_{t+1}/M_t = 0.99/1.03 = 0.96, \text{ approx.}$$

While the latter figure may require a degree of technical progress we are unlikely to be able to sustain, it would seem that the former (0.99) figure is far from unattainable.

The main lesson that follows for our purposes from the numerical illustration and the discussion of the time path of the variables is that indefinite preservation of the effective inventory of depletable resource in the face of continually growing demand requires no pathology or even complexity in the intertemporal behavior of the pertinent variables. True, the mechanism requires that the effective use of a depletable resource ultimately slow down toward zero. But we need never reach a date at which it actually becomes zero, and it may even continue to grow for a very substantial period of time.

X. CONCLUSIONS

The past hundred and fifty years have brought with them a burst of productivity growth and living standards in industrialized countries unprecedented in human history. It has been suggested that part of the explanation is the willingness of mankind, or at least of the portion of mankind that inhabits the industrialized countries, to deplete its natural heritage, obtaining its current prosperity at the expense of future generations. In this paper I have shown that such a conclusion is far from self-evident. Rising productivity, rather than drawing down humanity's stock of natural resource capital may, in an effective sense, actually augment it and may be able to continue to do so for the indefinite future. Resources which are not reproducible and whose quantities are finite may nevertheless be increased by technological advance in terms of their prospective economic contribution, and may do so for the indefinite future.

This is not only possible in theory. The evidence of trends in resource prices suggests that something of the sort is in fact going on. Indeed, it would seem that the real unresolved issue is the magnitude of the phenomenon and whether it is sufficient to result, on balance, in an actual expansion of the effective inventories of a substantial proportion of the world's resources.

REFERENCES

BARNETT, H.J. and MORSE, CHANDLER: *Scarcity and Growth.* Johns-Hopkins Press (Resources for the Future), Baltimore, 1963.

BAUMOL, WILLIAM J. and OATES, WALLACE E.: *Economics, Environmential Policy and the Quality of Life,* Prentice-Hall, Englewood Cliffs, New Jersey, 1979.

HOTELLING, HAROLD: 'The Economics of Exhaustible Resources', *Journal of Political Economy,* Vol. 39 (April 1931), pp. 137–175.

U.S. Bureau of Mines, Department of the Interior: *The Domestic Supply of Critical Minerals,* Washington D.C., 1983.

SUMMARY

Because technological change increases the efficiency of the extraction and use of natural resources it is shown that, despite the accelerated use of the world's finite resources since the Industrial Revolution, it is very possible that their effective remaining supply, measured in terms of the services they are still capable of providing in the future, is greater today than it was, say, two centuries earlier. In this paper it is shown that, paradoxically, measured in terms of their prospective contributions to human welfare, the available quantity of the world's exhaustible resources may rise forever, year after year. However, even though they may never approach disappearance, the consumption of their services will eventually have to decline and, ultimately, approach zero asymptotically.

CONTINUING EXPANSION OF FINITE RESOURCES

ZUSAMMENFASSUNG

Technische Veränderungen erhöhen die Effizienz der Gewinnung und Verwendung natürlicher Ressourcen. Deshalb ist es sehr wahrscheinlich, dass trotz dem beschleunigten Verbrauch der weltweit endlichen Ressourcen der von ihnen gestiftete Nutzen in Zukunft grösser sein wird als zum Beispiel vor zweihundert Jahren. Im vorliegenden Aufsatz wird nun aufgezeigt, dass paradoxerweise auch der Beitrag der natürlichen Ressourcen an die menschliche Wohlfahrt von Jahr zu Jahr ansteigt, auch wenn der Konsum der natürlichen Ressourcen sinken und assymptotisch gegen Null streben wird.

RÉSUMÉ

Le changement technologique accroit l'efficacité de l'extraction et de l'utilisation des ressources naturelles. Malgré l'emploi croissant des ressources finies mondiales depuis la révolution industrielle, cet article montre qu'il est très possible que les réserves de produits naturels, mesurées en termes de services qu'elles peuvent encore offrir, soient plus élevées aujourd'hui qu'elles ne l'étaient il y a, disons, deux siècles. L'auteur indique même – paradoxalement – que mesurées en termes de leur contribution prospective au bien-être de l'humanité, ces réserves peuvent même s'accroître, année après année. Cependant, la consommation de leurs services peut avoir tendance à décliner et enfin asymptotiquement tendre vers zéro.

[5]

Social Wants and Dismal Science: The Curious Case of the Climbing Costs of Health and Teaching*

WILLIAM J. BAUMOL

Director, C.V. Starr Center for Applied Economics
New York University
Professor Emeritus
Princeton University

Between 1981 and 1991 the University's health insurance costs . . . increased by 635%. This rapid and continuing inflation parallels the experience of most employers in the nation. . . . among [the] reasons . . . Doctors' and hospitals' charges for each procedure and operation increase each year at a rate that exceeds the rise in the cost of living (Karen Bradley, Director of Personnel, NYU, Memorandum to the Staff, 7 October 1991).

There were twelve postal deliveries on weekdays in Kentish Town [then in suburban London] at that time [the 1860s] and one on Sundays (Kapp [1972, 48n]).

Writings related to economic issues go back before the ancient Greeks. Yet, not without reason, there are many who regard the appearance of Adam Smith's *Wealth of Nations* in 1776(!) as the event representing the inauguration of the arena as a systematic discipline. Thus, it seems appropriate here to focus my few remarks on the history of my discipline in the period since then. This seems particularly apt, given the near coincidence of that publication date and that of the founding of the American Philosophical Society, as well as the frequent claim by specialists that Benjamin Franklin was Smith's source of information for his many observations on the economy of the American Colonies (for which Smith advocated independence, largely as an economical step for Britain).

Though my fellow economists have frequently pretended that their research is driven purely, as Veblen put it, by idle curiosity, they have tra-

* Read 30 April 1993. Sue Anne Batey Blackman's invaluable assistance in the preparation of this piece adds to my heavy debt to her. I am, of course, extremely grateful to the organizations that supported the research: the Alfred P. Sloan Foundation, the Price Institute for Entrepreneurial Studies, and the C.V. Starr Center for Applied Economics.

ditionally permitted themselves to be guided in their choice of research topics by the pressing social issues of the moment. This has been true since some of the earliest specialized studies of the economy, from the value and distribution theories of Ricardo and Malthus, that were hastily brought to fruition as contributions to the heated debate over the corn laws during the Napoleonic wars,[1] to the employment analysis of John Maynard Keynes, produced in 1936, obviously in response to the urgent problems presented by the Great Depression. One can even suggest that the *Wealth of Nations* itself was a response to the need for freedom of enterprise of the emerging Industrial Revolution.[2]

It is my belief that one cannot understand the history of economics except in this light. In the past, work in this discipline has been influenced heavily by economic, social and political developments that urgently demanded illumination of the accompanying economic issues, and the body of economists has generally responded as best it could. Though much of current work in economics, like that in a number of other disciplines, seems for the moment to be mired in formalism and technicality, I see little reason to expect that the ultimate course of research in economics will differ sharply from its past in terms of the susceptibility of its research topics to guidance by current social needs.

As always, I will eschew any attempt to foresee the future, leaving that to better qualified individuals such as storefront readers of palms and crystal balls. Rather, the remainder of this paper will be devoted to an illustration–to a social issue that most of us will readily consider to be pressing, and to an indication of what light the dismal science can shed on the subject and what it can contribute to the design of appropriate public policy.

---

[1] This issue was the strengthening of the protective duties on the importation of grain into the United Kingdom, the earlier duties having been eroded by wartime inflation. The pressure to provide an analysis that could shed light on the issue yielded no less than five major contributions on rent theory, two by Malthus and one each by Torrens, West and Ricardo, all published during the month of February 1815. For more details see Piero Sraffa's introduction to volume 4 of Ricardo's collected works, 1–5.

[2] Contemporaries focused on a different side of Smith's contribution toward solving the urgent problems of the time. As a reward for providing so many ideas for new taxes Lord North arranged a lucrative sinecure for Smith. Ironically, for this advocate of freedom of trade, the post he was given was that of collector of Scottish customs, whose duties he carried out assiduously, apparently to the surprise of those who had provided the position to him. Thus, this free trader, himself the son of a customs official, reverted to the family's arena of activity in the end.

Smith, incidentally, had many connections with the philosophical and scientific community of the time. A colleague of Joseph Black at the University of Glasgow, he also helped to provide a university job for James Watt (as "mathematical instrument maker" to the university); David Hume was Smith's closest friend, and he had substantial exchanges with persons as variegated as François Quesney, Samuel Johnson, James Boswell and (probably) Benjamin Franklin. For more on this see, e.g., Ray (1895).

1. The Cost Crisis of Health Care, Education, and Some Other Valuable Services

The exploding cost of health care is patently a matter eliciting widespread concern. There is hardly an election in an industrialized country nowadays in which commitment to containment of these costs is not expected of every viable candidate. In the United States the new president has repeatedly stressed this issue as one of the most critical facing society. The health care systems of other nations are cited as attractive models for this country, noting that the current U.S. arrangements exclude the poor and perhaps the lower middle class from the attainment of what are generally considered adequate standards of care, because rising costs raise the price beyond the means of a substantial proportion of the population.

Those of us who have children or grandchildren who attend private universities are only too painfully aware that education is beset by similar problems that already are also eliciting growing political attention. The discussion that follows will suggest that these two fields, health and education (and a number of others), not only share a problem but that this problem of growing costs has at least one source that is common. Until that source is recognized, it will be argued, programs to deal with the difficulty are likely to prove ineffective or worse. Once understood, however, promising courses of action for the problems or, rather, ways of living with them, do suggest themselves.

Thus, while the beginnings of the discussion will appear suitably grim, as one may expect of a product of the dismal science, the story, it can be promised, will have a rather happier ending–though one that does still depend on the rationality and insight with which policy makers are prepared to approach the matter.

It is often noted that the cost per capita (or cost as a share of average income) of health care in the United States is considerably higher than that in most other countries. We can be fairly certain from the statistical evidence that this is true, despite the well known pitfalls besetting comparison of prices in different countries with their different currencies. The shortcoming of this conclusion, in my view, is not that it is suspect, but that it focuses upon the wrong issue. The pain society experiences from the costs of health care and education does not derive primarily from their *levels* at some particular date but, rather, from their *growth rates.* What makes the problem so difficult to deal with is the fact that high as these costs may have been yesterday, they are considerably higher today, and will be substantially higher still tomorrow. Note that here I refer not to price inflation, but to what economists call "real price increases," that is, price increases *above and beyond* the rate of general inflation of prices in the economy.

The magnitude and persistence of the rates of growth of these real prices are sufficiently striking to leave little doubt that even if the time derivatives of the real costs of health care and education are not the only

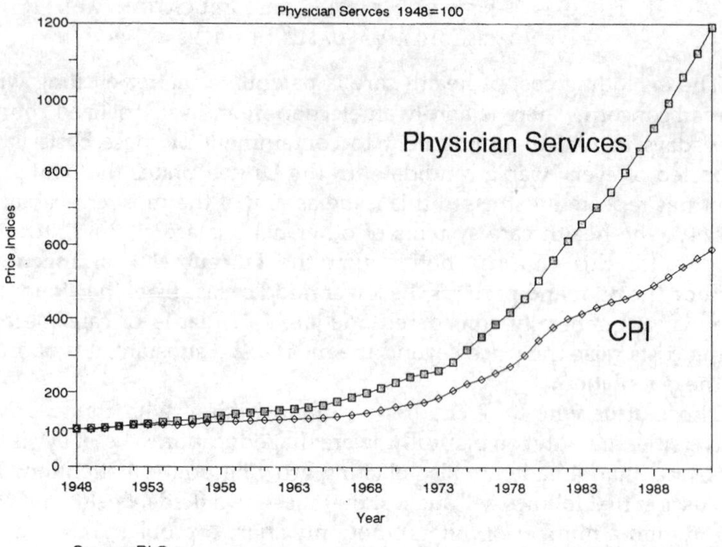

Source: BLS

FIGURE 1. Price Trends: Health Care vs. CPI, 1948–1992.

difficulty, they are surely a major component of the problem we are examining. Let me review some of the facts. From 1948 to 1992 the annual rate of increase in the price of a physician's services (the price charged by the doctor to the patient) was more than 5.5 percent per annum, compared to an average annual increase of 4 percent per year in the government's measure of overall inflation, the Consumer Price Index, or CPI (see Figure 1 for the graphs of these two series). This difference may not seem very large, but over the forty-four years in question it means that the price of a doctor's services has increased by approximately 1100 percent in absolute terms, or more than 100 percent in terms of dollars of constant purchasing power. In Figure 1 we see how the price of physicians' services (upper curve) has cumulatively outstripped the economy's rate of inflation (lower curve).

Over the postwar period, 1948–1992, the price of a hospital room increased even more rapidly, by a considerable margin, than the cost of a visit to a physician. The cost of a hospital room is reported by the U.S. Bureau of Labor Statistics to have risen at an average annual rate of 8.8 percent compounded, which over the forty-four-year interval cumulated to a nearly 5,000 percent increase. This amounts to a 700 percent rise in terms of dollars of constant purchasing power–that is, after full correction for the economy's overall inflation during this time interval. Figure 2 reports the hospital-room cost data and shows how it makes the rise in real price of a physician visit seem modest by comparison.

Increases of this magnitude clearly constitute a serious threat to the quality of medical care that middle and lower income persons, whether

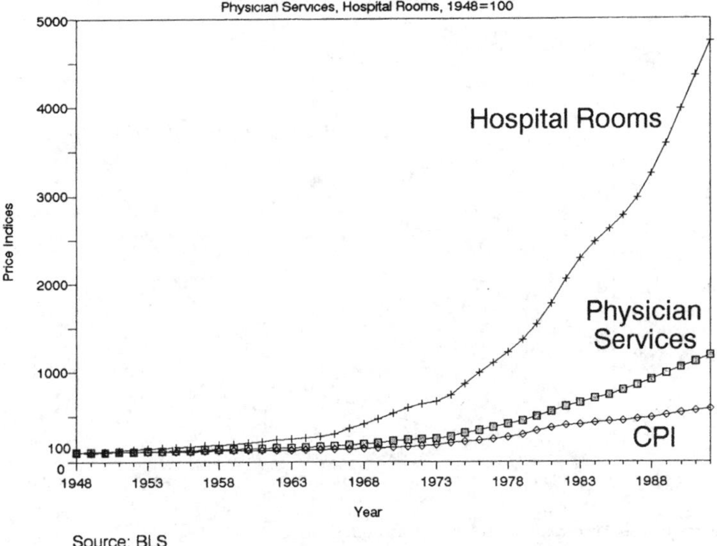

Source: BLS

FIGURE 2. **Price Trends: Health Care vs. CPI, 1948–1992.**

older or younger, can afford. In an affluent society such as ours, that is dedicated to promoting the general welfare–including the provision of medical care meeting some minimum standard of acceptability–the rising price of medical care clearly represents a problem of the utmost importance.[3]

The cost of education has shown patterns very similar to those of medical care. Education expenditure per student has also risen steadily and cumulatively at a rate markedly outstripping that of inflation. It increased at a rate of 7.6 percent for the postwar years, intermediate between that of a physician visit (5.5 percent), and that of a hospital room (8.8 percent). Figure 3 (constructed from data from the U.S. Department of Education) reports the information. Costs of higher education exhibit similar patterns.

There remains the question whether the problem of steadily growing real cost of health care and education is an issue peculiar to the U.S. It has been suggested that other countries exercise firmer control over their medical costs, and continue to offer better and more affordable public services. There is, undoubtedly, much truth to this contention, and it reflects, among other influences, a variety of public policies–a greater commitment to social services financed by tax rates far higher than those in the

---

[3] There have, of course, been some offsetting, beneficial developments. Growing scientific knowledge and improved medical techniques indisputably mean that patients are getting better care for their money than they were forty years ago. More than that. To the extent that innovation has reduced the length of treatment some illnesses require, expenditure *per illness* must have risen correspondingly less quickly than cost per patient-day.

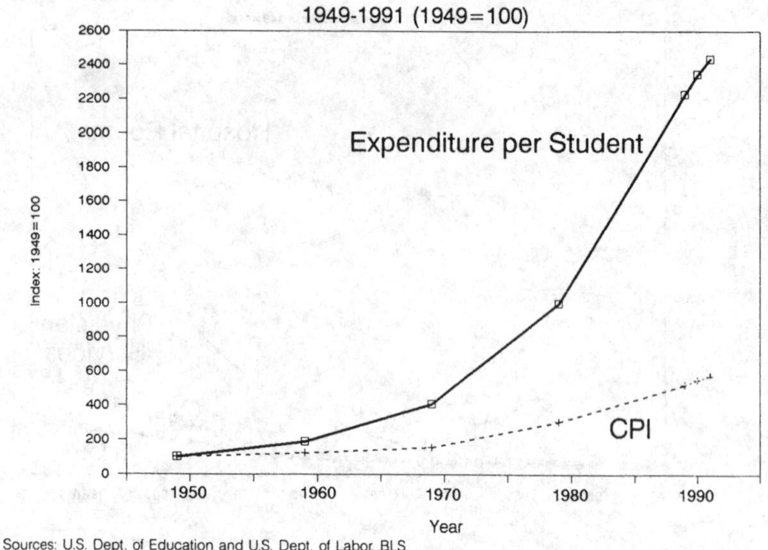

FIGURE 3. **Index of Education Expenditure per Student vs. CPI.**

United States, stricter controls on the fees charged by physicians, and so on. Still, it must be remembered that there are few industrialized countries in which similar complaints about *rates of cost increase* are not heard.

Let us, then, examine what the data show. Statistics for the required comparisons are surprisingly difficult to obtain. In part, this is attributable to measurement problems. There are a number of services, such as those of government, whose outputs are very hard to measure or even to define and observe. Others, such as health care, are so heterogeneous that the statistics are likely to be exceedingly difficult to compare from one country to another. Still, we have been able to obtain some such data for education and health care.

Figures 4a, 4b, and 4c show the cost of education per student for six countries: Japan, United Kingdom (1965–1988), Germany (1965–1989), Canada, France (1965–1990) and the U.S. (1965–1991).[4] The figures simply show indexes (1965 = 100) of total expenditures by educational institutions divided by total enrollment. Figure 4a provides indexes uncorrected for inflation (i.e., nominal expenditure per student). It shows that, for the

[4] The data for the U.S. include expenditures of all educational institutions, public and private, at all levels. The expenditure figures for the other countries are confined to public institutions, which constitute the bulk of their educational institutions.

The U.S. figures are from the U.S. Department of Education, while the source for the statistics for the other countries is the United Nations Educational, Scientific and Cultural Organization (UNESCO). The general price indexes—the gross domestic product (GDP) deflators—come from the Organization for Economic Cooperation and Development (OECD).

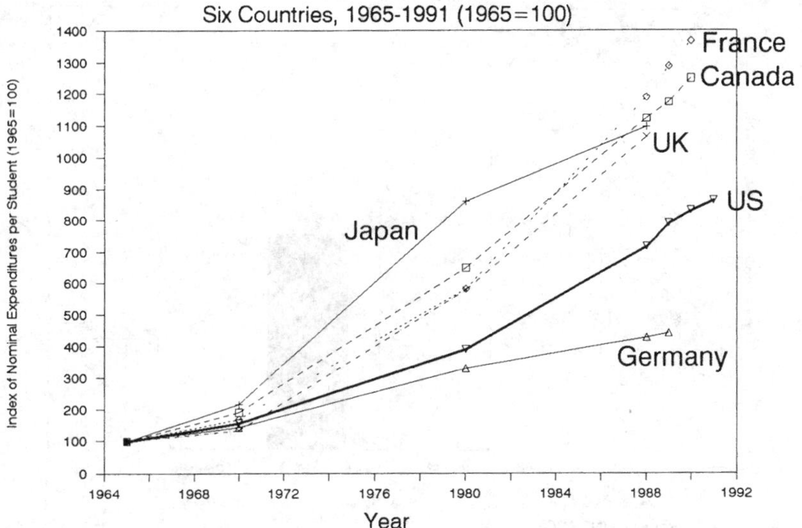

FIGURE 4a. Index of Nominal Education Expenditures per Student.

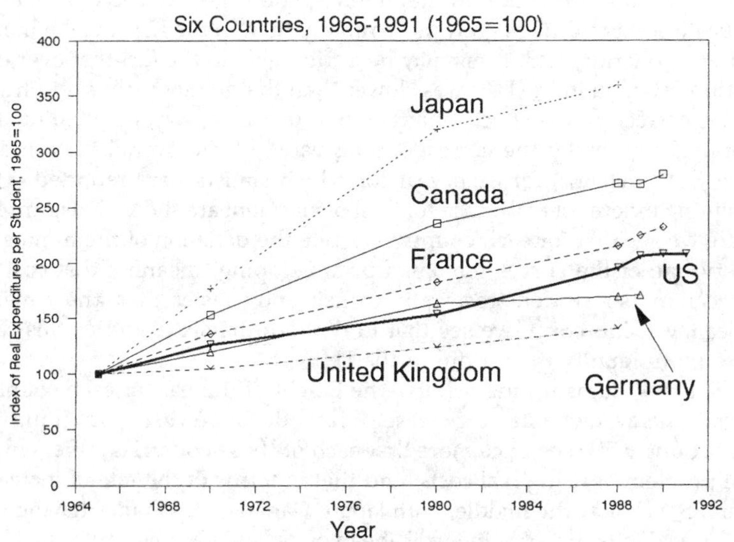

FIGURE 4b. Index of Real Education Expenditures per Student.

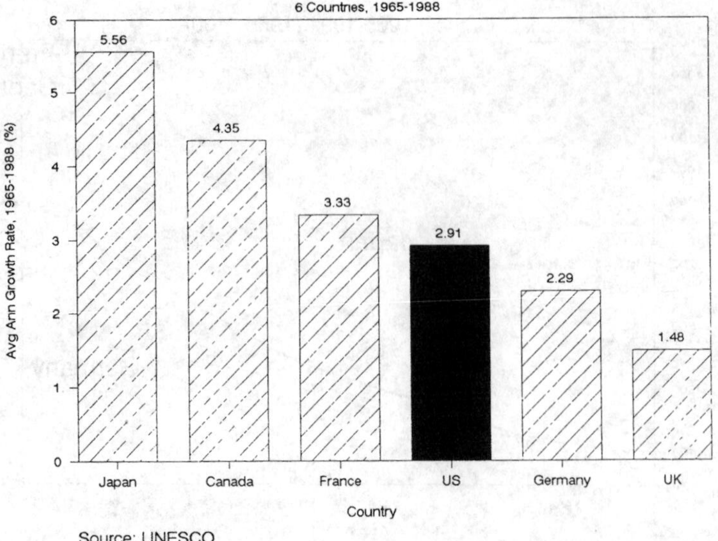

Source: UNESCO

FIGURE 4c. Real Education Price Growth Rates, Six Countries, 1965–1988.

most part, education costs rose at a substantial rate throughout most of the period. Since 1965 is selected as the base year, all of the countries are given the same initial point. In these terms, with no correction for the different rates of inflation in the different countries, we see that foreign education expenditures grew more rapidly than in the U.S. in all but one country–Germany. But this may be attributable to the fact that over the period inflation in the U.S. was slower than that in most other countries.

We correct for the effects of inflation in the usual way, by dividing the nominal figures by the corresponding value of the overall price index (the GDP deflator) for each year for which statistics are reported. The resulting indexes of real education cost per student are shown in Figure 4b. Here we see that for each country, despite the deflation of the numbers, every one of the curves remains upward-sloping, meaning that cost of education per student rose quite consistently faster than the general price level. Moreover, we see that in three of the six countries this cost rose more rapidly than it did in the U.S.

Figure 4c sums up the results. The height of the bar for each country shows the average rate of increase of *real* education costs per annum in that country. We see once more that each of these countries suffers from the problem of rising real costs, and that in terms of the rate of increase the U.S. is below the middle, with Japan, Canada, and France having the dubious distinction of being well ahead of us, and Germany and the U.K. lagging behind us.

We also have some comparative health care cost figures, for whatever they may be worth. In 1990 (updated 1993) the OECD provided, as they put it, "At a more aggregate level, a new 'total' medical-consumption price index . . ." (1990, p. 122). This price index is calculated for the years 1960 through 1990 for eighteen countries, including all of the major free-market industrial countries. In all of them the real health-care price index rose rapidly, as is hardly surprising. As Figure 5a (analogous to Figure 4c for education) indicates, after correction for inflation, in fourteen of the eighteen countries, health care prices rose more rapidly than prices in general. That is, in those fourteen countries the real cost of medical care rose (and rose quite steadily). The U.S. rate of increase was exceeded by that in seven of these countries: Austria, Australia, Canada, the Netherlands, New Zealand, Norway and Switzerland.[5] More recently, however, the growth rate of U.S. costs has accelerated relative to that of the other leading economies (Figure 5b). It must also be reported that in three of the countries, including the U.K. and France, the real medical price index fell. I am not in a position to judge whether this represents a fall in the quality of the services, a rise in the efficiency of their production or is merely a phenomenon that is purely statistical.[6]

At least two conclusions are suggested by our quick review of the data. First, it should be clear that the health care or educational systems of other countries provide no sure models for a quick fix of the problem of rising real cost of those services in the U.S. Second, the universality and persistence of the problem—the fact that it has endured for four decades at

[5] It should be reemphasized, however, that the *level* of U.S. per-capita medical care expenditures (in contradistinction to their *rate of growth*) is far higher than that in other countries. Using what economists consider the proper approach to translating foreign currencies into dollars (taking into account their relative purchasing power), it is estimated that, "Americans spend 2.8 times as much per capita as the British, 2.6 times as much as the Italians, 2.3 times as much as the Japanese, 1.7 times as much as the French, 1.5 times as much as the Swedes, and 1.4 times as much as the Canadians" (Schieber and Poullier [1987, p. 112]). A regression correlating per-capita health care spending with per-capita GDP for the twenty-four OECD countries in 1989 found a surprisingly tight relationship (health care spending per capita = $-419 + 107X$(per capita GDP), $R^2 = 0.85$, both parameters significant at the .01 level). Of the twenty-four countries, only the U.S. fell far from the regression line, exceeding its predicted outlay by about 25 percent (Scheiber, Poullier and Greenwald [1991, pp. 23–26]).

[6] One plausible explanation is that in periods of rapid inflation the prices of services that normally suffer from the problems of rising real costs described in the next section cannot overcome the forces that always cause lags in their cost-adjustment processes. In our initial study of the subject, on the economics of the performing arts, William Bowen and I found that in periods of rapid inflation, and only then, real costs of arts organizations fell (1966, p. 189 ff.). As is clear from Figure 5c (using slightly earlier data than those employed in Figure 5a), a similar relationship holds for health care costs. That graph plots for each of the nineteen countries the rate of inflation on the horizontal axis and the rate of increase of real health care price on the vertical axis. We see that all of the countries in which real health care cost fell between 1960 and 1987 were also countries in which the rate of inflation was high (they lie at the right hand side of the diagram). In general, the higher the rate of inflation, the more slowly a country's health care cost rose, with a one percent higher inflation corresponding, approximately, to a 0.25 percent fall in the rate of increase of real health care price.

It should also be noted that according to other studies France and the U.K. have not been immune from the problem of rising real health care costs. *The Economist* reports, "Over the past 40 years health spending in France has risen by an average of 7% a year in real terms" (22 June 1991, p. 52), while in the United Kingdom, ". . . throughout the 1980s [there has been] a real increase of 2.8% a year. . . ." (28 September 1991, p. 63).

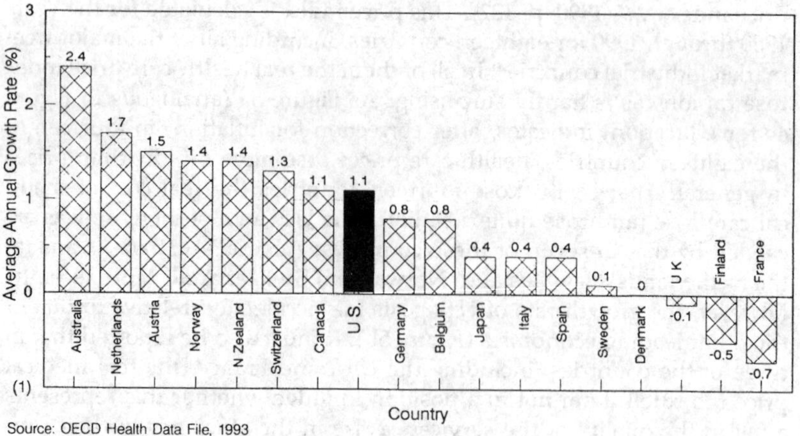

FIGURE 5a. Real Health Price Growth Rates, Eighteen Countries, 1960–1990.

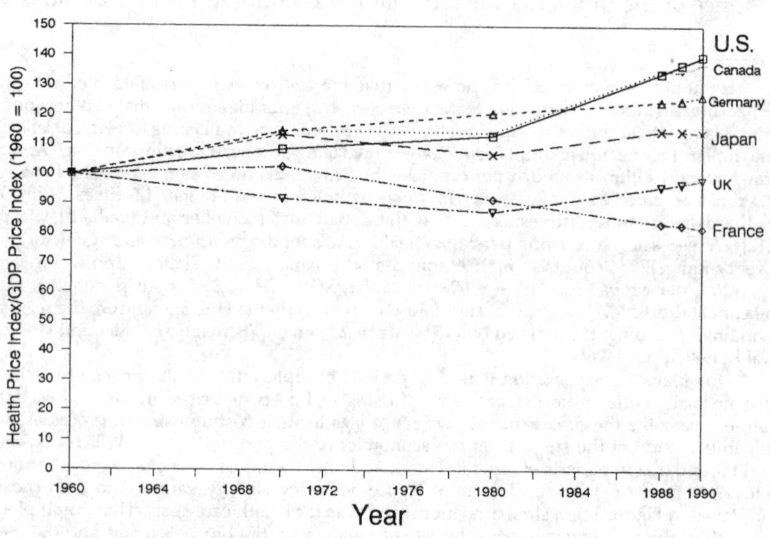

FIGURE 5b. Real Health Price Indices, Six Countries, 1960–1990.

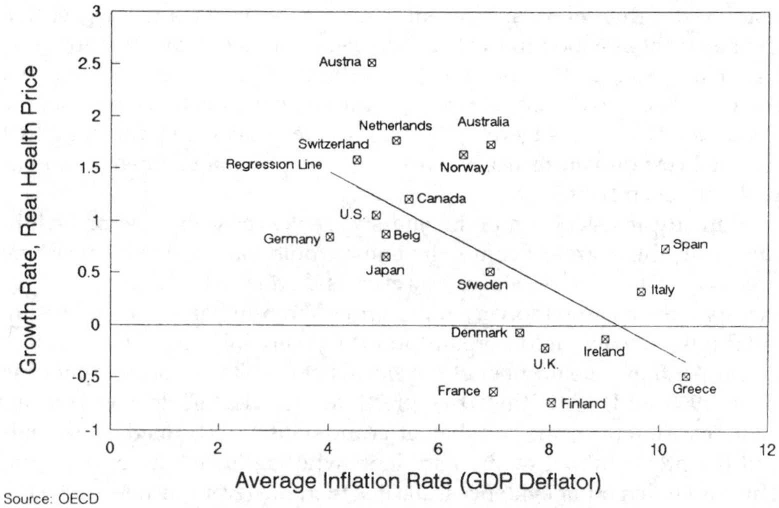

FIGURE 5c. **Real Health Price vs. Inflation, Growth Rates, 1960–1987.**

the very least, and has beset many countries beside the U.S.—indicate that it lies deeper than the particular administrative or other institutional arrangements adopted in this country. Let us, then, inquire into at least one possible source of the rising-cost phenomenon.

2. The Persistence of Productivity-Growth Differentials and the Cost Disease

The issue is surely complex, and no single explanatory hypothesis can pretend to account for a set of problems whose roots are undoubtedly sociological and psychological as well as economic. Still, there is one influence that goes far in accounting for the difficulties that have just been described, and that at the same time at least suggests the general directions one must pursue if a way out is to be found. It should be kept in mind that the following discussion focuses throughout, not upon the *level* of costs, but upon their real *rates of increase.* There are many influences, actual or alleged, notably lawsuits against doctors and others involved in health care, lack of competitiveness in the profession and high earnings of physicians, that clearly may help to explain the levels of those costs, but I am aware of none beside the one about to be described that seems to account for the many countries in which *growth* in health and education costs persistently outpaces the rate of inflation.

If litigation were to be capable of explaining the persistent rise in medical cost, it, and the size of jury awards, would have to have been increasing throughout the many decades during which the evidence indicates that real medical costs have been rising. I know of no evidence that this was so, or was so in the other countries in which costs have been rising faster than ours, and recent evidence even seems to suggest that the pertinent litigation in the U.S. has been leveling off or declining (see, e.g., Hay [1992, p. 121, Table 6.1]). Students of the subject indicate that there has been no discernible trend in the size of jury awards, but that the frequency of victories by the plaintiffs has been declining, meaning that the total cost of malpractice awards and other related payments also has probably been falling.

Similarly, if lack of competitiveness were the cause of growing health-care costs, the degree of competitiveness would have had to be declining over the years. The evidence, however, is distinctly to the contrary. For example, the advent and very rapid growth in number and membership of HMOs and comparable organizations has certainly added to the forces of competition. The number of physicians per capita has been expanding since 1960 and, with that, the pressures for doctors to compete for patients. Moreover, the number of admissions to U.S. medical schools and the proportion of medical students who graduate have also grown. This and much other evidence indicates that, however one may judge the presence or absence of competition in the field, it has certainly been increasing, not declining with the passage of time, as it would have had to have done if it were to constitute an explanation of rising health-care costs.[7]

Finally, if doctor's incomes were an explanation, they would have to be rising in real terms. Again, the facts indicate otherwise. Over much of the period after World War II the real (inflation-adjusted) earnings of doctors in the U.S. have been virtually constant. The 1991 *U.S. Statistical Abstract* reports the trends in median net physician incomes for the period 1975–1988. During these thirteen years, when the income figures are not corrected for the effects of inflation, we find that median incomes have approximately doubled, rising from $58,400 to $117,800 – an average annual rate of increase of about 5.4 percent. However, because during this time interval the Consumer Price Index more than doubled, real median physician income at the end of the period was somewhat less than where it had begun, at $53,600 in 1975 dollars.[8] This also shows that the problem cannot be attributed to physician greed and unscrupulous overcharging or other forms of villainy. While the ethics of doctors are probably no better than those of professors, or the members of other professions, the temptation to attribute the problem to villainy is surely misguided.

How, then, can one explain the source of the rising-cost problem? It is almost exactly a quarter century since William Bowen and I [1966] first

---

[7] For a much more thorough study of the subject by an economist employed by the Federal Trade Commission, see Noether [1986]. That study provides strong evidence for the conclusion in the text.

[8] During this same period teachers' salaries in elementary and high schools were increasing slightly in real terms (U.S. Department of Education [1992, p. 811]), so that doctors' incomes were actually falling behind those of schoolteachers.

reported our analysis of what is now called "the cost disease of the personal services," including health care, education and a number of other services, with its profoundly disturbing presage of the future. I remind the reader of this not to gloat over the accuracy of our depiction of the future (though I cannot deny that it is a source of some uneasy satisfaction). Indeed, we were not the first to offer such an analysis, and we explicitly denied at the time that we were providing a forecast. Still, the course taken by the economy since then, as it had for so long a period before, followed disturbingly closely the gloomier of the scenarios that our model suggests and undertakes to explain.

A major source of the cost disease was traced to the differences in the productivity growth rates of the various parts of the typical developed economy. It is productivity growth that, on this view, creates both private affluence and public squalor, and it is not by mere happenstance that at the same time, in the words of the poet, "wealth accumulates and men decay." For it is inherent in the technological structure of the economic growth process that a particular set of economic activities, many of them the very activities that are generally considered most critical for the health of the society, are condemned to a pattern of spiraling increases in their real prices that appears to put them beyond the reach of both the individual and the state.

It is hardly surprising that, while overall productivity in the industrial world has been growing rapidly, the pace of growth in different industries has varied substantially. What is more unexpected is the persistence of the pattern of differences in productivity growth between economic sectors. A given sector of the economy does not usually fluctuate haphazardly between periods of relatively slow and relatively rapid advance in productivity. Rather, the industries in which productivity was expanding slowly a century ago are, by and large, the very ones that are still the laggards today. And the endurance of productivity stagnancy in those industries has imposed upon them a distinctive price history that is the fundamental symptom of the cost disease of the personal services. This cost disease phenomenon shows up when the services, in a class that will presently be described, are plagued by cumulative and persistent rises in their costs, increases that normally exceed to a significant degree the corresponding rate of increase for commodities generally, i.e., almost always outstrip the economy's rate of inflation.

The services in question, which I call *the stagnant services,* include, most notably, health care, education, legal services, welfare programs for the poor, postal service, police protection, sanitation services, repair services, the performing arts, restaurant services and a number of others that will soon suggest themselves. The common element that characterizes them all is the handicraft attribute of their supply processes. None of them has, at least so far, been fully automated and liberated from the requirement of a substantial residue of personal attention by their producers. That is, they have resisted reduction in the amount of labor expended per unit of their output. Not that the growth rate of their labor productivity has always been zero. On the contrary, in almost every case there has been some rise in the productivity of these personal services with the passage of time; but over longer periods it has been far slower than the rate of productivity increase characteristic of the economy as a whole. That is why we call them the stagnant services.

There are at least two reasons why rapid and persistent productivity growth has eluded the stagnant services. First, some of them are inherently resistant to standardization. Before one can undertake to cure a patient or to repair a broken piece of machinery it is necessary to determine, case by case, just what is wrong, and the treatment must then be tailored to the individual case. The manufacture of thousands of identical automobiles can be carried out on an assembly line and much of the work done by industrial robots, but the repair of a car just hauled to a garage from the site of an accident cannot be entrusted completely to automated processes. A second reason why it has been difficult to reduce the labor content of these services is that in many of them quality is, or is at least believed to be, inescapably correlated with the amount of labor expended on their production. Teachers who cut down the time they spend on their classes or who increase class size, doctors who speed up the examination of their patients, or a police force that spends less time on the beat are all held to be shortchanging those whom they serve. This, then, is why the stagnant services have consistently proved unamenable to steady and substantial productivity growth, that is, to reduced labor content. To see the implications for costs and prices, let me return to a (slightly edited) quotation from our earliest description of the relationship (Baumol and Bowen [1966, pp. 167–171]).[9]

3. Cumulating Real Price Increases: The Fate of the Stagnant Sectors

Let us imagine an economy divided into two sectors: one, the progressive sector, in which productivity is rising, and another, the stagnant sector, in which productivity is constant. Suppose the first economic sector produces automobiles, and the second, performances of Mozart quartets. Let us assume that in automobile production, where technological improvements are possible, output per work-hour is increasing at an annual rate of 4 percent, while the productivity of quartet players remains unchanged year after year. Imagine now that the workers in the automobile industry recognize the growth in their own productivity and persuade management to agree to a matching rise in wages. The effect on the auto industry is easy to trace. Each year the average worker's wage

---

[9] There is little new in these observations on the effects of differential rates of productivity change on costs and prices. See, for example, Scitovsky and Scitovsky [1959]. Only the application of these to the state of the arts is relatively new. Some of the general ideas are suggested in Poggi [1964], in some of the annual reports of the Royal Opera, and in Toffler [1964, chap. 11, esp. 163 ff.]. See also Jean Fourastie's interesting comparisons of productivities, by century and nation [1960, chap. 4].

goes up by 4 percent, but her output increases by exactly the same percentage. Then the one effect on cost is exactly offset by the other—total cost and output both rise 4 percent. As a consequence, labor cost *per unit* (the ratio between total labor cost and total output) remains absolutely unchanged. This process can continue indefinitely in our imaginary world, with auto workers earning more and more each year, with cost per car remaining stationary, and with no rise in automobile prices necessary to maintain company profits.

But what of the other industry in our little economy? How is quartet performance faring in this society of growing abundance? Suppose that the quartet players somehow succeed in getting their wages raised, and that their standard of living, though below that of the auto workers, maintains its relative position, also increasing 4 percent per year. What does this situation imply for the costs of quartet performance? If the earnings of string players increase by 4 percent per year while their productivity remains unchanged, it follows that the direct labor cost per unit of their output must also rise at 4 percent, since cost per unit is equal to total cost divided by the number of units of output. If in a forty-hour week the string player provides just as many performances as he did the previous year, but his wage is 4 percent higher, the cost per performance must have risen correspondingly. Moreover, there is nothing in the nature of this situation to prevent the cost of performance from rising indefinitely and at a compounded rate. So long as the musicians are successful in resisting erosion of their relative incomes, the cost per performance must continue to increase along with the performer's income. Cumulatively rising costs will beset the performing arts with absolute inevitability.

Indeed, with productivity per work-hour roughly constant, *any* increase in the musicians' wage rates, however modest, must lead to a corresponding increase in costs. If wages go up 4 percent elsewhere in the economy, but performer incomes rise by only 2 percent, the direct labor cost of each performance must also increase by 2 percent unless there is an offsetting reduction in the number of labor-hours per performance, that is, an offsetting rise in productivity.

It is important to recognize that ordinary price inflation plays no role in the logic of our analysis. That is, so long as the wages of musicians in this two-sector economy continue to increase at all, the cost of a live performance will rise, cumulatively and persistently, relative to the cost of an automobile, whether or not the general price level in the economy is changing; the extent of the increase in the relative cost of the performance will depend directly on the relative rate of growth of productivity in the automobile industry.[10] Moreover, though it is always tempting to seek some villain to explain such a cumulative run of real price increases, there is no guilty party here. Neither wasteful expenditure nor greed

[10] Any overall price inflation in the economy, which affects the prices of *all* goods and services, contributes a separate, additional monetary cost increase on top of the stagnant services' innate price increases.

plays any role. It is the relatively stagnant technology of live musical performance—its inherent resistance to productivity improvements—that accounts for the compounding rise in the cost of performance of quartets.[11]

It will be evident that the foregoing analysis is applicable to many other personal services. In particular, the services that have been labeled "stagnant" all appear to have difficulties persistently impeding growth in their productivity very similar to those that beset the musicians in our parable. Clearly, health care has taken giant steps in quality improvement over the decades, but while the amount of physician time spent per patient-visit or per illness may have declined somewhat, it has done so only marginally; in education there has been no marked change in class size, and, actually, a small decline in number of students served per teacher-hour, and it is widely judged that there has been little if any improvement in quality. The output of an hour of police protection, or an hour of postal delivery time, or an hour of street cleaning time has probably been enhanced by the use of motor vehicles in terms of territory covered, but the increase has probably been modest (criminal activity has also been "enhanced" by the use of motor vehicles), and certainly has not been continuous and cumulative. The productivity of trial lawyers and actors or musicians engaged in live performances has risen to a minuscule degree at most, and while automotive repair services have done somewhat better, the increase in their productivity has still been well below that of manufacturing, as we will see presently. The circumstances of the insurance industry follow directly from what has just been said, for the purchaser of an insurance policy is simply acquiring a bundle of several stagnant services—health care, auto repair, legal services, and so on, and as we have just noted, productivity growth in the supply of this bundle has surely lagged. A final class of stagnant activities to be noted here is particularly significant in terms of the state of society. The care of the indigent, government welfare, and related programs seem to benefit from no significant source of productivity growth—they appear to remain fundamentally unchanged, handicraft activities.

The upshot is that all of these services suffer from a rise in their costs that is terrifyingly rapid and frighteningly persistent.[12] They threaten the strained budgets of the individual families, the municipalities and the central governments of the entire industrialized world. And, as

---

[11] The advent of mass media has, of course, contributed spectacularly to productivity in musical performance, increasing enormously the number of listeners reached by a given number of hours of performance. Yet, that has not solved the problem. The costs of television broadcasting, for example, are increasing at a compounded rate very similar to that of live performance. The reason is that the very rapid growth of productivity in the high-tech portion of broadcasting has made the cost of television transmission an ever-declining portion of the total budget of broadcasting activity, leading the live performance component to constitute a constantly *rising* share of the total. For a full discussion and the statistical evidence, see Baumol, Blackman and Wolff [1989, chap. 6].

[12] The cost disease analysis also has an implication that may help to account for the high relative *level* of health care cost in the U.S. It must be remembered that, despite wide-

financial stringency becomes more pressing, it is understandable that spending on these services is cut back or, at most, increased by amounts barely sufficient to stay abreast of the overall price inflation in the economy. But since the costs of the stagnant services are condemned to rise, persistently and cumulatively, with greater rapidity than the rate of inflation of the economy, the consequence is that the supply of these services tends to fall in quantity and quality. This undoubtedly is not the only source of increasing public squalor, but it must surely have made a significant contribution.

4. Some Further Evidence

There is another way in which one can seek pertinent evidence. If the lagging productivity explanation is valid, it should be valid in arenas other than health care and education. Some other services that are apt to have been infected by the cost disease have already been listed. If the analysis is valid, these arenas should also exhibit the rising real prices that are the symptom of the disease. The evidence suggests that this is in fact so.

For example, Figure 6 provides data obtained from the U.S. Bureau of Labor Statistics on the relative trends in the prices of automobile insurance, automotive maintenance and repair, and the CPI. For the entire period 1948–1992 the CPI grew at a compound rate a bit more than 4 percent per annum. For auto maintenance and repair the price increase averaged nearly 8 percent, while that for auto insurance was about 15 percent–presumably also reflecting the rising cost of litigation. The Bureau of Labor Statistics has also calculated a price index for legal services but only for the seven years 1986–1992. Still, it is suggestive that during this brief period it, too, grew consistently faster than the consumer price index, by about one percentage point per year, though at a rate nearly 1.5 percentage points more slowly than the price index for physician services.

The productivity growth record of these sectors (as reported in the U.S. government's Survey of Current Business) is consistent with our analysis. While the average growth rate of productivity in the auto repair subsector was a respectable 1.6 percent per annum over the period 1948–1986, it had declined significantly over the period, and that average productivity growth rate was only a bit more than half of the 3.1 percent rate achieved by the manufacturing subsector, motor vehicles and equipment.

The case of legal services is more extreme. Computerized information services have helped to save lawyers' time, as has air travel and the avail-

---

spread impressions to the contrary, productivity levels in all or virtually all other countries still remain well below those in the U.S. If that is so, we should expect that the graphs for their medical costs as well as those for other stagnant services should have intertemporal shapes very much like those shown for the U.S. in Figures 1-3, but that their heights should not yet have reached the levels of the American figures. The point is that we are all going rapidly uphill, but this country began climbing earlier.

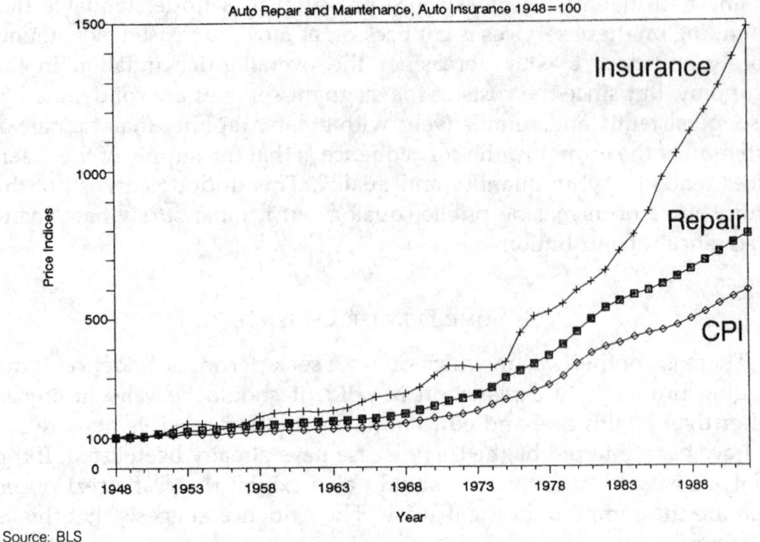

FIGURE 6. Price Trends: Auto Services vs. CPI, 1948–1992.

ability of telephones in automobiles. But such productivity-enhancing innovations are peripheral to the work of an attorney, whose research can perhaps be assigned to paralegal assistants but not left to machines, and whose planning of a case and its presentation in court must be done, in essence, the old-fashioned way—as an almost pure expenditure of labor time. There simply is no mechanical or electronic equipment capable of reducing the labor time expended, say, per legal case to any significant degree. And, as a matter of fact, the productivity growth (or, rather, decline) rate for the legal services subsector averaged -2.26 percent compounded (!) throughout our thirty-eight-year period. The implications for the time pattern of legal costs should by this point of the discussion have become all too obvious.

As for the insurance industry, the U.S. Department of Commerce provides labor-productivity growth figures for the U.S. economy for the entire period since the Second World War, dividing the economy into eleven sectors which, in turn, are divided into sixty-six subsectors. One of the eleven sectors is finance, insurance and real estate (FIRE), and it contains seven subsectors, including insurance carriers and insurance agents. In terms of average productivity growth over the postwar period this FIRE sector is one of the poorest performers (with only the categories dubbed miscellaneous services, government, and construction turning in a less exemplary record). Output per person-hour in the FIRE group of services increased at the very modest annual rate of 0.9 percent, while the average for all sectors was some 55 percent higher than this. Not only was the average growth rate of productivity in the FIRE sector low, but it fell through most of the period, and its rate of decline relative to its initial level was greater than that of any sector other than mining and construction.

The productivity pattern of the insurance agents and brokers subsector was very similar to that of the FIRE sector as a whole. Moreover, its productivity growth rate was actually negative: -0.99 percent per year over the thirty-eight-year period. In contrast, the productivity growth of the other insurance subsector, insurance carriers, showed no significant trend, downward or upward, and its average growth rate, 1.25 percent per year, was substantial (even if below the average for the economy), but well below the 2.77 percent growth rate for manufacturing and the 5.37 percent productivity growth rate for the telephone and telegraph subsector.

We see that the industries that are characterized by persistently rising real prices are precisely those that the cost disease analysis would lead us to expect to behave in this manner.

5. Toward Viable Policy: Can We Afford Abundant Health Care and Education?

The pervasive fiscal difficulties that threaten quality of life in the industrialized countries have many roots. However, the evidence that has been presented here indicates that a considerable share of the problem is attributable to the cost disease. If inflation proceeds at a rate of, say, 4 percent per year, but cost of education per pupil and other municipal services rise at a rate of 6 percent, then a tax base that expands only a little faster than the rate of inflation is sure to lead to growing financial problems for the city. And medical costs and insurance premiums that considerably outstrip the rate of inflation year after year would appear to put such vital services beyond the reach of all but the wealthiest families. If I am right in arguing that the cause of this predicament is the nature of the technology of the supply of these services, and that the course of development of such technology does not lend itself to easy modification, then the implication would seem grim indeed – the conclusion would appear to be one that befits the natural pessimism of a practitioner of the dismal science.

Yet, I shall argue now, far from there being no exit, the very structure of the problem is such as to offer society all the resources requisite for its solution. Contrary to appearances, we can afford ever more ample medical care, ever more abundant education, ever more adequate support of the indigent, and all this along with a growing abundance of private comforts and luxuries. It is an illusion that we cannot do so, and the main step needed to deal effectively with the fiscal problem underlying the growing public squalor is to overcome that illusion. This conclusion may strike the reader as implausible in light of all that has been said. Yet, the conclusion is inescapable, if only our future productivity record bears any resemblance to that of decades past which brought the U.S. and the rest of the industrial world ever-better health care and ever more education, despite rising costs. There are two fundamental reasons why this must be so, and I will describe them in turn.

A. *The small, but positive, growth rate of productivity in the stagnant services.* In *A Connecticut Yankee,* Mark Twain devotes an entire chapter to Sir Boss's unsuccessful attempt to explain the concept of real wages to his primitive hosts. He argues with some passion that the monetary magnitudes of wages are irrelevant; that, regardless of their value as expressed in terms of money, wages are really higher only when it takes fewer hours of labor to earn the wages needed to purchase a given set of goods. Yet, as I will show now, precisely that is true of the stagnant services. Their money prices are indeed rising ever higher, and their exchange rate against manufactured goods is constantly increasing, just as I have shown here. But in terms of the number of labor hours it takes to acquire them, over the longer run, their cost is decreasing steadily, albeit relatively slowly. If so, it is immediately obvious that the claim that we cannot afford them is simply a manifestation of what economists call "money illusion."

But how can that be? The answer is that even the most stagnant of services is undergoing some productivity growth–slowly, and not very steadily, but some growth nevertheless. The cost disease analysis does not claim otherwise; its workings merely require productivity in the stagnant services to grow substantially more slowly than that of the economy overall. To illustrate the point, let me return to my favorite example. If, in the earlier parable, the hypothetical Mozart string quartet had been scored for a half-hour performance, then its performance in 1990 required two person-hours of labor, just as it did in 1790, when it might have been written. Thus, there is apparently no scope for the slightest increase in labor productivity.[13] Yet that is only an illusion. To see why, assume that the more recent performance was by a Viennese group of musicians, and that it was played in Frankfurt am Main. A 1990 trip from their Austrian home base to the German auditorium surely would normally have taken no more than several hours. But when Mozart made the trip in 1790 it required six days of extreme discomfort (and, at that, Mozart wrote that he was surprised at the speed of the journey).[14] Certainly, technical progress has reduced the number of hours of labor required to provide a unit of the output in question, thus raising the labor productivity of every itinerant performer, even in live performance (and we know that performers are virtually all itinerant).

This example clearly suggests that there is no service whose productivity is not touched by technical progress to some degree. The conse-

---

[13] Or even for any increase in total factor productivity, for that matter; the latter appears frozen because the same number of instruments, the capital equipment, was required at the two dates.

[14] Letter of 28 September 1790.

quent rise in labor productivity means, by definition, that it requires ever less labor time to produce a unit of such a service. And every resulting reduction in labor time spent in producing the service means that those purchasing the service must expend that much less labor-time to acquire the wherewithal needed to purchase it. That is the sense in which even education and medical care have really grown steadily cheaper (albeit at a snail's pace, compared to other outputs), even as they appear to become steadily more unaffordable. Productivity growth in the stagnant services means that their real costs are steadily, if slowly, declining despite the dramatic inflation in their money prices. However, this, at best, can make only a minor contribution toward solution of the politico-budgetary problems that stem from the cost disease. More powerful aid must come from a second source.

B. *Productivity growth in the entire economy means we can afford more of everything.* There is a good deal more to the sanguine side of the cost disease story. Even if it were true that productivity in the stagnant services was not increasing one iota, their rising prices could still not put them beyond the reach of the community; on the contrary, it would remain true that society could afford ever more of them, just as it has in fact been getting ever more of the health care and education that seem steadily to become to an ever greater degree too expensive to afford.

As was pointed out some time ago by David Bradford [1969], in an economy in which productivity is growing in almost every sector and declining in none, it is a tautology that consumers can have more of every good and service. To achieve this goal, some *limited* quantity of the inputs used to produce goods whose productivity is growing relatively quickly (the "progressive" outputs) need merely be transferred into the production of the stagnant services. Then productivity growth will still permit expansion of the progressive output quantities, despite the limited decline in their inputs, while the outputs of the stagnant service will grow because more input is devoted to their production. To achieve such a goal – ever greater abundance of everything – society must change only the *proportions* of its income that it devotes to the different products. In these circumstances, it is a fiscal illusion that underlies the view that consumers as a group cannot afford to pay the rising costs of education, health care, and other such services.

We can suggest the magnitudes that may be involved by using current U.S. data on price trends and expenditures on health care and education to illustrate the point. We will now see what would be entailed if the real prices of education and health care continue to grow at their current rate for fifty years, if overall U.S. productivity rises for that period at its historic rate of (approximately) 2 percent, and if real educational and health care outputs maintain an unchanged share of GDP – that is, if the economy were to produce more of education, health care and everything else, keeping their relative outputs completely unchanged. It should be emphasized that the resulting numbers do not pretend to constitute any-

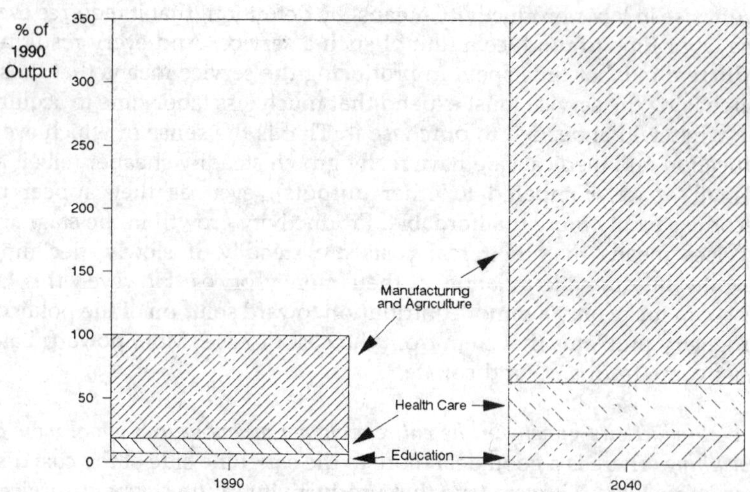

FIGURE 7. Hypothetical Changes in Total Outputs Over 50 Years, Assuming Historic Overall Productivity Growth Rate and Constant Sector Shares.

thing like a forecast—they are intended to be no more than a suggestive extrapolation. Or rather, they are intended as an indication of what the economy will be *capable* of achieving for the public, if historic price and productivity trends continue.

In Figures 7 and 8 the left-hand bar shows the 1990 actual shares of GDP constituted by health care, education, and the remainder. It shows

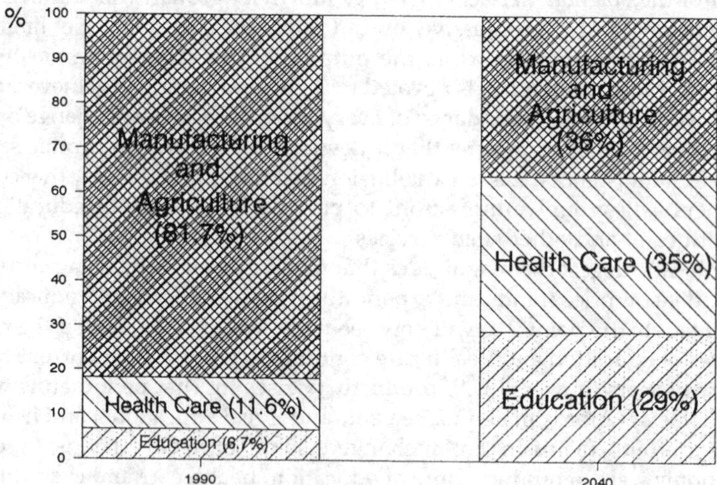

FIGURE 8. Hypothetical Changes in Total Spending, Over 50 Years, Assuming Historic Sectoral Productivity Growth Rates.

that the two services then constituted less than 20 percent of the total. In Figure 7 the right-hand bar reports what will happen to outputs if the number of hours of labor performed in the U.S. remains constant but productivity in the economy grows at its historic average rate and each industry's output level is adjusted to retain the same share of total output. It shows that in that period the output of every good and service, including education and health care, can increase to more than 3.5 times its 1990 magnitude. This growth is indicated by the relative heights of the corresponding segments of the two bars in Figure 7–that for 1990 and the one for the year 2040. That is, we see that the right-hand (2040) bar and every one of its segments is more than 3.5 times as tall as in the left-hand (1990) bar.

Figure 8, however, is the crucial one for our analysis, for it shows the modification of the apportionment of real expenditures required to achieve this result, in effect, measuring spending on each product by the relative number of hours of labor it requires to earn enough to purchase it. Our assumption that the total hours of labor do not change means that total spending on GDP, measured in terms of labor hours used, must also be constant. Thus, the 1990 bar and the 2040 bar, representing total (labor-hour) expenditure on GDP in the two years, must be exactly equal in height. However, expenditure proportions will have changed drastically. Medical outlays, instead of constituting 12 percent of the total, as they did in 1990, must rise to more than 35 percent of the total in 2040. And the share of expenditure devoted to education will have risen from under 7 percent of the total at the beginning of the period to nearly 30 percent at the end. In other words, if current relative price trends and output proportions continue as they are now, by the time four decades of the next century have passed, education and health care alone will absorb well over half of GDP! But that will not prevent consumers from nearly quadrupling their consumption of each and every good and service, including manufactured necessities and luxuries of every variety.

A little thought will confirm that this can continue indefinitely. As the *Washington Post* stated in an editorial (11 June 1991), "People sometimes say the country has no money to deal with the growing tragedy of the inner cities. That is incorrect. The country has a lot of money. It is only a question of how Americans choose to spend it."

An analogy can perhaps make the sanguine character of the basic conclusion clearer. Suppose we think of the public's consumption of goods and services as the purchase of a bundle containing many components, just as the purchase of a car includes the acquisition of seats, tires, steering wheel, etc. Imagine that the price of steering wheels is increasing at an impressive rate, but that because of the decline in the costs of the other components, cars (equipped with steering wheels) grow less expensive every year. Would one really conclude that steering wheels are growing unaffordable, even when their price grows to 65 percent of the price of the car?

6. Remaining Problems

Yet, this happy conclusion is just a bit simplistic. The path from theory to practice is beset by daunting difficulties. At least four of them require emphasis.

A. *Low-income groups and universal availability of health-care and education.* Even if the analysis is correct, and society will be able to enjoy an increasing abundance of health and educational services, their rising real prices can nevertheless deny them, increasingly, to the poor and, even more likely, to the middle classes. In a rich economy, that is hardly acceptable, and government will no doubt have to intervene to provide the means for the economically underprivileged to get their share of these and other vital services affected by the cost disease.

B. *Education of the public.* Not the least of the remaining problems is the difficult educational task of getting the public to recognize the difference between the reality and the illusion in the behavior of costs. It will not be easy to convince the intelligent nonspecialist that, even though prices of personal services appear to be rising at a rate that is out of control, in fact the costs of those services (in terms of their labor-time equivalent) are really gradually declining, because of increases in their labor productivity. One can hardly blame such persons for their reluctance to be taken in by what appears to be sleight of hand or mere theoretical gobbledygook. The difficulty of convincing those who have not thought about the matter analytically that an item really becomes cheaper when its price doubles if, at the same time, wages rise by a factor of 2.1 is, after all, the main moral that Mark Twain seems to want the reader to draw from Sir Boss's failure in his attempt to make the matter clear to his medieval hosts. Yet the task of explanation to the public should not be beyond the most skilled of journalists and others who specialize in the art of effective communication. And an indispensable task it is, for without it effective budgetary reorientation along the lines described will undoubtedly be impossible politically in a democratic society.[15]

C. *The large public-sector share of GDP.* A third critical problem besets effective treatment of the cost disease. The extrapolations in the previous section suggest that if the services in question are supplied largely by government, in half a century well over 65 percent of GDP may easily have to flow through the public sector, and be insulated from control by the market. The experience of the planned economies indicates that this is

---

[15] A recent and sophisticated empirical study based on the analysis presented here finds evidence that shortchanging of the services suffering from the cost disease is common. The study focuses on higher education and concludes, subject to a number of *caveats*, that ". . . underallocation of resources to higher education may have become widespread, with the most acute difficulties occurring in countries showing the greatest fiscal restriction, i.e., Denmark, New Zealand and the U.K." (Ryan [1992, p. 1]).

not a viable economic arrangement, for it is likely to handicap economic growth substantially. Moreover, the analysis implies that our municipal governments face a particularly difficult task in acquiring the revenues necessary to prevent municipal services from collapsing even more completely than they have already. A large portion of the budgets of city governments consists of education, health care, and other services likely to exhibit price behavior characteristic of the cost disease–police protection, libraries, welfare, and so on. This means that we can expect that the real outlays on these will have to treble and more (!) before the middle of the twenty-first century, if these service outputs are not to fall behind the outputs of the economy's remaining activities. The political task of acquiring such increases in government revenues will not be easy. And, as just indicated, even if it is achieved, the consequences for economic efficiency and bureaucratic control of so enormous an increase in the share of GDP that will have to flow through government channels rather than the private sector of the economy are hardly an attractive prospect.

D. *The privatization option and susceptibility to ill-advised price controls.* The popular answer of the hour to dangers such as the huge expansion of the public sector just described is greater reliance on privatization. But privatization, too, is no panacea. The public's opposition to any threat to the survival of the public school system can hardly be dismissed as groundless, and similar remarks apply to a number of other services, such as police protection, currently supplied by government.

In addition, any industry beset by the cost disease that is in private hands is sure to be suspected of greed and malfeasance. It is hard to believe that calls for price controls to limit their cumulatively rising prices will not become irresistible politically. But if the rising costs are caused by unavoidably slow growth in productivity, price controls can confidently be expected to lead to deterioration in the quality of those services or to their partial or total disappearance.

We must add to these considerations the likelihood that the cost disease affects many services besides health care and education vital for quality of life. For the same arguments apply to the live performing arts, to libraries, to police protection, to restaurants, to welfare support for the impoverished and to many other critical services. The implication is that if we do not think through the complex problems just described, or fail to do so in short order, we face a society increasingly characterized, in the words of J.K. Galbraith, by private affluence and public squalor. Already, unmistakable and disquieting signs are available for all to see.

This, then, concludes my story. It is meant to illustrate how economics in the present and future can be guided in its choice of subjects for research by pressing contemporaneous social issues, just as was true in the past. Perhaps what I am saying is that economics, at its core, is an applied discipline–we are not accompanied by a body of specialist engineers whose training prepares them to use the products of pure research wherever they are, by happenstance, applicable. Rather, the economist's predisposition is to design research in a way that is likely to yield applications, and the preceding discussion is intended to show by example how that can be done.

References

Baumol, W.J., and A. S. Blinder, *Economics: Principles and Policy*, San Diego: Harcourt Brace Jovanovich, 1982.

Baumol, W.J., and W. G. Bowen, *Performing Arts: The Economic Dilemma*, New York: Twentieth Century Fund, 1966.

Baumol, W.J., S.A.B. Blackman, and E. N. Wolff, *Productivity and American Leadership: The Long View*, Cambridge, Mass.: MIT Press, 1989.

Bradford, David, "Balance on Unbalanced Growth," *Zeitschrift für Nationalökonomie*, 29, 1969, 291–304.

Fourastiè, Jean, *The Causes of Wealth*, Glencoe, Illinois: The Free Press, 1960.

Hay, Iain, *Money, Medicine, and Malpractice in American Society*, New York: Praeger, 1992.

Kapp, Yvonne, *Eleanor Marx*, New York: Pantheon Books, 1972.

Keynes, J.M., *The General Theory of Employment, Interest and Money*, New York: Harcourt Brace, 1936.

National Center for Education Statistics, *Digest of Education Statistics 1992*, Washington, D.C.: U.S. Dept. of Education, October 1992.

Noether, Monica, "The Growing Supply of Physicians: Has the Market Become More Competitive?" *Journal of Labor Economics*, 4, 1986.

Organization for Economic Cooperation and Development (OECD), *Health Care Systems in Transition: The Search for Efficiency*, Paris: 1990.

Poggi, Emil J., "The American Theater: An Economic Study, 1870–1931," Dissertation: Columbia University, 1964.

Ray, John, *Life of Adam Smith*, London: Macmillan and Co., 1895.

Ricardo, David, *The Works and Correspondence of David Ricardo*, P. Sraffa, ed., Cambridge: Cambridge University Press, 1951 and subsequent years.

Ryan, Paul, "Unbalanced Growth and Fiscal Restriction: Public Spending on Higher Education in Advanced Economies Since 1970," *Structural Change and Economic Dynamics*, 3, no. 2, 1992, 261–88.

Scheiber, G.J., and J.-P. Poullier, "Trends in International Health Care Spending," *Health Affairs*, 6, Fall 1987, 105–112.

Scheiber, G.J., J.-P. Poullier, and L.M. Greenwald, "Health Care Systems in Twenty-Four Countries," *Health Affairs*, 10, Fall 1991, 22–38.

Scitovsky, Tibor, and Ann Scitovsky, "What Price Economic Progress?" *Yale Review*, Autumn, 1959.

Smith, Adam, *An Inquiry Into the Nature and Causes of the Wealth of Nations*, London: 1776.

Toffler, Alvin, *The Culture Consumers*, New York: St. Martin's Press, 1964.

United Nations Educational, Scientific and Cultural Organization (UNESCO), *Statistical Yearbook*, Paris: various issues.

U.S. Department of Education, *Digest of Education Statistics*, Washington, D.C.: National Center for Education Statistics, 1990.

[6]

Unbalanced Growth Revisited: Asymptotic Stagnancy and New Evidence

By WILLIAM J. BAUMOL, SUE ANNE BATEY BLACKMAN, AND EDWARD N. WOLFF*

Some years ago, Baumol (1967) presented a model of unbalanced growth in which an oversimplified economy was divided into productivity growth sectors, one "stagnant" and one "progressive." It was argued that relative costs and prices in the stagnant sector would tend to rise persistently and cumulatively, and that *if* the output proportions of the two sectors happened to remain fairly constant, the share of the economy's inputs used by the stagnant sector and the share of consumer expenditure devoted to outputs of the stagnant sector must both rise toward 100 percent. Finally, it was concluded that the net result must be a *ceteris paribus* decline in the economy's overall productivity growth rate.

Since then a variety of pertinent empirical materials and some further analysis have suggested that the model needs modifications, some of them of interest in themselves. But the behavior of prices, input-use patterns, and consumer outlays have followed the model's scenario to a remarkable degree.

I. Manifest Destiny of Relative Costs and Sectoral Inputs

In this paper we show that Baumol's earlier equation of the service sector of reality with the stagnant sector of the model requires modification. But there *is* a subclass of the services that is a better approximation to the model's stagnant activities. We also introduce a third set of economic activities, that we label "asymptotically stagnant," which are neither completely stagnant nor progressive. They use, in fairly fixed proportions, some inputs from the progressive sector and some from the stagnant sector. We will show that in their initial phases such activities are often outstanding in their rapid productivity growth and declining costs. However, with the passage of time, the cost and price behavior of these asymptotically stagnant activities *necessarily* approaches that of the stagnant sector.

We will also examine the empirical evidence relating to the model, showing that:

(*i*) In real terms, there happens to have been little shift in output shares between manufacturing and the services, not only with time, but with increasing wealth as one goes from less developed to industrialized countries. The model does not predict this, but the trend is not inconsistent with it.

(*ii*) As the model predicts, with these constant output proportions there was a marked simultaneous rise in relative prices and share of total expenditure on the services both with the passage of time and with increased industrialization.

(*iii*) The service sector happens to contain some of the economy's most progressive activities as well as its most stagnant.

(*iv*) As the model predicts, the U.S. labor force has been absorbed predominantly by the stagnant subsector of the services rather than the services as a whole.

(*v*) Television broadcasting and electronic data processing are examples of asymptotically stagnant activities, and the empirical budget and cost patterns for these activities are perfectly consistent with the model's predictions.

II. Basic Results on Stagnant and Progressive Outputs

Before summarizing the basic propositions to be evaluated empirically, we emphasize two crucial qualifications. First, the model is

*Baumol: Princeton and New York universities; Blackman: Princeton University; Wolff: New York University. We are extremely grateful to the Division of Information Science and Technology of the National Science Foundation, the Exxon Education Foundation, the Fishman-Davidson Center for the Study of the Service Sector, and the C. V. Starr Center for Applied Economics at New York University for support of the research reported here. We also thank David Dollar for his valuable suggestions.

obviously a gross oversimplification. Outputs, firms, and industries do *not* fall into black and white categories of stagnancy and progressivity—they are all shades of gray. Even the most stagnant sectors of the economy have undergone some technological change, varying from one period to another. Second, an activity which is, say, relatively stagnant need not stay so forever. It may be replaced by a more progressive substitute, or it may undergo an outburst of innovation previously thought very unlikely. Thus, there may be radical changes in the time paths predicted by the model. History shows the folly of predicting that some field of endeavor is beyond human inventiveness. When we speak of manifest destiny here, our claim is more modest. We merely maintain that things must go as predicted only so long as there is no major qualitative change in the distribution of innovation among industries.

The earlier paper on unbalanced growth provided some basic propositions whose proofs can now be generalized considerably. However, here we merely restate them and a few corollaries:

1) With the passage of time, the cost per unit of a consistently stagnant product (for example, live concerts) will rise monotonically and without limit relative to the cost of a consistently progressive product (for example, watches and clocks).

The reason for this phenomenon, which has been called the cost disease of the stagnant services, is obvious—the growing relative productivity of a more progressive output means that it will use relatively smaller and smaller input quantities per unit of output as time passes.

2) If the output ratio of a stagnant to a progressive product (the number of concerts performed divided by the number of watches produced) happens to remain constant or does not fall, the share of the combined inputs used by the stagnant activity must rise without limit.

This, too, is a tautology, since the progressive output must by definition employ relatively less and less input per unit of output, and the relative decline in its input use must compound with the passage of time.

3) If relative prices correspond to relative unit costs and if the ratio of the stagnant to the progressive output does not fall, then relative expenditure on the stagnant product must rise monotonically with time.

An example will make this clear and suggest the magnitudes that may be involved. Between the 1670's and the 1970's, the output per watchmaker in Geneva is estimated to have risen from about 12 watches to over 1,200 watches per year. Purcell wrote *Dido and Aneas* in the 1680's and today it takes as many person-hours and instruments to perform *live* as it did then. Hence, if the ratio of watches produced to performances of Dido had remained exactly the same, both the relative input quantities devoted to the musical performance and the relative expenditures on the performances must have risen about one-hundredfold.

From all this we conclude:

4) In an economy in which the productivity growth rates of the different sectors are unequal, it is impossible for both the output ratios and the input ratios to remain constant.

III. On Asymptotically Stagnant Activities

We come now to our third type of activity which was not included in the earlier 1967 model. These are the asymptotically stagnant activities like TV broadcasting and data processing that we think of as outstandingly progressive, but whose progressivity, as we will show, carries the seeds of its own destruction.

A pure asymptotically stagnant activity is one that uses in fixed proportions one group of inputs produced by progressive activities and another set of inputs produced by stagnant activities. A prime example is television broadcasting with, roughly, one hour of its progressive component (electronic transmission) required for one hour of its stagnant input (performance or program production). Characteristically, these are "high tech" industries, at the frontier of technical progress.

These activities are noteworthy for their behavior patterns. In their early stages, when progressive inputs dominate their budgets, their costs and prices fall rapidly, like those of progressive activities. Later, their fixed input proportions and the rapid fall in the relative prices of their progressive inputs *in-*

evitably give the stagnant inputs an ever-rising share of the total budget of the asymptotically stagnant activity, as a simple matter of arithmetic. For example, if the progressive input's cost is initially 80 percent of the budget and falls 25 percent per year, while the stagnant input is 20 percent of the budget and rises 6 percent per year (these, as we will see, are approximate figures for data processing), a pocket calculator will confirm that in just about ten years the budget proportions *must* be reversed, with the stagnant output now about 80 percent of the total. Third, as the stagnant component *must* come to dominate the activity's budget, its output cost and price must approach those of its stagnant component, and therefore have to rise, succumbing to the cost disease. Finally, the date when the activity sheds its progressive characteristics comes more quickly the more rapid the decline in the price of its progressive component. This is so because the more spectacularly successful is productivity enhancement in the production of the progressive inputs, the more rapidly they will distinguish themselves as significant components of the asymptotically stagnant activity's budget and, consequently, the more rapidly the relative cost of this activity must begin to rise.

These results can also all be derived via formal mathematics, but this is not the place to do so.

IV. Empirical Evidence from the U.S. Economy

We turn now to our empirical evidence—to test the implications of the basic model of unbalanced growth, and the asymptotic stagnancy construct. The first of these tasks requires classification of the actual sectors of the economy into progressive and stagnant categories, a division that is inevitably somewhat arbitrary. We base the classification on input and output data for the U.S. economy for 1947–76, since consistent national account data and input-output tables are available. A variety of measures of productivity growth rates were used to test the sensitivity of our classification scheme.

In Table 1, column 1 shows calculations of annual (compounded) rates of labor productivity growth using the official *National Income and Product Accounts*... (BEA, 1981).[1] The corresponding sectoral productivity concept is gross product originating (*GPO*) per person employed, and that of aggregate productivity is the ratio of gross domestic product (*GDP*) to total persons employed. The average annual rate of aggregate productivity growth was 2.16 percent over the period. Sectoral rates of productivity growth ranged from a high of 5.42 percent in communications and broadcasting, a service sector, to a low of −0.51 percent in government enterprises. Though there is a fairly wide spread in sectoral rates of productivity growth, there also appears to be a sharp break between the construction sector at 1.66 percent and the narrowly defined "general services" sector at 0.93 percent. By this criterion and these data, four sectors are stagnant: services (0.93 percent); finance and insurance (0.50 percent); government industry (0.31 percent); and government enterprises (−0.51 percent). Productivity growth in the remaining sectors was fairly rapid, putting them in the progressive group. Note that this group includes three service sectors: communications; trade; and real estate.[2]

The second column of Table 1 uses gross domestic output (*GDO*) in constant dollars as its sectoral output and number of persons employed as its labor input. *GDO* in constant dollars, an input-output concept, equals gross value of a sector's output or sales deflated by the *sectoral* price deflator. The new

[1] Here, as the total value of goods and services produced domestically, irrespective of ownership, *GDP* is actually preferable. The level of industry disaggregation was determined by the available statistics for the period. The output variable is gross product originating (*GPO*) in constant (1972) dollars. *GPO* in constant dollars is defined as the difference between the deflated value of output and the deflated value of interindustry inputs. The input concept is "persons engaged in employment" (L), defined as the sum of the number of full-time-equivalent employees and self-employed workers. This is perhaps the best available measure of labor input.

[2] The real estate data must be interpreted cautiously, since part of the "output" is the rent imputed to owner-occupied housing. However, where imputed rent enters official *GNP* and *GDP* statistics, the reported rate of productivity growth in real estate is the appropriate datum.

TABLE 1—AVERAGE ANNUAL RATE OF PRODUCTIVITY GROWTH BY SECTOR, 1947–76[a]

	Measure			
Industry	*GPO/L* (1)	*GDO/L* (2)	ρ (3)	λ (4)
1. Agriculture	3.59	4.47	1.56	3.95
2. Mining	2.70	2.76	0.08	1.38
3. Construction	1.66	1.19	−0.34	1.49
4. Manufacturing-Durables	2.52	2.80	0.58	3.08
5. Manufacturing-Nondurables	3.21	3.23	0.41	2.56
6. Transportation and Warehousing	1.74	2.74	0.68	2.42
7. Communication and Broadcasting	5.42	5.50	3.99	5.21
8. Utilities	4.96	4.77	1.53	2.96
9. Trade		2.17	1.09	2.19
a. Wholesale Trade	2.37			
b. Retail Trade	1.99			
10. Finance and Insurance	0.50	0.31	−0.27	0.57
11. Real Estate	2.72	3.10	1.21	4.86
12. General Services	0.93			
a. Hotels, Personal and Repair (except auto)		1.37	−0.31	1.35
b. Business and Professional Services		1.70	0.83	2.30
c. Auto Repair and Services		1.45	−0.84	1.04
d. Movies and Amusements		0.99	−0.56	0.64
e. Medical, Educational and Nonprofit		−0.46	−1.14	−0.19
f. Household Workers		−0.21	−0.21	−0.21
13. Government Enterprises	−0.51	1.10	−0.52	0.99
14. Government Industry	0.31	−0.18	0.08	−0.18
Overall: *GDP*	2.16			
GNP		2.18	1.17	2.18

Sources: Col. 1: BEA, *The National Income and Product Accounts of the United States*, 1929–76 Statistical Tables, September 1981, Tables 6.2 and 6.11. Col. 2: *GDO* for 1947 was obtained from the standard 87-order BEA input-output table for 1947; *GDO* for 1976 was obtained from BLS, *Time-Series Data for Input-Output Industries*, Bulletin 2018, 1979. Cols. 3–4: U.S. input-output data. See fn. 4 for details.

[a]Shown in percent.

estimated rates of sectoral productivity growth differ somewhat from those in column 1, though the rank orders are quite close. The major exception is the construction sector, whose 1.19 percent rate now places it in the stagnant category. The input-output data also permit disaggregation of general services into six subsectors, as shown in Table 1, and evaluation of their degrees of stagnancy. The range of sectoral productivity growth rates of these subsectors is fairly wide, though they all lie below the economy's 2.18 percent rate. The last three subsectors in this group all seem clearly to be stagnant. The first three are more marginal, though we will, somewhat arbitrarily, draw the line between business and professional services (1.70 percent) on the one hand, and hotels, personal and repair services (1.37) and auto services (1.45 percent) on the other, placing only the former in the progressive group.

Our third measure of productivity growth rates requires several symbols to describe the input-output framework. Let $X=$ (column) vector of gross output by sector; $Y=$ (column) vector of final demand by sector; $a=$ matrix of interindustry technical coefficients; $l=$ (row) vector of labor coefficients; $k=$ (row) vector of capital stock coefficients; and $p=$ (row) vector of prices showing the (current) price per unit of output of each industry. In addition, we use the following scalars: $w=$ the annual wage rate, in current dollars; $r=$ the rate of profit on the capital stock; $y=pY=GNP$ at current prices; $L=lX=$ total employment; and $K=kX=$ total capital stock.

The aggregate rate of total factor productivity (*TFP*) growth is given by

$$(1)\qquad \rho = (pdY - wdL - rdK)/y,$$

where d refers to the differential. The rate of *TFP* growth for sector j is given by

$$(2)\qquad \rho_j \equiv -\left(\sum_i p_i da_{ij} + wdl_j + rdk_j\right)/p_i.$$

This is the continuous analog of Wassily Leontief's 1953 measure of sectoral technical change.[3]

The U.S. input-output data for 1947 and 1976 were used to estimate this third set of growth rates (col. 3, Table 1).[4] The *TFP* measures were all lower than the corresponding labor productivity measures since capital-labor ratios were increasing. The overall rate of *TFP* growth was 1.17 percent per year, about one point lower than that of labor productivity, and the sectoral rates behaved similarly. Their relative magnitudes were virtually unchanged, except for mining.[5] By this measure, the line between the progressive and stagnant categories was drawn between nondurable manufacturing (0.41 percent), and government industry and the mining sector (both at 0.08 percent).

So far, our productivity measures evaluate productivity improvements within any one sector; one can also examine the changes in total input usage, direct and indirect, per unit of a sector's output. This also reflects productivity growth of the sector's input suppliers. One such total factor requirement measure (reported in col. 4, Table 1) is λ, which shows the total (direct plus indirect) labor requirements per unit of final output:

$$(3)\qquad \lambda = l(I-a)^{-1}.$$

Productivity growth based on λ is quite similar to the figures in column 2, Table 1, since changes in total factor requirements are dominated by those in direct factor requirements.[6] The classification of sectors uses cut-

[3]Also, see William Peterson (1979) and Wolff (forthcoming) for more details. Because discrete time periods are employed, a Turnquist-Divisia Index is used to estimate sectoral and the overall rate of *TFP* (see Frank Gollop and Dale Jorgensen, 1980, or Wolff, forthcoming).

[4]The 1947 input-output table is the standard 87-order Bureau of Economic Analysis (BEA) version. (See, for example, BEA *Survey of Current Business*, 1974, for methods and a listing of sectors.) The 1976 table was estimated using the so-called R.A.S. method on the 1972 table, with the gross domestic output figures in Bureau of Labor Statistics (BLS, 1979a). Estimates of the total capital stock in each input-output sector appear in BLS (1979b). Full capital coefficient matrices for 1947 were obtained from the Brandeis Economic Research Center (BERC); sectoral 1947 depreciation rates from BERC; and those for 1976 estimated from *Internal Revenue Service Corporation Tax Returns*. Sectoral price indices for 1947 were provided by BERC and for 1976 by the BEA. Additional details on data sources and methods are available from the authors.

The accounting framework was then modified as follows: 1) An "endogeneous export column" was created to balance the noncompetitive import row (sector 80). 2) For the estimation of Marxian labor values, the depreciation row that is normally part of value-added was treated as an endogenous input row (sector 88), and an "endogenous capital replacement" column was included to balance this row. 3) Five sectors (research and development (74), business travel (81), office supplies (82), scrap and used goods (83), and inventory valuation adjustment (87)) appeared in the 1947 table but not in the 1976 table. In order to assure consistency of the accounting framework, these sectors were eliminated from both gross and final output in 1947 by distributing their inputs to other sectors. 4) Indirect business taxes in value-added were eliminated in order to remove the biasing effect of indirect business taxes on relative prices. 5) The input-output matrices were finally converted to constant (1958) prices by multiplying each row of the matrix by the appropriate sectoral price deflator. For details, see Wolff (forthcoming).

[5]This reflects a large postwar influx of capital equipment into mining and increases in intermediate inputs. The mining sector is rather different from a more standard stagnant sector, since it is a process industry whose output is not directly related to its labor (or capital) input. Its low rate of *TFP* growth is attributable primarily to the nature of extraction, in which more accessible ores and petroleum are mined first and less accessible deposits later. The increasing difficulty of mining would have yielded a negative growth rate in *TFP* if technology had remained constant. The fact that *TFP* growth was zero in this sector over the period 1947–76 suggests that technical change (or the discovery of new accessible deposits) did occur.

[6]Three other measures were also used. The first, λ_m, differs from col. 4 only in λ's Marxian accounting framework. Capital, as a produced means of production, is valued by its depreciation rate (see Wolff, 1979). The second is ρ^*, the total factor requirement analog of ρ. Let $\gamma = k(I-a)^{-1}$ be the total capital requirements per unit of final output. Then the rate of change of total factor requirements per unit of final output can be estimated from $p_j^* \equiv -(wd\lambda_j + rd\gamma_j)/p_j$. The third

TABLE 2—SHARE OF EMPLOYMENT AND OUTPUT IN STAGNANT SECTOR, 1947 AND 1976[a]

	Measure			
	GPO/L (1)	*GDO/L* (2)	ρ (3)	λ (4)
A. Stagnant Sectors:				
2. Mining			×	×
3. Construction		×	×	×
10. Finance and Insurance	×	×	×	×
12. General and Services				
a. Hotels, Personal and Repair (except auto)	×	×	×	×
b. Business and Professional	×			
c. Auto Repair and Service	×	×	×	×
d. Movies and Amusement	×	×	×	×
e. Medical, Educational and Nonprofit	×	×	×	×
f. Household Workers	×	×	×	×
13. Government Enterprises	×	×	×	×
14. Government Industry	×	×	×	×
B. Annual Prod. Growth Rate, 1947–76:				
a. Progressive Sectors (all)	2.94	3.04	1.09	2.92
b. Stagnant Sectors	0.64	0.56	−0.84	0.73
c. Progressive Service Sectors	2.71	2.79	1.63	2.79
d. Overall	2.16	2.18	1.17	2.18
C. Percent of Employed Persons in Stagnant Sectors:				
a. 1947	27.6	30.7	32.4	32.4
b. 1976	41.2	42.0	43.0	43.0
D. Stagnant Sector Share of Final Output (1958 $):				
a. 1947	21.4	31.2	31.5	31.5
b. 1976	21.2	29.2	28.9	28.9
E. Stagnant Sector Share of Final Output (Current $):				
a. 1947	17.9	26.8	27.0	27.0
b. 1976	29.9	38.6	38.1	38.1
F. Stagnant Sector Share of *GDO* (1958 $):				
a. 1947	16.8	21.9	24.2	24.2
b. 1976	16.8	19.8	21.3	21.3
G. Stagnant Sector Share of *GDO* (Current $):				
a. 1947	13.7	18.3	20.4	20.4
b. 1976	22.9	24.5	26.7	26.7
H. Percent of Employed Persons in Progressive Services:[b]				
a. 1947	21.3	23.5	23.5	23.5
b. 1976	22.5	26.7	26.7	26.7

[a]Panels B–H results are shown in percent.
[b]In col. 1, progressive services are defined as communications and broadcasting, trade, and real estate. In cols. 2–4, they include the same three sectors and, in addition, business and professional services.

off points of 2.19 percent for the progressive category and 1.49 percent for the stagnant category, and is identical with that of column 2, except that the mining sector now falls into the stagnant category.

In Table 2, × indicates that a sector is classified as stagnant according to the measure of productivity growth (panel A). The average annual rate of productivity growth for the two aggregated sectors are shown in panel B.[7]

measure uses the rate of change in the (real) relative price of a sector's output to measure its relative rate of productivity growth. All three measures yielded the same classification scheme as shown in cols. 3 and 4 of Tables 1 and 2.

[7]It should be noted that the overall level of productivity growth corresponding to λ_m is the ratio of *NNP* to employment, since depreciation is treated as endogenous. The rate of growth is lower than that of *GNP* per worker.

V. Tests of the Model's Basic Implications

We are now in a position to test as hypotheses the main implications of our model. The first of these is the cost disease prediction that relative prices of the stagnant sector's outputs will rise at about the same rate as the shortfall in its rate of productivity growth. This is indeed confirmed by the data. By the measures of Table 2, the rate of productivity growth of the stagnant sector is from about two to two and one-half percentage points below that of the progressive sector.[8] Independently selected price data show that the price of stagnant output relative to progressive output increased at about 2 percent per year.

The next hypothesis is not an implication of the model, but was previously only a casual observation. This is the view that in real terms output shares have remained constant over time. This was examined using both final output and *GDO* shares (panels D and F, Table 2). The classification scheme of column 1 tells us that the real output shares remained constant over the period in terms of both final output and *GDO*. The other definitions, however, indicate a slight decline in the stagnant sector's real share of final demand and gross output.

We can now examine the other two main implications of the model. The first is that, since output shares have been fairly constant, the share of employment in the stagnant sector will rise over time. By all four definitions, the share of employment in the stagnant sector rose by over ten percentage points over the period and, by the first definition, by almost fourteen percentage points (panel C). The third basic prediction of our model is that, with output shares roughly constant in real terms, the share of output produced by the stagnant sector will rise in nominal terms over time. This is confirmed in panels E and G, which exhibit increases that range from 6 to 12 percent.[9]

[8]Both sectoral values of ρ are below the overall rate of *TFP* growth. This is correct, because as demonstrated in Peterson, $\rho = \Sigma_i (p_i X_i / y) \rho_i$, the ratio of total *GDO* to total final output (in current dollars) is about 2.0 in both years.

[9]We also found that the share of total capital stock in the stagnant sector declined by about five percentage points, indicating that the capital-labor ratio grew faster in the progressive sector. This result is consistent with the spirit of our model, since the progressive sector is characterized by more rapid changes in technology that can be expected to involve a more rapid displacement of labor by capital.

One final set of implications of the model can also be tested. As has been shown, the service sector includes both progressive and stagnant industries. In panel B, we have calculated separately the rate of productivity growth for progressive services. We find that the progressive services experienced slightly lower rates of growth of labor productivity than progressive goods producers but higher rates of total factor productivity growth. Moreover (panel H), we find that while employment in progressive services increased over the 1947–76 period, it rose very modestly, as our analysis might lead us to expect. Thus, progressive services behaved very differently from stagnant services over the postwar period and behaved very much like progressive goods sectors, and while it is true that the nation's labor force moved toward services, both stagnant and progressive, it was the former whose labor force increased most substantially. While the labor force of the progressive services rose somewhere between 5 and 14 percent, that of the stagnant services rose between 32 and 50 percent.[10]

[10]Some remarkable cross-sectional international comparisons provided by Robert Summers (1985) also offer

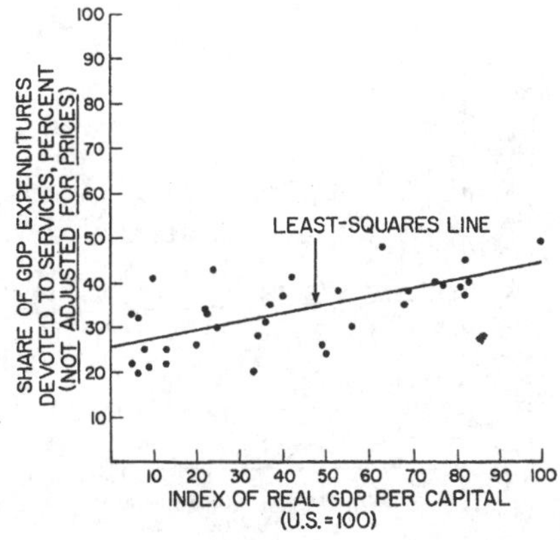

FIGURE F1

at least suggestive support for our model. The services' proportion of total real *GDP* expenditures, and their proportion of total nominal *GDP* expenditures were compared with real *GDP* per capita for a sample of 34 countries, ranging from very poor countries such as Malawi and India to highly industrialized states like Germany and the United States. As Figure F1 reports, at least in 1975, the real share of the services did not increase with a country's real per capita *GDP*, contrary to widespread belief. However, as our model suggests, since the real share of *GDP* devoted to services remained roughly constant among countries, the nominal share devoted to services nevertheless rose markedly with real *GDP* per capita (Figure F2). The results of a regression were completely consistent with these conclusions.

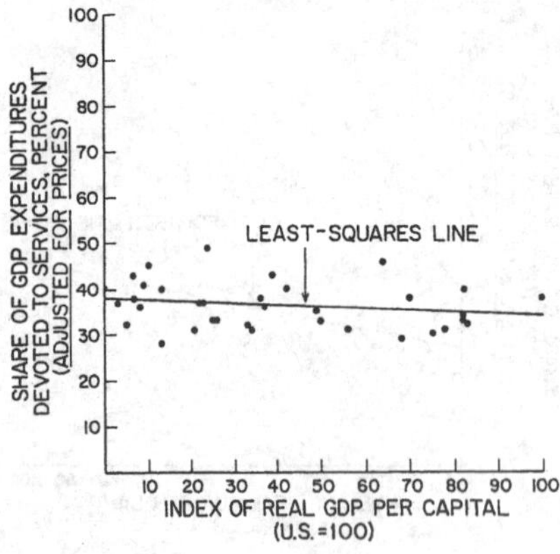

FIGURE F2

VI. Broadcasting, Electronic Computation, and Asymptotic Stagnancy

Our empirical evidence on two asymptotically stagnant activities, television broadcasting and data processing (computer services), shows that in both activities the progressive component's share of total costs diminished continually, while the stagnant component increased both in real terms and as a share of total cost.

A. *Electronic Computation*

In the last twenty years the cost of computer hardware per unit of processing power apparently fell some 25 percent per year (see, for example, W. J. Kubitz, 1980; S. Triebwasser, 1978; R. N. Noyce, 1977; and C. Burns, 1977). Meanwhile, the cost of (labor-intensive) computer software assumed an ever greater share of a computer system's total cost. Software was once a relatively minor element in computing cost—indeed, IBM once gave software away with its machines. Now, it is the hardware that is becoming almost incidental in total computation cost (see T. J. Gordon and T. R. Munson, 1980). By some estimates, software represented only 5 percent of system costs in 1973, had increased to 80 percent by 1978, and exceeded 90 percent by 1980 (see Kubitz; M. Schindler, 1979; and R. A. Minicucci, 1982). P. Grabscheid writes, that by 1985, "it will probably pay to substitute one hour of computer time for six minutes of staff time" (1982, p. 6). Software development remains essentially a handicraft activity, and is, so far, a stagnant service.

Some operating data from the Princeton University Computer Center (Figure 1) substantiate dramatically the growing importance of labor costs in total Center expenditures and the accompanying sharp drop in the dominance of the hardware component.[11] Between 1970 and 1983, total real labor costs at the Center rose at a compound rate of 2.6 per annum, while total real equipment costs fell at an annual rate of 4.6 percent.[12] Since the volume of computations has risen rapidly,

[11] In the three years (1976; 1979; 1981) in which the downward trend was interrupted, the increased share of hardware cost is ascribable to major equipment purchases and changes in equipment financing, rather than to increases in hardware prices. The Director of the Center does caution that, although the bulk of the drop in Center expenditures on hardware is attributable to actual hardware cost decreases, some part of it is the result of more favorable lease-purchase arrangements and an increase in the percent of equipment owned rather than rented.

[12] Some industry figures produce results that are less clear cut. For instance, the Diebold Group (1982) has studied computer operations of large U.S. corporations over the ten-year period, 1971–81. Their surveys showed that the average share of computer operations budgets devoted to hardware fell from 35 percent in 1971 to 27 percent in 1981; the share of expenditures on operations personnel (i.e., keypunchers whose work is most susceptible to automation and productivity increases) fell from 29 percent in 1971 to 18 percent in 1981; while the share of the budget spent on systems development personnel (the "brainpower" employees) remained essentially the same over the ten-year period (25 percent in 1971 and 24 percent in 1981).

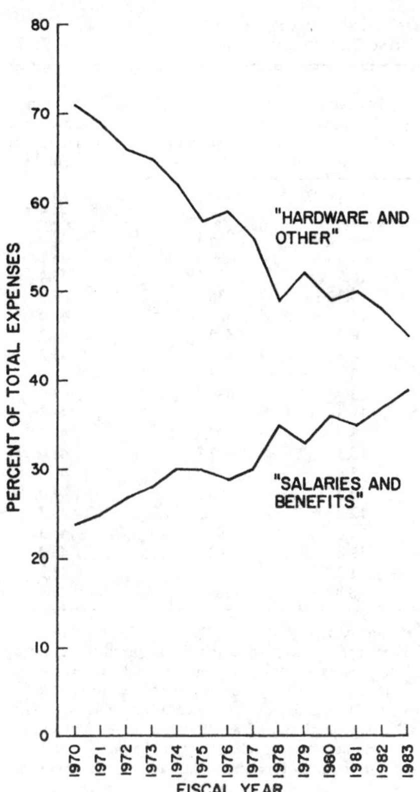

FIGURE 1. LABOR COSTS VS. HARDWARE COSTS AS A PERCENTAGE OF TOTAL COSTS, PRINCETON UNIVERSITY COMPUTER CENTER, 1970–83

Source: James Poage, Director, Princeton University Computer Center.

Notes: The cost category "Hardware and Other" is made up of approximately 80 percent computer hardware costs and 20 percent other costs, such as disposable supplies. Increases in hardware costs in 1976, 1979, and 1981 are largely ascribable to either the purchase of major new equipment, or the refinancing of equipment costs. Staff size at the Center has remained essentially unchanged over the period. Data for 1983 are estimates.

equipment cost per unit of output has fallen far more rapidly (and per unit labor costs have risen more slowly).[13]

[13]Although the number of computations performed at the Center is not recorded, according to the Director of the Center, this number has clearly increased dramatically. In particular, as the computer programs handled at the Center became ever more complex (i.e., as the "captured intelligence" in each program grew), each keystroke punched into the computer gave many more commands to the machine. We should note here that the other side of the phenomenon of the increasing domination of labor costs in computer budgets is the extraordinary increase in labor productivity brought about by computerization. Computer technology permits users to accomplish much more much faster. For example, a company that once paid a roomful of workers to tabulate year-end accounts can now computerize those operations and retrain the workers to analyze the data the computer puts out. At the Princeton University Computer Center the budget for salaries used to be dominated by keypunch personnel; today the staff there is far more skilled and professional. The data processing industry is seeking ways to enhance further the productivity of its personnel, for example, by finding ways to substitute hardware time for costly staff time and by creating software in so-called "fourth generation" computer languages which minimize the user's time and permit less-skilled (and lower-paid) operators to use the computer.

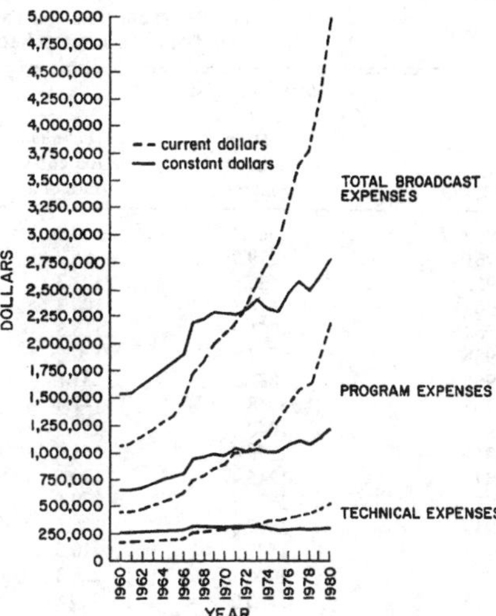

FIGURE 2. BROADCASTING EXPENSES PER AVERAGE TELEVISION STATION[a]

[a]Shown in current and constant dollars. Data exclude the three major networks, but include network owned and operated television stations.

Sources: U.S. Federal Communications Commission, *Annual Report*, various years, and "Television Financial Data 1980, FCC Financial Figures," August 10, 1981, No. 6, Vol. 101, p. 54. Source for price deflator is *Survey of Current Business*, various years.

TABLE 3—TECHNICAL AND PROGRAM EXPENSES AS A PERCENTAGE OF TOTAL TELEVISION BROADCASTING EXPENSES, 1960–80

Year	Total Broadcast Expenses (all TV stations,[a] in millions of dollars)	Technical Expenses (mil. of $)	Technical Expenses as Percent of Total	Program Expenses (mil. of $)	Program Expenses as Percent of Total
1960	563.3	92.9	16.5	239.1	42.4
1961	579.5	96.2	16.6	245.2	42.3
1962	626.6	101.3	16.1	265.4	42.3
1963	674.5	106.3	15.8	290.5	43.1
1964	725.4	113.8	15.7	315.1	43.4
1965	787.7	120.2	15.3	338.8	43.0
1966	885.0	131.1	14.8	380.1	43.0
1967	948.3	141.4	14.9	409.2	43.2
1968	1040.1	151.5	14.6	449.2	43.2
1969	1176.4	161.4	13.7	504.9	42.9
1970	1245.2	170.6	13.7	534.7	43.0
1971	1303.7	179.6	13.8	599.2	46.0
1972	1457.6	196.5	13.5	628.6	43.0
1973	1577.9	210.5	13.3	677.9	43.0
1974	1706.7	228.3	13.4	733.7	43.0
1975	1830.0	229.6	12.5	805.3	44.0
1976	2108.1	256.7	12.2	912.3	43.3
1977	2297.1	270.3	11.8	995.1	43.3
1978	2705.4	318.4	11.8	1162.5	43.0
1979	3100.6	346.3	11.2	1343.6	43.3
1980	3614.6	390.0	10.8	1588.3	43.9

Source: U.S. Federal Communications Commission, *Annual Report*, various years.
Notes: Technical expenses include payroll and other technical expenses such as circuit costs incurred in delivering programs to local stations. Program expenses include "talent" employees, other employees, rent and amortization of film and tape, records and transcripts, outside news service costs, payment to talent, music license fees, other performance and program rights, and all other program expenses. Other categories not listed in the table are selling expenses and general and administrative expenses (which includes general and administrative payroll, depreciation and amortization, interest, allocated costs of management from home office of affiliates(s), and other general and administrative expenses). These descriptions are taken from "Television Financial Data 1980, FCC Financial Figures," *Broadcasting*, August 10, 1981, Vol. 101, No. 6.
[a]Does not include the three major television networks but does include network owned and operated television stations.

B. *Television Broadcasting*

Television broadcasting also has progressive and stagnant components, such as transmission, which includes circuit costs, and programming, dominated by human labor. Here, too, the evidence on trends in costs, and trends in cost shares, is striking. Figure 2, using U.S. Federal Communications Commission data, shows the steep rise in average expenses of TV stations between 1960 and 1980 (in both current and constant dollars), and portrays the trends in the two relevant components of broadcasting expenses (technical and program expenses), showing that real program costs have climbed steadily, while real technical expenses have remained about constant over the twenty-year period. In Table 3 we see that, as a percent of total expenditures, technical costs have dropped continuously from 16.5 percent in 1960 to 10.8 percent in 1980. In constant dollars, over the twenty years in question total technical expenses per station have actually risen, but at the modest rate of 0.8 percent per year. However, the average rate of increase of real programming cost was 3.1 percent, and total real expenses increased at virtually the same annual rate, 2.9 percent.

VI. Concluding Comments

All the empirical data we have found seem consistent with the predictions of the amended unbalanced growth model. The "rising share of services" turns out to be somewhat illusory. The output shares of the progressive and stagnant sectors have in fact remained fairly constant in the postwar period, so that with rising relative prices, the share of total expenditures on the (stagnant) services and their share of the labor force have risen dramatically (their prices rose at about the same rate as their productivity lagged behind the progressive sectors), just as the model suggests. Similar trends are also found internationally.

We have also introduced into the model a type of activity we call asymptotically stagnant—economic enterprises which seem among the most high tech and progressive one can imagine. They contain both a technologically sophisticated component and a relatively irreducible labor-intensive component. Starting out as innovative activities dominated by their very productive technological side, as the labor component assumes an ever larger share of total cost (because the progressive component is innovating itself out of its cost-dominating position), ultimately the activity assumes all the characteristics of the stagnant services. Empirical data on two such activities—TV broadcasting and electronic computation—are also consistent with the model's predictions. This suggests that the progressivity of such activities may well prove transitory and somewhat illusory. In sum, the cost disease of the stagnant services may affect more of the economy than was previously thought.

REFERENCES

Baumol, W. J., "Macroeconomics of Unbalanced Growth: The Anatomy of Urban Crisis," *American Economic Review*, June 1967, *57*, 415–26.

Burns, C., "The Evolution of Office Information Systems," *Datamation*, No. 4, 1977, *23*, 60–64.

Gollop, Frank M. and Jorgensen, Dale W., "U.S. Productivity Growth by Industry, 1947–73," in John W. Kendrick and Beatrice N. Vaccara, eds., *New Developments in Productivity Measurement and Analysis*, Chicago: University of Chicago Press, 1980.

Gordon, T. J. and Munson, T. R., "Research Into Technology Output Measures," unpublished paper, The Futures Group for the National Science Foundation, November 1980.

Grabscheid, P., "The Economics of Information Processing," presentation for 1982–83 Chief Financial Officer Seminar Program Series, *Institutional Investor*, 1982.

Kubitz, W. J., "Computer Technology, A Forecast for the Future," in F. Wilfrid Lancaster, ed., *Proceedings of the 1979 Clinic on Library Applications of Data Processing, The Role of the Library in an Electronic Society*, Urbana-Champaign: University of Illinois Graduate School of Library Science, 1980, 135–61.

Leontief, Wassily, *Studies in the Structure of the American Economy*, New York: Oxford University Press, 1953.

Levin, H. J. *Fact and Fancy in Television Regulation*, New York: Russell Sage Foundation, 1980 (who cites Federal Communications Commission Network Inquiry Special Staff, *The Historical Evolution of the Commercial Network Broadcast System*, October 1979, p. 176).

Minicucci, R. A., "Sub-second Response Time: A Way to Improve Interactive User Productivity," *Systems Management Controls, SMC Newsletter* 82–19, November 1982.

Noyce, R. N., "Microelectronics," *Scientific American*, No. 3, 1977, *237*, 63–69.

Paik, N. J., "How to Keep Experimental Video on PBS National Programming," in *Independent Television-Makers and Public Communications Policy*, Rockefeller Foundation Working Papers, December 1979, ch. 2.

Peterson, William, "Total Factor Productivity in the U.K.: A Disaggregated Analysis," in K. D. Patterson and Kerry Scott, eds., *The Measurement of Capital: Theory and Practice*, London: Macmillan 1979.

Schindler, M., "Computers, Big and Small, Still Spreading as Software Grows," *Electronic Design*, No. 1, 1979, *27*, 88.

Summers, Robert, "Services in the International Economy," ARA/Wharton Conference on the Future of the Service Economy, University of Pennsylvania, Philadelphia, forthcoming 1985.

Triebwasser, S., "Impact of Semiconductor Microelectronics," *Computer Technology: Status, Limits, Alternatives*, New York: Institute of Electrical and Electronics Engineers, Inc., 1978, 176–77.

Wolff, Edward N., "The Rate of Surplus Value, the Organic Composition, and the General Rate of Profit in the U.S. Economy, 1947–1967," *American Economic Review*, June 1979, *69*, 329–41.

______, "Industrial Composition, Interindustry Effects, and the U.S. Productivity Slowdown," *Review of Economics and Statistics*, forthcoming.

The Diebold Group, "Management Information Services/Telecommunications Budgets, 1982," Document Number 211M, Abstract, p. 10 (also personal communication with David Dell, Director of Research Services, the Diebold Group, Inc., New York, NY).

U.S. Federal Communications Commission, *Annual Report*, various years.

U.S. Department of Commerce, Bureau of Economic Analysis, "The Input-Output Structure of the U.S. Economy: 1967," *Survey of Current Business*, February 1974; and various years.

______, ______, *The National Income and Products Accounts of the United States, 1929–1976*, Statistical Tables, Washington, 1981.

______, **Bureau of Labor Statistics,** (1979a) *Time-Series Data for Input-Output Industries*, Bulletin 2018, Washington, 1979.

______, ______, (1979b) *Capital Stock Estimates for Input-Output Industries: Methods and Data*, Bulletin 203, Washington, 1979.

KYKLOS, Vol. 49 – 1996 – Fasc. 4, 509 - 540

Inefficient and Locally Stable Trade Equilibria Under Scale Economies: Comparative Advantage Revisited

William J. Baumol and Ralph E. Gomory*

This paper explores and analyzes the inefficient trade equilibria that can be introduced by scale economies despite the workings of the market mechanism. It thereby seeks to enrich the standard analysis of efficiency of equilibrium, upon which so much of welfare theory has focused. Research in recent decades on trade in commodities whose production entails scale economies – goods that are often the focus of public concern and public policy – have revealed circumstances that are in marked contrast to those in the classical model. It has long been known that trade models with scale economies are characterized by multiple equilibria (see, e.g., Marshall, Matthews 1949–1950, Kemp 1964 and Ethier 1979). Indeed, as Krugman (1991, pp. 651–652) remarks,

> 'In the emerging literature on increasing returns and externalities, multiple equilibria are not a nuisance but a central part of the story'.

On this point the present authors have shown (1992, 1994) that multiple equilibria do not merely exist but are normally vast in number, increasing exponentially with the number of traded commodities. This paper demonstrates that these many equilibria display some surprising attributes, and describes some previously-unrecognized ways in which the market mechanism's performance can fall short of ideal where scale economies are present.

* Director of the C.V. Starr Center for Applied Economics at New York University, 269 Mercer Street, N.Y., N.Y. 10003, USA, and President, the Alfred P. Sloan Foundation. We are very grateful to the Alfred P. Sloan Foundation and the C.V. Starr Center for support of this work. Some of the material in this article is based on Baumol (1993).

We will show that in a world of scale economies (Section I) market forces cannot always drive the economy to an equilibrium that entails efficient use of the economy's resources or that follows the dictates of comparative advantage; (Section II) under scale economies *many equilibria can be inefficient* in the standard sense of the term; (Section III) In contrast, *equilibria can be efficient even if they violate the normal comparative advantage conditions.*

Usually, an equilibrium is either shown to be efficient or, if it does not meet this standard, it is simply said to be inefficient. In this paper we extend these notions by introducing a measure of *the degree* to which any particular equilibrium falls short of perfect efficiency. We then apply this new measure to provide suggestive results about the equilibria of some particular trade models. We also formulate a more-flexible definition of *comparative advantage*, one that is useful in understanding efficiency in this more complex world. We accompany that by another new concept: *local efficiency*, entailing a comparison of the efficiency of a particular equilibrium point with that of other points in the neighborhood. We think these concepts bring some order to the issue of efficiency in the presence of economies of scale.

I. EFFICIENT AND INEFFICIENT EQUILIBRIA AND COMPARATIVE ADVANTAGE

Although our general orientation is toward large problems with large numbers of equilibria, we will begin our analysis with some small examples. These simple geometric examples illustrate the results that offer the greatest contrast with the classical case: that equilibria are not always efficient, and that equilibria can be efficient even if they violate comparative advantage.

Two basic definitions. In this paper we will use the term *perfectly specialized assignment* to connote any division of the task of producing the world's outputs among producer countries in such a way that no commodity is produced in more than one country. An assignment will be said to satisfy the *classical comparative advantage* requirements if when Country J produces good I and Country J′ produces good I′ then the ratio of the average product of Country J labor (assumed in our model to be the only input) in the production of I to its average product in I′ is higher than the corresponding ratio in Country J′. We leave for later discussion the appropriate *range* of input quantity over which the average products should be measured. This issue of range will in fact be critical for the results of Section III.

In Gomory and Baumol (1994) we proved that in a theoretical world of universal scale economies each and every perfectly specialized assignment satisfies the requirements of equilibrium, and that, in addition, every such equilibrium is (locally) stable[1]. Moreover, the number of such specialized assignments is equal to the number of possible country-commodity combinations, and so it grows very rapidly when the number of goods or the number of countries in the model increases[2].

We will start our discussion with a small model which shows some of the properties of efficiency in the economies of scale case. The discussion is framed in terms of Ricardo's two countries, England and Portugal, but substitutes for his cloth and wine two more 'high-tech' products, computers and Walkman radios, in whose production we may expect scale economies. In such a two-good, two-country model it must be remembered that there are always exactly two perfectly specialized assignments. Portugal can produce all the Walkmans and England all the computers, or the reverse can be true.

1. It is an equilibrium at suitable prices and outputs because it then satisfies all the usual equilibrium requirements such as market clearing. The intuitive reason for the assignment's local stability is straightforward. Where there are scale economies, if Country J happens to be the exclusive producer of good I that will give it a cost advantage which Country J′ will be unable to overcome if it wants to embark on production of I, unless J′ launches into this activity on a large scale. The same will obviously be true if production of good I happens to be assigned exclusively to *any* other country. Thus any small (local) deviation from such a specialized assignment, implying that any attempted entry on a *small* scale into an industry by a country that is not currently supplying any of that industry's product, is foredoomed to failure. This means, of course, that the initial assignment is *locally* stable.
2. It is easy to show that with two countries and n commodities the number of perfectly specialized equilibria will be on the order of 2^n. This follows immediately from the argument of the previous footnote indicating why under substantial scale economies *every* perfectly specialized assignment of the production of the n goods between the two countries is a stable equilibrium. For labelling the goods 1,2,...n, it is obvious that there are two choices of the country in which good 1 will be produced, and for each such assignment there are two possible assignments of good 2, etc.

Figure 1

One Specialized Equilibrium Dominates the Other

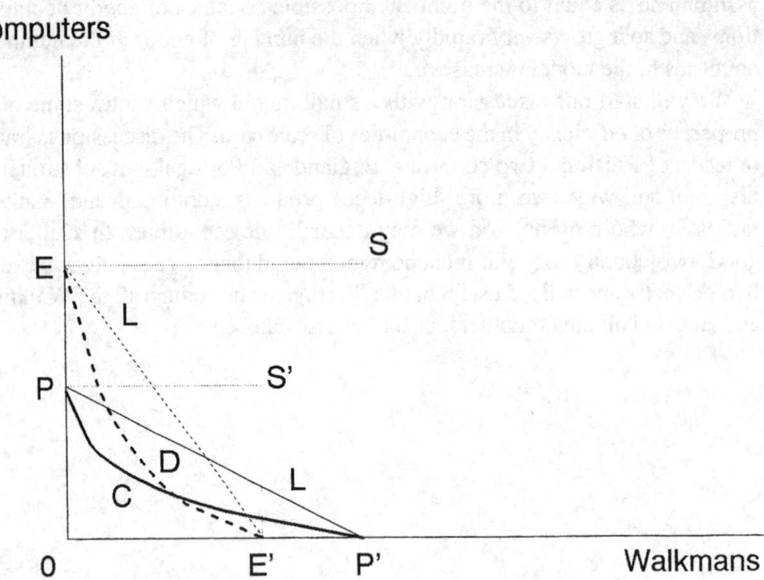

In *Figure 1,* PCP′ and EDE′ are the production frontiers for Portugal and England. Here, the convexity (downward) of the two frontiers represents the presence of scale economies, because towards the center of the frontier, where the country's production is unspecialized and the output of each good is relatively small, the output vector is held down (the output point is closer to the origin than it would be in the linear case)[3]. The two specialized solutions are S′ = (E′,P) and S = (P′,E). In the first of these England produces all the world's Walkmans and Portugal produces all of the computers, while in the second of these the production assignment is reversed. Both of these solutions are obviously locally stable equilibria at prices that clear the markets because if either country tries to produce a small quantity of the other's product it will fail because of its high costs. Yet, as shown in *Figure 1,* where the two frontiers intersect the one specialized point S clearly dominates the other, S′, so that the latter must be inefficient. This must always be so where the two countries'

3. In an unpublished paper Avinash Dixit has shown that convexity is sufficient but not necessary for scale economies.

production frontiers have an odd number of intersections, because then one country must be able to produce more Walkmans than the other and the other country must then be able to produce more computers than the first. Hence, the specialized equilibrium in which the first country produces all the Walkmans and the second country produces all the computers must then dominate the equilibrium in which the assignment of commodity production to the two countries is reversed. This example clearly shows that:

Theorem 1.1

In a world of scale economies an equilibrium can be inefficient.

Figure 2, in which the production frontiers of the two countries do not intersect, S and S′ remain the specialized solutions, but neither dominates the other. As a result, the efficiency of either of them is not immediately obvious. However, it is also possible to get some positive results, even for two-good problems. For example:

Theorem 1.2

One of the two production plans is always efficient. If the slope of chord EE′ is greater it is S and if the slope of chord PP′ is greater it is S′.

Proof: In *Figure 2* we have drawn the production frontier that would result if the chords were the actual production frontiers of the two countries, that is, if one were to make the problem linear in this way. It is, of course, well known that in such a two-by-two linear model one of the two specialized solutions will lie on the world production frontier, AS′B, and that point will satisfy the requirements of comparative advantage. In this case chord PP′ has the greater slope, meaning that Portugal's relative average product is greater in Walkman manufacture than in computer manufacture. For with a given supply of labor in each country (L_e and L_p, respectively), the slopes of the chords, EE′ and PP′ of the two countries are clearly $[(E/L_e) / (E'/L_e)]$ and $[(P/L_p) / (P'/L_p)]$, the ratios of the average products of labor in computer and Walkman production in the two countries. These ratios give us the traditional measure of comparative advantage. Thus, in a specialized equilibrium that satisfies comparative advantage Portugal will be the exclusive producer of Walkmans, as it is at S′. The point S′ is clearly efficient in this revised problem. It follows that it is *a fortiori* efficient in the original problem since, as the geometry clearly indicates, the production frontier of the original problem always lies at least as close to the origin as the production frontier of the problem based on the chords, so that any point of the original problem that lies on the linearized world frontier AS S′ B must obviously lie on the world frontier of the original problem. If the slopes were reversed we would apply the same reasoning and obtain the efficiency of the other specialized equilibrium S instead.

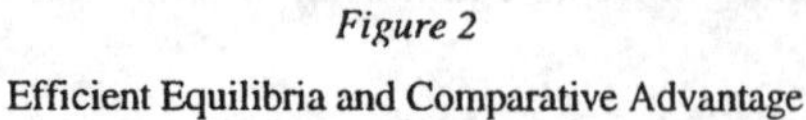

Figure 2

Efficient Equilibria and Comparative Advantage

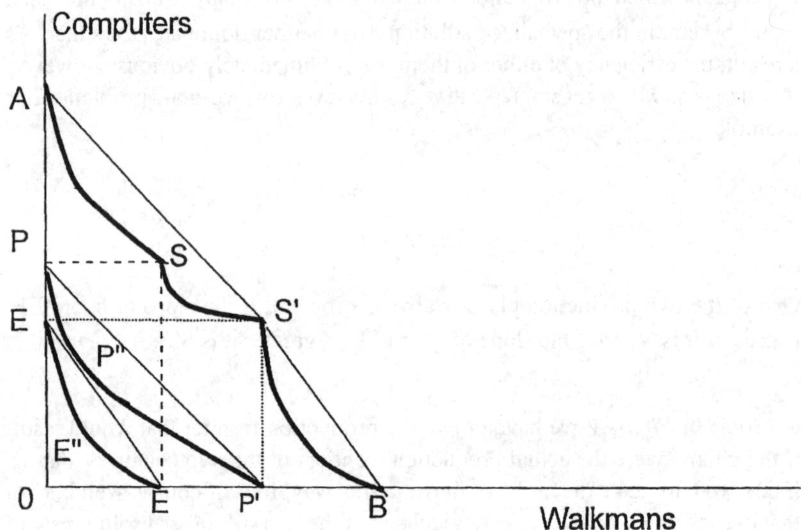

Having just shown that in small-scale models of the sort under discussion an equilibrium that satisfies comparative advantage is necessarily efficient, we can use similar reasoning to show that the converse relationship does not hold – an equilibrium can be efficient even if it violates comparative advantage. In *Figure* 2, where one of the frontiers, PP′, lies entirely above the other, EE′, neither equilibrium point dominates the other. We have just seen that in the linearized model derived from the chords of the individual country frontiers solution point

S′ is efficient because it lies on the world (linearized) production frontier while equilibrium point S is not, because in the linear model S lies below the world frontier. However, because as a result of their (downward) convexity in the original problem the individual country frontiers lie below their chords almost throughout, the world frontier, ASS′B does *not* lie above S (it should be obvious that numerical examples of this sort are easy to construct). So both S and S′ really are efficient in the case shown in the graph. Since the production pattern in each of the two equilibria is the reverse of the other, the production patterns of only one of the two equilibria (S′) can be in accord with the traditional criterion of comparative advantage, so the other (S) has a production pattern that violates comparative advantage (compare the slopes of EE′ and PP′), yet is efficient. This example shows:

Theorem 1.3

Under scale economies an equilibrium can be efficient even if it violates the traditional comparative advantage requirement.

The preceding discussion also suggests that there is a general tradeoff between (a) the magnitude of the loss incurred as a result of violation of comparative advantage in an efficient specialized equilibrium and (b) the strength of the scale economies needed to render that equilibrium efficient. In terms of our diagrams, the greater the difference between the slopes of the chords of the production frontiers of the two countries, the greater the degree of convexity of those production frontiers that is necessary for an equilibrium that violates comparative advantage to be efficient. This is easily demonstrated geometrically in the two-country two-good case and we conjecture that an effect of this sort is true generally. The intuitive reason for this relationship indicates how scale economies weaken the influence of comparative advantage. For if a country specializes in the production of a good in which it has a comparative *dis*advantage the resulting loss of efficiency can by made up for as a result of its large output of that good if and only if the economies of scale are sufficiently strong.

Inefficient Equilibria: Can the Free Market Eliminate Them? But can't market forces be counted upon to destroy the inefficient equilibria that have just been shown to exist in a world of scale economies? This, surely, is what economists have long been taught about perfectly competitive models with universally diminishing returns. Is there not something similar to be expected here? After all, any inefficient equilibrium is necessarily an unrealized opportunity for mutual gain. Should not arbitrageurs or other businesspersons be counted upon to recognize such an opportunity and find ways to take advantage of it?

There are two fundamental reasons why this is not true in a world of scale economies. First, there is the fact that market signals are all local – indicating such things as marginal costs and marginal revenues that correspond to the partial derivatives of the profit function. They tell us in what direction to move in order to go upward on the profit hill on which the decision maker is currently located. But where there are millions of equilibria, each of them the peak of efficiency in its own neighborhood (see Section IV, below) going uphill from an initial position fortuitously selected by history may merely lead us toward the highest point on a nearby little hill. It can easily lead us away from the true global maximum, the top of a much-higher hill that may be far away.

Second, practical reality gives us another key reason showing why the unaided market will not generally be up to the task. Moving from one perfectly specialized assignment to another requires firms and countries to embark on the production of goods they are not currently turning out, and about whose production they have little knowledge or experience. Moreover, scale economies mean that to have any chance of success in such an endeavor, one must enter on a large scale. This requires the investors to undertake a very great risk, betting on what constitutes a leap into the unknown. Anyone with much business experience will confirm that such opportunities are hardly always recognized, and when recognized they are hardly always pursued. In sum, there is no reason to expect the market mechanism to take automatic advantage of the unrealized opportunities provided by inefficient equilibria. Under scale economies such equilibria can exist and can be locally stable.

Having completed these preliminaries, let us proceed toward the construction of a more-general theory of economic efficiency in the presence of scale economies.

II. ORIENTATION AND THE BASIC MODEL

Orientation. Our orientation in this paper is toward large problems with very large numbers of equilibria. Although we discuss both specialized and non-specialized equilibria, our analysis will emphasize specialized equilibria. There is considerable plausibility to this emphasis since it has been known for over three decades that, from a purely theoretical point of view, specialized equilibria are likely to play a dominant role in models with economies of scale because of the instability of most non-specialized equilibria. Furthermore (Gomory 1994) showed that in large problems specialized equilibria play the dominant role in shaping the region of equilibria and determining the location of all equilibria, specialized and non-specialized alike. In this paper we will see once again the important role of specialized equilibria since we will show in Section IV that it is only the specialized and almost-specialized equilibria that are likely to be efficient in the usual sense.

However, in addition to specialized equilibria, there is one important class of non-specialized equilibria with properties that complement those of the specialized equilibria. These are equilibria with non-specialized (i.e., shared) production in some industries. These industries have production functions, that, after an initial range of rapidly decreasing average cost with increasing scale of production, eventually reach a minimum average cost, and thereafter become linear (the case of 'flat-bottomed average cost'). The instability that characterizes most shared equilibria is weak or non-existent for this type of industry. Equilibria that have shared production in some of these industries and specialized production in all the rest we will call *extended-specialized equilibria.*

The Basic Model. Our basic model consists of two countries (or two facilities) which we call Country 1 and Country 2. We will have production functions $f_{i,j}(l)$ that use the single input l to produce good i in Country j. If an amount of labor $l_{i,j}$ is used to produce the ith good in Country j, whose labor supply is L_j, the $l_{i,j}$ must satisfy the labor-availability inequalities

$$\sum_i l_{i,1} \leq L_1 \quad and \quad \sum_i l_{i,2} \leq L_2 . \tag{2.1}$$

Although we will sometimes refer to equilibria in our discussion or in our examples, the only property of an economic equilibrium that we will use is that its labor quantities satisfy (2.1)[4].

We define a *feasible production plan* P = $\{l_{i,j}\}$ for the quantities Q_i as a set of $l_{i,j}$ that satisfy (2.1) and has $f_{i,1}(l_{i,1}) + f_{i,2}(l_{i,2}) = Q_i$. We will say that the quantities Q_i are efficient if there is no set of $l_{i,j}$ that satisfy (2.1) and make more than the given output quantities, Q_i. We will assume that we have a feasible production plan P, possibly coming from an economic equilibrium. We would like to know if its resulting outputs, the Q_i, are an efficient set of goods.

There is one case that is completely straightforward. If P does not have equality in both the inequalities of (2.1), the unused labor can be used to make

4. For a full characterization of an equilibrium and proof that in our model *any* perfectly specialized assignment is a locally stable equilibrium, see Gomory and Baumol (1994).

additional goods. The total output would then strictly dominate the Q_i and they would not be efficient. In the remainder of this paper we will assume that the production pattern P that produces the Q_i does use up all the labor available in both countries.

We will say that the Q_i are efficient, or equivalently that P is efficient, if there is no feasible production plan that uses *strictly* less than the total labor of both countries[5]. In principle we could test for efficiency by solving a minimization problem: minimize the labor required subject to the non-linear conditions $f_{i,1}(l_{i,1}) + f_{i,2}(l_{i,2}) = Q_i$ for all i, and to (2.1), and see if that minimal amount is L_1+L_2. However, because of the non-linearities, this direct approach seems difficult and we will work instead with a linearized model.

III. THE LINEARIZED MODEL

This section of the paper deals with the classical efficiency concept and shows that in the case of scale economies comparative advantage, *defined in a somewhat different way*, is sufficient (but not necessary) to guarantee the efficiency of an equilibrium. We will also give a strong necessary condition.

Specialized Production. For a given i, one way to produce Q_i is to have it made solely in Country j. Then $Q_i = f_{i,j}(l'_{i,j})$ where $f_{i,j}$ is the production function for good i in Country j, and $l'_{i,j}$ is the amount of labor required in Country j to produce Q_i when Country j is the sole producer. If $Q_i > f_{i,j}(L_j)$ so that Q_i cannot be produced in Country j, even by all that country's labor, $l'_{i,j}$ is undefined. If $l'_{i,j}$ is defined we will say that $(i,j) \in D$, and if it is not defined we will say that $(i,j) \in D'$[6].

We will proceed by introducing related problems that replace the $f_{i,j}$ with linear production functions. These linearized production functions are related to, but are not the same as, those used in the proof of Theorem 1.1. We will refer to the problems obtained in this way as the *linearized problems*.

Efficiency in the linearized problems will turn out to be closely related to efficiency in the original non-linear problem. The linearized problems are both theoretically and computationally more tractable, and will be the natural basis for the concept of quantified efficiency (λ-efficiency) that we introduce in Section V.

5. One can, instead, use a dual approach that seeks $l_{i,j}$ employing all the labor of both countries and produces more than the Q_i.
6. While $(i,j) \in D'$ play a prominent role in very small problems they play a very small role in large problems where no single good uses up a large percentage of the labor force.

INEFFICIENT AND LOCALLY STABLE TRADE EQUILIBRIA

In defining a linearized problem the critical question is how to linearize. A natural answer is to take as the linearized production function the linear functions that make the Q_i with the same amount of labor as the $f_{i,j}$ themselves require. This is what we will do whenever possible. The exceptional cases, when the Q_i can't be produced even with the entire labor force of the country, we will handle slightly differently.

Figure 3

Production frontiers for Linearization

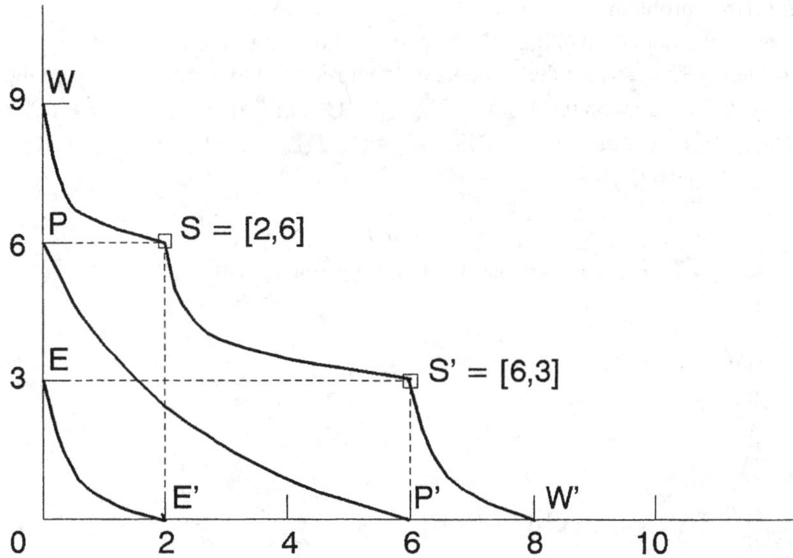

The Linearized Problem. We first define the *average productivities* $e_{i,j}$ by $e_{i,j} = f_{i,j}(l'_{i,j}) / l'_{i,j} = Q_i / l'_{i,j}$ for $(i,j) \in D$ and $e_{i,j} = f_{i,j}(L_j) / L_j$ for $(i,j) \in D'$. We then define the new linear production functions $L_{i,j}(l)$ by $L_{i,j}(l) = e_{i,j}l$. These linearized production functions clearly *depend on the choice of the Q*. The *linearized problem associated with the output quantities Q_i* is obtained by replacing the production functions $f_{i,j}(l)$ with the $L_{i,j}(l)$ defined from those Q_i. In *Figure 3* we see the original production frontiers for a typical economies of scale problem. Here, WSS′ W′ is the world frontier, obtained from the individual country frontiers EE′ and PP′. In *Figure 4* the linearized production functions associated with the quantities $(Q_1,Q_2) = (2,6)$ are shown as the dark lines. The individual country linearized production frontiers are obtained by putting a straight line through the two intersections of the original country production frontier with the rectangle whose vertices are (0,0) and $(Q_1,Q_2) = (2,6)$, because at those intersection points the original production frontiers represent the use of a quantity of labor in the production of the pertinent good lc sufficient to produce the given output, Q_i of good *lc*. In *Figure 5* we see the linear problem associated with the quantities $(Q_1,Q_2) = (6,3)$. Clearly, when we use this construct different linear problems are associated with different quantities Q_i.

We will say that *the* Q_i *are L-efficient* if they are efficient in the associated linearized problem.

Next we define quantities $l^*_{i,j}$ that are analogous to the $l'_{i,j}$ of the original problem. These $l^*_{i,j}$ are the amounts of labor required to make the Q_i using the linearized production functions so $L_{i,j}(l^*_{i,j}) = Q_i$. For $(i,j) \in D$, $L_{i,j}(l'_{i,j}) = e_{i,j}l'_{i,j} = (Q_i / l'_{i,j})l'_{i,j} = Q_i$, so $l^*_{i,j} = l'_{i,j}$. For $(i,j) \in D'$, $L(L_j) = e_{i,j}\ L_j = (f_{i,j}(L_j) / L_j)L_i = f_{i,j}(L_j) < Q_i$, so $l^*_{i,j} > L_j$.

Figure 4

Linearization Based on Assignment S = [2,6]

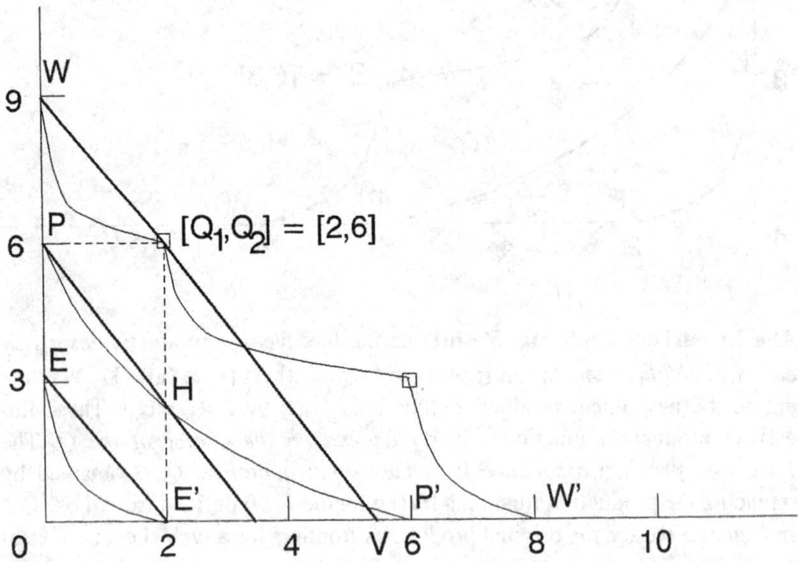

Since l' and l^* are used repeatedly throughout the following discussion, it is useful to summarize their meaning. $l'_{i,j}$ is simply the quantity of labor needed to produce the given quantity of good i if it is done in country j alone. $l^*_{i,j}$ is the same, except where the given output of i is so large that it requires more than country j's entire labor force to produce it. In that case, $l^*_{i,j}$ is the quantity of labor that would be necessary to produce the given quantity of i, using a linearized production function based on the average productivity obtained when using the entire labor force of the country to produce good i.

In contrast with the original problem, we can now easily characterize the labor inputs that will produce the Q_i using the linearized production functions. Consider any $y_{i,j}$ that satisfy:

$$0 \le y_{i,j} \le 1 \qquad y_{i,1} + y_{i,2} = 1.$$

$$\sum_i y_{i,1}\, l^*_{i,1} \le L_1 \quad and \quad \sum_i y_{i,2}\, l^*_{i,2} \le L_2. \tag{3.1}$$

Figure 5

Linearization Based on Assignment S′ = [6,3]

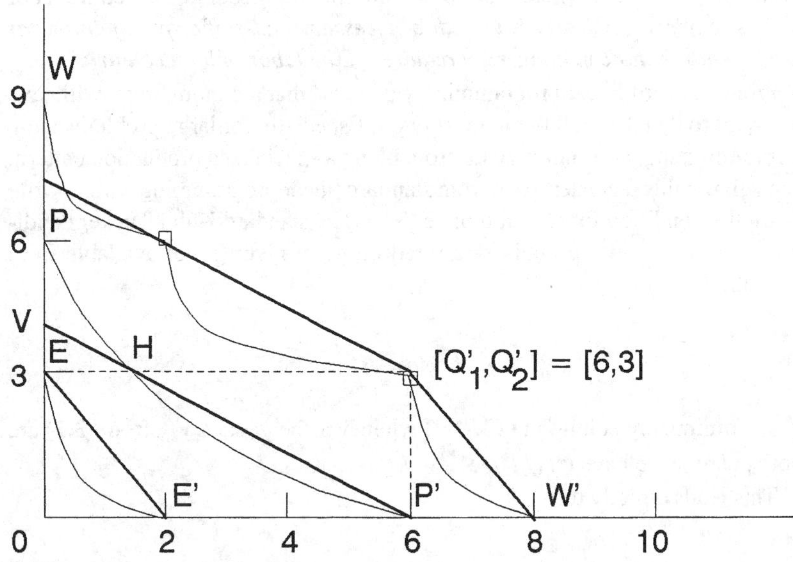

Each labor quantity $y_{i,j}l^*_{i,j}$ will, using the linearized production functions $L_{i,j}(l)$, produce exactly $L(y_{i,j}l^*_{i,j}) = e_{i,j}y_{i,j}l^*_{i,j} = y_{i,j}Q_i$. Therefore $y_{i,1}l^*_{i,1}$ and $y_{i,2}l^*_{i,2}$ together will produce $(y_{i,1} + y_{i,2})Q_i = Q_i$. Also the second line of (3.1) shows that these $y_{i,j}l^*_{i,j}$ will not overuse the quantities of labor available in the two countries. So the $y_{i,j}$ that satisfy (3.1) give the labor inputs $y_{i,j}l^*_{i,j}$ that produce the Q_i using the $L_{i,j}(l)$. We will often say that the $y_{i,j}$ produce the Q_i meaning that the labor quantities $y_{i,j}l^*_{i,j}$ do.

We can check for *L*-efficiency by solving the linear program that minimizes the total labor used in both countries to make the Q_i:

$$v = Min_y\, v(y) \quad v(y) = \sum_i (y_{i,1}\, l^*_{i,1} + y_{i,2}\, l^*_{i,2}) \text{ subject to}$$

$$0 \leq y_{i,j} \leq 1 \qquad y_{i,1} + y_{i,2} = 1.$$

$$\sum_i y_{i,1}\, l^*_{i,1} \leq L_1 \text{ and } \sum_i y_{i,2}\, l^*_{i,2} \leq L_2. \tag{3.2}$$

From this we can see whether or not the minimizing y requires the entire labor of both countries. *Clearly it is both a necessary and sufficient condition for L-efficiency that the minimizing y require all the labor of both countries.*

From standard linear programming we know[7] that a minimizing y will have $y_{i,j}$ equal to 0 or 1 for all but at most two i. Especially for large problems then, this minimizing y it is not very far from being a specialized production pattern. We will use this fact later. Also from standard linear programming we can write down the condition for y to minimize (3.2). The standard Kuhn-Tucker conditions applied to this specially structured program give: (proof available from the authors).

Lemma 3.1

y is a minimizing solution to (3.2) iff whenever the $y_{i,1}$ and $y_{k,2}$ from (3.2) are both positive we have $l^*_{i,1} / l^*_{i,2} \leq l^*_{k,1} / l^*_{k,2}$.

This leads directly to:

7. This must be so because if we use $y_{i,1} + y_{i,2} = 1$ to eliminate the $y_{i,2}$ we are left with n $y_{i,1}$ variables and n + 2 slack variables, call them S_i and T_j. We cannot have $y_{i,1} = 0$ and $S_i = 0$ for the same i since $S_i = 0$ means $y_{i,1} = 1$. Thus, in a basic solution, in which n variables = 0, we can have at most two cases where $y_{i,1} > 0$ and $S_i > 0$. Later we will see that there is at most one $y_{i,j}$ that is neither 1 nor 0.

INEFFICIENT AND LOCALLY STABLE TRADE EQUILIBRIA

Theorem 3.2: Necessary and Sufficient Condition for L-Efficiency

The necessary and sufficient conditions for $y_{i,j}$ to be *L*-efficient is that (1) the $y_{i,j}l^*_{i,j}$ use all the labor of both countries and (2) they entail ratios $l^*_{i,1} / l^*_{i,2}$ that satisfy $l^*_{i,1} / l^*_{i,2} \leq l^*_{k,1} / l^*_{k,2}$ when ever $y_{i,1} > 0$ and $y_{k,2} > 0$.

The inequality in Theorem 3.2 is in fact an average comparative advantage criterion. This becomes clearer if we express the result in terms of the average products, $e_{i,j}$ of the linearized problem. Since $e_{i,j} = Q_i / l^*_{i,j}$, $e_{i,1} / e_{i,2} = l^*_{i,2} / l^*_{i,1}$. That is, with Q_i given, the country that can produce it with the smallest relative amount of labor has a comparative efficiency advantage in producing good i relative to the other good, k. Theorem 3.2 can be restated as:

Theorem 3.3: Average Comparative Advantage and L-Efficiency

The necessary and sufficient conditions for the $y_{i,j}$ to be *L*-efficient are: (1) $y_{i,j}$ uses all the labor of both countries and (2) the productivities satisfy $e_{i,1}/e_{i,2} \leq e_{k,1} / e_{k,2}$ whenever i is produced in Country 2 and k is produced in County 1.

Efficiency in the Original Nonlinear Problem: We will now connect *L*-efficiency with efficiency in the original scale economies problem. To do this we attach to any feasible production plan $P = \{l_{i,j}\}$ (i.e., to any set of input quantities that can produce the Q_i), its linearized plan P* defined by $y_{i,j} = f_{i,j}(l_{i,j})/Q_i$. This linearized plan, as we are about to show, satisfies the linearized problem. Note that the linearized *problem* depends only on the set of Q_i while the linearized *plan* P* depends also on the particular production plan P chosen.

Sufficient Conditions: We will first work toward a sufficient condition for efficiency in the original problem. This is done in what amounts to two steps. The first shows that if any output vector Q_i is efficient in the linear problem then it is efficient in the original problem with scale economies. Next, we invoke the result (Theorem 3.3) that in the linear problem comparative advantage plus full employment of labor in both countries are necessary and sufficient for efficiency. It then clearly follows that the comparative-advantage requirements suffice for efficiency in the original problem.

Lemma 3.4: Relation between Efficiency in the Original and the Linear Plans

If P is any feasible production plan then P* satisfies (3.1) and uses no more labor for any good. Equivalently: if the $l_{i,j}$ are any feasible production pattern, then $y_{i,j} = f_{i,j}(l_{i,j}) / Q_i$ satisfies (3.1) and $y_{i,j}l^*_{i,j} \le l_{i,j}$.

Proof: Consider any production pattern $l_{i,j}$, with $f_{i,1}(l_{i,j}) + f_{i,2}(l_{i,2}) = Q_i$, and satisfying (2.1). Now consider $y_{i,j} = f_{i,j}(l_{i,j}) / Q_i$. We will show that $y_{i,j}$ satisfies the linearized problem (3.1) and uses no more labor, i.e., $y_{i,j}l^*_{i,j} \le l_{i,j}$.

Clearly, $0 \le y_{i,j} \le 1$ and $y_{i,1} + y_{i,2} = (f_{i,1}(l_{i,1}) + f_{i,2}(l_{i,2})) / Q_i = Q_i / Q_i = 1$. It remains to show $y_{i,j}l^*_{i,j} \le l_{i,j}$. This will show both that $y_{i,j}$ uses no more labor and that it satisfies the inequalities of (3.1).

For $(i,j) \in D$, $e_{i,j} = f_{i,j}(l'_{i,j}) / l'_{i,j}$. Using economies of scale and remembering that in this case $l_{i,j}^* = l_{i,j}' \ge l_{i,j}$,

$$L(y_{i,j}\, l^*_{i,j}) = y_{i,j} e_{i,j}\, l^*_{i,j} = y_{i,j} \frac{f_{i,j}(l^*_{i,j})}{l^*_{i,j}}\, l^*_{i,j} = y_{i,j} Q_i = f_{i,j}(l_{i,j}) \le \frac{f_{i,j}(l'_{i,j})}{l'_{i,j}}\, l_{i,j}.$$

$$\textit{eliminating the } \frac{f_{i,j}(l^*_{i,j})}{l^*_{i,j}} \textit{ gives } y_{i,j} l^*_{i,j} \le l_{i,j}. \tag{3.3}$$

For $(i,j) \in D'$, $e_{i,j} = F_{i,j}(L_j) / L_j$, so

$$L(y_{i,j}\, l^*_{i,j}) = y_{i,j} e_{i,j}\, l^*_{i,j} = y_{i,j} \frac{F_{i,j}(L_j)}{L_j}\, l^*_{i,j} = y_{i,j} Q_i = f_{i,j}(l_{i,j}) \le \frac{F_{i,j}(L_j)}{L_j}\, l_{i,j}$$

$$\textit{eliminating the } \frac{F_{i,j}(L_j)}{L_j} \textit{ gives } y_{i,j} l^*_{i,j} \le l_{i,j}. \tag{3.4}$$

This ends the proof of the lemma.

We have as an immediate consequence:

Theorem 3.5

If a set of Q_i are *L*-efficient then they are efficient.

Proof: We will prove the equivalent statement: if the Q_i are *not* efficient in the original problem, they are *not* efficient in the linearized problem. Let us assume that the Q_i are *not* efficient in the original problem so there is a feasible production pattern P using *strictly less* than the total labor of the two countries. Then Lemma 3.4 asserts that P* is a solution to the linearized problem that uses no more labor, so it too uses less than the total labor of the two countries. This shows that the Q_i are not L-efficient. Q.E.D.

Combining this with Theorem 3.3 gives us a sufficiency condition:

Theorem 3.6

Sufficient conditions for the production plan P to be efficient are (1) the productivities $e_{i,1} / e_{i,2}$ satisfy $e_{i,1} / e_{i,2} \leq e_{k,1} / e_{k,2}$ whenever i is produced in Country 2 and k is produced in County 1, and (2) the *linearized plan* P* uses all the labor of both countries.

The next theorem states that if the feasible production plan P *itself*, not P*, uses up the labor of the two counties, and satisfies average comparative advantage, it is efficient.

Theorem 3.7: Sufficiency of Average Competitive Advantage

Sufficient conditions for the specialized or extended-specialized production plan P to be efficient are (1) it has productivities $e_{i,1} / e_{i,2}$ that satisfy $e_{i,1} / e_{i,2} \leq e_{k,1} / e_{k,2}$ whenever i is produced in Country 2 and k is produced in County 1, and (2) it uses all the labor of both countries.

Proof: If P is extended-specialized (which includes specialized) we have for goods with specialized production, $f_{i,j}(l_{i,j}) = (f_{i,j}(l'_{i,j}) / l'_{i,j})l_{i,j}$ because $l_{i,j} = l'_{i,j}$. For goods with shared production we have either $f_{i,j}(l_{i,j}) = (f_{i,j}(l'_{i,j}) / l'_{i,j})l_{i,j}$ if $(i,j) \in D$ or $f_{i,j}(l_{i,j}) = (F_{i,j}(L_j) / L_j)l_{i,j}$ because $l_{i,j}$ is already in the linear range. In either case we obtain $y_{i,j}l^*_{i,j} = l_{i,j}$ instead of $y_{i,j}l^*_{i,j} \leq l_{i,j}$ in (3.2) or (3.4). Therefore, if P uses up all the labor so does P* and then Theorem 3.6 applies. Q.E.D.

Necessary Conditions: If we next consider necessary conditions there are certain things that are straightforward. A production plan P can not be efficient if an interchange of two industries between the two countries produces more of both goods, or equivalently, the same goods with less labor, so clearly n-good efficiency requires satisfaction of the two-good efficiency condition for every pair of goods as a necessary condition. However there is also a necessary condition related to the linear problem.

We start with this Lemma:

Lemma 3.8

Lemma: If the $y_{i,j}$ are integer (i.e., 0 or 1) and satisfy the labor-availability constraints (3.1), then, $P' = \{l_{i,j}\}$ where $l_{i,j} = y_{i,j}l^*_{i,j}$ is a feasible (specialized) production plan for the original problem.

Proof: Since the $y_{i,j}\ l^*_{i,j}$ satisfy (3.1) the $l_{i,j}$ clearly satisfy (2.1) – they use no more than the available labor. It only remains to show that $l_{i,j}$ can make the Q_i, i.e., that $f_{i,1}(y_{i,1}l^*_{i,1}) + f_{i,2}(y_{i,2}l^*_{i,2}) = Q_i$. For each i one of the two $y_{i,j}$ is 1, and the other is 0. Let us suppose $y_{i,1} = 1$ and $y_{i,2} = 0$. If $(i,1) \in D$, $l^*_{i,1} = l'_{1,1}$ so $f_{i,1}(l^*_{i,1}) = Q_i$ and $f_{i,2}(0) = 0$ so the $l_{i,j}$ make the Q_i. Clearly we have the same outcome if $y_{i,1} = 0$ and $y_{i,2} = 1$ provided that $(i,2) \in D$. We next consider the possibility $y_{i,1} = 1$ and $y_{i,2} = 0$ and $(i,1) \in D'$. As we remarked earlier when we were defining the linear problem, $(i,j) \in D'$ implies that $l^*_{i,j} > L_j$. This in turn implies, for $y_{i,1} = 1$, that $y_{i,1}l^*_{i,1} > L_1$. This means that the first inequality in (3.1) cannot be satisfied. That, however, contradicts the assumption that the $y_{i,j}\ l^*_{i,j}$ satisfy (3.1) so this case can not occur. The same reasoning applies to the remaining case $y_{i,1} = 0$ and $y_{i,2} = 1$ and $(i,2) \in D'$. Q.E.D.

This Lemma enables us to prove:

Theorem 3.9

If P is an *efficient* production plan, then the corresponding linear plan P* uses no more labor in (3.2) (or in (3.1)) than the minimizing *integer* solution to (3.2).

Proof: If we start with some efficient production plan, P, then by Lemma 3.4 its linearized plan, P*, satisfies the linearized problem and uses no more labor than P. If there were an integer y′ that solved the linearized problem with strictly less labor, it would give us by Lemma 3.8 a new feasible production plan P′ using no more labor than that, and therefore using less labor than the original P. This contradicts the assumed efficiency of the original P. Q.E.D.

INEFFICIENT AND LOCALLY STABLE TRADE EQUILIBRIA

If we start with a specialized P = { $l_{i,j}$ }, it produces a P* with $y_{i,j} = f_{i,j}(l_{i,j}) / Q_i$. However we can verify that these $y_{i,j}l^*_{i,j}$ are exactly the $l_{i,j}$ of P itself. For example if $f_{i,1}(l_{i,1}) = Q_i$, $y_{i,1} = 1$ so $y_{i,1}l^*_{i,1} = l^*_{i,1} = l'_{1,1} = l_{i,1}$ This leads immediately to:

Theorem 3.10: A Necessary Condition for Efficiency

If a specialized P is efficient, its P* must be integer (perfectly specialized) and must be minimal among *integer* solutions to (3.2).

In other words P* solves the *integer* programming problem represented by (3.2).

Proof: This is a restatement of Theorem 3.9 for specialized P using the fact that, for specialized P, P* is integer.

This theorem tells us that for a specialized plan, P, to be efficient in the original problem, its linearized counterpart, P*, must be the minimizing solution of the integer (perfectly specialized) version of the (efficiency) programming problem (3.2).

Special Cases: We will next discuss some illuminating special cases. These cases illustrate the variety of outcomes that can occur when the classical efficiency concept is used in the scale economies model. In particular, they demonstrate that the proportion of efficient specialized equilibria will in some cases be very large, and in other cases very small.

Identical Production Functions: Assume $f_{i,1}(l) = f_{i,2}(l)$ for all i. Any equilibrium or any feasible production plan P = { $l_{i,j}$ } point provides a set of Q_i, and satisfies our condition (2.1). Let us suppose that P is specialized and that Country 1 is the producer in the ith industry. Then $l_{i,1} = l'_{1,1}$ and $l_{i,2} = 0$. Clearly, $(i,1) \in D$. If we also have $(i,2) \in D$, it takes the same amount of labor $l_{i,1} = l_{i,2}$ to produce Q_i in both countries because the production functions are identical, so $e_{i,1} = e_{i,2}$. If on the other hand, $(i,2) \in D'$ and Q_i cannot be made by the entire labor force of Country 2, it must be true that $l_{i,1} > L_2$. Then we have from economies of scale $f_{i,1}(l_{i,1}) / l_{i,1} \geq f_{i,2}(L_2) / L_2$ so $e_{i,1} \geq e_{i,2}$. In either case, the producing country, Country 1, has an $e_{i,1} / e_{i,2} \geq 1$ and the non-producer, in this case Country 2, an $e_{i,2} / e_{i,1} \leq 1$. This argument can, of course, be repeated if Country 2 is the producer and for all i. We conclude that the comparative advantage conditions of Theorem 3.7 are necessarily satisfied and that we have efficiency. So if $f_{i,1}(l) = f_{i,2}(l)$ we have efficiency for all specialized production plans or specialized equilibria.

To explain the next two examples we must allude briefly to some of the results of Gomory (1991, 1992) and Gomory and Baumol (1992). In these papers we showed not only that the n-good model has 2^n-2 specialized equilibria, but also that if we calculate for each equilibrium its relative national income $Z_1 = Y_1 / (Y_1 + Y_2)$ and its (Cobb-Douglas) utility U_1 for Country 1, and then plot the points (Z_1,U_1) in the Z_1-U_1 plane, the resulting 2^n-2 points lie in a well-defined region of the plane. This region has a characteristic shape and well defined upper and lower boundaries that can be computed. We also showed that the region between the upper and lower boundaries tends to fill up solidly with these equilibria as n increases.

A similar statement can be made about a Z_2-U_2 plane, if we choose to plot the equilibria with $Z_2 = Y_2 / (Y_1 + Y_2)$ as the horizontal axis and U_2, the Cobb-Douglas utility for Country 2 as the vertical axis. In *Figure 6,* (and later in *Figures 7, 8,* and *9*), we combine the (Z_1,U_1) and (Z_2,U_2) plots. In *Figure 6* the dark dots are the points (Z_1,U_1) and the lighter dots the points (Z_2,U_2). The horizontal axis is Z_1 if read from left to right, and $Z_2 = 1\text{-}Z_1$ if read from right to left. *Figure 6* represents the equilibria for an 11-industry model. These equilibria give us a large set of specialized production patterns, whose efficiency has considerable natural interest.

With this background we can now discuss the next examples.

Productivity ratios that do not depend on the Q_i. Efficiency is also easier to understand when the $e_{i,j}$ depend on the size of the Q_i but the $e_{i,1}/e_{i,2}$ ratios do not. This occurs when, in each industry, one country has a consistent degree of advantage over the other over all Q_i or at least over a wide range of Q_i. An example of this is the case $f_{i,j}(l) = \varepsilon_{i,j}\, l^{\alpha_i}$. In this case we find directly that the $e_{i,1} / e_{i,2}$ ratios for each i are given by the expression $(\varepsilon_{i,1} / \varepsilon_{i,2})^{\alpha_i}$, which does not involve Q_i. These ratios are independent of the actual Q_i values and therefore are the same for all the different equilibria or specialized production plans. The ratios can be used to rank the industries in order of decreasing comparative advantage ratios, $e_{i,1} / e_{i,2}$. If we assign production of the first m industries in this ordering to Country 1 and the rest to Country 2, we obtain an equilibrium that certainly satisfies the comparative advantage condition of Theorem 3.7. We can create n-1 efficient equilibria in this way. These equilibria are shown in *Figure 7* for a 27-good model.

This example illustrates an important point. There are efficient equilibria that give very low utility for both countries, those that are near $Z_1 = 1$ or $Z_1 = 0$. At these equilibria one country makes almost everything and the other makes only one or two products. However, these products are made in such large quantities that the point is efficient, since there is no way to make more of those one or two while maintaining the quantities of the others. The disturbing implication is that efficiency and welfare are almost completely divorced, except where Z_1 is held fixed, i.e., at a *given* level of relative national income.

Ratios that depend on the Q_i. One might think at this point that there is always some string of efficient equilibria to be obtained by finding the equilibria whose ordering corresponds to the comparative advantage ordering of the productivity ratios, $e_{i,1} / e_{i,2}$. However, what has simplified our work to this point is that the $e_{i,1} / e_{i,2}$ ratios with which we have dealt have been independent of Q_i, while in general the $e_{i,1} / e_{i,2}$ depend also on the size of the Q_i. This dependence can in fact exclude the possibility of efficient equilibrium points over wide ranges of relative national incomes. We can provide an example in which there are no efficient specialized equilibria in the equilibrium region of the Z_1-U_1 plane for $Z_1 > 0.5$. While this example is somewhat artificial it does show the sensitivity to the details of the classical efficiency concept in this setting. It therefore seems worthwhile to consider other concepts that may generalize the classical concept and improve its adaptation to a world of scale economies.

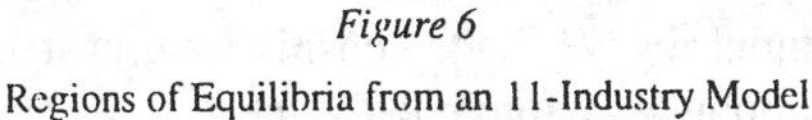

Figure 6

Regions of Equilibria from an 11-Industry Model

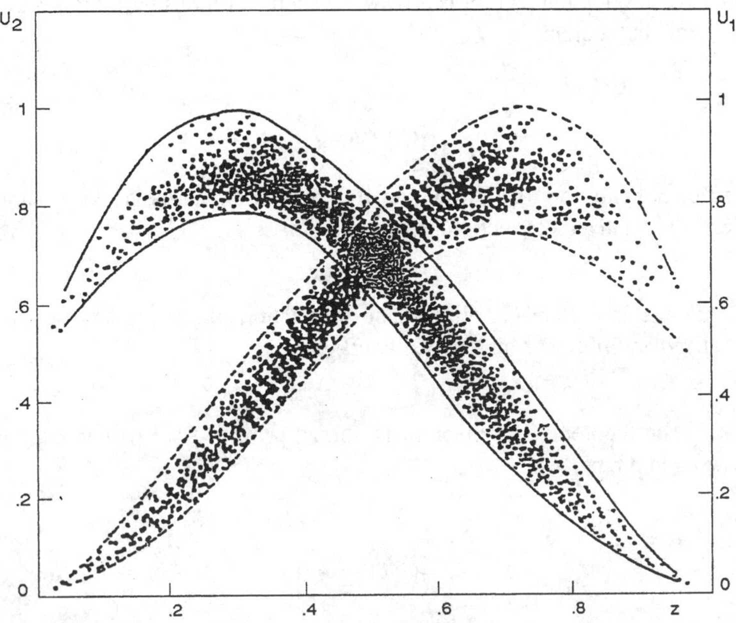

IV. LOCAL EFFICIENCY: THE EFFICIENCY COSTS OF NONSPECIALIZATION

We will call the $l_{i,j}$ *locally efficient* at Q if, roughly speaking, there is no nearby $l_{i,j}$, say, $l^{**}_{i,j}$, that provides more than the quantities Q_i. More precisely $l_{i,j}$ is locally efficient if there is some ε such that $| l^{**}_{i,j}-l_{i,j} | < \varepsilon$ implies that $f_{i,1}(l^{**}_{i,1}) + f_{i,2}(l^{**}_{i,2}) \leq Q_i$ for all i.

Local efficiency still rests on the idea that generates interest in the concept of efficiency. It still asks whether or not a better arrangement, i.e., one that generates larger quantities of goods than the Q_i, is possible. However, a *local* efficiency test only compares nearby arrangements, as common sense may suggest. Local efficiency makes behavior of our large numbers of equilibria much more coherent.

To see this we first need another concept – an *almost specialized production pattern* (aspp). In such a pattern, with the exception of at most one i, all production is specialized: $l_{i,1} > 0$ implies $l_{i,2} = 0$ and $l_{i,2} > 0$ implies $l_{i\,1} = 0$. We will also assume as part of the definition that for positive $l_{i,j}$, $f_{i,j}(l_{i,j}) > 0$, i.e., that a positive labor input always yields a positive output at the point in question, since otherwise the point is automatically inefficient. Note that a perfectly specialized production pattern is always an aspp. With this definition we can state the main theorem.

Theorem 4.1

A sufficient condition for $l_{i,j}$ to be locally efficient is that the $l_{i,j}$ be an almost perfectly specialized production pattern.

This has the important Corollary: The production pattern of any perfectly specialized equilibrium point is locally efficient.

Proof of the theorem: The theorem is almost proved if we demonstrate the following lemma:

Lemma 4.2

If $l_{i,j}$ is an aspp, then for ε sufficiently small, any changes $\delta_{i,1}$ that strictly decrease the total labor quantity in Country 1, while maintaining the total output of both countries at Q_i, will result in a strict increase in the labor used in Country 2.

Figure 7

Efficient Equilibria of a 27 Good-Model

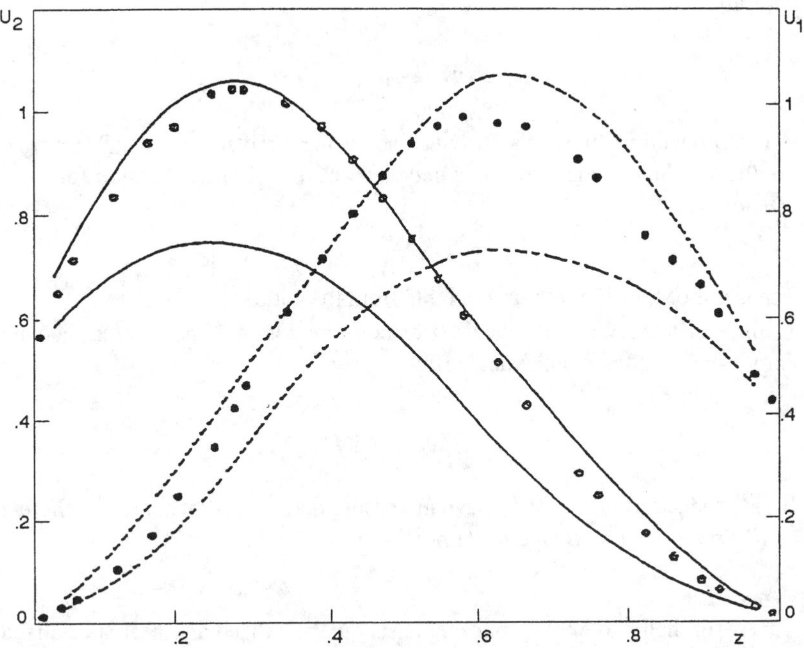

That the lemma is plausible can be seen in the following way: if we attempt to decrease the labor $l_{i,1}$ on the one non-specialized good, we must increase the amount of labor $l_{i,2}$ in Country 2 to maintain the output of the ith good. If we then try to avoid an increase in total labor use in Country 2 we must decrease the $l_{j,2}$ in some other industry. However in this industry Country 2 is the sole producer, so any decrease in $l_{j,2}$ will result in a *very large* increase in $l_{j,1}$ because this industry is starting from scratch in Country 1. Now we no longer have a decrease in Country 1's total labor use. This reasoning can be extended to every possible situation as is shown in a proof available from the authors.

If we accept 4.2, then to prove the theorem we need only observe that if there is a $l'_{i,j}$ that makes at least Q_i, in every industry using the same labor supply, and makes strictly more of Q_j, then by contracting the production of the jth good until it is exactly Q_j we will underuse the labor of one of the two countries. If we suppose that it is Country 1, then $l_{i,j}$-$l'_{i,j}$ would give us a set of $\delta_{i,j}$ that underuses the labor of Country 1, and which makes the Q_i while not increasing the use of labor in Country 2. This contradicts the lemma and proves the theorem.

That the aspp condition of Theorem 4.1 is not too arbitrary can be seen from the following theorem:

Theorem 4.3

If the production functions $f_{i,j}$ have increasing derivatives (rising marginal products of labor), then *aspp is a necessary and sufficient condition* for local efficiency.

The proof of this Theorem is available from the authors.

Since efficiency implies local efficiency Theorem 4.3 has as an immediate corollary a result about classical efficiency:

Theorem 4.4

If the production functions $f_{i,j}$ have increasing derivatives there are *no efficient equilibria with more than one shared industry.*

This result helps to explain our emphasis on specialized and near specialized (aspp) production patterns[8]. In the case of increasing derivatives they are the only production patterns with even the possibility of being efficient.

Examples of production functions with increasing derivatives are all production functions of the form $e_{i,j}l^{\alpha_{i,j}}$, with $\alpha_{i,j} \geq 1$, or any production function of that form preceded by an interval of zero output. An example of a reasonable production function *not* immediately meeting the criterion is a production function with a flat-bottomed average cost curve or one that starts out at zero, then increases sharply, and then becomes linear with a positive slope $e_{i,j}$ that is less than the derivative in the preceding steep portion. These are the functions of the type that underlies the extended-specialized production plans. However,

8. It is easy to show that in simple linear Ricardian model with two goods and two countries, varying only demand conditions, almost all efficient equilibria will be aspp, but *not* perfectly specialized, thus contradicting what the standard textbook examples suggest.

it can be shown that if the economy operates at a point in the linear range of such a production function, as it would be in an extended-specialized production plan, then we will generally have inefficiency with more than one shared industry. It can be shown that efficiency is not possible with more than one shared industry unless the $e_{i,1} / e_{i,2}$ ratios are the same in all the shared industries.

V. QUANTIFIED EFFICIENCY (λ-EFFICIENCY)

Although we see that all specialized production patterns are locally efficient, we are still interested in their efficiency in a more global sense. Now, however, we will not ask whether a given production pattern is efficient or not efficient but, rather, how bad or how good is it in terms of efficiency. We now seek a quantitative rather than a binary answer.

For this purpose we introduce as our quantitative measure, λ-efficiency. Consider any set of Q_i and its production pattern $l_{i,j}$. We will assume that the $l_{i,j}$ use up the total labor available in both countries. We will look for other production patterns $l_{i,j}$ that make the same set of Q_i, possibly using less of the total labor of the two countries, i.e., $\Sigma_{i,j} l_{i,j} < L_1 + L_2$. We propose the

Definition: $\lambda = (\min \Sigma_{i,j} l_{i,j}) / (L_1 + L_2)$ where the minimization extends over all production patterns that make the Q_i and do not require more than the available amount of labor in either country. We define λ to be the λ-efficiency of Q. Clearly $\lambda = 1$ coincides with the classical notion of efficiency, but now we can describe a point as having a λ-efficiency of, say, 0.77. This measures the percent of the total workforce required to make the original set of goods when they are made in the most efficient possible way. Thus, $1-\lambda$ is the proportion of the available labor wasted by the inefficiency of the equilibrium under study.

We will next discuss ways of finding the λ associated with a production pattern $P = \{l\}_{i,j}$. We will not be able to determine the magnitude of λ precisely, but will be able to obtain workable upper and lower bounds.

Underestimating λ: If v is the minimizing value of the linear programming problem (3.2) v is also an *underestimate* of the labor required to make the quantities Q_i using the $f_{i,j}$. This follows immediately from Lemma 3.4 which says that any feasible production plan P gives rise to a P* that satisfies the linearized plan and uses less labor. This gives us, by the definition of λ:

Theorem 5.1

$\lambda_u = v / (L_1+L_2)$ is an underestimate of λ.

Overestimating λ: Let v_I be the minimizing value of (3.2) when the minimization is not over all y but only over all integer y.

Theorem 5.2

$\lambda_o = v_I / (L_1+L_2)$ is an overestimate of λ.

Proof: By Lemma 3.8 any integer solution of (3.2) is a feasible production plan. Any feasible production plan is an overestimate of the minimal amount of labor required. Therefore the minimum integer solution is a production plan and therefore an overestimate.

Simplifying the Calculations: Both the linear programming solution to (3.2) which gives λ_u and the integer programming solution to (3.2) which gives λ_o can be greatly simplified. The first problem reduces to the well-known knapsack problem and the integer problem can be reduced to a dynamic programming problem with one state variable. A description of the method can be supplied to interested readers.

Convergence of λ_u and λ_o for large problems: λ_o and λ_u will tend toward each other, and therefore toward λ for large problems in which no one or two industries use up a large proportion of the total labor force. Intuitively, this reflects the fact, mentioned in Section III, that the linear programming problem will have at most two non-integer components, and so its solution will not be far from being an integer solution itself. Therefore, if the two components don't matter much, the linear programming underestimate is not far from an integer programming overestimate. While this is plausible there is considerable work in getting these thoughts to be precise. A formal description is available from the authors.

INEFFICIENT AND LOCALLY STABLE TRADE EQUILIBRIA

Figure 8

Equilibria with λ_u >0. 98

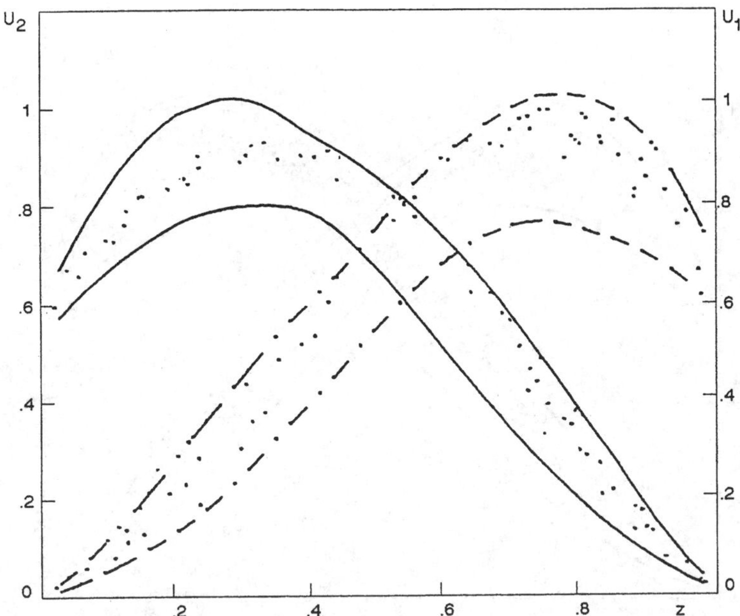

Efficiency in the Equilibria of a Region: We can now use the overestimates and underestimates to examine the efficiencies of the various equilibria populating the regions of equilibrium. In *Figure 8* we show the 98 equilibria in an 11-good model whose underestimate of λ, λ_u is > 0.98. In *Figure 9* we show the 449 equilibria whose overestimate of λ, λ_o is > 0.98. In these figures, and in other similar figures that we have examined, there is no particular tendency for the equilibria near the middle to be more efficient than the rest. There is, however, some tendency for the more efficient points to be near the upper boundary. This tendency is much more pronounced in the middle region than at either the right or left ends.

Figure 9

Equilibria with $\lambda_u > 0.98$

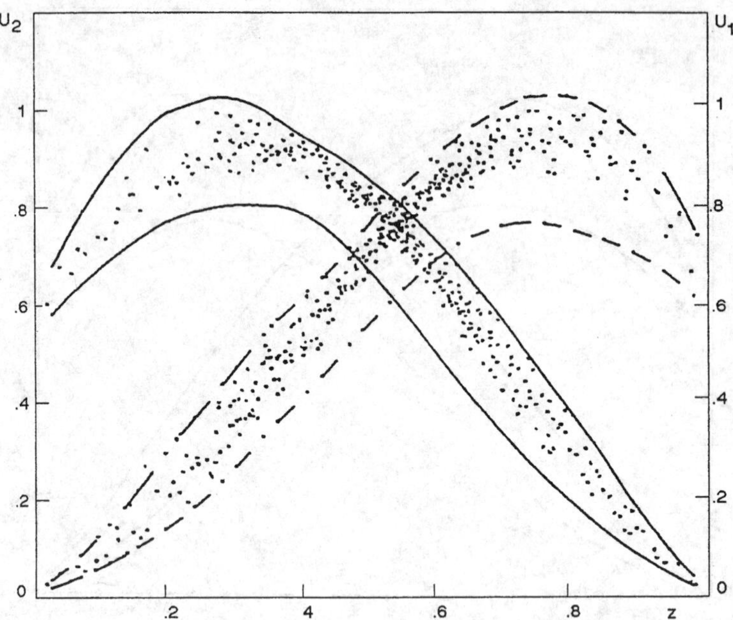

However, taking the region as a whole we may ask how efficient these equilibria are *on the average*. In *Figure 10* (a cumulative distribution) we have considered all the equilibria of the 11-good model. The height y of the upper curve gives the percent of the 2048 equilibria whose λ_u is $\leq$ x. The lower curve is a similar plot for λ_o. A plot of actual efficiency, if we could obtain it, would lie in between. The two vertical bars are the average λ_u on the left and the average λ_o on the right. The average efficiency lies in between, i.e., between 0.91 and 0.93. Considering the range of production efficiencies in the model parameters[9] the high average efficiency is a little surprising.

9. In the 11-country model the production function for the ith industry in the jth country was $e_{i,j}l^{\alpha_i}$. The α_i were between 1 and 2. The 11 values for the $e_{i,1}$ were (1.00, 1.02, 0.70, 0.94, 1.24, 0.60, 0.70, 0.77, 0.50, 1.10, 0.90) and the 11 values for the $e_{i,2}$ were (0.52, 0.71, 0.91, 0.92, 1.01, 1.23, 1.30, 1.02, 0.30, 1.20, 0.70). The 27-country model was similar.

INEFFICIENT AND LOCALLY STABLE TRADE EQUILIBRIA

Figure 10

λ_u and λ_o for an 11-Good-Model

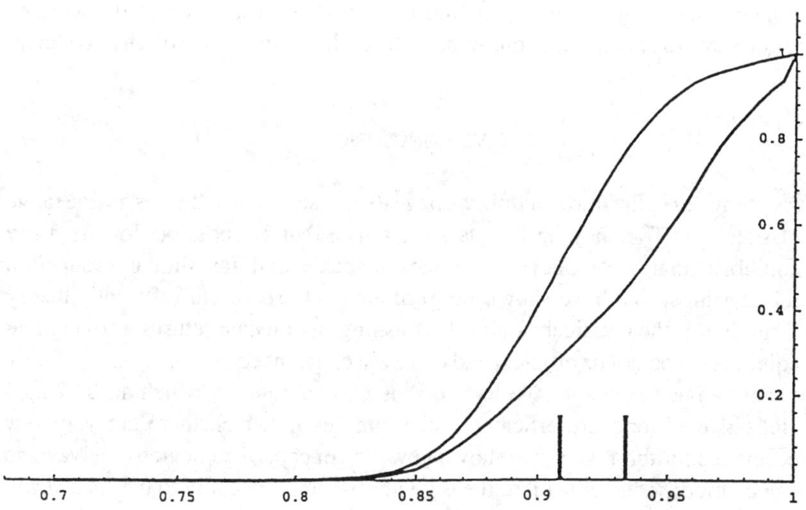

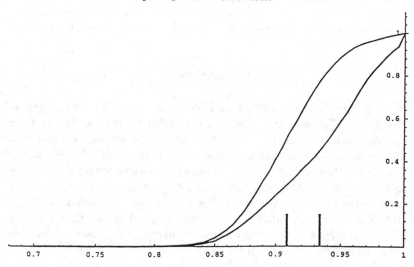

Figure 11

λ_u and λ_o for a Sample from a 27-Good Model

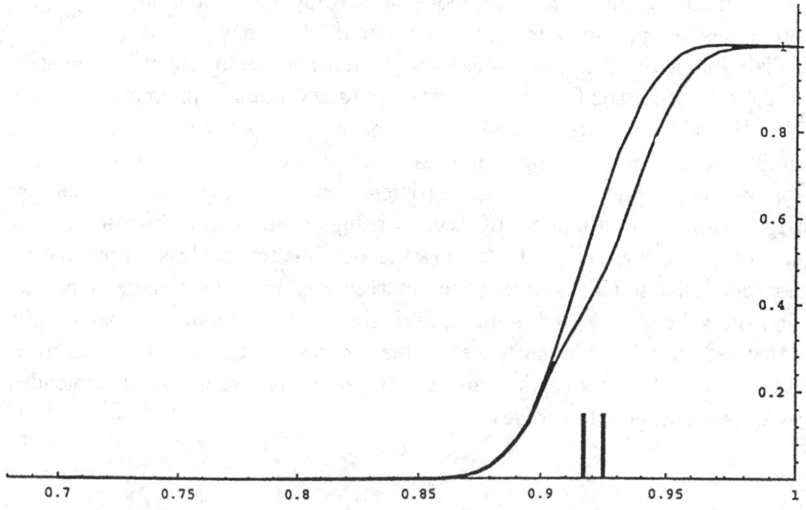

In *Figure 11* we have the same plot as that in *Figure 10* but this time we have taken a random sample of 2,000 points from a larger (27-good) model. The convergence of the two curves and the improved estimates of the average efficiency are exactly what one expects from the convergence discussed above.

VI. CONCLUSION

As promised in the introduction, we have demonstrated that there is a wide range of states of efficiency, in the classical sense, that are possible for the many equilibria that exist under economies of scale and for similar production relationships. We have shown the profound differences in efficiency theory from that in the classical case of diminishing or constant returns, proving that equilibria need not be efficient and that even efficient equilibria need not satisfy comparative advantage. We have discussed examples in which all 2^n-2 specialized equilibria are efficient, and examples in which there are very few efficient equilibria. We have shown how the concept of comparative advantage can be modified to adapt it to the n-good case and especially to the specialized or extended-specialized solutions that are important in a world of scale economies, demonstrating that comparative advantage is sufficient but not necessary for efficiency. We have introduced two new efficiency measures, local efficiency and λ-efficiency that seem to function more uniformly than the standard classical concept in the economies of scale setting, while retaining many of the properties that provide interest to the notion of efficiency.

The subject is clearly not of academic interest alone. It relates immediately to the role of laissez faire and government intervention in international trade. The classical analysis showed good reasons to believe that in a world of diminishing returns unimpeded market forces can be relied upon to do a reasonably good job in promoting efficiency in the trade process. The current paper, along with a number of recent writings dealing with the role of scale economies in international trade show that here matters are less simple. It does not follow that mindless government intervention, much less unfettered protectionism is the way to go. But the analysis shows that economic welfare may be enhanced in some circumstances if the governmental takes on some role. Exploration of the appropriate role is only beginning and this paper is intended as a contribution to the process.

INEFFICIENT AND LOCALLY STABLE TRADE EQUILIBRIA

REFERENCES

Baumol, W.J. (1993). On Location of Industries Among Trading Countries: Scale Economies as Possible Offset to Comparative Disadvantage, in: Hiroshi Ohta and Jacques-Francois Thisse (eds.), *Does Economic Space Matter? Essays in Honor of Melvin L. Greenhut.* St. Martins Press: 187-206.

Chipman, J. (1965). A Survey of the Theory of International Trade: Part 2, The Neo-Classical Theory, *Econometrica.* 33: 685-760.

Ethier, W.J. (1979). Internationally Decreasing Costs and World Trade, *Journal of International Economics.* 9: 1–24.

Ethier, W.J. (1982). Decreasing Costs in International Trade and Frank Graham's Argument for Protection, *Econometrica.* 50: 1243-1268.

Gomory, Ralph E. (1991). A Ricardo Model with Economies of Scale, *Proceedings of the National Academy of Sciences, U.S.A.* 88, Issue 18: 8267-8271.

Gomory, Ralph E. and W.J. Baumol (1992). Scale Economies, Regions of Multiple Trade Equilibria, and the Gains from Acquisition of Industries, *Economic Research Reports* (March), New York University: C.V. Starr Center for Applied Economics, RR# 92-10.

Gomory, Ralph E. (1994). A Ricardo Model with Economies of Scale, *Journal of Economic Theory.* 62: 394-419.

Grossman, G.M. and E. Helpman (1991). *Innovation and Growth in the Global Economy.* Cambridge, Mass.: MIT Press.

Helpman, E. and P.R. Krugman (1985). *Market Structure and Foreign Trade.* Cambridge, Mass.: MIT Press.

Kemp, M.C. (1969). *The Pure Theory of International Trade.* Englewood Cliffs, N.J.: Prentice Hall.

Krugman, P.R. (1991). History Versus Expectations, *Quarterly Journal of Economics.* 106: 651–667.

Matthews, R.C.O. (1949/50). Reciprocal Demand and Increasing Returns, *The Review of Economic Studies.* 17: 149-158.

Meade, J. E. (1952). *A Geometry of International Trade.* London: George Allen and Unwin.

SUMMARY

In the presence of scale economies a country that happens to be the exclusive producer of a commodity will be able to retain its monopoly against efforts of others to enter on a small scale even if that firm has neither absolute nor comparative advantage in its production. Hence equilibria can violate comparative advantage, be inefficient and yet be stable. Moreover, equilibria that violate comparative advantage can be efficient. In the article, sufficient efficiency conditions for the scale economies case are provided, and, two new concepts, local efficiency and (quantitative) degree of inefficiency are explained. The analysis confirms that in a world of scale economies market forces cannot be relied upon always to yield an efficient equilibrium.

ZUSAMMENFASSUNG

Ein Land, welches der exklusive Hersteller eines Gutes ist, wird beim Vorliegen von Skalenerträgen seine Monopolstellung gegenüber Konkurrenz von kleiner Grösse selbst dann halten können, wenn es weder absolute noch komparative Vorteile in der Produktion besitzt. Daher gibt es Gleichgewichte, die das Konzept der komparativen Vorteile verletzen, ineffizient aber trotzdem stabil sind.

Allerdings können solche Gleıchgewichte auch effizient sein. In diesem Aufsatz werden hinreichende Effizienzbedingungen für Skalenerträge aufgezeigt und zwei neue Konzepte, lokale Effizienz und ein (quantitativer) Grad an Ineffizienz erklärt. Die Analyse bestätigt, dass beim Vorliegen von Skalenerträgen die Marktkräfte nicht immer zu einem effizienten Gleichgewicht führen.

RÉSUMÉ

Au cas d'économies de l'échelle, un pays qui est le seul producteur d'un bien peut être capable de préserver son monopole malgré les efforts d'autres pays d'entrer dans la production à une échelle plus petite, même si le pays tenant le monopole n'a ni un avantage absolu ni relatif dans la prodution. Il en suit que ce genre d'équilibre peut contredire le principe de l'avantage comparatif, être non-efficient et ètre stable. De plus, des équilibres qui violent le principe de l'avantage comparatif peuvent être efficients. Dans l'article les conditions suffisantes pour le cas d'économies de l'échelle sont données, et deux conceptions nouvelles, celle de l'efficence locale et celle du degré (quantitatif) de l'inefficience sont expliquées. L'analyse confirme que dans un monde avec des économies de l'échelle les forces du marché ne produisent pas toujours des equilibres efficients.

PART II

INDUSTRIAL ORGANIZATION, REGULATION AND PRIVATIZATION

[8]

Contestable Markets: An Uprising in the Theory of Industry Structure

By WILLIAM J. BAUMOL*

The address of the departing president is no place for modesty. Nevertheless, I must resist the temptation to describe the analysis I will report here as anything like a revolution. Perhaps terms such as "rebellion" or "uprising" are rather more apt. But, nevertheless, I shall seek to convince you that the work my colleagues, John Panzar and Robert Willig, and I have carried out and encapsulated in our new book enables us to look at industry structure and behavior in a way that is novel in a number of respects, that it provides a unifying analytical structure to the subject area, and that it offers useful insights for empirical work and for the formulation of policy.

Before getting into the substance of the analysis I admit that this presidential address is most unorthodox in at least one significant respect—that it is not the work of a single author. Here it is not even sufficient to refer to Panzar and Willig, the coauthors of both the substance and the exposition of the book in which the analysis is described in full. For others have made crucial contributions to the formulation of the theory—most notably Elizabeth Bailey, Dietrich Fischer, Herman Quirmbach, and Thijs ten Raa.

But there are many more than these. No uprising by a tiny band of rebels can hope to change an established order, and when the time for rebellion is ripe it seems to break out simultaneously and independently in a variety of disconnected centers each offering its own program for the future. Events here have been no different. I have recently received a proposal for a conference on new developments in the theory of industry structure formulated by my colleague, Joseph Stiglitz, which lists some forty participants, most of them widely known. Among those working on the subject are persons as well known as Caves, Dasgupta, Dixit, Friedlaender, Grossman, Hart, Levin, Ordover, Rosse, Salop, Schmalensee, Sonnenschein, Spence, Varian, von Weiszäcker, and Zeckhauser, among *many* others.[1] It is, of course, tempting to me to take the view that our book is the true gospel of the rebellion and that the doctrines promulgated by others must be combatted as heresy. But that could at best be excused as a manifestation of the excessive zeal one comes to expect on such occasions. In truth, the immediate authors of the work I will report tonight may perhaps be able to justify a claim to have offered some systematization and order to the new doctrines—to have built upon them a more comprehensive statement of the issues and the analysis, and to have made a number of particular contributions. But, in the last analysis, we must look enthusiastically upon our fellow rebels as comrades in arms, each of whom has made a crucial contribution to the common cause.

Turning now to the substance of the theory, let me begin by contrasting our results with those of the standard theory. In offering this contrast, let me emphasize that much of the analysis rests on work that appeared considerably earlier in a variety of forms.

*Presidential address delivered at the ninety-fourth meeting of the American Economic Association, December 29, 1981. I should like to express my deep appreciation to the many colleagues who have contributed to the formulation of the ideas reported here, and to the Economics Program of the Division of Social Sciences of the National Science Foundation, the Division of Information Science and Technology of the National Science Foundation, and the Sloan Foundation for their very generous support of the research that underlies it.

[1]Such a list must inevitably have embarassing omissions—perhaps some of its author's closest friends. I can only say that it is intended just to be suggestive. The fact that it is so far from being complete also indicates how widespread an uprising I am discussing.

We, no less than other writers, owe a heavy debt to predecessors from Bertrand to Bain, from Cournot to Demsetz. Nevertheless, it must surely be acknowledged that the following characterization of the general tenor of the literature as it appeared until fairly recently is essentially accurate.

First, in the received analysis perfect competition serves as the one standard of welfare-maximizing structure and behavior. There is no similar form corresponding to industries in which efficiency calls for a very limited number of firms (though the earlier writings on workable competition did move in that direction in a manner less formal than ours).

Our analysis, in contrast, provides a generalization of the concept of the perfectly competitive market, one which we call a "perfectly contestable market." It is, generally, characterized by optimal behavior and yet applies to the full range of industry structures including even monopoly and oligopoly. In saying this, it must be made clear that perfectly contestable markets do not populate the world of reality any more than perfectly competitive markets do, though there are a number of industries which undoubtedly approximate contestability even if they are far from perfectly competitive. In our analysis, perfect contestability, then, serves not primarily as a description of reality, but as a benchmark for desirable industrial organization which is far more flexible and is applicable far more widely than the one that was available to us before.

Second, in the standard analysis (including that of many of our fellow rebels), the properties of oligopoly models are heavily dependent on the assumed expectations and reaction patterns characterizing the firms that are involved. When there is a change in the assumed nature of these expectations or reactions, the implied behavior of the oligopolistic industry may change drastically.

In our analysis, in the limiting case of perfect contestability, oligopolistic structure and behavior are freed entirely from their previous dependence on the conjectural variations of *incumbents* and, instead, these are generally determined uniquely and, in a manner that is tractable analytically, by the pressures of *potential* competition to which Bain directed our attention so tellingly.

Third, the standard analysis leaves us with the impression that there is a rough continuum, in terms of desirability of industry performance, ranging from unregulated pure monopoly as the pessimal arrangement to perfect competition as the ideal, with relative efficiency in resource allocation increasing monotonically as the number of firms expands.

I will show that, in contrast, in perfectly contestable markets behavior is sharply discontinuous in its welfare attributes. A contestable monopoly offers us some presumption, but no guarantee, of behavior consistent with a second best optimum, subject to the constraint that the firm be viable financially despite the presence of scale economies which render marginal cost pricing financially infeasible. That is, a contestable monopoly has some reason to adopt the Ramsey optimal price-output vector, but it may have other choices open to it. (For the analysis of contestable monopoly, see my article with Elizabeth Bailey and Willig, Panzar and Willig's article, and my book with Panzar and Willig, chs. 7 and 8.)

But once each product obtains a second producer, that is, once we enter the domain of duopoly or oligopoly for each and every good, such choice disappears. The contestable oligopoly which achieves an equilibrium that immunizes it from the incursions of entrants has only one pricing option—it must set its price exactly *equal* to marginal cost and do *all* of the things required for a first best optimum! In short, once we leave the world of pure or partial monopoly, any contestable market must behave ideally in every respect. Optimality is *not* approached gradually as the number of firms supplying a commodity grows. As has long been suggested in Chicago, two firms can be enough to guarantee optimality (see, for example, Eugene Fama and Arthur Laffer).

Thus, the analysis extends enormously the domain in which the invisible hand holds sway. In a perfectly contestable world, it seems to rule almost everywhere. Lest this seem to be too Panglossian a view of reality, let me offer two observations which make it clear that we emphatically do not believe that all need be for the best in this best of all possible worlds.

First, let me recall the observation that real markets are rarely, if ever, perfectly contestable. Contestability is merely a broader ideal, a benchmark of wider applicability than is perfect competition. To say that contestable oligopolies behave ideally and that contestable monopolies have some incentives for doing so is not to imply that this is even nearly true of all oligopolies or of unregulated monopolies in reality.

Second, while the theory extends the domain of the invisible hand in some directions, it unexpectedly restricts it in others. This brings me to the penultimate contrast I wish to offer here between the earlier views and those that emerge from our analysis.

The older theoretical analysis seems to have considered the invisible hand to be a rather weak intratemporal allocator of resources, as we have seen. The mere presence of unregulated monopoly or oligopoly was taken to be sufficient per se to imply that resources are likely to be misallocated *within* a given time period. But *where the market structure is such as to yield a satisfactory allocation of resources within the period*, it may have seemed that it can, at least in theory, do a good job of intertemporal resource allocation. In the absence of any externalities, persistent and asymmetric information gaps, and of interference with the workings of capital markets, the amounts that will be invested for the future may appear to be consistent with Pareto optimality and efficiency in the supply of outputs to current and future generations.

However, our analysis shows that where there are economies of scale in the production of durable capital, intertemporal contestable monopoly, which may perform relatively well in the single period, cannot be depended upon to perform ideally as time passes. In particular, we will see that the least costly producer is in the long run vulnerable to entry or replacement by rivals whose appearance is inefficient because it wastes valuable social resources.

There is one last contrast between the newer analyses and the older theory which I am most anxious to emphasize. In the older theory, the nature of the industry structure was *not* normally explained by the analysis. It was, in effect, taken to be given exogenously, with the fates determining, apparently capriciously, that one industry will be organized as an oligopoly, another as a monopoly and a third as a set of monopolistic competitors. Assuming that this destiny had somehow been revealed, the older analyses proceeded to investigate the consequences of the exogenously given industry structure for pricing, outputs, and other decisions.[2]

The new analyses are radically different in this respect. In our analysis, among others, an industry's structure is determined explicitly, endogenously, and simultaneously with the pricing, output, advertising, and other decisions of the firms of which it is constituted. This, perhaps, is one of the prime contributions of the new theoretical analyses.

I. Characteristics of Contestable Markets

Perhaps a misplaced instinct for melodrama has led me to say so much about contestable markets without even hinting what makes a market contestable. But I can postpone the definition no longer. A contestable market is one into which entry is absolutely free, *and exit is absolutely costless*. We use "freedom of entry" in Stigler's sense, not to mean that it is costless or easy, but that the entrant suffers no disadvantage in terms of production technique or perceived product quality relative to the incumbent,

[2] Of course, any analysis which considered the role of entry, whether it dealt with perfect competition or monopolistic competition, must implicitly have considered the determination of industry structure by the market. But in writings before the 1970's, such analyses usually did not consider how this process determined whether the industry would or would not turn out to be, for example, an oligopoly. The entry conditions were studied only to show how the *assumed* market structure could constitute an equilibrium state. Many recent writings have gone more explicitly into the determination of industry structure, though their approaches generally differ from ours.

and that potential entrants find it appropriate to evaluate the profitability of entry in terms of the incumbent firms' pre-entry prices. In short, it is a requirement of contestability that there be no cost discrimination against entrants. Absolute freedom of exit, to us, is one way to guarantee freedom of entry. By this we mean that any firm can leave without impediment, and in the process of departure can recoup any costs incurred in the entry process. If all capital is salable or reusable without loss other than that corresponding to normal user cost and depreciation, then any risk of entry is eliminated.

Thus, contestable markets may share at most one attribute with perfect competition. Their firms need not be small or numerous or independent in their decision making or produce homogeneous products. In short, a perfectly competitive market is necessarily perfectly contestable, but not *vice versa.*

The crucial feature of a contestable market is its vulnerability to hit-and-run entry. Even a very transient profit opportunity need not be neglected by a potential entrant, for he can go in, and, before prices change, collect his gains and then depart without cost, should the climate grow hostile.

Shortage of time forces me to deal rather briefly with two of the most important properties of contestable markets—their welfare attributes and the way in which they determine industry structure. I deal with these briefly because an intuitive view of the logic of these parts of the analysis is not difficult to provide. Then I can devote a bit more time to some details of the oligopoly and the intertemporal models.

A. *Perfect Contestability and Welfare*

The welfare properties of contestable markets follow almost directly from their definition and their vulnerability to hit-and-run incursions. Let me list some of these properties and discuss them succinctly.

First, a contestable market never offers more than a normal rate of profit—its economic profits must be zero or negative, even if it is oligopolistic or monopolistic. The reason is simple. Any positive profit means that a transient entrant can set up business, replicate a profit-making incumbent's output at the same cost as his, undercut the incumbent's prices slightly and still earn a profit. That is, continuity and the opportunity for costless entry and exit guarantee that an entrant who is content to accept a slightly lower economic profit can do so by selecting prices a bit lower than the incumbent's.

In sum, in a perfectly contestable market any economic profit earned by an incumbent automatically constitutes an earnings opportunity for an entrant who will hit and, if necessary, run (counting his temporary but supernormal profits on the way to the bank). Consequently, in contestable markets, zero profits must characterize any equilibrium, even under monopoly and oligopoly.

The second welfare characteristic of a contestable market follows from the same argument as the first. This second attribute of any contestable market is the absence of any sort of inefficiency in production in industry equilibrium. This is true alike of inefficiency of allocation of inputs, X-inefficiency, inefficient operation of the firm, or inefficient organization of the industry. For any unnecessary cost, like any abnormal profit, constitutes an invitation to entry. Of course, in the short run, as is true under perfect competition, both profits and waste may be present. But in the long run, these simply cannot withstand the threat brandished by potential entrants who have nothing to lose by grabbing at any opportunity for profit, however transient it may be.

A third welfare attribute of any long-run equilibrium in a contestable market is that no product can be sold at a price, p, that is less than its marginal cost. For if some firm sells y units of output at such a price and makes a profit in the process, then it is possible for an entrant to offer to sell a slightly smaller quantity, $y-\varepsilon$, at a price a shade lower than the incumbent's, and still make a profit. That is, if the price p is less than MC, then the sale of $y-\varepsilon$ units at price p must yield a total profit $\pi+\Delta\pi$ which is greater than the profit, π, that can be earned by selling only y units of output at that price. Therefore, there must exist a price just slightly lower than p which enables the entrant to undercut the incumbent and yet to earn at least as much as the incumbent, by eliminating the unprofitable marginal unit.

This last attribute of contestable equilibria —the fact that price must always at least equal marginal cost—is important for the economics of antitrust and regulation. For it means that in a perfectly contestable market, no cross subsidy is possible, that is, no predatory pricing can be used as a weapon of unfair competition. But we will see it also has implications which are more profound theoretically and which are more germane to our purposes. For it constitutes half of the argument which shows that when there are two or more suppliers of any product, its price must, in equilibrium, be exactly equal to marginal cost, and so resource allocation must satisfy all the requirements of first best optimality.

Indeed, the argument here is similar to the one which has just been described. But there is a complication which is what introduces the two-firm requirement into this proposition. $p < MC$ constitutes an opportunity for profit to an entrant who drops the unprofitable marginal unit of output, as we have just seen. It would seem, symmetrically, that $p > MC$ also automatically constitutes an opportunity for profitable entry. Instead of selling the y-unit output of a profitable incumbent, the entrant can now offer to sell the slightly larger output, $y + \varepsilon$, using the profits generated by the marginal unit at a price greater than marginal cost to permit a reduction in price below the incumbent's. But on this side of the incumbent's output, there is a catch in the argument. Suppose the incumbent is a monopolist. Then output and price are constrained by the elasticity of demand. An attempt by an entrant to sell $y + \varepsilon$ rather than y may conceivably cause a sharp reduction in price which eliminates the apparent profits of entry. In the extreme case where demand is perfectly inelastic, there will be no positive price at which the market will absorb the quantity $y + \varepsilon$. This means that the profit opportunity represented by $p > MC$ can crumble into dust as soon as anyone seeks to take advantage of it.

But all this changes when the market contains two or more sellers. Now $p > MC$ does always constitute a real opportunity for profitable entry. The entrant who wishes to sell a bit more than some one of the profitable incumbents, call him incumbent A, need not press against the industry's total demand curve for the product. Rather, he can undercut A, steal away all of his customers, at least temporarily, and, in addition, steal away ε units of demand from any other incumbent, B. Thus, if A and B together sell $y_a + y_b > y_a$, then an entrant can lure away $y_a + \varepsilon > y_a$ customers, for ε sufficiently small, and earn on this the incremental profit $\varepsilon(p - MC) > 0$. This means that the entrant who sells $y_a + \varepsilon$ can afford to undercut the prevailing prices somewhat and still make more profit than an incumbent who sells y_a at price p.

In sum, where a product is sold by two or more firms, any $p > MC$ constitutes an irresistible entry opportunity for hit-and-run entry in a perfectly contestable market, for it promises the entrant supernormal profits even if they accrue for a very short period of time.

Consequently, when a perfectly contestable market contains two or more sellers, neither $p < MC$ nor $p > MC$ is compatible with equilibrium. Thus we have our third and perhaps most crucial welfare attribute of such perfectly contestable markets—their prices, in equilibrium, must be equal to marginal costs, as is required for Pareto optimality of the "first best" variety. This, along with the conclusion that such markets permit no economic profits and no inefficiency in long-run equilibrium, constitutes their critical properties from the viewpoint of economic welfare. Certainly, since they do enjoy those three properties, the optimality of perfectly contestable equilibria (with the reservations already expressed about the case of pure monopoly) fully justifies our conclusion that perfect contestability constitutes a proper generalization of the concept of perfect competition so far as welfare implications are concerned.

B. *On the Determination of Industry Structure*

I shall be briefer and even less rigorous in describing how industry structure is determined endogenously by contestability analysis. Though this area encompasses one of its most crucial accomplishments, there is no way I can do justice to the details of the analysis in an oral presentation and within my allotted span of time. However, an intuitive view of the matter is not difficult.

The key to the analysis lies in the second welfare property of contestable equilibria—their incompatibility with inefficiency of any sort. In particular, they are incompatible with inefficiency in the *organization* of an industry. That is, suppose we consider whether a particular output quantity of an industry will be produced by two firms or by a thousand. Suppose it turns out that the two-firm arrangement can produce the given output at a cost 20 percent lower than it can be done by the 1,000 firms. Then one implication of our analysis is that the industry cannot be in long-run equilibrium if it encompasses 1,000 producers. Thus we already have some hint about the equilibrium industry structure of a contestable market.

We can go further with this example. Suppose that, with the given output vector for the industry, it turns out that *no* number of firms other than two can produce at as low a total cost as is possible under a two-firm arrangement. That is, suppose two firms can produce the output vector at a total cost lower than it can be done by one firm or three firms or sixty or six thousand. Then we say that for the given output vector the industry is a *natural duopoly*.

This now tells us how the industry's structure can be determined. We proceed, conceptually, in two steps. First we determine what structure happens to be most efficient for the production of a given output vector by a given industry. Next, we investigate when market pressures will lead the industry toward such an efficient structure in equilibrium.

Now, the first step, though it has many intriguing analytic attributes, is essentially a pure matter of computation. Given the cost function for a typical firm, it is ultimately a matter of calculation to determine how many firms will produce a given output most efficiently. For example, if economies of scale hold throughout the relevant range and there are sufficient complementarities in the production of the different commodities supplied by the firm, then it is an old and well-known conclusion that single firm production will be most economical—that we are dealing with a natural monopoly.

Similarly, in the single product case suppose the average cost curve is U shaped and attains its minimum point at an output of 10,000 units per year. Then it is obvious that if the industry happens to sell 50,000 units per year, this output can be produced most cheaply if it is composed of exactly five firms, each producing 10,000 units at its point of minimum average cost.

Things become far more complex and more interesting when the firm and the industry produce a multiplicity of commodities, as they always do in reality. But the logic is always the same. When the industry output vector is small compared to the output vectors the firm can produce at relatively low cost, then the efficient industry structure will be characterized by very few firms. The opposite will be true when the industry's output vector is relatively far from the origin. In the multiproduct case, since average cost cannot be defined, two complications beset the characterization of the output vectors which the firm can produce relatively efficiently. First, since here average cost cannot be defined, we cannot simply look for the point of minimum average costs. But we overcome this problem by dealing with output bundles having fixed proportions among commodity quantities—by moving along a ray in output space. Along any such ray the behavior of average cost *is* definable, and the point of minimum ray average cost (*RAC*) is our criterion of relatively efficient scale for the firm. Thus, in Figure 1 we have a ray average cost curve for the production of boots and shoes when they are produced in the proportion given by ray *0R*. We see that for such bundles y^m is the point of minimum *RAC*. A second problem affecting the determination of the output vectors the firm can produce efficiently is the choice of output proportions —the location of the ray along which the firm will operate. This depends on the degree of complementarity in production of the goods, and it also lends itself to formal analysis.

We note also that the most efficient number of firms will vary with the location of the

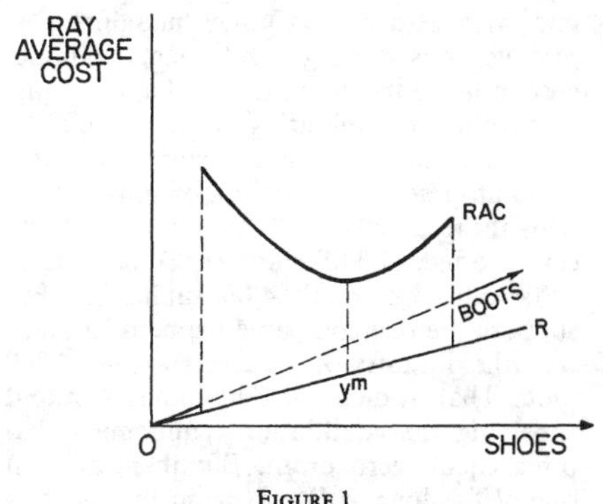

FIGURE 1

industry's output vector. The industry may be a natural monopoly with one output vector, a natural duopoly with another, and efficiency may require seventy-three firms when some third output vector is provided by the industry.

This, then, completes the first of the two basic steps in the endogenous determination of industry structure. Here we have examined what industry structure is least costly for each given output vector of a given industry, and have found how the result depends on the magnitudes of the elements of that output vector and the shape of the cost function of the typical firm. So far the discussion may perhaps be considered normative rather than behavioral. It tells us what structure is most efficient under the circumstances, not which industry structure will emerge under the pressures of the market mechanism.

The transition toward the second, behavioral, stage of the analysis is provided by the observation that the optimal structure of an industry depends on its output vector, while that output vector in turn depends on the prices charged by its firms. But, since pricing depends on industry structure, we are brought full circle to the conclusion that pricing behavior and industry structure must, ultimately, be determined simultaneously and endogenously.

We are in no position to go much further than this for a market whose properties are unspecified. But, for a perfectly contestable market, we can go much further. Indeed, the properties of perfect contestability cut through every difficulty and tell us the equilibrium prices, outputs, and industry structure, all at once.

Where more than one firm supplies a product, we have already characterized these prices precisely. For we have concluded that each equilibrium price will equal the associated marginal cost. Then, given the industry's cost and demand relationships, this yields the industry's output quantities simultaneously with its prices, in the usual manner. Here there is absolutely nothing new in the analysis.

But what is new is the format of the analysis of the determination of industry structure. As I have already pointed out, structure is determined by the efficiency requirement of equilibrium in any contestable market. Since no such equilibrium is compatible with failure to minimize industry costs, it follows that the market forces under perfect contestability will bring us results consistent with those of our normative analysis. Whatever industry structures minimize total costs for the equilibrium output vector must turn out to be the only structures consistent with industry equilibrium in the long run.

Thus, for contestable markets, but for contestable markets *only*, the second stage of the analysis of industry structure turns out to be a sham. Whatever industry structure was shown by the first, normative, portion of the analysis to be least costly must also emerge as the industry structure selected by market behavior. No additional calculations are required by the behavioral analysis. It will all have been done in the normative cost-minimization analysis and the behavioral analysis is pure bonus.

Thus, as I promised, I have indicated how contestability theory departs from the older theory which implicitly took industry structure to be determined exogenously in a manner totally unspecified and, instead, along with other recent writings, embraces the determination of industry structure as an integral part of the theory to be dealt with simultaneously with the determination of prices and outputs.

At this point I can only conjecture about the determination of industry structure once we leave the limiting case of perfect contestability. But my guess is that there are no sharp discontinuities here, and that while the industry structures which emerge in reality are not always those which minimize costs, they will constitute reasonable approximations to the efficient structures. If this is not so it is difficult to account for the similarities in the patterns of industry structure that one observes in different countries. Why else do we not see agriculture organized as an oligopoly in any free market economy, or automobiles produced by 10,000 firms? Market pressures must surely make any very inefficient market structure vulnerable to entry, to displacement of incumbents by foreign competition, or to undermining in other ways. If that is so, the market structure that is called for by contestability theory may not prove to be too bad an approximation to what we encounter in reality.

II. On Oligopoly Equilibrium

I should like now to examine oligopoly equilibrium somewhat more extensively. We have seen that, except where a multiproduct oligopoly firm happens to sell some of its products in markets in which it has no competitors, an important partial monopoly case which I will ignore in what follows, all prices must equal the corresponding marginal costs in long-run equilibrium. But in an oligopoly market, this is a troublesome concept. Unless the industry output vector happens to fall at a point where the cost function is characterized by locally constant returns to scale, we know that zero profits are incompatible with marginal cost pricing. Particularly if there are scale economies at that point, so that marginal cost pricing precludes financial viability, we can hardly expect such a solution to constitute an equilibrium. Besides, we have seen that long-run equilibrium requires profit to be precisely zero. We would thus appear to have run into a major snag by concluding that perfect contestability always leads to marginal cost pricing under oligopoly.

This is particularly so if the (ray) average curve is U shaped, with its minimum occurring at a single point, y^m. For in this case that minimum point is the only output of the firm consistent with constant returns to scale and with zero profits under marginal cost pricing. Thus, dealing with the single product case to make the point, it would appear, say, that if the *AC*-minimizing output is 1,000, in a contestable market, equilibrium is possible if quantity demanded from the industry happens to be exactly 2,000 units (so two firms can produce 1,000 units each) or exactly 3,000 units or exactly 4,000 units, etc. But suppose the demand curve happens to intersect the industry *AC* curve, say, at 4,030 units. That is, then, the only industry output satisfying the equilibrium requirement that price equals zero profit. But then, at least one of the four or five firms in the industry must produce either more or less than 1,000 units of output, and so the slope of its *AC* curve will not be zero at that point, precluding either *MC* pricing or zero profits and, consequently, violating one or the other of the requirements of equilibrium in a perfectly contestable market.

It would appear that equilibrium will be impossible in this perfectly contestable market unless by a great piece of luck the industry demand curve happens to intersect its *AC* curve at 2,000 or 3,000 units or some other integer multiple of 1,000 units of output.

There are a variety of ways in which one can grapple with this difficulty. In his dissertation at New York University, Thijs ten Raa has explored the issue with some care and has shown that the presence of entry costs of sufficient magnitude, that is, irreversible costs which must be borne by an entrant but not by an incumbent, can eliminate the existence problem. The minimum size of the entry cost required to permit an equilibrium will depend on the size of the deviation from zero profits under marginal cost pricing and ten Raa has given us rules for its determination. He has shown also that the existence problem, as measured by the required minimum size of entry cost, decreases rapidly as the equilibrium number of firms of the industry increases, typically attaining negligible proportions as that number reaches, say, ten enterprises. For, as is well known, when the firm's average cost curve is U shaped the industry's average cost curve will approach a horizontal line as the

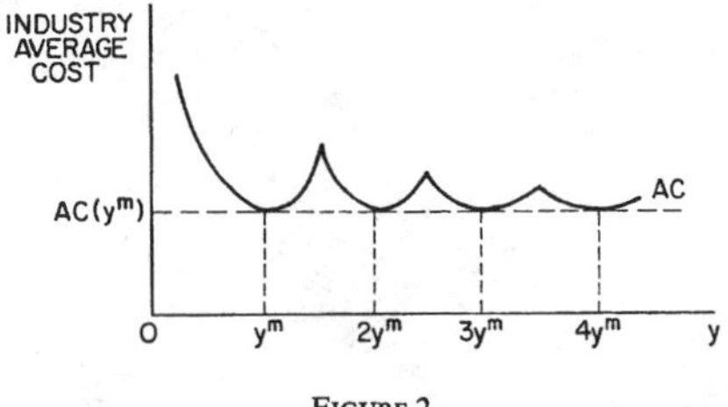

FIGURE 2

size of industry output increases. This is shown in Figure 2 which is a standard diagram giving the firm's and the industry's AC curves when the former is U shaped. As a result, the deviations between average cost and marginal cost will decline as industry output increases and so the minimum size of the entry cost required to preserve equilibrium declines correspondingly.

However, here I want to describe another approach offered in our book to the problem of existence which I have just described—the difficulty of satisfying simultaneously the zero-profit requirement and the requirement of marginal cost pricing. This second avenue relies on the apparently unanimous conclusion of empirical investigators of the cost function of the firm, that AC curves are not, in fact, characterized by a unique minimum point as they would be if they had a smooth U shape. Rather, these investigators tell us, the AC curve of reality has a flat bottom—an interval along which it is horizontal. That is, average costs do tend to fall at first with size of output, then they reach a minimum and continue at that level for some range of outputs, after which they may begin to rise once more. An AC curve of this variety is shown in Figure 3. Obviously, such a flat segment of the AC curves *does* help matters because there is now a *range* of outputs over which MC pricing yields zero profits. Moreover, the longer the flat-bottomed segment the better matters are for existence of equilibrium. Indeed, it is easy to show that if the left-hand end of the flat segment occurs at output y^m and the right-hand end occurs at ky_m, then if k is greater than or equal to 2 the existence problem disappears altogether, because the industry's AC curves will be horizontal for any output greater than y_m. That

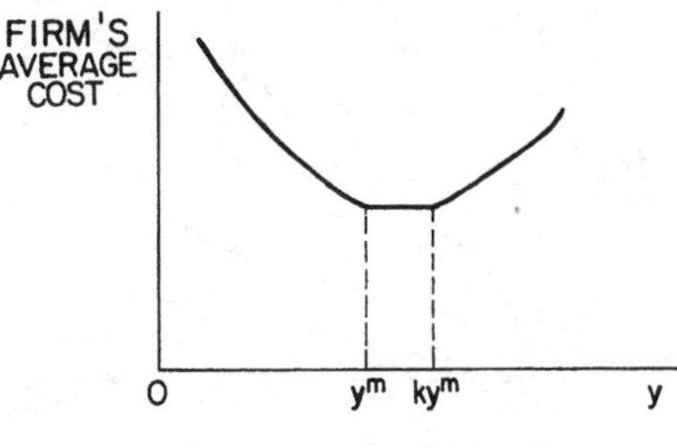

FIGURE 3

is, in any contestable market in which two or more firms operate the industry AC curve will be horizontal and MC pricing will always yield zero profits. To confirm that this is so, note that if, for example, the flat segment for the firm extends from $y = 1,000$ to $y = 2,000$, then any industry output of, say, $9,000 + \Delta y$ where $0 \leqslant \Delta y \leqslant 9,000$ can be produced by nine firms, each of them turning out more than 1,000 but less than 2,000 units. Hence, each of them will operate along the horizontal portion of its AC curve, as equilibrium requires.

Thus, if the horizontal interval (y^m, ky_m) happens to satisfy $k \geqslant 2$, there is no longer any problem for existence of equilibrium in a contestable market with two or more firms. But fate may not always be so kind. What if that horizontal interval is quite short, that is, k is quite close to unity? Such a case is shown in our diagram where for illustration I have taken $k = 4/3$.

I should like to take advantage of your patience by dealing here not with the simplest case—that of the single product industry—but with the multiproduct problem. I do this partly to offer you some feeling of the way in which the multiproduct analysis, which is one of the hallmarks of our study, works out in practice.

Because, as we have seen, there is no way one can measure average cost for all output combinations in the multiproduct case, I will deal exclusively with the total cost function. Figure 4 shows such a total cost function for the single firm, which is taken to manufacture two products, boots and shoes.

Let us pause briefly to examine its shape. Along any ray such as OR, which keeps

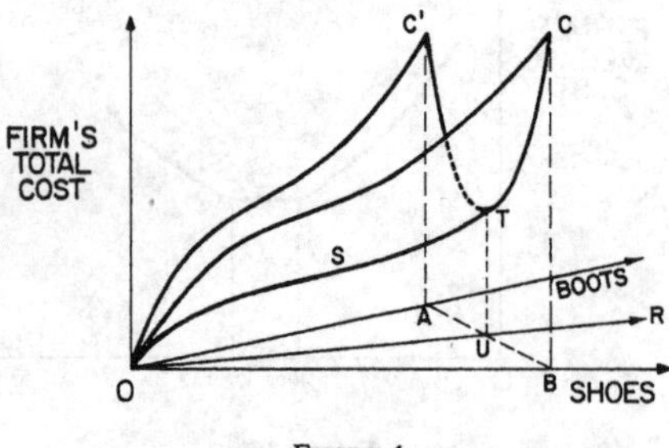

FIGURE 4

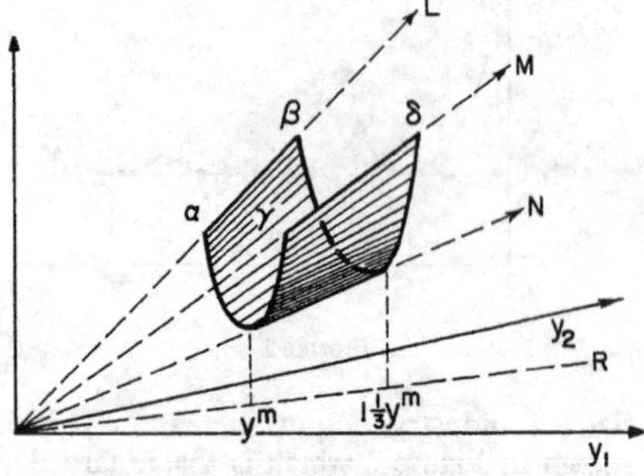

FIGURE 5

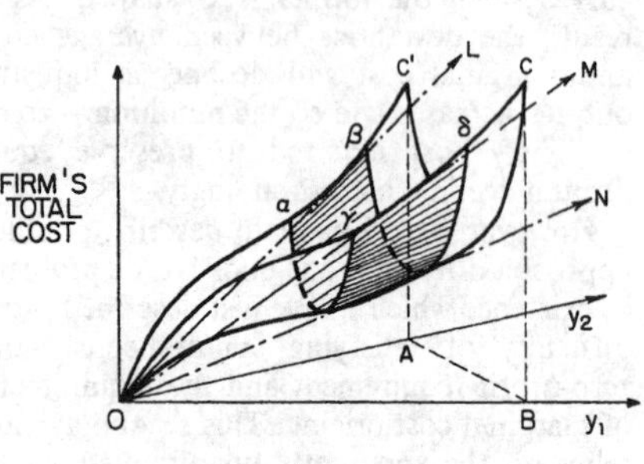

FIGURE 6

output proportions constant, we have an ordinary total cost curve, *OST*. With one exception, which I will note soon, I have drawn it to have the usual sort of shape, with marginal costs falling near the origin and rising at points much further from the origin. On the other hand, the trans ray cut above *AB* yields a cross section *C′TC* which is more or less U shaped. This means that it is relatively cheaper to produce boots and shoes together (point *U*) than to produce them in isolation (point *A* or point *B*). That is, this convex trans ray shape is enough to offer us the complementarity which leads firms and industries to turn out a multiplicity of products rather than specializing in the production of a single good.

Now what, in such a case, corresponds to the flat bottom of an *AC* curve in a single product case? The answer is that the cost function in the neighborhood of the corresponding output must be linearly homogeneous. In Figure 5 such a region, $\alpha\beta\gamma\delta$, is depicted. It is linearly homogeneous because it is generated by a set of rays such as *L*, *M*, and *N*. For simplicity in the discussion that follows, I have given this region a very regular shape—it is, approximately, a rectangle which has been moved into three-dimensional space and given a U-shaped cross section.

Now Figure 6 combines the two preceding diagrams and we see that they have been drawn to mesh together, so that the linearly homogeneous region constitutes a portion of the firm's total cost surface. We see then that the firm's total cost does have a region in which constant returns to scale occur, and which corresponds to the flat-bottomed segment of the *AC* curve.

Moreover, as before, I have deliberately kept this segment quite narrow. Indeed, I have repeated the previous proportions, letting the segment extend from a distance y^m from the origin to the distance $1\frac{1}{3}y^m$ along any ray on the floor of the diagram.

Let us now see what happens in these circumstances when we turn to the total cost surface for the *industry*. This is depicted in Figure 7 which shows a relationship that may at first seem surprising. In Figure 7 I depict only the linearly homogeneous portions of the industry's cost surface. There we see that while for the firm linear homogeneity prevailed only in the interval from y^m to $1\frac{1}{3}y^m$, in the case of industry output linear homogeneity also holds in that same interval but, in addition, it holds for the interval $2y^m$ to $2\frac{2}{3}y^m$ and in the region extending from $3y^m$ to infinity. That is, everywhere beyond $3y^m$ the industry's total cost function is linearly homogeneous. In this case, then, we have three regions of local linear homogene-

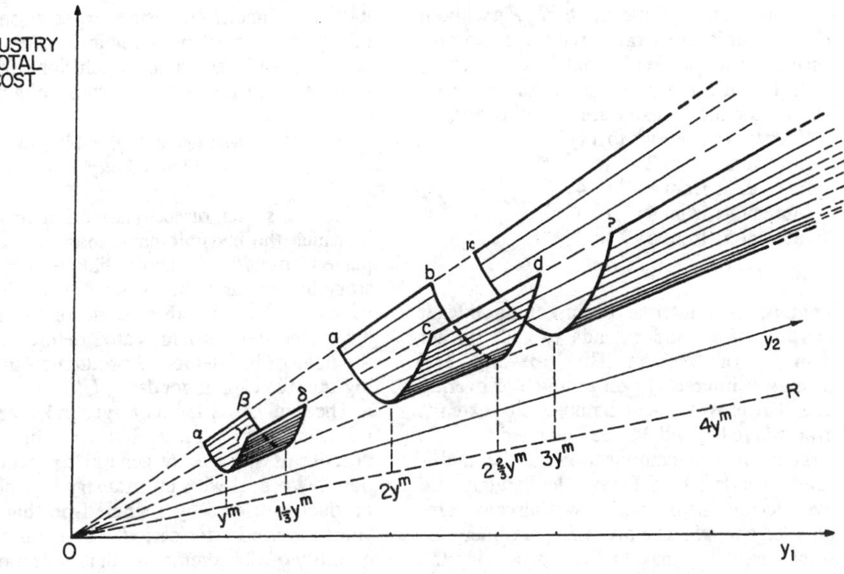

FIGURE 7

ity in the industry's cost function, $\alpha\beta\gamma\delta$, which is identical with that of the individual firm, the larger region *abcd*, and the infinite region *aleph beth*....

Before showing why this is so we must pause to note the implications of the exercise. For it means that even a relatively small region of flatness in the AC curve of the individual firm, that is, of linear homogeneity in its total cost function, eliminates the bulk of the existence problem for oligopoly equilibrium in a contestable market. The problem does not arise for outputs nearer to the origin than y_m because such outputs are supplied most efficiently by a monopoly which is not required to price at marginal cost in a contestable market equilibrium. The problem also does not arise for any industry output greater than $3y^m$ in this case, because everywhere beyond that marginal cost pricing yields zero profits. There are two relatively narrow regions in which no equilibrium is, indeed, possible, but here we may conjecture that the vicissitudes of disequilibrium will cause shifts in the demand relationships as changing prices and changing consumption patterns affect tastes, and so the industry will ultimately happen upon an equilibrium position and remain there until exogenous disturbances move it away. Thus we end up with an oligopoly equilibrium whose prices, profits, and other attributes are determined without benefit of the conjectural variation, reaction functions, and the other paraphernalia of standard oligopoly analysis.

To complete this discussion of oligopoly equilibrium in a contestable market, it only remains for me to explain why the regions of linear homogeneity in the industry's cost function are as depicted in Figure 7. The answer is straightforward. Let $C(y)$ be the firm's total cost function for which we have assumed for expository simplicity that in the interval from y^m to $1\frac{1}{3}y^m$ along each and every ray, total cost grows exactly proportionately with output. Then two firms can produce $2y^m$ at the same unit cost, and three firms can produce $3y^m$ at that same unit cost for the given output bundle, etc. But by exactly the same argument, the two firms together, each producing no more than $1\frac{1}{3}y^m$, can turn out anything up to $2\frac{2}{3}y^m$ without affecting unit costs, and three firms can produce as much as $3\frac{3}{3}y^m$, that is, as much as $4y^m$. In sum, the intervals of linear homogeneity for the industry are the following:

Interval 1: from y^m to $1\frac{1}{3}y^m$
Interval 2: from $2y^m$ to $2\frac{2}{3}y^m$
Interval 3: from $3y^m$ to $4y^m$
Interval 4: from $4y^m$ to $5\frac{1}{3}y^m$
Interval 5: from $5y^m$ to $6\frac{2}{3}y^m$
. . . .

That is, each interval begins at an integer multiple of y^m and extends $1/3\ y^m$ further than its predecessor. Thus, beyond $3y^m$ successive intervals begin to touch or overlap and that is why linear homogeneity extends everywhere beyond $3y^m$ as I claimed.[3]

There is one complication in the multiproduct case which I have deliberately slid over, feeling the discussion was already complicated enough. The preceding argument assumes implicitly that the firms producing the industry output all employ the same output proportions as those in the industry output vector. For otherwise, it is not legitimate to move outward along a single ray as the number of firms is increased. But suppose increased industry output were to permit savings through increased specialization. Might there not be constant returns with fixed output proportions and yet economies of scale for the industry overall? This problem is avoided by our complementarity assumption used to account for the industry's multiproduct operation—our U-shaped trans-ray cross section. This, in effect, rules out such savings from specialization in the regions where linear homogeneity also rules out savings from increased scale.

This, then, completes my discussion of oligopoly equilibrium in perfectly contestable markets, which we have seen, yields a determinate set of prices and outputs that is not dependent upon assumptions about the nature of incumbent firm's expectations relating to entrants' behavior and offers us a concrete and favorable conclusion on the welfare implications of contestable oligopoly.

III. Intertemporal Vulnerability to Inefficient Entry

Having so far directed attention to areas in which the invisible hand manifests unexpected strength, I should like to end my story by dealing with an issue in relation to which it is weaker than some of us might have expected. As I indicated before, this is the issue of intertemporal production involving durable capital goods.

The analysis is far more general than the following story suggests, but even the case I describe is sufficiently general to make the point. We deal with an industry in which a product is offered by a single firm that provides it period after period. The equilibrium quantity of the commodity that is demanded grows steadily with the passage of time in a manner that is foreseen without uncertainty. Because of economies of scale in the production of capacity the firm deliberately builds some excess capacity to take care of anticipated growth in sales volume. But there is some point, let us say, $z=45$ years in the future, such that it would be uneconomic to take further growth in sales volume into account in the initial choice of capacity. This is so because the opportunity (interest) cost of the capacity that remains idle for 45 or more years exceeds the savings made possible by the economies of scale of construction. Thus, after 45 years it will pay the firm to undertake a second construction project to build the added capacity needed to produce the goods demanded of it.

Suppose that in every particular period our producer is a natural monopolist, that is, he produces the industry's supply of its one commodity at a cost lower than it can be done by any two or more enterprises. Then considering that same product in different periods to be formally equivalent to different goods we may take our supplier to be an intertemporal natural monopolist in a multiproduct industry. That is, no combination of

[3] The reader can readily generalize this result. If the flat-bottomed segment for the firm extends from y^m to $y^m(1+1/w)$, where w is an integer, then there will be w regions of linear homogeneity in the industry cost function and it will be linearly homogeneous for any output $y \geqslant wy^m$.

two or more firms can produce the industry's intertemporal output vector as cheaply as he. I will prove now under a set of remarkably unrestrictive assumptions that despite its cost advantages, there exists no intertemporal price vector consistent with equilibrium for this firm. That is, whatever his price vector, his market will at some time be vulnerable to partial or complete takeover by an entrant who has neither superior skills nor technological superiority and whose entrance increases the quantities of resources used up in production. In other words, here the invisible hand proves incapable of protecting the most efficient producing arrangement and leaves the incumbent producer vulnerable to displacement by an aggressive entrant. I leave to your imaginations what, if anything, this says about the successive displacements on the world market of the Dutch by the English, the English by the Germans and the Americans, and the Americans, perhaps, by the Japanese.

The proof of our proposition on the intertemporal vulnerability of incumbents to entry that is premature from the viewpoint of cost minimization does require just a little bit of algebra. To keep our analysis simple, I will divide time into two periods, each lasting $z=45$ years so that capacity in the first period is, optimally, just sufficient to satisfy all demand, but in the second, it requires the construction of added capacity to meet demand growth because, by assumption, anticipatory construction to meet growth more than z years in the future simply is too costly. Also for simplicity, I will assume that there are no costs other than cost of construction. Of course, neither this nor the use of only two periods really affects the argument in any way. My only three substantive assumptions are that demand is growing with time, that there are economies of scale, that is, declining average costs in construction, and that there exists some length of time, z, so great that it does not pay in the initial construction to build capacity sufficient for the growth in quantity demanded that will occur beyond that date.

The argument, like the notation, is now straightforward. Let y_t be output in period t, p_t be price in period t, and $K(y)$ be the cost of construction of capacity sufficient to produce (a maximum of) y units per period. Here, both p_t and $K(y)$ are expressed in discounted present value.[4]

Then, by assumption, our firm will construct at the beginning of the first period capacity just sufficient to produce output y_1 at cost $K(y_1)$ and at the beginning of the second period it will produce the rest of the capacity it needs, $y_2-y_1>0$, at the cost $K(y_2-y_1)$.

The first requirement for the prices in question to be consistent with equilibrium is that they permit the incumbent to cover his costs, that is, that

$$(1)\quad p_1y_1+p_2y_2 \geqslant K(y_1)+K(y_2-y_1).$$

Second, for these prices to constitute an equilibrium they must protect the incumbent against any and all possible incursions by entrants. That is, suppose an entrant were to consider the possibility of constructing capacity y_1 and not expanding in the future, and, by undercutting the incumbent, selling the same output, y_1, in each period. Entry on these terms will in fact be profitable unless the prices are such that the sale of y_1 in each period does not bring in revenues sufficient to cover the cost, $K(y_1)$, of the entrant's once-and-for-all construction. That is, entry will be profitable unless

$$(2)\qquad p_1y_1+p_2y_1 \leqslant K(y_1).$$

Thus, the prices in question cannot constitute an equilibrium unless (2) as well as (1) are satisfied.

Now, subtracting (2) from (1) we obtain immediately

$$p_2(y_2-y_1) \geqslant K(y_2-y_1)$$

or

$$(3)\qquad p_2 \geqslant K(y_2-y_1)/(y_2-y_1),$$

[4]That is, if p_1^*, p_2^*, represent the undiscounted prices, $p_1=p_1^*$, $p_2=p_2^*/(1+r)$, where r is the rate of interest, etc.

but, by the assumption that average construction cost is declining, since $y_1 > 0$,

$$(4) \quad K(y_2 - y_1)/(y_2 - y_1) > K(y_2)/y_2.$$

Substituting this into (3) we have at once

$$p_2 > K(y_2)/y_2$$

or

$$(5) \qquad p_2 y_2 > K(y_2).$$

Inequality (5) is our result. For it proves that any prices which satisfy equilibrium requirements (1) and (2) must permit a second-period entrant using the same techniques to build capacity y_2 from the ground up, at cost $K(y_2)$, to price slightly below anything the incumbent can charge and yet recover his costs; and that in doing so, the entrant can earn a profit.

Thus, our intertemporal natural monopolist cannot quote, *at time zero*, any prices capable of preventing the takeover of some or all of his market. Moreover, this is so despite the waste, in the form of replication of the incumbent's plant, that this entails. That, then, is the end of the formal argument, the proof that here the invisible hand manifests weakness that is, perhaps, unexpected.

You will all undoubtedly recognize that the story as told here in its barest outlines omits all sorts of nuances, such as entrants' fear of responsive pricing, the role of bankruptcy, depreciation of capital, and the like. This is not the place to go into these matters for it is neither possible nor appropriate here for me to go beyond illustration of the logic of the new analysis.

IV. Concluding Comments

Before closing let me add a word on policy implications, whose details must also be left to another place. In spirit, the policy conclusions are consistent with many of those economists have long been espousing. At least in the intratemporal analysis, the heroes are the (unidentified) potential entrants who exercise discipline over the incumbent, and who do so most effectively when entry is free. In the limit, when entry and exit are completely free, efficient incumbent monopolists and oligopolists may in fact be able to prevent entry. But they can do so only by behaving virtuously, that is, by offering to consumers the benefits which competition would otherwise bring. For every deviation from good behavior instantly makes them vulnerable to hit-and-run entry.

This immediately offers what may be a new insight on antitrust policy. It tells us that a history of absence of entry in an industry and a high concentration index may be signs of virtue, not of vice. This will be true when entry costs in our sense are negligible. And, then, efforts to change market structure must be regarded as mischievous and antisocial in their effects.

A second and more obvious conclusion is the questionable desirability of artificial impediments to entry, such as regulators were long inclined to impose. The new analysis merely reinforces the view that any proposed regulatory barrier to entry must start off with a heavy presumption against its adoption. Perhaps a bit newer is the emphasis on the importance of freedom of exit which is as crucial a requirement of contestability as is freedom of entry. Thus we must reject as perverse the propensity of regulators to resist the closing down of unprofitable lines of activity. This has even gone so far as a Congressional proposal (apparently supported by Ralph Nader) to require any plant with yearly sales exceeding $250,000 to provide fifty-two weeks of severance pay and to pay three years of taxes, before it will be permitted to close, and that only after giving two years notice!

There is much more to the policy implications of the new theory, but I will stop here, also leaving its results relating to empirical research for discussion elsewhere.

Let me only say in closing that I hope I have adequately justified my characterization of the new theory as a rebellion or an uprising. I believe it offers a host of new analytical methods, new tasks for empirical research, and new results. It permits reexamination of the domain of the invisible hand, yields contributions to the theory of oligopoly, provides a standard for policy that is far broader and more widely applicable than that of perfect competition, and leads to a theory that analyzes the determination of industry structure endogenously and simultaneously with the analysis of the other variables more traditionally treated in the theory of the firm and the industry. It aspires to provide no less than a unifying theory as a foundation for the analysis of industrial organization. I will perhaps be excused for feeling that this was an ambitious undertaking.

REFERENCES

Bain, Joe S., *Barriers to New Competition*, Cambridge: Harvard University Press, 1956.

Baumol, William J., Bailey, Elizabeth E., and Willig, Robert D., "Weak Invisible Hand Theorems on the Sustainability of Multiproduct Natural Monopoly," *American Economic Review*, June 1977, *67*, 350–65.

______, Panzar, John C., and Willig, Robert D., *Contestable Markets and the Theory of Industry Structure*, San Diego: Harcourt Brace Jovanovich, 1982.

Bertrand, Jules, Review of *Théorie Mathematique de la Richesse* and *Récherches sur les Principes Mathèmatiques de la théorie des Richesses*, *Journal des Savants*, 1883, 499–508.

Cournot, A. A., *Researches into the Mathematical Principles of the Theory of Wealth*, New York: A. M. Kelley, 1938; 1960.

Demsetz, Harold, "Why Regulate Utilities?," *Journal of Law and Economics*, April 1968, *11*, 55–65.

Fama, Eugene F. and Laffer, Arthur B., "The Number of Firms and Competition," *American Economic Review*, September 1972, *62*, 670–74.

Panzar, John C. and Willig, Robert D., "Free Entry and the Sustainability of Natural Monopoly," *Bell Journal of Economics*, Spring 1977, *8*, 1–22.

ten Raa, Thijs, "A Theory of Value and Industry Structure," unpublished doctoral dissertation, New York University, 1980.

Reprinted from

THE AMERICAN ECONOMIC REVIEW

[9]

ON THE PERILS OF PRIVATIZATION

William J. Baumol

C.V. Starr Center for Applied Economics, New York University and Princeton University

> The bureaucracy often conceives that...a mind [capable of drawing up a faultless and exhaustive economic plan] is at its disposal; that is why it so easily frees itself from the control of the market.
>
> — Leon Trotsky

Just a year or two ago privatization was widely regarded as the true panacea for many of the world's economies. The countries of the British Commonwealth joined the former Soviet nations and those of Latin America in the attempt to toss their nationalized industries, naked, into the marketplace. The market appeared to be accepted as the elixir that would transform moribund industries into gushing sources of abundance, and would do so overnight. Now, many are no longer so sure. Poland and the Czech Republic seem to have remained faithful, at least until recently, when the Polish Parliament rejected a critical piece of privatizing legislation. But in the United Kingdom regulators are interceding between the market forces and newly privatized firms; in New Zealand the courts are intervening; in Puerto Rico at least some privatization attempts have been called off; and in more than one former Soviet land, victory at the polls either has gone or threatens to go to representatives of the *ancien régime*, presumably an indicator of growing public disenchantment with moves toward a market economy.

The fact is that privatization has proved to be less easy to carry out and less magical in its accomplishments than seems earlier to have been believed. Disappointment has been engendered by the slow pace of privatization, the accompanying reduction in jobs, the wealth accumulated by those who are successful at the task, and the apparently long delays before its benefits emerge. These difficulties, of course, are the result of illusion and misunderstanding by the public. They do not recognize that even in the miracle economies of the Far East decades were required before the invested effort began to display fruit of noticeable dimensions. Nor is it recognized that efficiency and competitiveness require elimination of redundant jobs and that the market's incentive mechanism is founded upon the prospects of wealth for those who succeed. Never having recognized these less prepossessing attributes of the market mechanism, the public is understandably distressed when they show themselves.

Perhaps most disturbing, however, is the propensity of even well-intentioned public servants to sabotage the process. It is they who are likely to have made the privatized firm into a monopoly. It is they who, believing that they are encouraging competition, create what are, in effect, governmentally sponsored cartels, in which there coexist many enterprises, each of which is prohibited from competing with the

Eastern Economic Journal, Vol. 19, No. 4, Fall 1993

others, and in which the most inefficient of the firms in the industry are kept alive at the consumer's expense by impediments to price reductions by more efficient rivals. It is the bureaucrats who, paying lip service to the market mechanism, but often distrusting it profoundly, seek to take away the power of the privatized firms to make decisions for themselves, under the constraining influence of market forces. Finally, it is they who are prone to restrict the profits of the privatized firms and the incomes of their entrepreneurs, without recognizing that they are thereby destroying the very engine that can in time yield the benefits so widely expected to flow from privatization.

The central issue here, of course, is what government should and what it should not do if privatization is to have a chance of fulfilling its earlier promise. The first part of the discussion will focus on privatization in the venerable market economies such as the U.K., New Zealand or France. Then, it will turn to the very different problems in the economies in transition from central to market control.

A FEW WORDS ON THE MARKET MECHANISM

Economists recognize a number of critical features of the market mechanism of which the general public is unaware. There is, however, one crucial attribute of the market in which, in my view, the nonspecialists have a more accurate view of the workings of the market than do many members of our profession.

The public does not seem to recognize that the market serves the consumer effectively and is able to produce its abundance by virtue of its merciless system of rewards and penalties. The impersonal forces of the market accept no excuse for failure, and bankruptcy is their prescribed penalty. The market is also discomfortingly generous in its rewards to those who succeed in serving the public with the products that it wants at costs as low as are currently attainable. Here it does not distinguish merit; the firm that simply stumbles on a popular new product is rewarded as handsomely as the one that invested long and heavily in product development. Efficiency may be repaid even if it is just the result of the happenstance that the enterprise is large and is in an industry that offers economies of scale and scope.

Misapprehensions on these subjects tempt the public to clamor for the imposition of limits on the wealth of those whose are most successful. They elicit political support for public sector rescue of failing enterprises and dying industries. Above all, they engender opprobrium for those driven by greed to conquer new economic worlds and expand the economic horizon. One cannot quarrel with such preferences. But one can deplore the public's failure to recognize that it cannot have things both ways.

Where, in my opinion, the nonspecialist does have the better grasp of the market is in identifying its main accomplishment. We economists have been prone to emphasize its power to achieve static allocative efficiency and have tended to conclude because of spillovers of innovation and for other oft-discussed reasons, that it is rather defective as an engine of growth. The view in the former Soviet economies is very different. There, the contrast between the economic abundance of the free-enterprise economies and their own poverty is probably the most pressing reason for their admiration of the market. Static efficiency is not the focus. Rather, despite defection from other Marxist ideas, there remains agreement with the judgment of Marx and Engels that "The bourgeoisie, during its rule of scarce one hundred years, has created more massive and more colossal productive forces than have all previous generations together" [the *Communist Manifesto*]. Historical evidence supports this view abundantly.

THE VENERABLE MARKET ECONOMIES: DEFEAT FROM THE JAWS OF VICTORY

The Tendency To Monopoly in Western Firms Picked for Privatizing

Thus, those who view the market as a means to improve the flow of abundance have solid grounds for the belief that output and efficiency can be enhanced greatly by a transfer of nationalized firms from the stultifying control of government to the tender mercies of the market. Yet, this transfer seems often to be accompanied by the erection of impediments to the productive contribution of the privatized enterprises. I will argue now that this is hardly fortuitous.

In the older market economies the key problem is the considerable proportion of the candidates for privatization that are firms with monopoly attributes, for which there are at least four reasons, none of them accidental.

Monopolies as Targets of Previous Nationalization. In the free-enterprise economies, it is the monopolies and near monopolies that have been prime targets of takeover by government because it has long been recognized that market forces are apt to be incapable of constraining them effectively. Consequently, when it was proposed to return nationalized firms to the private sector it is not surprising that a considerable proportion of the candidates held either a monopoly position or a position that seemed to confer some degree of monopoly power. This is notably true of the public utilities — the suppliers of electricity, gas, and telecommunications in Latin America and Europe.

Management's Desire for Protection from Competition. A second powerful influence that skewed public enterprises toward monopoly has been the predictable behavior of their public sector managements. Most persons enthusiastically favor competition when it affects others, but not when it constrains themselves and invariably makes their lives more difficult. Bureaucrats are no exception, but they are in a better position than most to make their wish come true. A governmentally owned utility is often protected by law from all but the most insignificant forms of rivalry. The state telephone company, the post office and the electricity supplier are generally secured from the threat of entry — by government decree.

A Monopoly's Assets Command Higher Prices. When a nationalized firm is put up for sale, those who are responsible for overseeing the transaction are likely to consider themselves obligated for the sake of the public interest to seek to obtain for the property as high a price as can be gotten. But it is obvious that higher price bids can be elicited if the property is offered along with a monopoly license that is protected against the entry of rivals. This temptation is sometimes too great to resist, with the consequence that the newly private firm enters the economy with the grant of a monopoly. But it is not often acknowledged by the government that this automatically entails the threat of close regulation in the future.

Competition Undermines Popular Cross Subsidies. A fourth and more subtle influence skews the nationalized firms toward possession of monopoly power. The agencies that run them, like the regulators in the United States, have strongly and persistently favored a policy known in the business as "universal service." They are moved in this direction by an amalgam of natural inclination and political pressure. Particularly where the firm in question is a public utility and its product is widely desired, it has been considered bad policy to require classes of consumers whom it is particularly difficult to supply to pay the high cost of serving them. It was deemed appropriate for the same price per unit to be offered to everyone — to isolated farmers who could be reached by telephone only by long and underutilized stretches of wire, to inner city firms to which mail delivery costs are increased by congestion, crime and other impediments, and to any other user whose service is extraordinarily difficult and expensive. More than that, some nationalized services such as telecommunications are less costly to deliver to large firms because of the scale economies available in such transactions than to small-volume residential customers. Dedication to universal service impelled those who control nationalized enterprises to price the residential services at levels considerably lower than what the relative cost of serving those customers appeared to require. Characteristically, all this ended up in a complex system of cross subsidies, with the supplier of electricity, for example, required to charge big business customers prices sufficiently high to yield the revenues that could cover losses incurred in serving isolated farmers or inner city user firms or household customers in general.

Nothing in the preceding paragraph is to be construed to imply that these cross subsidies are indefensible or that their social purposes are unworthy. Rather, the point is that such cross subsidies are incompatible with competition and freedom of entry. An electricity supplier that overprices, relative to the pertinent costs, the power it supplies to large business customers, and supplies electricity to farmers at a loss, can continue to do so only as long as it possesses an unchallenged monopoly.

But if the field is opened to entrants, those new rivals are likely to spring up soon enough and to focus their efforts upon sales to the highly profitable business customers. The monopoly incumbent can be expected to denounce this selective entry strategy as "cream skimming," but it is precisely what economists usually hope the entrants will do. The result, of course, is that the high profits of the business segment of the market will soon be forced down by competitive pressure, and the original incumbent will find itself deprived of the source of funds out of which it previously made up for the losses incurred in serving rural firms and households. The cross subsidy must come to an end either by choice of the original incumbent firm or as the result of its bankruptcy. To avoid this, those who set the rules for the operation of nationalized firms, like the regulators in the U.S., found a variety of reasons for the prohibition of competition and entry. This influence, too, contributed to the high frequency with which candidates for privatization turned out to be monopolies. It is an influence that, as we will see, continues to haunt the process of privatization, and even its sequel, in the West.

The Tendency to Tight Regulation of the Privatized Firms

The result of all this is that when a government enterprise is transferred to private ownership it often finds itself suspect. Its goals are often taken to be exploitation of the public and subversion of competition, and it is widely prejudged to have the power to attain those goals. The forces of the market are deemed, sometimes with good reason, to be too weak to constrain that enterprise adequately. Hence, private it may be permitted to become, but only under the heavy hand of regulation. Individuals are allowed to *own* it but they are given little opportunity to *control* it.

In practice, in Western economies problems at this stage seem to have arisen primarily from inexperience with economic regulation, its pitfalls, and the practices that will keep its social costs within reasonable bounds. The nations that have substantial numbers of nationalized firms to be privatized are obviously those which in the past have chosen nationalization over regulation as the instrument for control of monopoly power. Thus, it is hardly accidental that the privatizing economies are the ones least prepared by experience to institute and carry out a rational regulatory regime. In the process they have tended to want to learn for themselves, many of them possessing a very competent civil service, experienced and effective business managers and a group of highly qualified economists. Yet, in a number of cases, they have simply repeated many of the mistakes of U.S. regulation that it has taken decades to begin to ameliorate.

Perhaps the central error besetting the process has been what amounts to complete distrust of the market on the part of the novice regulators, even those who consider themselves to be avid partisans of the free enterprise system. They do believe that *elsewhere in the economy* the market does a good job of directing business activity in accord with the general welfare, but they seem to feel that the market loses all of those salutary powers to circumscribe the firm under the regulator's oversight. The regulatory agency resists attempts to offer any significant range of discretion to the management of the privatized firm in making its economic decisions.

Prices, accounting methods, perhaps investment and other decisions are constrained closely, so that the firm may be left with less freedom to act and the market may be given hardly more influence over those acts than they possessed when the enterprise was a property of the government. For then the firms were run by bureaucrats whose actions were supposedly driven by devotion to the public interest, while once privatized they are in the hands of individuals believed to be driven only by greed. Thus, the private owners, on this view, must be restricted even more tightly than their public sector predecessors had been. In these circumstances it should cause little surprise that the market provides less of the benefits to that industry than might have been expected of it, for the market forces have for all practical purposes been exiled from the arena.

Recipes for Misguided Regulation

One encounters in some form in the regulation of the newly privatized enterprises virtually all of what economists consider to be the mistakes that had long plagued regulation in the United States. Thus, the following list of questionable actions will seem familiar to those who have studied American regulatory history. These include (1) prevention or limitation of effective competition, (2) ossification of cross subsidy, (3) use of cartelization and other inefficient devices to protect competitors at the expense of competition, (4) injection of costly and avoidable regulatory risk, (5) restriction of freedom of decision making by management even within limits competitive conditions would permit, (6) use of discredited criteria such as fully distributed cost for regulation of prices. This list is readily extended, but it is already sufficiently long to illustrate the point.

Prevention or Limitation of Effective Competition. One of the central problems that has plagued the adoption of rational regulatory policy has been the conflict between two of its goals — the encouragement of competition and the promotion of "universal service." The desire to nurture competition in the privatized arenas is, of course, the natural consequence of the fear of monopoly power that underlies the decision to regulate. Competition, if it can be introduced and expanded, is the obvious way to put an end to monopoly power and to limit its exercise. But two problems beset this approach. First, the mere introduction of additional firms into the market is no guarantee of effective competition or of any competition at all, either if market or technological conditions such as scale economies impede or preclude it, or if regulatory restrictions all but prevent competition. Second, as we have just seen, effective competition is incompatible with retention of the cross subsidies that are valued so highly by many regulators. This has been known to impel regulators to adopt rules that protect the cross subsidies by undermining or prohibiting competition.

Thus, in a recent report on privatization in the U.K.[1] *The Economist* tells us that

> More subtly, the government has modified its policy. The original plan was to open [rail] passenger services to competition...[with] trains...run by franchised providers, offering competing services on each line....The government is backing away from that. Its fear is that the entrepreneurs would pick the best peak-time services. Off peak services would be left to British Rail, or disappear altogether.
>
> So ....Only on a few routes will "open access" (that is, competition) be allowed. Even in those cases, the core service will be provided by one operator who will be eligible for government subsidy. Any other operator running a train on the route will have to compete without subsidy....

> [Another] big privatization, that of **the Post Office**, could soon get a green light....[But ministers] worry that privatization threatens the universal postal rate, which ensures that it costs the same to post a letter to any part of Britain. [1993, 53]

Ossification of Cross Subsidy. British Rail and the British Post Office are by no means the only organizations for which policymakers have undertaken to preserve the historic cross subsidies. In postal service the uniformity of charges, regardless of distance or cost of delivery, is widely considered sacred, and one can hardly imagine a privatized post office anywhere that stands a good chance of being freed from this restriction. However, it applies to other arenas as well, and in some of these, different approaches have been taken by the regulators. That is, they have not all sought to protect the monopoly or the monopoly power of the private firm, as is at least contemplated for some industries in the U.K.

Thus, in New Zealand, when the telephone company, New Zealand Telecom, was transferred to private hands, a condition of the sale was that the firm taking over the company from the government continue the price advantages the nationalized predecessor firm had offered to residential subscribers. This stipulation, referred to as "the Kiwi Share," is believed to entail losses in the supply of at least some of the residential services. That is, those services are said to bring in revenues at the Kiwi-Share prices that fall short of the incremental costs of the services in question. Profitability of the enterprise then requires a cross subsidy from other customers of New Zealand Telecom, presumably the business subscriber. This has led to litigation with Clear Communications, the new rival of Telecom, as to whether Clear should somehow bear part of the cost burden. More to the point for the current discussion, such enshrined cross subsidies seem to have had marked effects on the prices of services other than those that the universal service goal seeks to promote, and those prices may well have been driven far out of line with those that economic efficiency requires.[2]

Imposed Cartelization. Despite the fact that continued monopoly permits retention of the cross subsidies, the monopolistic character of many of the privatized firms has elicited a schizophrenic reaction from regulators. Since monopoly is accepted as an evil, many of them have undertaken to destroy it by the introduction of competitors into the regulated industry. But apparently driven by a desire, conscious or unconscious, to have it both ways, they have in at least some cases ended up with an arrangement entailing a multiplicity of firms as well as continued cross subsidy. In what *appears* to be a compromise they have carried out what in the U.S. courts has been described as "protecting competitors while undermining competition." This they have done by imposing some form of cartel arrangement upon the industry, one in which continued coexistence of two or more firms is ensured, but none is given the freedom to compete with the others in prices and related matters.

This is sometimes accomplished in subtle ways. For example, the price ceilings imposed on British Telecom have resulted in very low prices on rental of telephone lines for which the company felt forced to make up by means of high prices on number and duration of calls. Large business customers normally keep their lines very busy with calls, resulting in a high call/line ratio, so that this pricing arrangement made it difficult for British Telecom to compete for business customers with its relatively unregulated rival, Mercury. The call/line ratio pattern is reversed for residential and small business users, so that Telecom found itself with a considerable price advantage in this segment of the market. The result was virtually a split market, with Mercury in effect assigned the large-volume business customers, and there granted near immunity from competition, while Telecom found itself in the same position in the residential market. It was as though Mercury had been assigned an exclusive license for operation in Scotland, and Telecom had received the franchise for Wales.

The net cost to society of imposition of a cartel arrangement is likely to be high. It clearly does little or nothing to curtail monopoly power. In addition, it creates inefficiencies that a monopoly is likely to avoid, for any particular segment of the market may not happen to be assigned to the firm that can serve it at lowest cost. Moreover, in a cartel there may be costly replication of facilities, and facilities that are withdrawn from service by each firm because of the limited market segment assigned to it may not be those that are the most inefficient in the industry. That is, plant *A* of firm *X* that is shut down may be more efficient than firm *Y*'s plant *B* that continues in operation. Yet the regulator whose actions have created such a cartel is likely to congratulate himself for having injected competition into the arena without endangering universal service.

Imposition of Avoidable Regulatory Risk. Risk is costly to firms, and that cost is usually passed on to consumers, at least in part. In addition to the risks that normally face an enterprise, the regulated firm faces the danger that regulators will change their minds unpredictably, causing costly and avoidable errors in the regulated firms' decisions. This is true of all regulation but it affects privatized Western firms in a distinctive way.

An infant-firm argument often leads regulators to extend special protection to an entrant enterprise. The privatized firm — the earlier sole incumbent — may be required to supply services to the entrant at especially low prices, or to offer it other forms of implicit subsidy, or still other forms of protection may be provided. It is usually promised that all of these will be phased out at a suitable time, but normally no date is specified, nor is anyone told the precise circumstances under which that will occur (e.g., when the entrant's sales reach *X* percent of the industry's). No one is told whether subsidies will all be removed at once or whether it will be done gradually, and if the latter, at what rate. This has happened, for example, in the case of Mercury and British Telecom. All this imposes unnecessary uncertainty not only upon the privatized firm, *but also upon its new rival.* And as indicated, much of that cost will be borne by consumers.

Pointless Restriction Upon Management's Freedom of Decision. The large privatized firm is predictably distrusted by the regulator. Even when the latter adopts rules ostensibly designed to reduce restrictions upon management, steps will often be taken to curtail that freedom or eliminate it altogether. For example, regulation has in recent years made use of floors and ceilings upon prices, with the bounding magnitudes based in a rough and ready way upon economic analysis. This suggests that once such limits are determined the privatized firm will be left free to select the intermediate price that best suits its interests and changing market conditions. However, in my presence regulators have more than once expressed shock at the idea that management should be given such unrestricted license. They seek to narrow the firm's options further, or require a waiting period before the proposed prices can be put into effect, or subject the prices adopted to *ex post* review and penalties.

There are at least two costly consequences. First, it restores a feature of traditional regulation which has long been criticized — the delays it imposes on the decisions of the regulated firms and the resulting lag in adaptation of its decisions to evolving market conditions. Second, it all but removes the influence of the market upon the price-setting process, ensuring that privatization does not serve as an effective step toward adoption of the market mechanism as the prime guide of economic activity.

Adoption of Discredited Regulatory Criteria. The privatized firms often find themselves regulated with the aid of accounting conventions, notably *fully-distributed (fully-allocated) costs*, that are universally admitted to be arbitrary, that only by happenstance will bear the slightest resemblance to the costs economic analysis has shown to be pertinent to economically efficient decisions, that undermine incentives for innovation, and that often serve as protectionist devices inhibiting true efficiency.

Fully-allocated costs are the accountant's attempt to provide figures resembling average costs for each of the firm's products in a multi-product enterprise. The results are always arbitrary because there are typically substantial costs fixed and common to two (or more) company products, *A* and *B*, and there is no way based on the pertinent facts to determine what share of those costs is properly attributable to *A*, and what share to *B*. The result is that speciously associated criteria, e.g., the value of the output of *A* relative to that of *B*, or the relative weights of the products, are used to apportion those costs arbitrarily.

Because the resulting figures generally bear no resemblance to marginal costs or any other real and pertinent cost figures, prices based by the regulator on fully-distributed costs will generally lead to outputs, sales, investment levels, etc., that have no resemblance to those required for economic efficiency. Because those prices are set with absolutely no consideration of the different demand conditions faced by the various products, those prices will therefore often prove uncompensatory. Because such prices are "cost plus" in character, they eliminate any incentive for process innovation or other cost cutting efforts. Moreover, because of their arbitrary character, the fully-distributed cost figures lend themselves to manipulation and they have often been used in litigation before regulatory agencies by firms determined to protect themselves from the setting of low prices by more-efficient rivals. All this was experienced in the U.S. for many decades in virtually every regulatory arena. And much of this is now being reexperienced by the newly privatized enterprises in other countries.

Are More-Promising Regulatory Principles Available?

The New Regulatory Principles. Out of the discussion that has accompanied the period of deregulation in the U.S., the years since the mid-1970s, and the subsequent experience, there has emerged a new body of principles for the guidance of economic regulation. These principles are designed to minimize interference with economic efficiency, to expand the role of the market as far as seems advisable in areas of the economy where the strength of competitive forces is suspected of being inadequate and, incidentally, to reduce litigation. These principles have already been used in the U.S. in regulation of railroad freight rates, and in telecommunications pricing, and they are under discussion elsewhere. There is reason to believe that what may be dubbed "the new regulatory principles" have, at least so far, largely lived up to their promise, and lightened the burden of regulation significantly, while contributing to efficiency. It would appear that those who regulate the newly privatized industries can profit from a study of those principles.

On the Objective of Economic Regulation. This is not the place to lay those principles out in any detail, but they can be summarized rather briefly.[3] The underlying premise is that the sole purpose of economic regulation is to facilitate and encourage effective competition where that is feasible and to provide an effective substitute for competition where competition is not possible, at least for some substantial period. In a later section appropriate means for the encouragement of competition will be considered. Here I focus on the latter regulatory task, that of serving *in loco competitio* — as a substitute for the absent competitive forces.

If it is agreed that this is the proper task of the regulators, then two things follow. First, it is their obligation, in markets where the strength of competition is deemed inadequate, to constrain regulated firms to adopt only such decisions and act only in such ways that effective competition would permit if, contrary to fact, the markets were effectively competitive. Second, the regulators' role as proxy for competition requires that *they must not constrain the firms under their jurisdiction any further than this*, that is, the regulators must accept a self-denying ordinance obligating them never to prevent managements from any action that they could have carried out in an effectively competitive market.

The task of the regulator, then, consists of two parts. First, it must determine which choices competitive markets do and which they do not leave open to firms, and second, it must adopt procedures to ensure that the firms will act in a manner consistent with the competitive standard. The literature of economics provides considerable help in carrying out the first of these tasks, for it contains very substantial discussions of the behavior of competitive industries. Here, one *caveat* applies. The industries containing newly privatized firms will often be characterized by scale economies, at least up to some rather substantial level of output. Hence, a large multiplicity of firms probably will neither be feasible nor desirable, and marginal cost pricing will very likely be incompatible with solvency of the firms. Thus, the competition that serves as the standard for regulators here is not the model of perfect competition. Rather, the equally theoretical concept of perfect contestability, with its totally unimpeded freedom of entry and exit, must serve as the model because it is compatible with the presence of scale economies and the existence of only a small number of firms, and contestability theory does lay out the requirements of economic efficiency in such circumstances.

The New Rules for Price Regulation. We can now summarize very briefly the rules and principles that emerge from the analysis, providing even a short explanation only where it seems necessary:

1. In any market where there is evidence that competition is sufficiently powerful to protect the public interest, regulators should refrain from intervention.

2. In markets in which adequate competition (rather than the mere presence of a multiplicity of non-competing firms) can be stimulated, that should be done.

3. Prices should not be permitted in the long run to exceed the levels that in a perfectly competitive market would make entry profitable, entry that would subsequently drive those prices back down. These price ceilings are referred to in the literature as the "stand-alone costs" of any product or combination of products.

4. Prices should not be permitted to go below those that would be viable for any substantial period in a competitive or contestable market. This generally means that those prices should not fall short of the marginal cost of any product or the per unit incremental cost of the entire output by the firm of any homogeneous product.

5. Because in a contestable market one may encounter prices close to the stand-alone cost ceiling or the marginal-average incremental cost floor, the firm should be left free to adopt any price within these limits, adjusting that choice to current demand conditions in accord with the judgment of management.

6. Price ceilings are not to be adjusted downward immediately to correspond to any reduction in costs the regulated firm is able to achieve. Rather, in accord with the Schumpeterian model of the market's incentives for innovation and enhanced efficiency, price ceilings are to be unchanged for substantial periods, except for a built-in inflation escalator that automatically increases the ceiling in accord with some standard price index such as the consumer price index (CPI), *after subtraction of some number corresponding*

to the industry's past record of rate of reduction of cost per unit of output per year. Thus, an industry with an average record of productivity growth of 2 percent per year would, in a year when the CPI grew 6 percent, find its price ceilings increased by 4 percent, so that it would earn profits exceeding the competitive level if and only if it managed to exceed its past 2 percent productivity growth record. During a grace period of several years the firm is able to keep those profits as its reward for innovation. But, just as competition ensures in an unregulated Schumpeterian world, prices will ultimately be adjusted to eliminate the enhanced profits so that, thereafter, the benefits are passed on to consumers. This is referred to in the regulatory literature as "the price-cap" approach to rate regulation.

7. When inputs are supplied by a regulated firm, both to itself as a component of one of its final products, X, and to a competitor producer of X, then the regulated firm should charge the rival the same price for that input that the former implicitly charges to itself. This rule is called "the parity principle," "the optimal input-pricing rule" or "the profit-imputation rule." The price of the input should equal the (incremental) cost entailed in supplying it, as usual in a competitive or contestable market, *including any associated opportunity cost*. That opportunity cost, in the circumstances under discussion here, includes any profit the regulated firm forgoes by the sale of a unit of input to its rival because that permits the rival to take away some sales of final product X. Thus the price of the input to a rival should include all of the profit contribution the regulated firm obtains from the sale of a unit of final product X.

Note that many of these rules are counterintuitive to the layman. For example, the parity principle (rule 7) requires the price of a widget input, whose direct incremental cost constitutes only 2 percent of the cost of final product X, should nevertheless compensate the widget maker firm for *100 percent* of the profit it forgoes from the sales of X as a result of its supply of widgets to competitors.

These rules call for regulatory behavior very different from that often encountered by privatized firms. Characteristically, in practice less has been left to the control of the market and less freedom has been given to management. Fully distributed cost is often used, sometimes as a price floor, sometimes as a ceiling and sometimes as *the* imposed price, with marginal, incremental and stand-alone costs often mentioned in hearings but often disregarded by the regulator. Input prices, rather than following the parity principle, are often set so as to pass on part of the regulated firm's profits from the final product to its competitor that purchases the input from it. That is, the input price is not permitted to include all of the opportunity cost entailed in the sale of the input. It seems clear that all of these procedures used by regulators of privatized firms offer considerable room for improvement from the point of view of economic efficiency and utilization of the market mechanism.

IS COMPETITION REALLY POSSIBLE?

None of what has been said is intended to impugn the good intentions of those who regulate the privatized firms. Thus, when entry of a new firm has been facilitated or even elicited by the regulators, they are undoubtedly convinced that they have thereby contributed to competition, even in cases where this has occurred through the imposition of a cartel arrangement that shields the entrant from effective competitive pressures. Once entry has occurred, the regulators' dedication to competition is adjoined to their natural predisposition to ensure the survival of every enterprise under their jurisdiction, no matter how inefficient and costly to the public.

Though these views are critical, it must be conceded that those regulators do have a valid point. If it is ever to be appropriate to free the privatized firms from regulation, and thrust them, unfettered, into the free market, true competition must somehow be made viable in the arena. One is led naturally to ask, then, is this really possible? More specifically, in cases where one cannot be confident that competition will evolve by itself, or there are good grounds to fear that it will do so on too modest a scale or too slow a pace, what measures are suitable for its facilitation and encouragement? The comments that follow are offered only as provisional and rather abstract ruminations, because the evidence on these matters has not really been explored.

One can hardly dispute the standard conclusion that in fields in which scale economies are strong, universal and prevalent through all of the relevant ranges of output quantities, monopoly is "natural." That is, in these circumstances, it is unlikely that a multiplicity of firms will be able to survive, and it is, moreover, probable that their survival is undesirable. The reasons are well-known and need no repetition here.

Casual observation suggests, however, that such cases may be rare. The evidence indicates that scale economies do arise in a considerable number of industries, but that evidence relates only to a narrow range of output levels in the neighborhood of current output vectors. The econometric studies, quite understandably, provide little evidence about the range of outputs over which economies of scale and scope prevail, and offer no indication of the points at which they are exhausted. But one does notice that while oligopoly is a fairly common phenomenon, monopoly that has not been imposed by government seems rather rare. Indeed, outside a few public utilities, it is difficult to think of examples.

This would seem consistent with what empirical studies indicate — that in a number of industries scale economies are substantial, that they prevail over a considerable range of outputs, but that beyond some output levels they are replaced by approximately constant returns to scale that themselves hold over significant output ranges. This is the equivalent of the observation for the (theoretical) single-product firm that the average cost curve is more realistically taken to be flat-bottomed rather than U-shaped.

The hypothesis implicit in the preceding paragraph, then, is that among privatized industries the multiproduct equivalent of flat-bottomed average cost curves is common, but that the flat-bottomed range follows only after a considerable interval of substantial scale economies. If this hypothesis proves correct, it has implications for the prospects for competition in the privatized industries that are not necessarily in conflict with the views of regulators described earlier in this section. First, it follows that at least oligopolistic competition is very possible in these industries and that such competition can be expected to endure. Second, it suggests that successful entry is likely to require the assembly of large quantities of capital and other resources, because only firms of considerable scale will be able to compete successfully. Third, it suggests, because of the considerable region of constant returns to scale, that the successful firms in the industry need not be of similar size, and that relatively large and *relatively* small firms may be able to coexist. Finally, it follows that even the smallest firms in a long-run equilibrium in such an industry may prove to be effective competitors, able to exert a very effective constraining influence upon the pricing of the larger enterprises in the same market.

In such privatized industries it follows that at least some degree of competition can be achieved and that the eventual presence of a number of competing firms can be hoped for. If collusion can be prevented or is inherently unlikely, the prospect, even with a small number of rivals, is that the firms will compete vigorously and effectively, though such competition may make use of strategic courses of action that yield public benefits short of those expected from a perfectly competitive or contestable industry. Yet, particularly where entry requires substantial sunk investments, one cannot be fully confident that one will experience the establishment of the new firms requisite for transformation of the market into one that is highly competitive or at least highly rivalrous.

Experience suggests that such entry will in fact often take place. For example, the establishment of MCI, Sprint and other carriers in U.S. telecommunications so soon after entry was permitted suggests that private initiative will often suffice to carry out the task. Still, there are at least three reasons why it may not happen, even in arenas in which it is called for by the public interest. All of them relate to the impossibility of successful entry on a small scale in our scenario.

First, in the scenario under discussion successful entry requires the establishment, in one initial step, of a firm already sufficiently large to be able to compete effectively in the scale-economies industry. But the entry of a full-blown second or third supplier into the particular industry in question may well entail types of activity that go well beyond anything experienced in the industry before. In that case, private investors may have as little accurate information about an entrant's prospects as does any government agency seeking to encourage entry into the field. Either of these is consequently apt to overlook a promising entry opportunity or to overvalue an opportunity whose prospects are really modest or worse.

Second, entry may be desirable to society even though it is unable to attract sufficient private investment, because the risk to the latter is considerably greater than the risk to society. There are many reasons why this may be so. Most notably, there is the possibility that the new enterprise may become insolvent and be lost to the original investors, but that it will then undergo reorganization under new ownership and continue to yield benefits to the economy. Where this scenario is a possibility it follows that, other things being equal, the expected payoff to society will be greater than that to private investors, so that the undertaking may be worthwhile socially, but not to any private group. A particular variant of this problem arises when there is any likelihood of successful strategic countermoves to entry by the earlier incumbent. If entry requires sunk outlays, that possibility will increase the risk facing the new firm and is likely to raise the cost of funds to the entrant, though its assets may continue to serve society even if the strategy of the predecessor firm is successful.

Finally, there is the possibility that externalities, perhaps the most usual cause of market failure, will be present — that the act of entry will yield socially beneficial spillovers from which the investors do not profit. The most obvious form that this can take occurs when entry frees the economy from the costly burdens of regulation in this arena. If the presence of a multiplicity of firms is deemed to render regulation redundant in the industry in question then that may benefit both the earlier incumbent and the body of customers, a benefit that is not reflected in the earnings of the entrant. Once again, it follows that entry may be unprofitable even if it is socially beneficial.

All of these observations can constitute justification for some public sector intervention to facilitate the entry of new firms and encourage their growth. In general, the externalities problem aside, it is to be expected that the danger to survival against which they should be protected will be temporary, for otherwise there is a real question as to whether their presence will ever constitute a significant contribution to competition, or any contribution at all. The issue, then, is a variation on the infant industry theme. Enough has been written on this subject to make redundant any further discussion of the validity of the infant industry argument and its implications. There are, however, some observations that may be illuminating that grow out of experience of attempts by regulators of privatized firms to provide protection to infant entrants.

There are forms of protection that are extremely and unnecessarily costly to society. For example, rules that force the incumbent firm's prices substantially higher than is called for by its costs are sources of inefficiency because they reduce the incentive for the entrant to invest in productivity growth. Similarly, the imposition of a cartel arrangement for the purpose, in the manner described in an earlier section, clearly impedes efficiency, beside contributing little or nothing to competition. Yet both of these devices are apt to recommend themselves to the regulatory agency in its well-intentioned attempt to foster competition.

The discussion in earlier paragraphs of this section of the reasons the market may fail to elicit all the entry that is socially desirable also suggests more efficient ways to provide public sector encouragement to the entrants. As we have seen, the difficulty seems to have two primary sources: excessive private cost of the capital required for entry and externalities deriving from the presence of the entrant. But externalities and differences between private and social costs more generally are well understood by economists, and efficient remedies for them are described even in the elementary texts. In the case under discussion what is clearly called for is a Pigouvian subsidy for the entrant's borrowing. Ideally, of course, it should be financed by the public treasury, but that is unlikely to be feasible politically. In practice, it has proven far easier to impose such burdens on the incumbent privatized firm for whom it is hoped to elicit new competitors. Economic analysis indicates that such a required subsidy of the entrant by the incumbent has efficiency costs of its own. However, if there is no alternative, it is surely least damaging to require the incumbent to establish a capital subsidization fund for the entrant, without constraining the incumbent to employ governmentally specified sources of funding, e.g., uneconomically-high prices for particular products. The flexibility called for here is directly analogous to the flexibility permitted by Pigouvian charges as compared to the use of direct controls as means to control pollution, with the superiority of the Pigouvian approach deriving in good part from the freedom that it gives to polluting firms to seek low cost ways to reduce emissions.

One final point is appropriate here. If governmental assistance to entrants is to be a temporary affair there is much to be gained if the time path of reduction of such assistance is made as clear as possible in advance, and the date at which it is scheduled for elimination or the circumstances in which it will be terminated announced well in advance, as a commitment of the regulator. Such precommitment offers three clear benefits. First, it eliminates the well-recognized danger that the infant firm will never be deemed to have grown up and that its protection will be continued indefinitely. Second, it eliminates unnecessary uncertainty, reducing this source of substantial cost for incumbent and entrant alike. Finally, it provides an added incentive for the entrant to prepare itself for the rigors that will be entailed in having to fend for itself in a competitive market place, and thereby encourages the entrant to invest in efficiency and strengthening of its competitive position.

ON PRIVATIZATION IN FORMERLY CENTRALLY-DIRECTED ECONOMIES[4]

I turn finally to privatization in the former Soviet countries, where I have no direct experience, and must rely on the reports of others for my observations. My remarks will, consequently, be relatively brief.

Privatization in Eastern Europe is beset by problems that make those in the West seem minor and tractable by comparison. In each country there are many thousands of firms in the hands of the governments, and it is proposed to privatize a very substantial proportion of them. Thus, the number of candidate enterprises swamps the small number of firms that have been transferred to the private sector in Western countries. In addition, there is no functioning capital market, little experience with the working of the market mechanism and no cadre of entrepreneurs trained by experience to pursue profit through the promotion of industry. All this is well-known, but Eastern privatization programs also face difficulties that are less familiar. Most of those that are now recognized by students of the subject are not matters of post-privatization regulatory oversight, as in the West. Rather, they arise at an earlier stage — the very process of transfer of the properties from public to private hands. The essence of the matter is that Eastern governments have found that it just is not easy to rid themselves of the assets.

There are at least six problems that occur at this stage:

1. ***Valuation of the Assets.*** If government firms are to be sold it is necessary to set a price or at least to have some idea of an appropriate price with which one can bargain or one can decide whether an offer is worth considering. However, in the Eastern countries, firms have not been sold for a very long time, so there is no experience on which to base an estimate of market value, and there are no well-organized securities exchanges where the firms can be valued on the basis of the prices of their stocks.

2. ***Obsolete and Deteriorated Plant.*** The problem of valuation is exacerbated by the fact that plant and equipment is typically obsolete and seems often to be worth little more than its value as scrap. It is difficult for ministers responsible for the sales to reconcile themselves to such a low valuation. Much more valuable, apparently, is the land on which the firm is located, but Eastern governments have shown some reluctance to part with the land and have sometimes agreed only to offer a short-term lease to prospective owners of the firms, thereby ensuring lower bids and the likelihood of even further deterioration of the assets because investment in repair and maintenance, let alone upgrading and modernization, are thereby rendered extremely risky.

3. ***Unavailability of Domestic Purchasing Power.*** Even if a reasonable estimate of appropriate price can be obtained, it is generally difficult to find buyers among citizens of the country in question for anything near that price, at least for larger firms that are candidates for privatization. The requisite purchasing power simply is not available. Sometimes willing purchasers can be found, but these are usually foreigners. For the usual reasons, the Eastern governments fear that it is dangerous to sell off any substantial share of the nation's assets to foreigners.

4. ***Viable Procedures for Giveaway of Assets.*** An alternative to sale of the assets — one that has frequently been adopted as a partial solution, is to give away ownership of the properties. Such a transfer, clearly, has to be carried out in an egalitarian manner, excluding no group of adult citizens. But it is impractical to divide up each and every factory among the millions of citizens of the country, and so a way has to be found to keep numbers manageable, without discriminating against anyone. The manner in which this has been done will be discussed presently.

5. ***Arrangement for Oversight of Management.*** Even with the giveaway programs that have been adopted, unavoidably the number of shareholders in each firm has been large, with the danger that none of them will hold any substantial proportion of the equity. The result that is thereby threatened is that no owner or organized set of owners of the privatized firm will be in a position to exercise any control over the actions of management. In the older capitalist economies, the resulting principal-agent problem is very familiar, particularly after the takeover wars of the 1980s. Managements may turn out to be incompetent, or they may simply pursue their own interests at the stockholders' expense. In the former Soviet bloc, the problem is even more serious. For management is often in the hands of the bureaucrats who formerly ran the firms and who have not yet been replaced. Experienced in dealing with the hierarchy of the party and the planning apparatus, these individuals generally have little familiarity with market pressures, with forces driving the firm constantly toward adoption of the latest or the most efficient technology and toward energetic pursuit of customers. It therefore becomes urgent to devise arrangements that will prevent the old line management from performing in its accustomed manner and that will provide the power to replace management if that is called for.

6. ***Vested Managerial Interests.*** The old managements have frequently been active in trying to protect their vested interests. They have often tried to arrange to purchase their firms themselves, and to do so at giveaway prices. For example, assets have been sold to them at book value in Russia, with book value expressed in rubles unadjusted for inflation. Since the country is experiencing something close to hyperinflation, this means the properties were made available virtually free. The old managements have also been known to favor having a very large body of tiny stockholders, presumably to ensure that the body of equity owners is powerless to control or influence management.

All of these matters will obviously have to be dealt with effectively if privatization is not to prove disappointing or even disastrous. A good deal of progress has occurred here, at least in principle, though there is still a long way to go before execution is completed. There is a sharp distinction between what has happened to the smaller firms such as farms and retail establishments, and what has been accomplished for the larger enterprises.

Privatization of the small firms has reportedly been handled with considerable success. Stanley Fischer tells us that there are now nearly 200,000 private farms in Russia and that 40 percent of all small enterprises have applied for privatization [*New York Times,* 6 April 1993, A23]. In Hungary there are "66,000 small private firms and 180,000 one-man firms [which] account for 40% of output" [*The Economist,* 1993].

> Poland has succeeded in leasing or selling more than 40,000 shops to private operators by mid-1991. It is estimated that as a result of this 'small-scale privatization' as well as the rapid growth of new private firms in the service sector, roughly 80 percent of retail trade is now carried out by the private sector! Privatization has also been very rapid in trucking, construction, and small industrial units, where privatization has occurred in part by auctions, and in part by leasing the enterprises to the workforce. [Sachs, 1992, 6]

The small enterprise conversion has been easier for several reasons. First, because so many new owners benefited, the program was favored by a fairly large constituency. Second, there was little need to worry about monopoly or market power in the case of these enterprises. Third, the capital requirements for the process were modest. Finally, because they are generally owner-managed and are, in any event, easily subject to owner oversight, they did not raise the difficult problems of control that beset large-enterprise transfers to the private sector.

> Part of the reason why "small privatization" has been a relative success in some countries is that it raises few of the hugely complex corporate governance problems endemic in all efforts to reform larger industries. The privatized shops and service outlets are usually owner-managed, and the low capitalization requirements make for a potentially lively secondary market which is able to correct for many mistakes in the initial allocation. For this reason, it may not be particularly important whether the state withdraws from running small businesses in favor of workers employed by them (as is commonly the case) or whether it sells them to the highest bidder in an open competitive process (as was the case in Czechoslovakia), so long as there are no crippling transferability restrictions on the privatized assets. [Frydman and Rapaczynski, 1993, 4]

Still, even here there were obstacles, partially avoidable; for example,

> [In most] stores and service outlets in Eastern Europe...constant shortages meant that their inventory was not worth very much, and their substandard services did not make for a great amount of valuable "goodwill". What these stores and outlets did have was their very valuable premises that needed to be reallocated to better uses. In this context, it is interesting to note that, in most cases, the "privatization" of the retail sector did not entail a transfer of the ownership right to the premises; instead, the state retained the title and the premises have been most often merely leased for relatively

> short periods of time, often with no secure right to renew and a number of burdensome restrictions. [ibid., 3]

This is the arena in which privatization has, by all accounts, been relatively successful. "Unfortunately, privatization of large industrial enterprises has proceeded much more slowly, indeed far too slowly" [Sachs, 1992, 6]. With the apparent exception of the Czech Republic this experience seems to be universal.

> ...in the case of larger industries, where privatization encounters very serious technical and political obstacles [the] initial difficulty ... [is] the need to find and empower new owners. The first instinct of East European policymakers ... was to follow well known precedents, such as British style privatizations, involving a sale of shares to the public or to a selected number of private investors ... [but] the attempts to emulate Western privatizations were, by and large, a failure. With a few notable exceptions of sales to foreign investors ... the unattractiveness of investment in East European state enterprises, the slowness of the process, the problems of valuation, the shortage of domestic capital, and the unwillingness of foreign investors to enter at a large enough scale account for the fact that very few East European [large] enterprises have in fact been sold to outside private investors. [Frydman and Rapaczynski, 1993, 4-5]

There have been a number of arrangements that have been devised to deal with some of the problems posed by the task of transfer of ownership of a large nationalized firm and its subsequent governance. These plans follow approaches that naturally recommend themselves to economists[5] and, while not or at least not yet universally adopted, they have been considered with surprising rapidity in a surprising number of countries, and have actually been put into practice in the Czech Republic. The key elements of these programs are the use of vouchers and the role assigned to financial intermediaries.

In order to solve the problems entailed in division of ownership of the large firms among the entire population, it was proposed to offer for sale sets of vouchers at minimal prices, with the vouchers usable by the purchaser to acquire an equity interest through bidding at auction in any of the large state enterprise that had been declared eligible for this process. The first of such auctions, held in the Czech Republic in December of 1992, is reported to have transferred 2,000 firms with a book value of $7 billion to the public [*The Economist,* 1993, 14]. At first, sales of the vouchers to the public were slow, but when the low prices and favorable conditions of the transfers were publicized demand picked up rapidly. Similar procedures have been proposed in Poland and Russia, but the parliaments have so far frustrated these attempts.

In order to prevent excessive diffusion of ownership and to provide for the presence of some stockholders possessing equity sufficient to give them some power to control management, another provision was proposed. It was suggested that incentives be provided to have the securities purchased with the vouchers held by financial intermediaries, that is, quasi mutual funds, in which the stocks bought with vouchers could be deposited. This has been proposed in Poland, and actually put into practice in the Czech Republic. There,

> ...spurred by rather irresponsible promises of spectacular returns on the part of many investment funds, over 70 per cent of the voucher recipients decided to place their vouchers with the funds. As a result, while the choice of the voucher route of privatization led to a very speedy transfer of title, the plan also produced a significant concentration of ownership, giving rise to a hope that the new owners will exercise effective control over the management of the privatized enterprises. [Frydman and Rapaczynski, 1993, 7]

Thus, the problems of transfer of ownership to the private sector that have been mentioned are clearly not beyond solution. It is yet possible that many of these transfers will be carried out in a manner that effectively promotes the public interest. Yet so far, lack of resources, inexperience with markets, fear of the unknown and political considerations have led to a host of problems. Thus, one pair of observers note several such difficulties that have appeared during the first three years of the privatization process in Eastern Europe:

> First, ... Instead of the expected clarification of property rights and the establishment of a system of economic incentives characteristic of capitalist society, the intended privatization process has so far resulted in many countries in a maze of complicated economic and legal relations that may sometimes even impede a speedy transition to a system in which the rights of capital are clearly delineated and protected.
>
> Second, the conflict between the interests of insiders, intent on retaining authority over their enterprises, and the right of outside investors to acquire control has often overlooked consequences....insider control and barriers to the entry of outsiders may also retard the development of a system of property rights, including the rights of the insiders as owners of capital. [ibid., 13]

In addition to all this there remain dangers that threaten to bring the entire process to a halt. The illusion on the part of the public that transition to a market system can bring prosperity overnight when the process required decades even in the miracle economies in the Far East and the equally illusory belief that a market mechanism can work without the promise of generous and enviable financial rewards to those who are successful may yet lead to disillusionment and unwillingness to proceed with the privatization process. Even if that does not happen, the Eastern

European economies will later undoubtedly run into the difficult regulatory problems of privatization in Western Europe that have already been described. But these are difficulties only for the future.

NOTES

The author is deeply grateful to the Alfred P. Sloan Foundation and the C.V. Starr Center for their support of this work. He is most indebted to his colleague, S. A. B. Blackman for her capable assistance in the research.

1. For a fuller and very illuminating discussion of the privatization process in the U.K. see Johnson [1991, Chapter 5]
2. In the U.S., adherence to the goal of "universal service," with its accompanying cross subsidies, has eroded as deregulation spread. It eventually became clear in telecommunications, for example, that as entry occurred the cross subsidies would become unsustainable. Yet even here, as in a number of public utility arenas, some vestigial cross subsidy was retained. The suppliers, ostensibly voluntarily, agreed to supply what are called "lifeline services," that offer the elderly or the impoverished, or the residents of slum areas some basic services, with all luxury enhancements eliminated, at highly reduced prices. Because the magnitude of the cross subsidy is kept to moderate levels by this approach, and because several, if not all, of the suppliers of the services in question have more or less voluntarily followed it, it does not appear to have led regulators to try to restrict entry, and it apparently has not greatly affected the prices of other services. Still, political pressures have not permitted an end to regulatory intervention to preserve popular cross subsidies.
3. For a fuller discussion see the forthcoming monograph, by Gregory Sidak and myself [1993].
4. For details on the process in the different countries see the excellent treatment in Frydman, Rapaczynski and Earle [1993].
5. Indeed, the proposals were formulated and introduced by economists. The ideas were initially formulated by Frydman and Rapaczynski [1991], though similar proposals may well have been made independently by other Western economist advisers to the East European countries and by other economists in those countries.

REFERENCES

Baumol, W. J. and Sidak, G. *Toward Competition in Local Telephony.* Cambridge, MA: MIT Press, 1993.

The Economist. A Survey of Eastern Europe. 13 March 1993, 1-22.

Fischer, S. America's Allies in Serbia. *The New York Times,* 6 April 1993, A23.

Frydman, R. and Rapaczynski, A. Markets and Institutions in Large-Scale Privatization: An Approach to Economic and Social Transformation in Eastern Europe, in *Reforming Central and Eastern European Economies,* edited by V. Corbo, F. Coricelli and J. Bossak. Washington: the World Bank, 1991.

__________ **and** __________. Privatization in Eastern Europe: is the State Withering Away? New York University, C.V. Starr Center for Applied Economics, 1993 (forthcoming in the World Bank, *Finance and Development*).

Frydman, R., Rapaczynski, A. and Earle, J. S. *The Privatization Process in Central Europe* (two volumes). Budapest: The Central European University Press, 1993.

Johnson, C. *The Economy Under Mrs. Thatcher, 1979-1990.* London: Penguin Books, 1992.

Sachs, J. The Economic Transformation of Eastern Europe: the Case of Poland. *The American Economist,* Fall 1992, 3-11.

[10]

PREDATION AND THE LOGIC OF THE AVERAGE VARIABLE COST TEST*

WILLIAM J. BAUMOL
New York University

ABSTRACT

This article explores principles for execution of the widely accepted Areeda-Turner test of predatory pricing. Defining an Areeda-Turner price as one that does not threaten to exclude any more-efficient supplier, I conclude that (1) any individual price that is not below average avoidable cost cannot be predatory; (2) thus, *average avoidable cost,* not *marginal cost,* is crucial in testing predation; (3) sets of prices of different products of the firm can violate the test if the revenues of any *combinations* of the firm's products fall short of the combined avoidable costs of those products; and (4) a firm's failure to maximize its profits during some relatively brief period is not by itself legitimate evidence of predation.

EVER since the appearance in 1975 of the classic Areeda-Turner article, average variable cost (AVC) has played a key role in adjudication of charges of predatory pricing. This is so despite the conclusion by Phillip Areeda and Donald Turner that it is *marginal* cost (MC) rather than any form of average cost that constitutes the defensible borderline between a price that is predatory and one that is not.[1] As in their article, the courts have accepted the view that marginal cost is exceedingly difficult to determine in practice, so that, faute de mieux, one must apologetically accept average variable cost as an imperfect proxy, even though one knows full well that the magnitudes of the two costs can differ substantially.

I have previously suggested that, in taking this position, those authors and their followers had undervalued average variable cost itself as an independent and perfectly legitimate test for the purpose.[2] This article presents what I believe to be even stronger grounds for that position and for the more unorthodox view that some variant of the AVC test is more to the point than one based on marginal cost.

* I am extremely grateful to Holly J. Gregory of Weil, Gotshal and Manges for her very valuable comments. I must also thank the C. V. Starr Center for Applied Economics, New York University, for its support of the preparation of this article.

[1] Phillip Areeda & Donald Turner, Predatory Pricing and Related Practices under Section 2 of the Sherman Act, 88 Harv. L. Rev. 637 (1975).

[2] William J. Baumol, Superfairness: Applications and Theory 126–27 (1986).

[*Journal of Law & Economics,* vol. XXXIX (April 1996)]

Perhaps the more important objective of this article is to explore the principles that should guide proper execution of the Areeda-Turner test, thereby dealing with a number of issues that have been matters of contention in the courts.[3] Starting from the premise that a proper Areeda-Turner price is one that does not threaten the existence (or at least the presence) of any equally efficient or more efficient supplier, this analysis leads to the following rules: (1) no price that equals or exceeds average avoidable cost can be predatory; (2) "average total cost" is a figure that is undefinable and unmeasurable in a multiproduct firm and must therefore be rejected as part of any legitimate test of predatory pricing; (3) the firm can violate the Areeda-Turner test not only if the price of an individual product is below average variable (avoidable) cost, but also if, at the prices in question, the revenues of any *combinations* of the firm's products fall short of the combined avoidable costs of those products; (4) the time period appropriate for use in an Areeda-Turner test is either the period during which the price at issue actually prevailed or the period during which it could, ex ante, reasonably have been expected to prevail; (5) where the firm practices differential pricing—for example, by negotiating different contract terms with different customers—sales of a product at different prices should be treated as sales of different products and subjected to combinatorial rule 3; (6) a firm's failure to maximize its profits during some relatively brief period is normal and beneficial business practice and is not legitimate evidence of predation; and (7) the average avoidable cost used in the Areeda-Turner test should include any opportunity costs incurred when proprietors of the firm supply inputs to the firm but should not include revenue forgone if the price at issue entails a reduction from some previous price because the previous price is irrelevant for determining whether the price at issue is a threat to the viability of an efficient competitor.

In all this it should be recognized that the problem of determining an

[3] Thus, it is not the purpose of this article to reexamine the issue of predation in general and to review the large body of literature of the subject, encompassing such noteworthy contributions as John S. McGee, Predatory Price Cutting: The Standard Oil (New Jersey) Case, 1 J. Law & Econ. 137 (1958); Lester G. Telser, Economic Theory and the Core (1978); Oliver E. Williamson, Predatory Pricing: A Strategic and Welfare Analysis, 87 Yale L. J. 284 (1977); and Paul L. Joskow & Alvin K. Klevorick, A Framework for Analyzing Predatory Pricing Policy, 89 Yale L. J. 213 (1979). Moreover, this article makes no attempt to follow up on the view I have suggested elsewhere in William J. Baumol, Quasi-Permanence of Price Reductions: A Policy for Prevention of Predatory Pricing, 89 Yale L. J. 1 (1979), that there is much to be said for an intertemporal analysis of the process of predation, considering the sequence of deliberate losses by the predator, the exit of rivals, and the subsequent attempt at recoupment of the earlier losses as a useful basis for rules for the prevention of predatory acts. Here, however, my focus is on the widely adopted Areeda-Turner rule, its logic, and its proper execution.

appropriate lower bound for price, as the Areeda-Turner test of predatory pricing undertakes to do, is very much like the problem of selecting such a price floor as a criterion of cross subsidy. That is why much of the content of this article is apt to remind the reader of the literature on price regulation that clearly has suggested a number of the conclusions offered here.

I. In Praise of Areeda-Turner

Before getting to the substance of my discussion it is important for me to emphasize that nothing said here is intended in any way to undermine or even to criticize the Areeda-Turner test. It is easy, with years of afterthought, to quibble with details of their original argument, and that will occur here. But none of what is said is intended to belittle the authors' accomplishment or to advocate restriction of the use of their standard. In a world in which vigorous competition is all too easily mistaken for predation, and in which firms can unintentionally overstep the line, it is important to provide managers with guidelines as unambiguous as the issue permits, to enable them to tailor their decisions in a way that ensures compliance with the law and minimizes vulnerability to anticompetitive lawsuits intended to handicap vigorous competition. Of course, in the complex world of reality, one cannot hope to formulate a test that does so with perfection, but Areeda-Turner comes as close to success in doing so as could reasonably have been hoped, and more. There seems to be general consensus among informed observers that genuine cases of predation are very rare birds. As Areeda and Turner note, that does not relieve us of the necessity of guarding against those rare occurrences, of taking steps to prevent them and to rectify any damage they produce. But there is a painful trade-off here. Rules that make it excessively easy to secure conviction on charges of predation invite anticompetitive and rent-seeking litigation. Such rules tempt firms that cannot make it in the marketplace by virtue of superior products or greater efficiency and lower costs, to seek success over their more efficient rivals in the courts instead. There they can hope to constrain the vigor of rivalrous acts by competitors and to transmogrify the character of their rivals from energetic enterprise to timidity and hesitance. This can sometimes be accomplished by mere threat of a lawsuit, but if the lawsuit is indeed undertaken and won there is a rich additional bonus awaiting the plaintiff—trebled damages, which, in a total victory, can amount to many years of net earnings by either the plaintiff or the defendant. Long study of the subject has led me to the conclusion that litigation of this sort is a major handicap to the growth and competitiveness of the nation's economy. Thus, I conclude that Areeda and Turner have made a substantial contribution to our economic well-being by helping to reduce ambiguity in the concept of predatory pricing and decreasing the vulnerability of vigorous competitors to lawsuits that threaten to undermine the effectiveness of their competition and their entrepreneurship.

Still, there are a number of instances in which the odor of predation is strong, as when an entrant airline with its six-plane fleet, operating on almost as many routes, proposes to fly a route coveted by a large incumbent airline, whereon the latter announces that it will open for business (for the first time) along each of the most promising of the entrant's routes. Analogous examples in which predatory *pricing* is the issue are also easily imagined. There is reason to provide the entrant in such a scenario effective recourse against overaggressive acts by the large incumbent. Accordingly, the rules for proper execution of an average variable cost test that are described in this article are designed not to offer undue protection to the firm suspected of predatory pricing. Indeed, we will see that some of those rules facilitate the task of the plaintiff, by making clearer what that entity must prove, just as an Areeda-Turner type of rule makes clearer to the firm making a pricing decision what it must do to ensure that its choice of price is free of any taint of predation.

II. Two Possible Roles of Cost Tests of Predatory Pricing

Discussions of the subject can generally be interpreted to imply that there are three necessary conditions that must be satisfied before a price can legitimately be deemed to be predatory. Indeed, one can, perhaps, *define* a price to be predatory if and only if it meets all three of the following conditions. First, the choice of that price must have no legitimate business purpose.[4] Second, that price must threaten the existence or the entry of rivals that are at least as efficient as the firm (call it "firm F") that has adopted the price at issue ("price P"). Third, there must be a reasonable prospect of recoupment of at least whatever initial costs to firm F were entailed in the company's adoption of the price in question, that recoupment taking the form of monopoly profits made possible by reduction (as a result of price P) in the number of competitors facing F.

[4] In an article in the American Lawyer, Roger Parloff takes issue with my views on legitimate business purpose, saying, "There is, of course, no 'legitimate business purpose' exemption in the antitrust laws" (Roger Parloff, Fare's Fair, 65 Am. Law. (October 1993)). But, then, the laws, so far as I know, also provide no exemption for prices that exceed AVC, yet many courts clearly accept that criterion. Moreover, the courts have, I believe, repeatedly emphasized that normal business acts undertaken in pursuit of profit constitute no violation of the law, even if they *happen* to harm rivals incidentally. But that is just what I mean by legitimate business purpose.

Here, I will not be concerned with the third of these necessary conditions for pricing to be deemed predatory—the prospect of recoupment. Rather, I will focus on the other two necessary conditions, to which I will refer, respectively, as *legitimate business purpose* and *threat to efficient rivals*. I will suggest that the *cost* tests of predatory pricing have generally been interpreted to direct themselves to the first of these two requirements, while, in my view, they throw light far more dependably on the second. If this is granted, I will show that it is to AVC, or one of its close relatives, rather than to MC, that we must turn for guidance.

III. Areeda-Turner and Legitimate Business Purpose

The original Areeda-Turner article never seems to come down squarely on one of the two roles as primary justification for the test. However, one comes away with the distinct impression that legitimate business purpose is a foundation on which the authors propose to rest their argument. This seems implicit in their criterion of predation that rests on the relationship between price and marginal cost where, I note for later discussion, marginal cost (as well as marginal revenue) must, of course, include the present values of the effects of today's decisions on future costs (or revenues). It is implied that a price as low as marginal cost is legitimate business practice because, in equilibrium in a regime of perfect competition (the economist's theoretically ideal—if practically unattainable—state of affairs), the firm will always adopt a price that is equal to marginal cost, and "a higher price would result in a reduction in output and thus deprive some buyers of a commodity for which they were willing to pay the cost of production."[5] At the other extreme, the monopolist will maximize profit by selecting an output at which marginal cost is equal to marginal revenue. Since, as is well known, when the demand curve is downward sloping, as is normally assumed, price will necessarily exceed marginal revenue, that price will always exceed marginal cost as well.[6] And, it may be added, if the demand curve, though downward sloping, is nearly horizontal (a small rise in price reduces quantity demanded substantially) price, marginal revenue and, hence, marginal cost will all very nearly be equal. Thus, even for the monopolist, a normal pricing act will entail $P >$ MC, though possibly by a very small amount. In contrast, "[b]y definition, a firm producing at an output where marginal cost exceeds price is selling at least part of that output at an out-of-pocket loss. It could eliminate that loss by reducing its output."[7] The authors

[5] Areeda & Turner, *supra* note 1, at 702.
[6] *Id.* at 703.
[7] *Id.* at 712.

go on to note, "A monopolist may attempt to justify prices below marginal cost by claiming either that the price is being used for promotional purposes or that he is simply meeting an equally low price of a rival. We conclude, however, that these justifications are either so rarely applicable or of such dubious merit for a monopolist that the presumption of illegality for prices below both marginal and average cost[8] should be conclusive."[9]

To sum up, the argument seems to be that in normal and legitimate business transactions price will at least sometimes exceed marginal cost by only a very small amount but that it will only very rarely fall short of marginal cost in transactions that are clearly legitimate. The inference that seems to be drawn from this is that marginal cost is the knife-edge border between pricing that constitutes legitimate business practice and pricing that can be presumed to constitute acts of predation.

Yet the choice of marginal cost as the borderline between price as legitimate and illegitimate business act is not altogether convincing. It is at once too permissive and excessively demanding. At the one extreme, suppose demand for the product at issue happens to be brisk and that it is clearly profitable for the firm to price 50 percent above MC. Is it then normal and legitimate business practice for the firm to eschew this profit opportunity and select a price that exceeds MC by, say, only 2 percent? Such a decision does not imply that the choice is predatory, but it also does not constitute proof that it constitutes legitimate business practice. In contrast, it is hard to imagine a firm that has never found it expedient or even necessary to sell products for at least a brief period at a price below marginal cost, for reasons ranging from product introduction to distress sales of products that are perishable or subject to obsolescence. Thus, on the one side, we cannot casually accept the unsupported assertion that sales at prices below marginal costs constitute a presumption that the act is without legitimate business purpose. On the other side, we cannot confidently conclude that any sale at a price above marginal cost has a legitimate business purpose.

The problem with use of marginal cost as the criterion for testing legiti-

[8] As I presently show, the concept "average cost" in a multiproduct firm is treacherous nonsense. Because costs that are fixed and common are characteristically substantial, and because they can only be allocated among the firm's different products on a totally arbitrary basis, they have always been subject to manipulation by "creative accounting procedures" and have commonly been used to inhibit competition.

[9] *Id.* at 713. A curious feature of the Areeda-Turner article is its exclusive focus on the two polar cases of monopoly and perfect competition, with little said about anything in between. This is particularly surprising since (hardly by accident) litigation on predatory pricing usually arises in industries composed of a multiplicity of firms whose number can be fairly small.

macy of business purpose is that it simply does not get at the issue. We can define an act by a firm to have a legitimate business purpose if it promises to yield a net addition to the firm's profits over the long run, a profit that does not depend on the exit of any at least equally efficient rivals or on prevention of entry of efficient firms. But there is simply no way in which one can infer from the fact that the firm adopts a price that exceeds MC that this will constitute a net addition to long-run profits relative to what the firm might otherwise have earned, nor can one legitimately conclude that a price that falls short of MC must reduce those profits in the absence of destruction of competitors or entrants. Promotional prices for new products are examples that are real and exceedingly common, and the temporary losses they entail are a feature they share with heavy outlays on innovation, or radical plant modernization and retooling, and a host of other patently legitimate business acts that are prime examples of productive entrepreneurship. Mere comparison of price and marginal cost is simply not very effective in discriminating between legitimate and illegitimate business acts.

IV. Areeda-Turner as Test of Threat to Efficient Rivals

I will argue now that the Areeda-Turner test is entirely defensible as a criterion to determine whether the price at issue constitutes a threat to efficient rivals of firm F. But I will show that for this purpose it is average variable cost or a near relative, rather than marginal cost, that provides the requisite information.

Areeda and Turner do discuss the role of their criterion in helping to distinguish whether efficient rivals are threatened by price *P*. They conclude, quite correctly, that the marginal cost test performs this task imperfectly. They consider "instances where marginal cost is below average cost, a situation that will not occur unless the monopolist possesses 'excess capacity.' Only then will the monopolist's marginal cost price deprive equally efficient rivals, actual or potential, of 'normal' returns on their capital. Although narrowed, the problem remains: the equally efficient rival might be destroyed or dissuaded from entering. . . . Admittedly [this] poses some threat to competition in the long run. . . . However, we see no satisfactory method of eliminating this risk."[10]

There is, however, a method that is satisfactory, and, as a matter of fact, it is the method by which the courts have chosen to carry out the Areeda-Turner test. For there is a well-known principle in elementary economics telling us that a firm will minimize its losses (maximize its

[10] *Id.* at 710–11.

profits) by exiting from a market (using the term in an economic rather than a legal sense) when and only when the total revenue it can obtain by remaining in that market falls short of its total *variable* cost. If that revenue exceeds the firm's variable cost it should nevertheless remain in the market even though by doing so it does not cover its *total* cost. Here, the term "variable cost" is defined to include all *fixed* costs that are not *sunk*, so that they can be escaped if the firm exits from the market.

To see this,[11] we must first examine the relation between cost and the incentive for exit that faces a firm. It will be recalled that costs are defined to be sunk if the firm cannot escape them in the short run, either because of a contract (say, with the landlord or the union) or because it has already signed a contract to buy the item whose cost is sunk (for example, a machine). If the firm stops producing, its revenue will fall to zero. Its short-run variable costs will also fall to zero. But its sunk costs—such as rent—will remain to plague it. If the firm is losing money, it will be better off continuing to operate if the resulting revenues produce *any* surplus above variable costs, thereby making *some* contribution to sunk cost. However, it should be obvious that, if the revenues the firm can earn by remaining in operation fall short of variable costs the shortfall will simply add to the losses resulting from its sunk-cost obligations.

The pertinence of all this for the Areeda-Turner test as a criterion of threat to efficient rivals follows from one more observation. Consider two firms, A and B, that are vying to serve as suppliers of a given quantity, Q, of some good or service. Which of them will be the more efficient supplier of Q? The answer is that it will be the firm for which the supply of Q causes the smallest addition to cost. That addition to cost is what economists call the *incremental cost* of Q. For the moment, let us simply equate AIC (average incremental cost) with average variable cost (a subject to which we will return presently). Then, if $\mathrm{AVC}(Q)_{\mathrm{A}}$ is the average variable cost of Q when produced by firm A, and so on, firm B will be the more efficient supplier of Q if and only if

$$\mathrm{AVC}(Q)_{\mathrm{B}} < \mathrm{AVC}(Q)_{\mathrm{A}}.$$

But, then, if A charges a price P_{A} for Q that at least equals its average variable cost of Q production, then that price cannot possibly drive its efficient competitor B out of business because then

$$P_{\mathrm{A}} > \mathrm{AVC}(Q)_{\mathrm{A}} > \mathrm{AVC}(Q)_{\mathrm{B}}.$$

[11] The next few paragraphs contain material that is obvious to an economist. However, since the point is central to my argument, and because a number of wise and erudite lawyers with whom I have worked have nevertheless wanted the matter explained, I have not excised the material altogether.

For, then, B can charge a price equal to A's or even a little lower, and still cover its own variable cost, which, as we have seen, ensures that exit is not the more profitable alternative for firm B. We obtain the generalized Areeda-Turner result:

RULE 1. Any price above the pertinent average variable cost for the output quantity in question cannot be predatory because it can never cause the exit (prevent the entry) of an efficient, profit-seeking rival.[12]

This rule is still vague in two respects. It has not yet indicated what output quantity is pertinent, and it has not shown what average variable cost is relevant. The latter, for example, entails the proper choice of time period (the pertinent short run) in which to calculate the cost. The output quantity issue is this: is the relevant quantity that of firm F, whose price is under investigation, or is it the output of its complaining rival? Perhaps surprisingly, I argue later that, at least for part of the role of the test, it is the output quantity of the rival that matters.

V. WHICH COST? AVERAGE VARIABLE COST? AVERAGE INCREMENTAL COST? AVERAGE AVOIDABLE COST?

Though average variable cost is the concept that seems to be used universally in carrying out the Areeda-Turner test, that cost is not well defined. It seems to refer to the variable portion of the total cost of production of the entire quantity of a commodity supplied by a firm divided by that output quantity. But this statement is not as clear-cut as it appears. First, it does not make clear what is to be done about outlays that have been called "product-specific fixed costs,"[13] that is, costs that

[12] One can still object that a price that just equals or slightly exceeds the firm's average variable cost can be used to drive out a rival that is marginally less efficient than the incumbent. If the latter then is able to raise its price well above the competitive level, one may have good reason to conclude that the original price was predatory in its consequences. Elsewhere I have recognized the pertinence of such intertemporal pricing patterns and have proposed a criterion of predatory behavior to deal with them (Baumol, *supra* note 3). Such a possibility, however, affects *every* cost test that is designed to determine the borderline between a level of price that is predatory and one that is not. For any price that is above the selected borderline can nevertheless serve to drive out a firm so inefficient that it cannot meet the price set at that level. It seems to me that despite the valid concern raised here, the average variable cost criterion remains a legitimate borderline.

[13] There is considerable confusion in the literature about two pertinent concepts, fixed costs and sunk costs, which are really very different. There are, in fact four types of cost that are relevant here, and they can be defined thus: *fixed costs* are costs that must be incurred in a lump in order for any output at all to be provided, and they do not vary when the magnitude of output changes. These costs are not variable either in the short or the long run. Any cost that is not fixed is defined to be *variable*. A *sunk cost*, however, is a cost that cannot be avoided for some limited period of time, but after that period it becomes *avoidable* or *escapable*. A cost that is fixed may or may not be sunk, and a cost that is sunk may not be fixed. For example, one cannot operate an airline between, say, New York and Milwaukee without investing in at least one airplane, an outlay whose amount

are incurred *exclusively* on behalf of one particular product but whose magnitude is not increased when the output of that product rises.

The economist's concept, average incremental cost, is unambiguous on this subject. The average incremental cost of any given increment in output always includes *any* product-specific outlay (that is, any outlay that does not serve several products in common) that is caused by the output increment in question. It seems clear that, if one is testing whether price P is in some sense compensatory, such incremental costs must be included in the calculation, even if they are fixed in character. But that is not quite the answer we seek. The issue, in terms of the notation of the preceding section, is whether P_A, the price charged by firm A, can drive an efficient firm, B, out of the field of endeavor. The pertinent cost here is what may be thought of as the decremental rather than the incremental cost to firm B if it decides to exit. That is, the issue is the cost that B can *escape* or *avoid* by leaving. Thus P_A will not be able to drive firm B from the production of X (or some portion of the production of X) if it exceeds AAC_B, firm B's average avoidable cost (AAC) incurred in producing the pertinent increment of X (in the discussion that follows, the terms "avoidable cost" and "escapable cost" will be used interchangeably).

Now, it will generally be true that AAC $\leq$ AIC for any given quantity of output. That is, when expanding output X by a given increment, it is necessary to incur some sunk outlays (that are typically quite substantial and) that cannot entirely be escaped or avoided except in the very long run. So AIC includes those sunk outlays, but AAC does not. Thus, a price that exceeds the average incremental cost of some output can confidently be expected to exceed its average avoidable cost. Thus we arrive at:

RULE 2. The proper AVC figure to be used in the Areeda-Turner test to determine whether some price constitutes a threat to an efficient rival is the average avoidable cost of the pertinent output increment (decrement). If the average incremental cost is used instead, and the price nevertheless passes the test, one can be confident that the price is not predatory, because in general AIC $\geq$ AAC. The AAC figure must, how-

does not vary with number of passengers until capacity is reached. Thus, this cost is fixed, and does not become variable even in the long run, because one cannot run an airline on the route with zero airplanes. In contrast, this cost is not sunk because, if traffic between New York and Milwaukee declines drastically, the plane can be shifted to serve another route. A large factory with a 10-year useful life, however, constitutes a cost that is sunk for that period, but it need not be fixed because at the end of 10 years it may be desirable to produce less than before, using a smaller factory whose investment cost is lower. The distinction is not mere semantics—the two types of cost have very different implications for market performance and economic efficiency.

ever, include all pertinent portions of the product-specific fixed but avoidable costs, that is, all portions of such costs that can be escaped in the pertinent period of time.

VI. Digression: Nonexistence of Average Total Cost in Multiproduct Firms

Since the concept of "average total cost" (ATC) intrudes so often in discussions of predation, it is worth noting briefly that in the case of a multiproduct firm it violates all economic logic. Outside a textbook, there probably exists no such thing as a single-product firm, and all multiproduct firms have fixed costs incurred in common on behalf of two or more of their products. There is, however, no economically defensible way of dividing such costs up among the firm's various products. As is well known, all methods for the allocation of common fixed costs are arbitrary.

Before the courts or regulatory agencies, ATC (fully allocated costs) are always manipulated to produce whatever answers are desired by the party that puts them forward. Moreover, as I show elsewhere,[14] the amounts by which these contrived cost figures can easily be manipulated is enormous. Thus, though to economists it may seem obvious, for practitioners in the antitrust arena it is hardly redundant to suggest:

Rule 3. Any conclusion about the predatory character of a price that is based on a calculation of average total cost must be disregarded. The ATC numbers can offer absolutely no substantive economic information, and they are apt to constitute an invitation to anticompetitive action.

VII. Product Combinations and the AVC Test

How, then, should fixed and common costs be dealt with? Are the fuel bill and the pilot's salary simply to be ignored in a test to determine whether air fares are predatory? Surely, those costs are avoidable. By canceling a flight the fuel expenditure can be avoided and perhaps also the salary of the pilot. Economists have, indeed, worked out a rigorously defensible way to take them into account. To make the procedure clear one must begin the explanation, as it were, one step earlier. We must start off with the incremental cost (or the avoidable cost) of the individual services supplied by the airline—in this case, the two services: first-class transportation and economy transportation. The point is that for *neither*

[14] See William J. Baumol, Michael F. Koehn, & Robert D. Willig, How Arbitrary Is Arbitrary?—or, Toward the Deserved Demise of Full Cost Allocation, 120 Pub. Util. Fortnightly 16 (September 3, 1987).

of these services does the incremental cost or the avoidable cost include any of the pilot's income or any (substantial) part of the fuel bill. If the airplane is to fly in order to transport the economy passengers, it adds little or nothing to either of those costs to fly the first-class passengers as well. The same argument holds for the incremental (avoidable) cost of flying the economy passengers. Thus, none of the common fixed cost enters the incremental cost of any *one* individual service.

However, matters are quite different if we consider the cost of the two services together, which, it will be remembered, are assumed to constitute the full set of services offered by our hypothetical airline. The incremental cost of transporting both first-class and economy passengers combined clearly includes both pilot compensation and fuel outlay on the flight, and much of that combined cost could be avoided if the airline chose not to serve first-class and economy passengers alike, and simply canceled the flight. Thus, these common fixed costs must be included in their entirety in the incremental cost of the *combination* of the two airline services, and whatever portion of those costs is escapable in the pertinent period must be included in the avoidable cost of the service combination.

It is easy to see now that the price of first-class service can exceed its average avoidable cost, and the same can be true for the economy fare, yet the two together may fail to cover their combined avoidable cost. A numerical example will make that clear. Suppose that the incremental food, ticketing, and other avoidable costs for the trip in question is $50 for each of the 200 economy passengers and $80 for each of the 40 first-class passengers, and that the escapable portion of the fuel and pilot costs amount to $15,000. Then an economy fare of $60 and a first-class fare of $100 will clearly cover their average incremental (avoidable) costs, which are $50 and $80, respectively. But at those prices the total incremental revenue yielded by the flight is 200 × $60 + 40 × $100 = $16,000, and hardly covers the total escapable cost whose amount is 200 × $50 + 40 × $80 + $15,000 = $28,200. For the individual fares together do not contribute enough to cover the common escapable costs.

The implication of all this is the following. The price of an individual product may fail what we may call the *generalized Areeda-Turner test* if it does not cover the average avoidable cost of that product alone. But it can also fail the test if the incremental revenues provided by that service together with that of any subset of the company's other services are insufficient in total to cover the avoidable costs of that combination of services. Thus, a firm that supplies, say, five different services can fail the test on the basis of the price of some individual service, or because it fails the corresponding test for any pair of the firm's services, or because it does so for any triad of the firm's services, and so on.

Of course, it is totally impractical, and an unreasonable burden, for a defendant to be required to supply an estimate of the avoidable cost for each and every combination of such services. Indeed, such a requirement would invite anticompetitive "fishing expeditions" by prospective plaintiffs. However, this combinatorial feature of the generalized Areeda-Turner test does offer that plaintiff a very legitimate advantage. As is done in regulatory arenas that use such combinatorial criteria to determine whether prices are compensatory, the plaintiff is required to specify, *in advance,* what service or what one combination of services he believes to have predatory prices, and the plaintiff and defendant alike are expected to provide avoidable cost information about the one service or the one combination of services that has been deemed predatory in the complaint. Sometimes this test can, in practice, be extended to encompass several services or service combinations, but that set is always required to be small, and the procedure is, consequently, entirely manageable, as experience in regulation has demonstrated. This leads to:

RULE 4. The proper Areeda-Turner test to determine whether a firm's prices constitute a threat to an efficient rival must extend to combinations of the firm's products. The price of each product by itself must equal or exceed that item's average avoidable cost. Moreover, any combination of the firm's products must be priced so as to yield an incremental revenue that exceeds the avoidable cost incurred by that combination of products. In practice, a plaintiff should be required to specify in advance what products or product combinations it has reason to believe will fail this criterion, and litigation should take into consideration only the avoidable costs of the preselected products or product combinations.

VIII. SEQUENCES OF TIME PERIODS AND THE AREEDA-TURNER TEST

Just as the generalized Areeda-Turner test must logically be extendible to combinations of products, it must also be extendible to sequences of time periods. The issue arises because the magnitude of avoidable cost for a product or combination of products varies with the time period under consideration. Generally, the longer the pertinent time period, the greater the total avoidable cost and average avoidable cost figures will be. The reason is that as time passes, the larger the set of costs that were formerly sunk now become escapable. A firm may have signed a 2-year lease for a building, for example. At the end of the 2-year period, if the firm wants to remain in production, it will have to continue the rent payments. But only then, if it decides to cease production, can it escape those outlays altogether. Similarly, as time passes the firm has more of an opportunity to sell or lease redundant equipment, thus avoiding part of the cost which it cannot escape in a shorter period.

Since the longer the period considered, the higher we can expect avoidable cost to be, in a predation case we can expect the plaintiffs to press for a long period as the time interval suitable for the cost calculation, while the defendant can be relied on to argue for a brief period. The choice, however, is not arbitrary, and the principle for its selection follows unambiguously from the use of the Areeda-Turner criterion to determine whether a price or a combination of prices is a threat to an efficient rival. The answer, simply, is that, if the price at issue is in force for, say, 3 months, the period pertinent to the cost calculation is 3 months. For if that price alone is to drive a competitor from the arena, it then has just 3 months in which to do so. And on the principle explained in an earlier section, it will be capable of driving a rival from the field only if that price is less than the per-unit cost that a rival can escape in that period—it is the average avoidable cost calculated for a 3-month horizon. Logic permits no other answer.

However, that is not the end of the story. Suppose that the defendant adopted a \$50 price for 3 months, a \$52 price for the following 2 months, and a \$47 price for the 5 months following that. Suppose, moreover, that the three prices in combination are claimed to be predatory, on the hypothesis that no one of them or no pair of them could have driven out an efficient rival but that, by persistently proffering such a sequence of low prices, the rival allegedly could be forced from the arena. This is clearly a tenable hypothesis that can justify examination on its merits. And this can be done in a manner analogous with the procedure for combinations of outputs. That is, one must compare the incremental revenue provided by the sales that occurred at those prices to the firm that charged them, with the costs escapable over the entire period during which the prices prevailed. That is, one should compare the discounted present value of the incremental revenues with the discounted present value of the costs that could have been escaped, taking each such cost avoided to occur at the date at which the escape could reasonably be expected to occur. We then have:

RULE 5. The time horizon pertinent for the calculation of the AAC for an Areeda-Turner test is the time period over which the price in question prevailed or could reasonably have been expected to prevail. Where a sequence of prices is alleged to be predatory in combination the pertinent horizon is the end of all the time periods during which those prices prevailed, and the test should require that the present value of the incremental revenues for this extended period equal or exceed the present value of the avoidable costs. Once again, it should be the obligation of the plaintiff to specify in advance what pertinent time period or sequence of time periods it is challenging.

IX. The Size of the Pertinent Increment (Decrement) under Differential Pricing

Up to this point I have spoken of a comparison of *the* (unique) price of the product in question with the average avoidable cost entailed in continued production of that good or service. In practice, however, firms often do not charge the same price for a given product to all customers. For example, if the product serves primarily as an input to the production processes of a number of large business customers, each of the buyers may negotiate its own contract, with its purchase price dependent on the outcome of the negotiations and possibly quite different from the prices paid by other purchaser firms. This is said to entail *differential pricing*. It is also referred to as "price discrimination." Because differential pricing is so widespread in industries with scale economies, and arises so often in regulatory arenas, in the next section I will digress once more to see why such differential pricing may be necessary for the achievement of economic efficiency. That is, the discussion in the next section will show why one cannot solve simply by prohibition of differential pricing any special problems related to predatory pricing that may arise because differential prices are present. Here, however, we will simply recognize the existence of such prices and see what they imply for the choice of output increment to be used in the calculation of AAC for use in the Areeda-Turner test.

To illustrate the point, suppose that the firm sells 7,000 units of commodity *X* at a price of $500 and that, in addition, it sells 3,000 units of the same good at a price of $375. What price, or what incremental revenue, is appropriately to be compared with what avoidable cost? The answer, in brief, is that the two sales should be treated as the sales of two different commodities sold by the same firm. That is, the appropriate rule for the generalized Areeda-Turner test for this case is rule 4 above. Thus, the $500 sale of 7,000 units of *X* must cover its own avoidable cost, and the same must be true of the sales at the $375 price. In addition, the combined sales must provide enough incremental revenue to cover their combined incremental costs. The reason is straightforward. Consider an efficient rival that is competing for one or both of our firm's customer groups. Since, by definition of efficiency, that rival firm must have avoidable cost no higher than our firm's, it follows that, if the prices at issue pass the generalized Areeda-Turner test procedure just described, that rival cannot be driven out of the competition for either customer group or from competition for their combined purchases.

Here a confusion can easily arise. If there are scale economies in the production of *X*, a rival that seeks to compete only, say, for the business of the $500 customers will find itself at a cost disadvantage because it seeks to produce only the 3,000 units demanded by those customers at that price, while our firm produces the 10,000 units demanded by the two customer groups together. But this simply means that the rival is *not* an efficient supplier of the 3,000 units of product by themselves. The issue for customers is which of the two sellers can provide them with good *X* more cheaply, regardless of the reason that explains why one firm happens to produce at a lower cost than the other. Superior efficiency may be attributable to harder work or greater ability, but it may also result from luck (for example, one of the firms happened to pick what later turned out to be a better location, say, one closer to a superhighway entrance that had not been constructed or even planned when the site was chosen). Similarly, large scale (or, sometimes, small scale) can give one of the firms a cost advantage. But all of that is immaterial to customers—they simply want the lower-priced supplier regardless of whether its efficiency was achieved by merit or happenstance, and the market mechanism parcels out its rewards accordingly. We obtain:

RULE 6. Where differential pricing is practiced, the generalized Areeda-Turner test should be carried out in accord with rule 4, treating sales of a given product at different prices as sales of different commodities supplied by the same firm.

Before leaving the subject of the pertinent increment (decrement) to be considered in the Areeda-Turner test, I note that one additional observation is appropriate, this time for the case where differential pricing is not practiced. The point to be made now is offered for analytical completeness, though in practice it will probably prove wise to disregard it. Consider a case in which the defendant, firm D, is producing 8,000 units of good *X*, while the plaintiff, firm P, is producing only 2,500 units. The efficiency issue entailed in the possibility that the plaintiff will be forced to exit is whether the public is better off if the 2,500-unit output continues to be produced by firm P or if that production is taken over by D. Obviously, the public will be better off when P stays in the business if P has the lower incremental cost of producing 2,500 units. Moreover, if the same is true of avoidable costs, a price by D that covers its own incremental or avoidable costs of producing the 2,500 units cannot threaten the existence of firm P. The point to be noted here is that the avoidable cost to be considered in the test is that of the defendant and that is the cost that has usually been examined in practice in carrying out the Areeda-Turner test. But the output quantity in question is not the 8,000-unit output of the defendant, *but the 2,500 unit output quantity of the plaintiff.*[15] The reason for this rather surprising observation is that the pertinent

[15] That is, the pertinent cost is the defendant's avoidable cost entailed in producing the 2,500 units after they are, hypothetically, added to its initial 8,000-unit output.

issue for the public interest here is who is the more efficient producer of the plaintiff's output because the choice of producer of the defendant's output is simply not at issue. Yet, as has been noted, this observation is probably only of theoretical interest. In practice, it will probably not be easy to determine the incremental or avoidable cost that would be incurred by the defendant if it were, hypothetically, to take over the production of the plaintiff, in addition to its own. Moreover, unless there are very sharp scale economies or sharp diseconomies in the production of the good at issue, the cost figure will not be affected much by the choice between the output quantities of the two firms as the increment in output to be used in the calculation. In any event, if average variable cost is being used to determine, not whether a particular price by firm Y is a threat to its competitor, but to investigate whether it is compensatory to Y and, hence, a legitimate business decision, then it is clear that it is the output of Y, and not that of a rival, that is pertinent.

X. Digression: Differential Pricing and Economic Efficiency

Let us pause to see now why it is not in the public interest to rule out differential pricing altogether. For simplicity, the discussion of this section will deal with the imaginary case of single-product firms. I will show that a role arises for differential (that is, discriminatory) prices if, as is widely considered to be the normal case, the firm's average cost[16] curve is U-shaped. Figure 1 represents a case of two-firm production (by firms 1 and 2) with a U-shaped AC curve for each of the firms. The graph is a bit unusual in that the horizontal axis does not measure physical output but instead measures the share of total industry output that accrues to each firm. For example, the 60 percent point on the *x*-axis means that at that point firm 1 produces 60 percent of total industry output, so that firm 2 produces the remainder, 40 percent, of that output. At the left end of the axis, there is the 0 percent point at which firm 1 produces nothing, and so firm 2 produces 100 percent of industry output, while at the right end of the axis, at the 100 percent point, the opposite is true. The purpose of this somewhat unusual construction is that it enables us to compare the costs and sales of the two firms directly. For firm 1, rising output share means moving from left to right on the graph, in the usual manner. For firm 2, however, rising output share means moving from right to left.

Clearly, the allocation of the task of production will be efficient at point *b* on the horizontal axis, where the marginal costs of the two firms are

[16] Note that here we are entitled to talk about average costs (or average total costs) because we are dealing with single-product firms for which there can be no unattributable common costs (see Section VI *supra*).

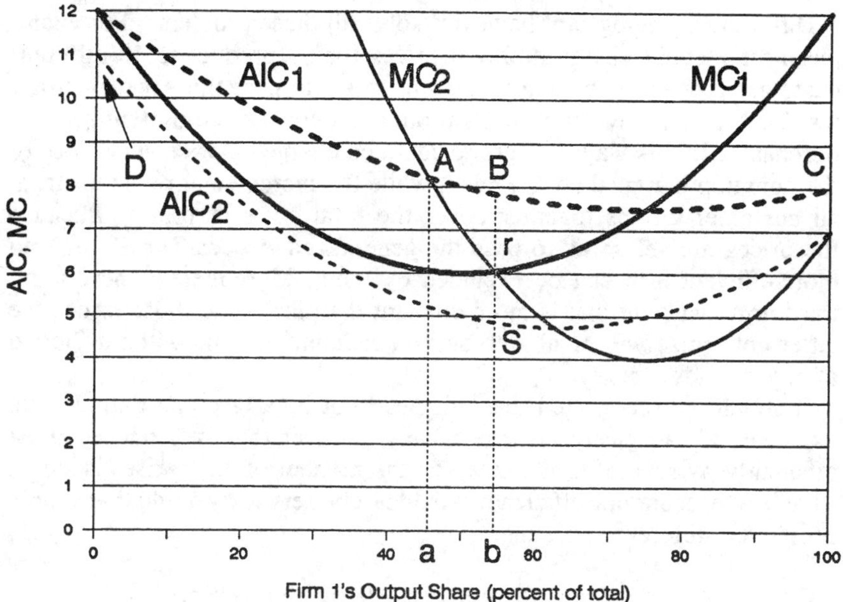

FIGURE 1.—Differential pricing required for efficiency

equal (point *r*). For in this case sharing of the output task clearly results in lower total output cost than production of the entire product by either firm alone. This is clear because at efficient output share *b* the average cost of firm 1 (point *B*) is lower than when firm 1 serves 100 percent of the market (point *C*), and the same is true for firm 2 (point *S* is substantially lower than *D*).

Yet there is no undifferentiated price that will lead to efficiency. It is true that a fixed price equal to the common marginal cost at point *r* will lead both firms to select the outputs that place them at the efficient output-share point, *b*. But since *r* lies below *B*, it is clear that this price will be below the average cost of firm 1. This means, most obviously, that firm 1 will be unable to survive at the marginal-cost price, so that, even though it is inefficient, the industry will be driven to monopoly, or a price will have to be set at some level above *r*—a level that is incompatible with an efficient allocation of output between the two firms. Moreover, even if firm 1 is able to survive a price equal to *r* by virtue of some form of subsidy, that price can exclude a third firm more efficient than firm 1; that is, it will exclude a third firm whose average cost of producing firm 1's output at point *b* is less than 1's average cost, *B*, but higher than the marginal-cost price, *r*.

Differential pricing can, however, solve all these problems. For example, firm 1 could charge different prices for its product to 10 different customer groups, with each group's price set to pass the Areeda-Turner test for the increment in firm 1's production constituted by that group's purchases. In this way, one group could be charged a price very close to the common marginal cost level, *r*, while the incremental revenues from all customer groups together cover the total costs of firm 1. Because the prices are set so as to pass the generalized Areeda-Turner test, no more-efficient firm can be excluded by them. Moreover, if there is no third firm available that is more efficient than firm 1, at those prices the latter enterprise will be able to survive indefinitely, and without the aid of any subsidy.

It should be recognized that this need not be a rare and pathological example. It can easily be true of any product that is produced most efficiently by several firms, in which the number of enterprises is small. That is why economic efficiency would not be served by a rule that simply prohibited differential pricing.[17]

XI. On Short-Run Profit Maximization Criteria of Predatory Pricing

Two ancillary topics remain to be dealt with here. One is the role of short-run profit maximization in a test of predatory pricing, an issue that has arisen in several discussions. The second is the proper role of opportunity cost in the generalized Areeda-Turner test.

The notion that failure to maximize short-run profits is somehow associated with predation has arisen in the Areeda-Turner discussion from the very beginning. Thus, Areeda and Turner themselves remark, "A necessary but . . . not sufficient condition of predation is the sacrifice of short-run profits."[18] However, the U.S. Court of Appeals, Fifth Circuit, has gone well beyond Areeda-Turner on this matter. It has asserted that, to prevail in a complaint of predation, "a plaintiff must at least show that either (1) a competitor is charging a price below his average variable cost in the competitive market or (2) the competitor is charging a price below its short-run, profit-maximizing price and barriers to entry are great

[17] It should be noted that the famous Ramsey pricing rule, which is the recognized rule for efficient pricing in circumstances where prices equal to marginal costs are incompatible with survival of the firm, uses differential pricing to obtain its optimality results. That is, Ramsey analysis shows that, where marginal-cost prices are not feasible financially, then differential pricing is required for optimality. On all this see, for example, William J. Baumol & J. Gregory Sidak, Toward Competition in Local Telephony ch. 3 (1994).

[18] Areeda & Turner, *supra* note 1, at 703.

enough to enable the discriminator to reap the benefits of predation before new entry is possible."[19] This would seem to imply that in the circumstances noted, failure to maximize profit is also *sufficient* to prove predation.

Now, there is a sensible interpretation of this short-run profit-maximization test, and there is also one that makes no sense. If one means by it that normal business behavior requires the firm always to seek the price that maximizes the profits that the firm will earn before some nearby horizon date, then the proposition is, indeed, nonsense. Every rational and successful firm has at some time forgone near-term profits in the expectation that the temporary sacrifice constitutes what amounts to an investment that will later pay off in spades. Rare is the firm that did not lose money during the weeks or months after it was first established. Every firm that decides to shut down a factory in order to retool and modernize deliberately elects to sacrifice short-term profits in the sense we are now using the term. Every firm that undertakes to invest heavily on an innovation whose payoff is expected only several years in the future is making a similar choice. It is not only silly but destructive of effective exercise of entrepreneurship to determine that such an act is suspect. As said, if this view were accepted, there would be few if any firms that would not qualify as suspects.

There is, however, a second interpretation of the term, "failure to maximize short-run profits." This sensible connotation is the adoption for some limited period of a price that reduces the present value of the firm's future profits. Here, the term "short-run" pertains to the limited period of time the price is in force. It places no time constraint on the period during which any resulting effects on the profits that are earned can be taken into consideration. In this sense, a new product price that will last for 2 weeks, and that entails $10,000 in net costs during those 2 weeks, but which is expected eventually to stimulate demand sufficiently to make up for this outlay many-fold, need not be a departure from short-run profit maximization. Only if that 2-week outlay cannot reasonably be expected to be made up in the future, or if it can be made up only through later monopoly profits after rivals are driven from the field by the price cut, is that requirement violated. There is, indeed, some reason to suspect predatory behavior if short-run profits are deliberately satisfied in the second of these senses, but not in the first. These observations can be summarized as:

RULE 7. There is absolutely nothing predatory about a price decision

[19] International Air Ind. Inc. v. American Excelsior Co. 517 F.2d 714, 724 (5th Cir. 1975); Adjustors Replace-A-Car v. Agency Rent-A-Car, Inc. 739 F.2d 884, 889–90 (5th Cir. 1984).

by a firm that fails to maximize the profits it can expect to earn during some brief proximate time period, provided that this price passes the (average variable cost) Areeda-Turner test and that this act can be expected to yield returns in the future that make up for whatever has been sacrificed in this way.

However, one can perhaps agree that a "necessary . . . condition of predation" is the adoption for some limited period of a price that will reduce the present value of the firm's stream of expected future profits, constituting a short-run action by the firm that is inconsistent with maximization of the present value of present and future profits.

Some courts have taken the position that the preceding argument is troublesome. For it seems to allow a defense holding that short-run losses are acceptable if only they raise the present discounted value of the firm. However, this is precisely what rational predation does. How, then, does one distinguish between predation and its absence if short-run losses are considered unobjectionable? Surely, the average variable cost test is the appropriate way to deal with the dilemma. That is, a price that exceeds average variable cost as defined here cannot be predatory, even if it does not maximize short-run profit. For, as has been shown in Section IV above, no price by an incumbent that at least equals its average variable cost can force the exit or prevent the entry of any rival that is at least equally efficient in terms of the incremental cost of the output in question.

XII. On the Role of Opportunity Costs in the Areeda-Turner Test

Economists agree that the type of sacrifice that they call "opportunity cost" is a legitimate part of any cost calculation. Indeed, they (including myself) assert that any cost calculation that totally ignores the opportunity cost component is likely to be illegitimate. The courts have not generally committed themselves on this issue in their dealings with the Areeda-Turner test. I show here that the matter is somewhat complex and that if the test is used to determine whether the price at issue constitutes a threat to the existence of an efficient rival, the opportunity cost component of avoidable cost must be treated in a particular way that will be spelled out presently.

The *opportunity cost* of an act such as the adoption of some price is defined to consist of any earnings implicitly or explicitly forgone as a result of that decision. For example, the opportunity cost of a student's decision to attend college includes any earnings forgone because that decision prevents the student from accepting full-time employment. It is a real cost that must be weighed in the decision to attend college because, if that decision is not taken, the prospective student will be better off financially by the amount of those wages. This, then, must be weighed in along with the other costs and the benefits of college attendance.

In business decisions, opportunity cost takes two primary forms that play an important and very different role in our discussion. The first is the opportunity cost of *owner-supplied inputs,* and the second is the cost of *revenues forgone* as a result of the decision in question. For example, suppose a single-proprietor firm decides to reduce the price of its product and this results in an increase in sales whose production requires some additional investment. If the owner supplies the funds out of her own savings, those funds cannot be considered to be free. The decision to tie them up in the company means that they cannot be invested in bonds where they would have earned, say, $9,000 per year in interest. On this account, then, the proprietor is $9,000 per annum poorer than she otherwise might have been, and failure to take this into consideration can clearly lead to an irrational decision.

The same price cut means that the goods that would otherwise have been sold at the previous higher price—say, 1,000 units of product at a price of $30 per unit—will now be sold at the reduced price of $25, for example, resulting in a forgone revenue of $5 × 1,000 units = $5,000. This loss of revenue, that is, this opportunity cost, too, must be weighed against the other gains and losses that can be expected to stem from the price cut before deciding whether or not the price reduction should be adopted.

Turning now to our central issue, suppose it is alleged that the price cut is predatory and that the new price should consequently be subjected to an Areeda-Turner test comparing the price with avoidable cost. Obviously, the inclusion of opportunity cost can only increase the avoidable cost figure and make the Areeda-Turner test more difficult to pass. Should all the opportunity costs be included in the calculation?

The answer, that may be unexpected to economists, is that if the Areeda-Turner test is used (as it is argued here it should be) to determine whether the price constitutes a threat to efficient competitors, then the opportunity cost of owner-supplied inputs *should* be included, but the revenues forgone as a result of the price cut *should not.*

The reason the cost of the owner-supplied income should be included is that any funds that our firm uses to produce its pertinent input must have their counterpart if that same output is instead produced by an efficient rival. If additional investment is required to provide that output, the rival, too, will have to provide such funds, either by borrowing or some other such means or by obtaining them from the rival's proprietors. If our firm's price does not cover the cost of its own invested funds, it is also likely to be unable to cover the rival's required investment cost, even if the rival is the more efficient supplier and can carry out its production cost with a (slightly) lower investment. In other words, a price of firm F that does not cover the opportunity cost of that firm's avoidable investment can constitute a threat to a more efficient rival and should be considered to fail the generalized Areeda-Turner test.

In contrast, the revenue firm F forgoes by reducing its price has no relevance to determination of whether the new price constitutes a threat to the presence of an efficient rival. If, in our example, the new price of $25 covers all of firm F's pertinent and avoidable input costs, both its opportunity costs and its other costs, then that price should by definition cover the corresponding costs of the lower input quantities needed by an efficient rival to produce the output in question. True, the higher revenue that the higher $30 price would have offered might also have constituted a benefit to the rival, but it is irrelevant to whether the lower price, in itself, is or is not a threat to an efficient rival. That gives us, finally:

RULE 8. In carrying out the generalized Areeda-Turner test of a price or set of prices, it is essential to include all opportunity costs of owner-supplied inputs in the calculation of associated avoidable cost, but it is necessary to omit the opportunity cost of any revenue forgone if the price in question constitutes a reduction from an earlier price.[20]

XIII. FINAL COMMENT: THE HETERODOX POSITIONS ON AREEDA-TURNER

This article has departed from standard views of the Areeda-Turner test in a number of ways. For example, the possibility that combinations of services can fail the modified Areeda-Turner test, even if all the individual services pass, seems not to have arisen in the literature. Still, it should be recognized that in practice courts do seem to have been willing to consider the prices of a set of outputs in combination or an intertemporal sequence of prices in predation lawsuits, just as my proposed rule on this subject requires. Similar comments apply to other rules in this article, such as that on the proper role of opportunity cost in the Areeda-Turner calculation. Perhaps the most novel element in the discussion is the proposed treatment of the Areeda-Turner test as a means to determine whether the price at issue constitutes (or constituted) a threat to efficient rivals, and my deduction from this point of departure that average vari-

[20] There are at least two cases in which the courts have explicitly rejected forgone revenues of profits as a type of opportunity cost that must be considered in a predatory pricing case. These are Continental Airlines, Inc. v. American Airlines, Inc., 824 F. Supp. 689 (S.D. Tex. 1993) (in a predatory pricing case, rejecting forgone revenues as an opportunity cost that must be included in determining defendant's relevant costs); In re IBM Peripheral EDP Devices Antitrust Litigation, 459 F. Supp. 626 (N.D. Cal. 1978) (same).

able cost, interpreted as average avoidable cost, is really the pertinent criterion, and not merely an inferior proxy for marginal cost.

Bibliography

Areeda, Phillip, and Turner, Donald. "Predatory Pricing and Related Practices under Section 2 of the Sherman Act." *Harvard Law Review* 88 (1975): 637–733.

Baumol, William J. "Quasi-Permanence of Price Reductions: A Policy for Prevention of Predatory Pricing." *Yale Law Journal* 89 (1979): 1–26.

Baumol, William J. *Superfairness: Applications and Theory*. Cambridge, Mass.: MIT Press, 1986.

Baumol, William J.; Koehn, Michael F.; and Willig, Robert D. "How Arbitrary Is Arbitrary?—or, Toward the Deserved Demise of Full Cost Allocation." *Public Utilities Fortnightly* 120 (September 3, 1987): 16–21.

Baumol, William J., and Sidak, J. Gregory. *Toward Competition in Local Telephony*. Cambridge, Mass.: MIT Press, 1994.

Joskow, Paul L., and Klevorick, Alvin K. "A Framework for Analyzing Predatory Pricing Policy." *Yale Law Journal* 89 (1979): 213–70.

McGee, John S. "Predatory Price Cutting: The Standard Oil (New Jersey) Case." *Journal of Law and Economics* 1 (1958): 137–69.

Parloff, Roger. "Fare's Fair." *American Lawyer* 65 (October 1993): 60–66.

Telser, Lester G. *Economic Theory and the Core*. Chicago and London: University of Chicago Press, 1978.

Williamson, Oliver E. "Predatory Pricing: A Strategic and Welfare Analysis." *Yale Law Journal* 87 (1977): 284–340.

[11]

Having Your Cake: How to Preserve Universal-Service Cross Subsidies While Facilitating Competitive Entry

William J. Baumol[†]

Differential pricing for access to bottleneck inputs such as local telephone facilities or electricity transmission facilities is shown to solve the old dilemma of deregulation: facilitating competitive entry without destroying cross subsidies indispensable for "universal service" programs. If bottleneck facilities are inputs to two services, one of which subsidizes the other, entrants that provide the subsidized service must receive the same subsidy in the access price as consumers receive when they purchase those services. Rivals in the supply of the other service must contribute an equivalent subsidy through paying a higher access price. Differential access pricing allows efficient competitors to find it equally profitable to supply either service because any motive for "cream skimming" disappears. Such differential pricing, coupled with access pricing consistent with the Efficient Component Pricing Rule, is shown to be necessary for economic efficiency.

---

† Director, C.V. Starr Center for Applied Economics, New York University; and senior research economist and professor emeritus, Princeton University. I am grateful to the C.V. Starr Center for its support of this work. I am exceedingly indebted to Scott Bohannon of Sidley & Austin for his invaluable contribution in finding appropriate references to the legal literature and related matters. I must also thank the editors of this Journal for their very helpful suggestions and, as always, Sue Anne Batey Blackman, who deserves much credit and bears none of the guilt.

Introduction

Regulators have long suffered from an apparently irreconcilable dilemma. Their own understandable predilections, supplemented by powerful political pressures, have led them to impose a set of cross subsidies on the prices of the firms they regulate. Cross subsidies systematically favor particular groups of customers, such as household customers or isolated farmers, at the expense of other groups, such as business customers or those near supply sources, by forcing the latter group to subsidize the former.[1] At the same time, however, regulators have also sought to stimulate entry and competition in regulated industries. For example, the Telecommunications Act of 1996[2] requires a monopoly local telephone service provider to lease parts of its network to its competitors at cost-based rates, thereby allowing entrant firms to offer service without incurring the tremendous expense of building a duplicative network before beginning service. The dilemma is that the twin goals of imposing cross subsidies and promoting competition are ordinarily incompatible. Effective competition tends to eliminate the source of cross subsidies by driving down the prices of items that yield particularly large profits.

A number of misguided expedients have been adopted in an effort to reconcile these two conflicting objectives. Most notably, some regulators have taken actions that severely handicap incumbent firms in some portions of the regulated market while impeding entrant firms in other parts. The result is the creation of a cartel in which each firm is assigned its own monopolized terrain.[3] Of course, this gives the *appearance* of

---

1 For example, suppose it costs Bell Atlantic only $10 to provide most customers in New Jersey with local telephone service. Suppose further that the cost of service for some rural customers is considerably higher, say $50, and that the average cost of statewide service is $15. Rather than setting local rates near $10 for the majority of customers and $50 for the more costly rural customers, regulators may require Bell Atlantic to charge approximately $15 for all of its customers. The low-cost customers are then said to be cross-subsidizing the rural customers.

2 Pub. L. No. 104-104, 110 Stat. 56 (codified in scattered sections of 47 U.S.C.).

3 For example, it can be argued that in the U.K., telephone rates were set by regulation in a way that favored entrants in dealing with large business firms but handicapped entrants in sales to

competition but ultimately helps only to protect cross subsidies from the eroding effects of true competition.

In this Article, I propose a regime of *non-uniform* and competitively neutral pricing of access to bottleneck services owned by an incumbent monopoly. By "bottleneck" services, I refer to services that are indispensable to both the incumbent and its competitors in the production or delivery of the final product. I will show that the proposed arrangement is *competitively neutral*, meaning that it does not favor either the incumbent or the entrants in the final-product market. Moreover, I will prove that the arrangement is the only access pricing rule that can achieve neutrality in the presence of cross subsidy and price discrimination in final-product sales. Lastly, I will argue that all affected parties can gain from this arrangement, since it offers full access to efficient suppliers in each and every pertinent market. Both incumbents and entrants will gain by having access to all markets. The public will gain because competition will pervade the industry. Finally, regulators will gain because their apparently inconsistent goals will be reconciled: Pervasive competition will coexist with the cross subsidies they deem to be in the social interest.

This Article is divided into two parts. Part I provides relevant background information on bottleneck pricing issues. It discusses the importance of bottleneck pricing for regulatory policy, the parity-pricing formula for competitively neutral access to a single product market, and previous approaches to bottleneck pricing. Part II shows how parity pricing can be adapted to ensure competitive neutrality in a multi-product industry with cross-subsidies or differential pricing. It demonstrates that competitive neutrality requires differential access pricing that precisely replicates the price-cost differences among the final products for which the bottleneck facility is an input.

---

households. *See* ELI NOAM, TELECOMMUNICATIONS IN EUROPE 110-13 (1992); JOHN VICKERS & GEORGE YARROW, PRIVATIZATION: AN ECONOMIC ANALYSIS 229-30, 238-39 (1988). In the United States, some electricity cogenerators were not permitted to compete for customers with the utilities, but the utilities were forced to buy electricity from the cogenerators at prices set by regulatory formula. *See* MICHAEL E. SMALL, A GUIDE TO FERC REGULATION AND RATEMAKING OF ELECTRIC UTILITIES AND OTHER POWER SUPPLIERS 148-51 (3d ed. 1994).

I. Background: The Bottleneck Pricing Issues[4]

A. *Current Importance of the Issue for Privatization and Facilitation of Competitive Entry*

How to price bottleneck services is an issue that is being debated vigorously before courts and regulatory agencies throughout the industrial and industrializing world, with the formulas presented in this Article often being the focus of these litigative proceedings.[5] In the United States, the issue of pricing is at the forefront of discussion of means to facilitate competitive entry into activities that have traditionally been run by franchised monopolies.[6]

Bottleneck pricing is now a pivotal issue in at least three industries: telecommunications,[7] electric power,[8] and rail transportation.[9] In telecommunications, the equipment of the monopolist local telephone company become bottleneck facilities. Entrants are not able to operate without them, and the facilities are available from only one owner. In response, the government has required current monopoly providers of local telephone services to rent their facilities to entrants who desire to use them.[10] This allows entrants to avoid having to build expensive plants and equipment of their own, making entry a practical possibility. While this solution *seems* to solve the entry barrier problem, the regulating government agency must also specify the *price* at which the facilities will be offered to entrants. If the owner of the facilities is permitted to charge any price, it can protect itself from entry by setting the price at such an exorbitant level that no entrant can afford to pay it. In State Commission

4 For references to the current literature on the issue, the reader may want to consult William J. Baumol et al., *Parity Pricing and Its Critics: A Necessary Condition for Efficiency in the Provision of Bottleneck Services to Competitors*, 14 YALE J. ON REG. 145 (1997).

5 *See, e.g.*, Telecom Corp. v. Clear Communications, Ltd. [1995] 1 N.Z.L.R. 385; St. Louis Southwestern Ry.—Intertrackage Rights Over Mo. Pac. R.R.—Kan. City to St. Louis, 8 I.C.C.2d 80 (1991); Alternative Regulatory Frameworks for Local Exch. Carriers, 33 C.P.U.C.2d 43 (1989).

6 *See, e.g.*, Implementation of the Local Competition Provisions in the Telecommunications Act of 1996, 11 F.C.C.R. 15,499, ¶¶ 3-5, at 15,505-06 (1996) (presenting this issue as one that the Telecommunications Act of 1996 seeks to address) [hereinafter *Local Competition Order*].

7 *See id.* ¶¶ 625-766, at 15,814-83.

8 *See* Inquiry Concerning the Commission's Pricing Policy for Transmission Services Provided by Public Utilities Under the Federal Power Act, 59 Fed. Reg. 55,031, 55,033-35 (1994); WILLIAM J. BAUMOL & J. GREGORY SIDAK, TRANSMISSION PRICING AND STRANDED COSTS IN THE ELECTRIC POWER INDUSTRY 115-58 (1995) (discussing the efficient pricing of electric transmission facilities and past pricing decisions by the Federal Energy Regulatory Commission).

9 *See, e.g.*, FMC Wyo. Corp. v. Union Pac. R.R., S.T.B. Fin., No. 33467, 1997 WL 768315 (S.T.B. Dec. 12, 1997); Central Power & Light Co. v. Southern Pac. Transp. Co., No. 41242, 1997 WL 299703 (S.T.B. Apr. 28, 1997).

10 *See* 47 U.S.C. § 251(c)(3) (Supp. II 1996); *Local Competition Order*, *supra* note 6, ¶¶ 342-365, at 15,671-83.

arbitrations and in proceedings before the Federal Communications Commission, carriers such as Bell Atlantic, GTE, and AT&T have advocated various cost standards, including both book (or historic) costs and forward-looking cost standards such as the Efficient Component Pricing Rule and Total Service Long-Run Incremental Cost.[11]

In electricity, the issue has been raised by the inauguration of competition in power *generation.* Today, and increasingly so in the near future, the established electric utility firms in the United States will face the competition of rival generators of electricity.[12] However, before electricity can be sold as a final product, it must be transported to customers. The large capacity and high cost of electricity transmission facilities make rivalry in electricity *transmission* (as distinguished from generation) impractical. Transmission facilities are often owned by electric utilities; these companies and their competitors in generation must use the same facilities to transport electricity from generating stations to customers. Thus, the transmission facilities are bottleneck inputs to the supply of the final product—delivered electric power—and the pricing issue is clearly analogous to the setting of a fee for use of a telecommunications facility as a bottleneck input.

The rail transportation case will bring out the issue most clearly.[13] Consider two railroads, *A* and *B*, which want to compete in serving cities *C* and *D*. The cities are separated by high mountains with a single pass, through which railroad *A* owns tracks and in which there is no room for a second set of tracks. Railroad *B* therefore rents permission to traverse (or trackage rights over) that portion of *A*'s route. The mountain pass is clearly a bottleneck input to the transportation of freight between the two cities. In these circumstances, the question is what is the efficient price that railroad *A* should charge its potential rival, *B*, for use of the tracks? Too high a price will patently exclude competition, while too low a price will entail a competition-distorting subsidy from the pass-owning railroad to the

11 *See, e.g.*, AT&T Communications, Inc. v. Bellsouth Telecomms., Inc., 20 F. Supp. 2d 1097 (E.D. Ky. 1998); Southwestern Bell Tel. Co. v. AT&T Communications Inc., No. A97-CA-132-SS, 1998 WL 657717 (S.D. Tex. Aug. 31, 1998); GTE South Inc. v. Morrison, 6 F. Supp. 2d 517 (E.D. Va. 1998).

12 *See, e.g.*, Promoting Wholesale Competition Through Open Access Non-Discriminatory Transmission Servs. by Public Utils., 61 Fed. Reg. 21,540 (1996) (discussing several Federal Energy Regulatory Commission proceedings initiated to facilitate a more competitive electric industry); Ralph Cavanagh, *California Scores with New Electricity Choices*, SACRAMENTO BUS. J. (Aug. 11, 1997) <http://www.amcity.com/sacramento/stories/081197/editorial5.html>.

13 The simple example provided in the text has been litigated on numerous occasions. The most famous case, *United States v. Terminal Railroad Ass'n*, 224 U.S. 383 (1912), established the essential facilities doctrine in antitrust law. There, a group of railroads that jointly owned a bottleneck railroad terminal in St. Louis were denying their competitors access to the terminal. The Supreme Court found that this practice violated Section 1 of the Sherman Antitrust Act because it denied access to a facility essential for their competitors to compete. Today, railroad mergers continue to concern agencies such as the Surface Transportation Board. *See, e.g.*, *Central Power & Light Co.*, 1997 WL.

entrant.

The bottleneck pricing issue has arisen similarly in Australia,[14] the United Kingdom,[15] Hong Kong,[16] and the European Union.[17] Indeed, it appears wherever privatization initially leaves an industry in the hands of a monopoly or, at the very least, a large firm that possesses substantial market power. The issue of pricing is also likely to become an international matter of great urgency in the near future as a result of the Telecommunications Agreement of 1997, under which approximately seventy countries agreed to open their telecommunications markets to foreign competition.[18] If international competition is to become a reality, obstacles that impede entry by foreign rivals must be removed or reduced.

B. *Parity Pricing (ECPR): The Rule for Efficient Pricing of Bottleneck Services*

The most discussed solution to the problem of determining an efficient price for a bottleneck service is based on a result I call the Level-Playing-Field Theorem. This theorem tells us that only by using certain formulas (equations (1a) or (1b) below) can we *neutrally* price a monopoly-owned bottleneck service required by both the bottleneck owner and its final-product competitors. This rule is called the Efficient Component Pricing Rule (ECPR) or the *parity pricing* formula. The term "parity price" refers to the price at which a competitor neither receives nor gives up a competitive advantage to the owner of a bottleneck service for using that service. According to the theory, a level playing field, and hence efficiency in the competition between the bottleneck owner and its

14 To resolve the issue, the Australian Competition & Consumer Commission chose to use Total Service Long-Run Incremental Cost, the standard advocated by many potential entrants, over the Efficient Component Pricing Rule. *See* AUSTRALIAN COMPETITION & CONSUMER COMM'N, ACCESS PRICING PRINCIPLES (1997).

15 OFTEL, the telecommunications regulatory agency in the U.K., has embraced long-run incremental cost principles for pricing of bottleneck facilities owned by dominant carriers such as British Telecommunications. *See* OFFICE OF TELECOMM., OFTEL'S SUBMISSION TO THE MONOPOLIES AND MERGERS COMMISSION INQUIRY INTO THE PRICES OF CALLS TO MOBILE PHONES ¶ 3.2 (1998) ("OFTEL believes that the most appropriate and economically efficient basis for assessment of charges for a bottleneck service is that derived from forward looking Long Run Incremental Costs (LRIC).").

16 *See* 1 INTERNATIONAL TELECOMM. UNION, GENERAL TRENDS IN TELECOMMUNICATIONS REFORM 1998, at 96 (1998).

17 *See* Directive 97/51/EC of the European Parliament and of the Council of 6 October 1997 Amending Council Directives 90/387/EEC and 92/44/EEC for the Purpose of Adaptation to a Competitive Environment in Telecommunications, 1997 O.J. (L 295) 23; Council Directive 92/44/EEC of 5 June 1992 on the Application of Open Network Provision to Leased Lines, 1992 O.J. (L 165) 27; Directive 97/33/EC of the European Parliament and of the Council of 30 June 1997 on Interconnection in Telecommunications with Regard to Ensuring Universal Service and Interoperability Through Application of the Principles of Open Network Provision (ONP), 1997 O.J. (L 199) 32.

18 *See* World Trade Organization: Agreement on Telecommunications Services (Fourth Protocol on General Agreement on Trade in Services), 36 I.L.M. 354, 366 (1997).

competitors, can only arise if the bottleneck service in question is priced as follows:[19]

Bottleneck service price per unit = Bottleneck owner's final product price minus the incremental cost to the owner of all final-product inputs, other than bottleneck service, (1a)

or, in convenient symbols:

$$P_b = P_{bf} - IC_{br} \qquad (1b)$$

where the subscript f refers to *final* product, so that P_{bf} is the price of the bottleneck owner's final product, and r refers to the *remaining* inputs (other than the bottleneck input) that enter into the incremental cost of the final product.

Exhibit 1, below, demonstrates that at any other price for the bottleneck service, a competitor's minimum viable final product price will not be equal to the bottleneck owner's price plus (or minus) the competitor's cost advantage (or disadvantage) in supplying the inputs other than the bottleneck service needed for the final product. In other words, at any other bottleneck service price, one of the suppliers will be unable to achieve the final product price advantage to which its own efficiency entitles it.

19 As I have previously written and emphasized, this pricing rule is necessary but not sufficient for economic efficiency or protection of the public interest. In addition to equations (1a) or (1b), these goals require either effective competition or regulation in the final-product markets to ensure that the final-product prices yield no monopoly profits and no other efficiency-undermining distortions. For a summary of the discussion and references, see Baumol et al., *supra* note 4, at 147-48. It should be noted that the pertinent output increment for which the cost is calculated is the volume of business that is expected to be lost to competitors. I am grateful to Robert Graniere of the National Regulatory Research Institute for discussion related to this point.

Yale Journal on Regulation Vol. 16:1, 1999

EXHIBIT 1
The Level-Playing-Field Theorem:
Derivation of the Competitive Neutrality Formula for Access Pricing[20]

To derive competitive-neutrality formula (1), we define a **level playing field** in the pricing of access to require the following:

Suppose a firm's incremental cost (IC) per unit of output of supplying the non-bottleneck components of the final product is X dollars less than that of a bottleneck-owning competitor (or the reverse). Then, this more efficient firm should just be able (without losing money) to price the final product by X dollars less than the price charged by its less efficient competitor.

More formally, we have as the definition of a level playing field:

bottleneck owner final-product price – minimum competitor final-product price = IC of owner-supplied remaining inputs – IC of competitor-supplied remaining inputs. (2)

But we know that the competitor's minimum (financially-viable) price is:

minimum competitor final-product price = price of bottleneck service + IC of competitor-supplied remaining inputs. (3)

Adding these two equations we immediately obtain the **competitive neutrality formula**:

the only price of bottleneck service that provides a level playing field = bottleneck owner final-product price – IC of owner-supplied remaining inputs. (4)

Competitive neutrality formula (4) is clearly the same as formula (1), so that any bottleneck service price that violates equation (4) or its equivalent (1) must tilt the playing field, favoring either the bottleneck owner at the expense of its competitors or the reverse.

It should be noted that the rule is not very difficult to carry out in practice or for the regulator to monitor. Nowadays in regulatory arenas, estimates of incremental costs are provided fairly routinely and appear to be determinable to a reasonable degree of approximation without

20 This formula was originally contributed by Robert Willig, with the current author participating in dissemination and adaptation to particular regulatory and analytic issues. For an early description of the analysis, see Robert D. Willig, *The Theory of Network Access Pricing*, *in* ISSUES IN PUBLIC UTILITY REGULATION 109 (Harry M. Trebbing ed., 1979).

enormous cost or effort. For example, telecommunications regulatory agencies in the United States (and possibly other countries as well) can use a number of off-the-shelf models such as the HAI Model, the Benchmark Cost Proxy Model, and the Hybrid Cost Proxy Model, to calculate universal service subsidies or incremental cost of telecommunications network components.[21] In addition, most of the state regulatory commissions have conducted a number of incremental cost studies over the past two years to determine unbundled network element prices.[22] Thus, if the rule is correct, to calculate the efficient price of a bottleneck service, one merely needs to observe the final-product price currently charged by the owner of the bottleneck facility and subtract from it the pertinent incremental cost.

C. *Previous Approaches to the Pricing of Bottleneck Services*

It is not possible to offer a general characterization of the methods previously used to determine the prices charged for bottleneck services. These prices were often arrived at by informal negotiation between the owner of the facility and its users. As far as I know, there were no generally accepted regulatory rules, but where the issue of pricing did arise, its resolution was based on what was deemed to be the pertinent cost, which generally meant the "fully allocated cost." The fully allocated cost of any product or activity may be described as the cost directly attributable to the item in question (in practice, an approximation to its incremental cost) plus some share of the firm's remaining costs. These remaining *common costs* range from the salary of the company president to the cost of a railroad track's construction and maintenance, which is attributable in common to the various commodities carried over the given route. Since no unique allocation standard is possible for costs that inseparably serve several purposes simultaneously, the share of common cost assigned to a particular product or activity was determined on the basis of an arbitrarily selected accounting criterion. The result was frequent litigation over the cost calculations.

21 *See* Federal-State Joint Bd. on Universal Serv., 12 F.C.C.R. 18,514 (1997) (analyzing a variety of models that use forward-looking cost methods for calculating universal service support). Many parties have submitted extensive comments and reply comments on how those models should be refined. *See id.* The FCC has recently released its guidelines on telecommunications cost modeling. *See* Federal-State Joint Bd. on Universal Serv., 1998 WL 751153 (F.C.C. Oct. 28, 1998)

22 *See, e.g.*, Petitions by AT&T Communications, Inc., MCI Telecomm. Corp. and MCI Metro Access Transmission Servs., Inc., for Arbitration of Certain Terms and Conditions of a Proposed Agreement with GTE Florida, Inc. Concerning Interconnection and Resale Under the Telecomm. Act of 1996, No. 970847-TP, 1997 WL 41243, at *63-*64 (Fla Pub. Serv. Comm'n May 21, 1997); AT&T Communications, Inc., No. P-140, Sub 50, 1996 WL 769763, at *30-*34 (N.C. Util. Comm'n Dec. 23, 1996), *aff'd*, No. P-140, Sub 50, 1997 WL 233035 (N.C. Utils. Comm'n Apr. 11, 1997).

A simple example will bring out most clearly the contrast between such procedures and parity pricing, using a rough characterization of earlier practice. I refer again to my railroad case, in which railroads *A* and *B* compete in serving cities *C* and *D*.[23] Railroad *A* owns the only tracks that can fit in the pass through the high mountains that separate the cities. Therefore, the mountain pass is clearly a bottleneck input to the transportation of freight between the two cities. Suppose railroad *A*'s incremental cost of carrying a carload of lumber between the two cities is $1,000, with $10 of this amount attributable to wear and tear of track when a carload of lumber crosses the pass. Railroad *A* has been charging shippers $1,500 per carload for this traffic and using the $500 surplus over the incremental cost of lumber transport for the entire route to cover costs common to lumber and other types of freight—costs such as track maintenance and replacement. The railroad earns no more than competitive profit overall.

Under these circumstances, the ECPR price for the right of railroad *B* to send a carload of lumber over the mountain pass is, by formula (1), the $1500 price charged by *A* for transport over the route, minus the $990 incremental cost of the non-bottleneck portion of the shipment ($990 = $1000 total IC minus the $10 bottleneck IC). Thus, the parity price is $510, which equals $1500 minus $990. However, at least until very recently, the regulators would have calculated the fee quite differently. For example, since the $10 incremental cost of *B*'s traversal is only one percent of the total incremental cost of the route, they can be expected to have reasoned that railroad *A* is entitled only to one percent of the contribution to common costs that flows from *B*'s shipment between the two cities, making the regulatory fee $15 rather than the $510 price required by the parity principle.

We see that the two prices can be dramatically different because one is based on a regulatory concept of equity and the other (the ECPR price) is based on the requirements of economic efficiency. At first glance it may appear that the far higher ECPR price is unfair because it extracts so high a fee for traversal of a small portion of the route. However, as Exhibit 1 implicitly demonstrates, the fee set at this level allows one to say that both railroads are paying the same price for traversal of the mountain pass. The lower, more traditional fee is therefore not only a subsidy to the other railroad that can permit it to take business away from a more efficient competitor; it also treats the two railroads differently, permitting railroad *B* to rent use of the mountain-pass tracks at a cost far lower than what it costs railroad *A* to provide the tracks.

---

23 *See supra* note 13 and accompanying text.

II. The Differential-Pricing Issue for Bottleneck Services

We come at last to the central issue of this Article: How can regulators permit competition in regulated industries without making it impossible to retain the cross subsidies that commonly serve as the instruments of universal service? Regulators seek to maintain cross subsidies in deregulated industries. However, universal service often makes this difficult, since it requires very low prices to impecunious consumers or consumers whose location makes them extremely costly to serve. These prices often fail to cover the costs of serving these customers, who are expected to refrain from purchasing the regulated service if the price of the service is not subsidized. But where such cross subsidies exist, competition will be driven to engage in "cream skimming." Competitors will focus on the more lucrative products of the regulated firm, which are the products that provide the revenues that finance the cross subsidies. Thus it may appear, at first glance, that competition is incompatible with the cross subsidies of universal service. This Part will show that competition and cross subsidies can, in fact, be made to coexist.

It should be noted here that cross subsidies may have a defensible social purpose. For example, an increase in the number of subscribers to telephone service increases the value of telecommunications facilities to retailing firms. Since these indirect benefits ("positive externalities" in the jargon of economics) accrue to the firms rather than to the subscribers who pay for the service they receive, both equity and efficiency can call for some subsidy from business subscribers to household subscribers. As another example, it may well be agreed that impecunious elderly persons should be ensured access to telephone service or to electric power, and that this requires that such services be provided to them at prices that do not cover the pertinent costs. But it may only be politically feasible to provide the funding for such low prices from the buyers of other services of the firm in question. Other reasonable grounds for the preservation of cross subsidies, both economic and sociological, can readily be suggested. There is nothing new in the observation that cross subsidies can sometimes be justifiable. Rather, the novel point is that such desirable cross subsidies can be made sustainable, despite the presence of competition, by appropriate access pricing rules.

An extension of the Level-Playing-Field Theorem demonstrates that it is possible to make competition and cross subsidies compatible. The Theorem shows that where there is cross subsidy or price discrimination of any sort in final product prices, then any *uniform* price for access to a bottleneck service cannot be competitively neutral. Such a uniform price *must* tilt the playing field by favoring some of the rival suppliers of final products at the expense of the others.

This observation is pertinent because, in practice, bottleneck inputs are rarely used only to produce a single product. A railroad bridge that all competitors along a given route must use can carry coal and wheat and many other products. A local telecommunications loop carries business and household telephone messages, data and voice messages, and messages from California and Connecticut. The question, then, is whether the price of a homogeneous bottleneck service should be fixed and independent of the final product in whose production it is used, or should *differential pricing* of the bottleneck service be permitted or even required, depending on the pricing of the final product for which it is employed. Here, I will argue that:

a) If there is discrimination in the bottleneck owner's prices of the final products, *I* and *J*, for which the bottleneck input is used, so that the difference between the bottleneck owner's prices for *I* and *J* is not equal to the difference between the incremental costs for *I* and *J* (that is, $P_{fbi} - P_{fbj}$ is not equal to $IC_{rbi} - IC_{rbj}$), then uniform pricing of the bottleneck service will either force the bottleneck owner to end its discriminatory pricing of the final product, or the market must, in effect, be transformed into a cartel in which different suppliers specialize in the supply of different products and do not compete with one another.

b) On the other hand, if there is differential pricing of the bottleneck service, so that the competitive neutrality formulas (1) are satisfied for *each* product for which the bottleneck service is required, then the differential pricing of the final product can be preserved, and effective competition can continue in the market for each of the final products. Specifically, such a differential pricing arrangement will be the only viable solution in a regulated market in which the regulator seeks to preserve effective competition and to impose some cross subsidy that is deemed to serve the public interest or to be required by political pressures

A. *Interfirm Discrimination Through Uniformity Of Access Price*

The analysis is straightforward. I will show that if differential prices are charged for final products that use the bottleneck service but the bottleneck service is priced uniformly in all uses, the playing field cannot be level. To show this, suppose that the bottleneck input is used to produce (at least) two final products, *I* and *J*, that are sold by the bottleneck owner at prices that are discriminatory in the sense that the price for product *I* minus the incremental cost for product *I* is greater than the price for product *J* minus the incremental cost for product *J*:

$$P_{fbi} - IC_{rbi} > P_{fbj} - IC_{rbj} \qquad (5)$$

where the subscript *r,* again, refers to the cost of the *remaining* (non-bottleneck) inputs, assuming for simplicity that the incremental cost of bottleneck use is the same for both products. If the price of the bottleneck service, P_b, is set at the average (perhaps weighted) of the difference between the final price and the incremental cost ($P_f - IC_r$) for the two products, then the price of bottleneck service is greater than the price for product *J* minus the incremental cost for *J*:

$$P_b > P_{fbj} - IC_{rbj} \qquad (6)$$

So, if a competitor, *C*, has the same cost for the remaining inputs (that is, $IC_{rbj} = IC_{rcj}$), then

$$P_{fbj} < P_b + IC_{rcj} = min\ P_{fcj} \qquad (7)$$

meaning that a competitor who is just as efficient as the bottleneck owner in supplying product *J* will be unable, without losing money on sales of *J*, to charge a final-product price, P_{fcj}, that is as low as that of the bottleneck owner. Clearly, the playing field for sale of *J* will not be level, and the competitor will find itself unable to compete in the product-*J* market, even though it is an equally efficient producer of *J*. Of course, the problem is that the uniform price of the bottleneck service must exceed the competitively-neutral price for that input when it is used to produce output *J*. The competitor will be saddled with what amounts to an excessive discriminatory price for the bottleneck service that handicaps or prevents its competition with the bottleneck owner in the supply of product *J*.

The same reasoning shows that the uniform averaged competitively-neutral price for the bottleneck service will render the bottleneck service owner's price for product *I* greater than the competitor's minimum price for product *I*,

$$P_{fbi} > min\ P_{fci} \qquad (8)$$

if the bottleneck owner and the competitor are equally efficient in supplying product *I*. Thus, the averaged uniform price for the bottleneck service must tilt the playing field in the competitor's favor in the supply of product *I*.

More generally, we have the Uniform Access-Price Theorem: If the final-product prices for two goods that use a bottleneck service as an input are discriminatory in the sense of (5), then no uniform bottleneck-service price can satisfy the competitive neutrality requirement (4) for every final product, so that for those products for which it is not satisfied one of the suppliers of those products must be handicapped in a discriminatory manner.

The implications are clear. The competitor will be forced to supply those products in which the net yield to the bottleneck owner, $P_{fb} - IC_{rb}$, is greatest. This is another way of saying that the competitor will have no option but to engage in cream skimming.

There are two possible scenarios for the sequel:

a) The bottleneck owner will reduce its price for final-product *I*, and (particularly if it is losing money on *J*, meaning that a cross subsidy is involved) it may be forced to raise its price for final product *J* until the two sides of inequality (5) are made equal to one another. Then the discrimination in final-product prices will have been ended by competition—the expected sequel to cream-skimming competition.

b) Alternatively, either regulatory fiat or self-interest or some other exogenous force may keep the final-product prices of *I* and *J* at their discriminatory level. Then the bottleneck owner will find itself the sole supplier of product *J*, while the other firm (if there are only two firms) will become the sole supplier of *I*. In that case, the result will be, in effect, the establishment of a cartel in which each firm finds itself assigned an exclusive territory that is immune from direct competition. Some truncated competitive force will remain in the market, since each firm will have to keep the price of its final product below the level that will make entry into that field by the other firm financially feasible. But up to that limit each firm will be shielded from the constraint of effective competition. There will be more than one firm in the industry, but there will be no real competition.

B. *Consequences of Differential Competitively-Neutral Prices for Bottleneck Services*

As an alternative, the regulator can impose strict compliance with competitive neutrality for a bottleneck service, final product by final product. By now, it should be evident that this requires the price charged by the bottleneck owner to vary with the use to which the bottleneck service is put by a competitor. It may require a bottleneck service fee of X dollars per minute when the bottleneck is used to carry calls from business customers and Y dollars per minute if it transmits calls from households. Competitive-neutrality formula (4) tells us, *ceteris paribus*, that the bottleneck service price must vary from one bottleneck use to another precisely by the amount that the corresponding final product prices vary. For example, given two final products with equal incremental costs for which the price of one product is 0.2 dollars more than the other, the competitively-neutral prices of bottleneck service for the two uses must also differ by exactly 0.2 dollars. Several consequences follow from such a pricing arrangement.

1. Bottleneck-Owner Indifference Among Suppliers

With these access prices, the bottleneck owner will be *indifferent*, so far as profits are concerned, between use of its facilities by itself and use of those facilities by its competitors. The competitive neutrality pricing formula guarantees that the bottleneck owner will obtain exactly the same profit whichever of the two courses is taken. For with price set in accord with formula (4), the sale of I by a rival will yield bottleneck price:

$$P_{bi} = P_{fbi} - IC_{rbi} = R \qquad (9)$$

where R is defined as the cost of providing a unit of bottleneck service for product I *plus* the profit the bottleneck owner would obtain from its own sale of a unit of I.

Thus, for each product I, the price charged by the bottleneck owner to competitors for bottleneck services will give the owner exactly the same profit as if it had used the services to supply product I itself. This result is well known in the literature on parity (ECPR) pricing.[24]

2. Access Prices for Cross-Subsidized Products

The second implication of differential and competitively-neutral pricing is more surprising: It follows from (9) that if final-product J is the recipient of a cross subsidy and is therefore priced below incremental cost (its profit yield to the bottleneck owner is negative), then the competitively-neutral price for bottleneck service to be used in the production of J *must also be less than the incremental cost* of supplying the bottleneck service for the purpose!

24 *See, e.g.*, Baumol et al., *supra* note 4, at 146.

Though this result may seem bizarre at first, its logic is straightforward. Cross subsidy by the bottleneck owner means that in order for rivals to compete effectively with the bottleneck owner, replication of this cross subsidy must be available to them in some way. If the bottleneck owner sells product J to consumers at a price below cost, then it must provide its rivals with bottleneck service at a price that does not cover cost as well. In other words, if product J is the recipient of a cross subsidy when sold by the bottleneck proprietor, then competitive neutrality requires that the same cross subsidy be made available to rival suppliers of J through access pricing. Otherwise, rivals that have no other source of cross subsidy will not be able to compete in the supply of J because of their inability to match the bottleneck owner's final-product price of J. In these circumstances, if the bottleneck service price covers the entire incremental cost of providing the service for output J production, the playing field cannot be level.

3. Open Competition in all Industry Products

Differential and competitively-neutral prices offer entrants and other rivals of the bottleneck owner the prospect that they will be able to compete in every market in which the bottleneck owner offers products. Thus, unless their entry or survival is threatened by the inefficiency of their *own* operations, they will not find themselves excluded from any branch of the regulated industry.

4. Cream Skimming Prevention—Competitor Indifference Among the Different Products That Are Supplied with the Aid of the Bottleneck

The fourth consequence of differential and competitively-neutral prices is that they eliminate any incentive for cream skimming by competitors. The differential bottleneck service price is adjusted so that when a final product price is relatively high, the bottleneck service price for use in making that product will be elevated by exactly the same amount, other things being equal. Consequently, the competitor will have no incentive to favor high-priced products over low-priced products.

5. Preservation of Cross Subsidies Despite Effective Competition

The final implication of differential and competitively-neutral pricing should now be obvious. In contrast to what is normally expected, such a pricing arrangement is consistent with continued competition in each and every one of the bottleneck owner's products, along with preservation of any and all cross subsidies in the bottleneck owner's final-product prices. Thus, these access prices enable the regulator to have it both ways. They enable competition to survive and even to permeate every branch of the regulated industry. They also permit retention of the cross-subsidies characteristically favored by regulators. Regulators can now require impoverished families, or isolated farmers and other customers whom it is especially costly to serve, to be granted subsidized prices. They can also demand that prices favor household over business customers. In short, differential and competitively-neutral pricing promotes universal service by means of cross subsidy without precluding the forces of competition that otherwise undermine universal service.

Conclusion

It is this last feature of differentiated, competitively-neutral pricing that may make it most attractive to regulators in practice and that may be most relevant for practice. It reconciles the goal of promoting competition with the objective of helping particular classes of customers. Moreover, it opens the regulated fields to entrants and permits them and other rivals to compete in every product market on the basis of relative efficiency. The public can benefit from the pervasive competition that it makes possible. Even the bottleneck owner has something to gain from the arrangement. Although the owner will end up facing rivals in the sale of every one of its products, it will not find itself effectively excluded from any of those markets by distorted prices. Furthermore, its legitimate profits will be protected through the competitively-neutral character of the bottleneck prices. It has been proven here that in an industry that is characterized by differential final-product prices and cross subsidy, as most regulated industries are in reality,[25] any uniform access price for bottleneck services cannot be competitively neutral. Productive efficiency is necessarily undermined when less efficient firms are allowed to undercut suppliers that are more efficient in their use of resources. Despite its advantages, differential competitive neutrality has rarely been considered as an option by either practitioners or analysts. This option should not be overlooked. Although it may prove to have shortcomings that have not yet been recognized, it merits careful consideration at the very least.

---

25 *See* W. KIP VISCUSI ET AL., ECONOMICS OF REGULATION AND ANTITRUST 532 (2d ed. 1995).

[12]

USE OF ANTITRUST TO SUBVERT COMPETITION*

WILLIAM J. BAUMOL and *JANUSZ A. ORDOVER*
Princeton and New York Universities — *New York University*

> The day after Congress passed the changes in the clean air legislation which substantially tightened emissions standards the Japanese automakers called an emergency meeting of their engineers. On the same day the carmakers in Detroit called an emergency meeting of their lawyers. [JOKE CIRCULATING AT THE TIME]

THERE is a specter that haunts our antitrust institutions. Its threat is that, far from serving as the bulwark of competition, these institutions will become the most powerful instrument in the hands of those who wish to subvert it. More than that, it threatens to draw great quantities of resources into the struggle to prevent effective competition, thereby more than offsetting the contributions to economic efficiency promised by antitrust activities. This is a specter that may well dwarf any other source of concern about the antitrust processes. We ignore it at our peril and would do well to take steps to exorcise it.

The problem is not an easy one. In a sense it is inherent in the very nature of the antitrust process. There is no doubt, for example, that mergers can sometimes inhibit or undermine competition and that predatory pricing can sometimes serve as an instrument of monopolization. But then, because of that, a merger that promises to introduce efficiencies that make it necessary for other firms in the industry to try harder is vulnerable to challenge by those rivals, who will claim that it is anticompetitive. Similarly, a firm that by virtue of superior efficiency or economies of scale or scope is able to offer prices low enough to make its competitors uncomfortable is all too likely to find itself accused of predation. Such attempts

* We thank the C. V. Starr Center for Applied Economics at New York University for assistance in the preparation of this paper. Professor Ordover's research has been financed in part by the National Science Foundation. We also thank W. Baxter, J. Miller, and the other participants at the Conference for helpful comments. E. F. Glynn of the FTC vastly improved our discussion of antitrust in Japan and in the EEC Member States.

[*Journal of Law & Economics*, vol. XXVIII (May 1985)]

to use the law as an instrument for the subversion of competition do not confine themselves to private lawsuits. All too often the enterprise seeking to erect a protective umbrella about itself will be tempted to try to subvert the antitrust authorities, Congress, and even the president's office as partners in its purpose. One suspects that the costs in terms of the efficiency of the firm and the economy that is subject to this sort of attack are high. One knows that the costs in terms of the time of management, lawyers, economists, and others absorbed in the litigation process itself are enormous. And it is almost all economic waste.

I. Protectionism as Rent Seeking

Few observers will deny that some firms succumb to the temptation to seek governmental protection from the unpleasantness of effective competition. The blatant attempts by some steel and auto firms to have foreign imports restricted, the transparent purpose underlying a number of private antitrust suits, among other examples, can leave little doubt that the phenomenon is a reality. Yet, at least in some discussions, the volume of such protectionist activity is viewed as fortuitous, explainable largely in terms of cultural characteristics, political climate, and other influences beyond the purview of economic analysis. For example, American litigiousness is sometimes contrasted with Japanese distaste for direct confrontation as an explanation of the differences in the volume of private suits in the two countries.

Economic theory nonetheless has a good deal to say about the matter. The theory of rent seeking contributed by James Buchanan and extended to a variety of legal issues by Richard Posner tells us just how much protectionist effort one can expect in any particular set of circumstances. To summarize the argument very briefly, rent is defined by economists as any earnings by the supplier of an activity that exceed the minimum amount necessary to elicit the services of that supplier. Any supercompetitive (monopoly) profits of a firm are a rent. The theory of rent seeking tells us that where entrepreneurs are free to spend money in an attempt to gain control of such a source of rent, that is, when entry into a rent-seeking activity is completely free, when rent seeking is perfectly competitive or at least perfectly contestable, the resources devoted to the attempt will reach just the amount necessary to consume the entire rent. Rent seekers suing one another to gain control of a source of monopoly profit will spend so much on lawyers, consultants, and so on, that they will dissipate the entire expected monopoly profit in the process. That is just a corollary of the theorem that under perfect competition (excess) profits must be zero. In the circumstances posited, the struggle for the monopoly profits is a perfectly competitive process (or, at least, one that is perfectly contestable).

The result may seem to constitute a mere transfer of wealth from the monopolist to lawyers and economists, but it is much worse than that. In the process the latter are led to devote considerable (and valuable) time in a way that yields no socially valuable product. In other words, here rent seeking transforms into pure waste a quantity of resources equal in value to the rent that is sought.

The search for protection, which is the subject of this paper, is rent seeking (or rent preserving), as we now show. But it is not necessarily competitive, and so the analysis requires some modification. Envision the following scenario. Firm A offers generous salaries to its management, and firm B, with a leaner compensation package, undercuts A's prices, thereby eliminating the rents constituted by the overcompetitive salaries. A can hope to force B to cease and desist and perhaps even to collect treble damages from B by suing it for predatory pricing. What quantity of resources will A devote to this purpose?

First we note that even if other firms in the industry are hurt by A's pricing behavior, there is no competitive pressure driving A to use up its entire expected gain in its rent-preserving outlays. To see what will occur, let us first assume that A is the only firm affected by B's prices and then consider the case where several enterprises have their rents threatened.

Where A alone is involved, and assuming that its chances of achieving its protectionist goal increase monotonically with the quantity of resources it devotes to the purpose, then, as usual, profit maximization requires it to spend on its litigation effort up to the point where an additional dollar in outlay increases the expected rent yield by no more than $1.00. This may well leave firm A with a considerable expected gain from the undertaking. But it is also likely to involve a very substantial total outlay, that is, a very large amount of waste.

Where several other firms C, D, and E will benefit along with A if B is forced to end its "unfair competition," each of them will find it profitable to spend some money to increase the probability of victory. The joint profit-maximizing outlay will be greater, in general, than when only A's rents are at stake, since the marginal expected yield to the group as a whole must be at least as great as the marginal yield to A alone. However, in the absence of effective collusion, the behavior of the group may well not be (joint) profit maximizing, and it may involve outlays by the group lower than those that maximize their joint profits. This is so because an externality (free-rider) issue is involved. Any increment in probability of success against B achieved by an increase in A's expenditure will also benefit firms C, D, and E. As a result, when the marginal net benefit of such outlays to firm A reaches zero, its marginal benefit to the group of firms will still be positive. It follows that the total rent-seeking expenditure of the group can be expected to be less than that which maximizes their combined expected rent return.[1] The group's outlay will almost certainly be at least as large as the largest of the outlays of any one of the four rent-seeking firms would have been had it been the only competitor of B. To see this, it would have paid, say, firm C to spend X dollars in litigation if A and D were not spending anything for the purpose. If C finds that A and D together are spending only $X - \Delta$ for the purpose, then surely it will pay C to obtain the same probability of success as it would have in isolation since now it only costs him $\Delta < X$ dollars to do so. The Slutsky theorem for the firm not subject to a budget constraint tells us that this must be so because what is involved is a reduction in the price of increased probability of success in the rent-seeking undertaking.

We conclude from all this that while protectionist activity is a form of rent seeking, its expected benefits to the rent seeker are not likely to be dissipated completely in wasteful litigation expenditure. But the theory suggests nevertheless that the expenditures may typically be very substantial and that the social costs stemming from such direct waste may well prove very high.[2]

This is by no means the only type of social cost of protectionism. There are at least two other sorts of cost: monopolistic resource misallocation, and disincentives for internal operating efficiency for the individual firms, which may prove far more serious. The nature of the first of these is obvious to anyone familiar with welfare economics. After all, the immediate purpose of the protectionist activity is to subvert the forces of competition, and if the effort succeeds, it will lead to pricing and other decisions that are different, perhaps very different, from those that would emerge under competition. It follows that resources can be expected to be misallocated, as is always true under unregulated monopoly in a market that is not contestable.

[1] We cannot be certain of this since it depends on the concavity-convexity properties of the pertinent relationships. The presence of externalities themselves is likely to cause problems on that score. On this see William J. Baumol & David F. Bradford, Detrimental Externalities and Non-Convexity of the Production Set, 40 Economica 160 (n.s. 1972); or William J. Baumol & Wallace E. Oates, The Theory of Environmental Policy (1975), at ch. 8.

[2] The astonishing outlays by major firms on the antitrust litigations in which they have been involved confirms that these expenditures can indeed be substantial. For example, Alan A. Fisher & Robert H. Lande, Efficiency Considerations in Merger Enforcement, 71 Calif. L. Rev. 1580, 1673 (1983) estimate that Du Pont, Seagram, and Mobil spent about $13.5 million in private legal fees to acquire Conoco. In addition, they estimate at 1673 n.308 that an average merger antitrust case costs anywhere between $700,000 and $1.4 million. To this one must add costs incurred by the DOJ, or the FCC, and the courts.

The second social cost takes the form of inefficiency in the protected firm. First, if a company is insulated from competition, the pressures that would otherwise force it to operate with maximal efficiency are simply removed.[3] It is freer than it otherwise would be to engage in nepotism and sloppy supervision, to display excessive caution in risky decisions, and to avoid innovations that require management to exert itself. In short, protectionist activity frees the firm to engage in the degree of inefficiency that suits the proclivities and abilities of its management.

The third social cost of protectionism is its effect on the immediate objectives, and hence the organization, of the firm. If such rent seeking is the easier way to increase its profits or to achieve other managerial objectives, the firm's energies will be directed toward preparation for its litigative ventures, which will receive priority over efforts to increase productivity or to improve the product line. Engineers will become relatively less numerous in the ranks of top management, and lawyers will assume a correspondingly larger share.[4]

In sum, the social costs of rent-seeking protectionism can be very high (though we have no estimate of their magnitude). Indeed, if it is true that productivity growth in the United States is suffering from a serious longer-term malaise, it is not implausible that the incentives for firms to undertake the sort of rent seeking we are discussing has played a role that is not negligible.

We repeat that the antitrust and regulatory institutions have shown

[3] Some sense of magnitude of the expenditures that insulation from competition can elicit is suggested by the surprising size of the cut in wage and salary outlays in aviation that followed airline deregulation.

[4] A simple model making use of the Slutsky theorem readily confirms that if the antitrust laws increase the expected returns to litigation, they will also increase the firm's outlays on lawyers and other inputs that contribute to the probability of success in such litigation. A very elementary model for the purpose maximizes the profit function.

$$\Pi^*(\mathbf{Z}, x) = \Pi(Z) + vr - x \tag{1}$$

subject to

$$r = f(x), f'(x) > 0, \tag{2}$$

where $\mathbf{Z}$ = the vector of the firm's inputs and outputs, x = its litigation-related expenditure, r = its probability of victory in litigation, v = its expected increase in profit as a result of victory, $f(x)$ = probability of litigative success as a function of the firm's expenditure on litigation, and $\Pi(Z)$ = the firm's profit from its normal production activities in the absence of litigation.

We may regard r, the probability of success, as an additional output of the firm and v as the per unit return to an increase in the value of r. Then, if the sufficient conditions for the Slutsky theorem are satisfied, we know that we must have $\partial r/\partial v > 0$. That is, if the availability of the antitrust rules increases the payoff to litigative rent-seeking activity, the profit-maximizing firm will act to increase the probability of success in this arena. But by (2), in order to do so it must increase x, so that we have our result, $\partial x/\partial v > 0$.

themselves to be sources of substantial incentives and opportunities for such rent-seeking activity. Whenever a competitor becomes too successful or too efficient, whenever his competition threatens to become sufficiently effective to disturb the quiet and easy life his rival is leading, the latter will be tempted to sue on the grounds that the competition is "unfair." Every successful enterprise comes to expect almost as a routine phenomenon that it will sooner or later find itself the defendant in a multiplicity of cases. It is an enchanted topsy-turvy world in which vigorous competition is made to seem anticompetitive and in which "fair competition" comes to mean no competition at all.

The runners-up, the firms that despair of succeeding through superior efficiency or more attractive products, use different instruments in seeking protection from rivals. The antitrust laws are not always useful as means to handicap competition from abroad, but they are apparently a prime instrument for the creation of impediments to effective competition by American rivals. The reason the antitrust laws can be used in this way is clear. The borderline between measures that are legitimate competitive moves and those that are destructive instruments of monopolization is often difficult to define even in principle (witness, for example, the intricacies of the concept of predatory innovation). Moreover, whatever the criteria adopted, in practice they rarely lend themselves to clear-cut evidence and unambiguous conclusions. The runner-up firm then finds itself with the opportunity to claim that almost any successful program by a rival is "anticompetitive" and that it constitutes monopolization. Antitrust, whose objective is the preservation of competition, by its very nature lends itself to use as a means to undermine effective competition. This is not merely ironic. It is very dangerous for the workings of our economy.

II. Antitrust Provisions That Encourage Protectionism

We cannot hope to provide an exhaustive list of the antitrust institutions that lend themselves to the purposes of the protectionist. We simply offer several illustrations. We discuss the treble-damages provisions, vagueness of criteria of predation and other types of unfairness of competition, and excessive severity of tests of anticompetitiveness.

Treble Damages[5]

The availability of trebled damages payments to the plaintiff has several arguments in its favor. First, there is evidence that in antitrust suits pri-

[5] See Kenneth G. Elzinga and William Breit, Private Antitrust Enforcement: The New Learning, in this issue, and Frank H. Easterbrook, Detrebling Antitrust Damages, in this issue, for an extensive discussion of the social costs and benefits of the trebling of damages.

vate plaintiffs have a relatively low probability of winning their cases.[6] If private antitrust suits are considered desirable in at least some cases, the plaintiffs must be offered an expected return at least equal to the heavy litigation costs they are likely to incur. While treble damages do not generally increase the probability of victory (and may well decrease it by forcing the defendant to expend larger resources to protect his interests), they almost certainly increase the expected award to a plaintiff. Second, in some cases (such as successful price fixing), in addition to the culprit's ill-gotten gains, his victims suffer a deadweight loss in the form of distorted relative purchase quantities which the courts do not recognize in their damage calculations. A multiplied damage payment then serves as very rough compensation for such deadweight losses, though any resemblance between the two magnitudes is certain to be purely coincidental. Third, no doubt some violators of the antitrust laws escape unscathed and sometimes are not even brought to trial, let alone convicted and punished. Optimal deterrence requires such firms to face ex ante a probable punishment that does fit the crime. This means that the higher the probability that any particular violator of the law will get away with it, the higher must be the fine exacted from those who are brought to justice.

All of these arguments are legitimate so far as they go, but they neglect the other side of the matter. From the point of view of society, escalated damages awards also increase the probable payoff to protectionist activity. The runner-up who hopes to impose legal obstacles on the vigorous competitive efforts of his all-too-successful rival is offered the prospect of also acquiring a substantial amount of funding in the process. It has even been charged that runners-up have been known to start such suits in the hope of acquiring the funding that the capital market denied them.

Trebled damages also increase the amounts it pays both defendant and plaintiff to expend in combating the case, for such damages increase the pool of rents to be disputed. And, as usual, the waste of economic resources elicited can be expected to be proportional to the size of the available rents. It is noteworthy that, as in the case of rivalrous advertising, such enhanced outlays on a legal battle will tend to cancel one another, at least in part. They will benefit neither the plaintiff nor the defendant, while raising the cost to society.

All in all, the case against trebled damages is far from clear-cut. Yet the fact that they provide a direct incentive for protectionist activity suggests that the issue requires reconsideration. We will return to this subject

[6] See Richard A. Posner, A Statistical Study of Antitrust Enforcement, 13 J. Law & Econ. 365 (1970); National Economic Research Associates, Statistical Analysis of Private Antitrust Enforcement, Final Report (1979).

later, when we discuss policy appropriate for the phenomenon of protectionist misuse of antitrust institutions.

Vagueness of Antitrust Criteria

Knowledgeable students of antitrust issues often are impressed with the difficulty of determining and defining in a manner that is universally applicable the borderline between acceptable and unacceptable behavior. Scherer's attack on the famous Areeda-Turner article is a classic illustration, carefully cataloguing a variety of circumstances under which almost any reasonable but explicitly defined standard of predatory pricing can be expected to condone activities that are anticompetitive or to condemn activities that are innocent or even benign.[7] No categorical rule can fully encompass intentions, antecedent and subsequent circumstances and developments, interdependence with actions other than those under immediate consideration, and the host of other pertinent considerations. Such a point of view would seem to lead toward heavy reliance on the good judgment of the courts, toward a universal reign of some form of rule of reason. It leaves matters subject to vague and general guidelines derived from the obscure admonitions of the pertinent law and the available precedents, and beyond that it gives the courts the duty of deciding matters case by case, on the basis of individual judgment and in light of attendant circumstances.

Here is not the place to examine all the likely consequences of such a procedure or to consider the implications of wide range in capability and economic sophistication that one encounters among judges. Rather, our concern here is that obscurity and ambiguity are convenient tools for those enterprises on the prowl for opportunities to hobble competition. As we know, it is not always necessary to win cases in order to blunt a rival's competitive weapons. Harassment by lawsuit or even the threat of harassment can be a marvelous stimulus to timidity on the part of competitors. The potential defendant who cannot judge in advance with any reasonable degree of certainty whether its behavior will afterward be deemed illegal is particularly vulnerable to guerrilla warfare and intimidation into the sort of gentlemanly competitive behavior that is the antithesis of true competition.

Thus, to continue with our example, whatever one may think of the Areeda-Turner test (and we do consider it to constitute a major infusion of

[7] F. M. Scherer, Comment on Areeda and Turner, 89 Harv. L. Rev. 869 (1976). Phillip Areeda and Donald F. Turner, Predatory Pricing and Related Practices under Section 2 of the Sherman Act, 88 Harv. L. Rev. 697 (1975).

logic into the arena), it seems to us certainly to have made a critical and beneficial contribution simply by reducing vagueness in the criterion of predation in pricing. This makes protectionist misuse of the antitrust laws much less easy.

Severity of the Tests of Anticompetitiveness

A third phenomenon that facilitates protectionist efforts is reliance on rules increasing the range of private activities subject to condemnation as "anticompetitive." Here, too, the Areeda-Turner contribution provides an excellent illustration. The long debate between advocates of fully distributed cost tests of anticompetitiveness in pricing and advocates of incremental or marginal costs for this purpose has a straightforward interpretation in terms of our discussion. Though we are not disinterested observers of this debate, we are reasonably confident that it is not bias alone that leads us to interpret advocacy of the fully distributed cost approach as a systematic protectionist onslaught. We believe the evidence strongly supports the thesis that it is a standard put forward almost exclusively by firms that were unlikely to compete successfully on the merits of their performance alone. They advocate their costing approach as a device to limit the price-cutting opportunities of rivals rendered more efficient by economies of scale or scope, by superior management, or by other legitimate sources of superiority. This is surely attested to by the frequency of cases in which full distribution has been used to argue that some prices are unacceptably low, when the pricing behavior that should most be feared by guardians of the public interest in the presence of market power is overcharging, not underpricing.

Thus, rules that make vigorous competition dangerous clearly foster protectionism. That point is obvious enough. What is perhaps only a bit less obvious is that protectionists are not prone to wait passively for such overrestrictive rules to fall into their laps. Rather, a central element in their strategy is persistent expenditure of money and effort to change the rules in ways that favor their cause, and resistance to any attempt to reduce impediments to effective competition. When an agency such as the FTC proposes to hold hearings on the advisability of revision of one of its rules that may be suspected of discouraging competition, those who stand to bear the brunt of any enhanced competitive pressures can be expected to resist energetically.

In sum, it seems plausible that rules defining unacceptable competitive practices that lean toward potential plaintiffs are a major source of encouragement to protectionist efforts. The presence of such rules is not happenstance. They are often attributable to the deliberate efforts of those who stand to gain by using the antitrust mechanism to emasculate competition.

The preceding paragraphs are intended to suggest that the search for protection from competition by runner-up firms, and the use of antitrust institutions for the purpose, is encouraged by a number of attributes of those institutions themselves. We do not mean to apportion blame or even to claim that any one group can be said to be at fault. Our purpose is to look for strategic points that lend themselves to modification and that are therefore appropriate foci for ameliorative policy—a subject to which we will return presently.

It must, however, be pointed out that even if antitrust rules were modified to make them less susceptible to rent-seeking activities described here, such activities might not disappear or even decline materially. More likely, firms might merely divert their rent-seeking resources to other political and legal arenas.

III. Case Examples of Strategic Uses of Antitrust

The purpose of this section is to illustrate by means of a few actual cases the protectionist uses of antitrust and associated forms of government intervention such as regulation. Our examples involve mergers and joint ventures, as well as monopolization cases.

A. *The GM-Toyota Joint Venture*

The GM-Toyota joint venture illustrates clearly the strategic role of antitrust litigation. Here, it is Chrysler and Ford, the horizontal competitors of the joint venturers, that have pressed the Federal Trade Commission to reject the joint venture on the ground that it will restrain competition in the automobile market in general and in the subcompact segment of the market in particular. Recently the FTC approved the joint venture. Undeterred, Chrysler has been pressing a private antitrust action in an attempt to accomplish what it failed to do at the FTC.

This sort of opposition is predictable, and in a manner that is rather ironic it can signal clearly the likely effects of the joint venture. If the enterprise were in fact likely to acquire monopoly power and charge excessive prices, other U.S. auto firms undoubtedly would benefit from the resulting protective umbrella, which would enable them to raise their prices as well. If this is the probable outcome, then those rivals can be expected to view the joint venture with equanimity and silent acquiescence. But if the joint venture really is likely to introduce economies or improve product quality, it is sure to make life harder for the domestic rivals of the participants who will then have to run correspondingly faster in order to stand still.[8] Paradoxically, then and only then, when the joint venture is really beneficial, can those rivals be relied on to denounce the undertaking as "anticompetitive."[9] That is exactly the response of Chrysler and Ford, who have presented themselves here as defenders of consumers' interests even though before other forums they have not hesitated to argue for blatantly protectionist measures such as higher trade barriers. Once again, consistency has given way to expediency.

B. MCI v. AT & T: The Economics of Price Inflexibility[10]

MCI was perhaps the first firm to challenge AT & T's monopoly in the long-distance telecommunications market. Beginning in 1963, MCI embarked on an extensive investment program in microwave transmission facilities. Because of its (and the FCC's) policy of "universal service" or "nationwide averaging," AT & T's relative rates along different routes did not correspond closely to relative costs, with service along sparsely used routes comparatively underpriced. This was a clear invitation for "cream skimming" entry. Understandably, MCI at least initially attempted to specialize in serving the high-density routes in which AT & T earned more substantial profit margins.

MCI's moves to enter these routes predictably led to an attempt by AT & T to adjust its relative rates to correspond more closely to costs. MCI alleged that these responses were anticompetitive. Litigation ensued.[11] Of course, MCI's initial entry primarily into AT & T's more profitable routes is unobjectionable. The benefits of competition depend on the willingness of entrants to seek out profitable opportunities. What is far more questionable is MCI's attempt to use antitrust litigation as a means to restrain AT & T's ability to respond to competitive incursions. It was charged that by adjusting its prices on different routes to correspond more closely to

[8] Admittedly, it is possible that the joint venture will make GM a more formidable competitor not because of any gains in economic efficiency but merely because it will make it easier for GM to satisfy the asinine Company Average Fuel Efficiency (CAFE) regulations.

[9] Steven Salop suggested to one of us that a merger of joint venture may be a part of a strategy employed by the merging partners, or co-venturers, to elevate the rivals' costs and thereby harm competition. We doubt that "predatory" mergers or joint ventures are a frequent occurrence. In such a rare instance, the rival would have to assume the standard of proof of a potential anticompetitive effect that is appropriate for monopolization cases, rather than that which is appropriate for a merger case.

[10] We are not disinterested discussants of this case. Both of us have carried out work for AT & T. One of us not only served as a witness for AT & T in the MCI case but also recommended the type of price response to MCI's entry that AT & T later adopted.

[11] MCI Communications Corp. v. AT & T, 369 F. Supp. 1004 (E. D. Pa. 1973) vacated and remanded, 496 F.2d 214 (3d Cir. 1974); MCI Communications Corp. v. AT & T, 462 F. Supp. 1072 (N. D. Ill. 1978), rev'd, 708 F.2d 1081 (7th Cir. 1983).

costs, even on routes where competition had not yet appeared, AT & T was launching "preemptive strikes." One can imagine what would have been said if instead AT & T had reduced prices *only* on the routes where MCI had opened for business.

MCI insisted during the trial and in its appellate brief that a "full-cost" approach should be used to calculate AT & T's costs and to perform the tests of predatoriness.[12] Indeed, according to MCI, citing Dr. William Melody's testimony, many "economists advocate the use of fully distributed costs as the proper test for below-cost predatory pricing in the telecommunications industry."[13]

There is no need to dwell here on the inefficiencies that result from the use of fully allocated costs as constraints on the price responses of regulated and unregulated firms. It suffices to note that insistence that such costs are the appropriate price floors invites socially inefficient entry that is elicited not by genuine cost advantages and productive efficiencies but by false profitability signals. There is no doubt that potential and actual entrants (such as MCI) have a strong incentive to rigidify the price responses open to an incumbent who is confronted with newly emerging competition. It seems clear that the staunchest advocates of full-cost pricing have been firms anxious to hobble their disquietingly effective rivals.

C. *Strategic Uses of Antitrust in Takeover Cases*

The targets of tender offers frequently initiate antitrust suits against their unwanted suitors. The critical issues are whether the targets should be allowed to institute injunction proceedings or whether instead the enforcement of merger statutes should be left to the government and to customers who are likely to be injured if the merger brings competition to an end, elevates prices, and causes resource misallocation. The issue is not straightforward. While the incentive for management to bring an antitrust case need not coincide with the interests of the consumers,[14] it is nevertheless true that the management of the target is probably better informed than any other group about the likely consequences of the acquisition for future competition.

There is no question that a target's management, bent on derailing the tender offer, has a potent weapon in the antitrust laws. The two most

[12] Brief of Appellees, MCI Communications Corp. and MCI Telecommunications Corp. (March 5, 1981), at 112.

[13] *Id.* at 113–14. The court of appeals disagreed and decided against MCI on most points.

[14] This point is made in Frank H. Easterbrook & Daniel R. Fischel, Antitrust Suits by Targets of Tender Offers, 80 Michigan L. Rev. 1155 (1982).

recent instances in which highly lucrative offers were defeated with the aid of the antitrust laws were *Grumman Corp. v. LTV Corp.*[15] and *Marathon Oil Co. v. Mobil Corp.*[16] The latter case illustrates the problem clearly. Marathon's management possessed extensive, firsthand information about the scope of its geographic operations and about the marketing of gasoline to independents, which was at issue in the antitrust proceedings. On the other hand, Marathon's management hardly shared the interests of the automobile owners in cheap and plentiful gasoline.[17] Indeed, if the target's management were truly guided by shareholders' interests, it ought to sell the company to the bidder likely to obtain the highest profit from the transaction.[18] But when such enhanced profits result from the elevation of market power in the postmerger market, the interests of the consumers and of the target's stockholders clash directly.

IV. Alternative Enforcement Procedures: Japan and the EEC

In this section we briefly compare antitrust procedures in the United States with those of our major trading partners: Japan and the EEC. We do not claim any expertise on the antitrust laws of other countries. However, expertise is not required in light of our limited objective—to explore how other countries have held in check the use of antitrust litigation as a strategic weapon in the hands of competitors. (Of course, none of the discussion is meant to imply that the antitrust policies in other countries constitute ideal models for the United States that should recommend themselves to American scholars and policymakers.)

A. *Japan*[19]

Japan has dealt with the problem of strategic use or abuse of the antitrust laws by largely consolidating enforcement in its Fair Trade Commission (JFTC). In Japan a person injured by acts in violation of the antimonopoly laws has a right to sue for damages under Section 709 of the Civil Code. And any person injured by conduct found illegal by the JFTC has a right, under Section 25 of the Antimonopoly Act, to recover dam-

[15] 665 F.2d 10 (2d Cir. 1981).

[16] 669 F.2d 378 (6th Cir. 1982).

[17] In fact, if the management had wanted to trigger an auction for Marathon by impeding Mobil's actions, it might have been implying that it was expecting another oil company as the next suitor.

[18] That is, if the target's managers can somehow share in these incremental profits.

[19] Information in this section is culled from notes by Matsushita; see M. Matsushita, Informal Notes for the Conference on Japan's Antimonopoly Legislation and Doing Business with Japan, Japan Society (January 5, 1978).

ages.[20] Yet as of 1983 only five damage suits had been filed under Section 25. The reasons for the reluctance of private Japanese plaintiffs to seek damages in court are not easy to determine. We think that the national distaste for litigation cannot explain it fully. In particular, the fact that damages are not readily awarded in Japan and that plaintiffs can sue under Section 25 only if the JFTC has found the conduct complained of to be illegal surely discourages private actions for damages.[21]

Japan's FTC is basically an administrative agency with some quasi-judicial powers. Its judicial powers are exercised only rarely. According to the Japanese antitrust expert M. Matsushita of Sophia University, only four antitrust criminal cases have occurred in the past thirty years of antitrust enforcement. The main channel through which the JFTC shapes competition is informal. The JFTC may issue "warnings" that are usually respected. In addition, the JFTC provides "guidance" that helps the companies to avoid conflict with the antitrust laws, especially in international contracts.

When the JFTC brings a formal action, it usually ends with the company (or companies) accepting the JFTC's recommendation decision. Available estimates indicate that some 90 percent of these recommendations are accepted. Those that are not accepted usually are resolved during trial through consent decisions that embody the proposals of the respondent.

Private complaints are filed with the JFTC. The JFTC must then investigate but need not take an enforcement action. However, according to the Japanese experts, frequently investigation alone suffices to induce the investigated firm (or firms) to stop the activity that has been challenged.

[20] Hiroshi Iyori & Akinori Uesugi, The Antimonopoly Laws of Japan 127 (2d ed. 1983). We are grateful to Edward Glynn of the FTC for correcting our earlier discussion of private enforcement in Japan.

[21] Economists are usually loath to seek explanations in alleged differences in "national character" to explain the Japanese record. Arguments based on national character are difficult to test and are, in any event, treacherous, as the following illustrative story suggests: "An Australian expert, invited by the Japanese government, had this to say in his Report, as excerpted in the *Japan Times* of August 18th 1915: 'Japan commercially, I regret to say, does not bear the best reputation for executing business. Inferior goods, irregularity and indifferent shipments have caused no end of worry . . . My impression as to your cheap labour was soon disillusioned when I saw your people at work. No doubt they are lowly paid, but the return is equally so; to see your men at work made me feel that you are a very satisfied easy-going race who reckon time is no object. When I spoke to some managers they informed me that it was impossible to change the habits of national heritage . . . First class managers . . . are required to wake things up and get out of the go-as-you-please style that seems universal at present.' " Cited in J. N. Bhagwati, Development Economics: What Have We Learnt (mimeographed, Columbia Univ. 1984), at 27.

Thus, here there does remain some scope for strategic use of the JFTC investigatory powers.

Yet the incentives for the allegedly harmed petitioners to use this process are limited. They receive no financial recompense for any harm they have suffered. Their only benefit derives from the JFTC's ability to require cessation of the allegedly anticompetitive activity. The incentive to use the JFTC for protection from competition is thereby weakened, especially if the cost of filing the complaint is high.

It is noteworthy that in a few cases complaining parties have attempted to sue the JFTC for the failure to act on their complaints. However, appellate authorities have ruled that only respondents can appeal a JFTC decision and have thereby severely restricted the complainants' standing to sue.

In sum, in Japan antitrust enforcement is placed almost exclusively in the hands of its JFTC, which relies heavily on informal mechanisms such as warnings and reviews. The strategic use of the antitrust mechanism is circumscribed because the parties who claim they were harmed must first convince the JFTC to act and cannot appeal from the JFTC decisions.

One may well feel that this arrangement goes too far and that its protection of anticompetitive activities is excessive. However, it does certainly help to check the litigiousness of business firms and their use of antitrust as a means to restrain effective competition.

B. The EEC Member States

It would add unduly to the length of this paper, and strain the information at our disposal, to analyze the vulnerability to strategic abuse of the national laws on competition where they exist in the EEC countries. It is safe to say, however, that the incentives for abuse probably are significantly weaker in the EEC member states than they are in the United States, at least for the following reasons. First, in the EEC member states the plaintiff who wins a case is not entitled to treble damages. Second, in the EEC member states contingent fee arrangements with lawyers do not exist in antitrust cases. Third, discovery procedures are less developed in Europe than they are in the United States, which may make it more difficult for a plaintiff to obtain the "incriminating" evidence with which to fuel rent-seeking anticompetitive activities.[22] Fourth, in the EEC mem-

[22] However, as Edward Glynn has noted, extensive "discovery" available under American law can at times also be used to "bludgeon" a financially weak plaintiff into dropping his case.

ber states the right to trial by jury in money damage cases is not available. Fifth, in Britain especially an unsuccessful plaintiff must bear the defendant's costs.[23] And, finally, in Europe some aspects of the competition law, for example merger statutes, fall only within the purview of governmental bodies. This greatly reduces the opportunity for strategic use of these laws.

Having said all this, we must emphasize one important continuing development in the EEC member states that bears directly on the issues raised in this paper. It has by now become fairly well established through judicial authority that "actions for injunctions and for compensation may be brought in national courts by plaintiffs claiming to suffer loss as a result of infringements of Articles 85–86 and 90 EEC Treaty. . . . This confirms that Articles 85–86 are laws for the protection of individual interests and *not* merely laws for the protection of the public interest or the community."[24] Thus, for example, rivals now can avail themselves of EEC statutes on competition if they can claim to have been affected in their intracommunity business activities by allegedly anticompetitive actions of a dominant firm.

This extension of the enforcement of the EEC competition statutes in general, and of Article 86 in particular, opens an opportunity for strategic use of the statutes. The leading United Kingdom case that has established that plaintiffs can, in fact, sue shows that the EEC competition statutes can be used to retard rather than promote allocative efficiency.[25] In that case, the plaintiff was purchasing most of its "bulk butter" from the Milk Marketing Board (which apparently had a dominant position in the relevant market) for resale to a single purchaser in the Netherlands. At some point the defendant changed its marketing strategy and decided to sell its bulk butter to four distributors in England and Wales. The plaintiff was instructed to purchase its butter requirements from the designated distributors. Allegedly, this would have rendered its resale activities unprofitable. The plaintiff sued and asked for injunctive relief. The relief was not granted. Nevertheless, the case set a precedent for future suits.

The preceding sequence will be familiar to the American students of

[23] We note, however, that the effects of fee shifting on litigation incentives are not as clear as one might expect. See Steven Shavell, Suit, Settlement and Trial: A Theoretical Analysis under Alternative Methods for the Allocation of Legal Costs, 11 J. Legal Stud. 55 (1982); and Janusz A. Ordover & Ariel Rubinstein, A Sequential Concession Game with Asymmetric Information (mimeographed, C. V. Starr Center for Applied Economics, New York Univ., July 1984).

[24] John Temple Lang, Enforcement in National Courts of Community Competition Rules on Enterprises, Notes for Lecture, Brussels (March 1983).

[25] Garden Cottage Foods, Ltd. v. Milk Marketing Board (1983) 2 ALL ER 770.

antitrust. Vertical relations between a manufacturer and his dealers have been a subject of frequent litigation, often of doubtful merit. It appears that now, by involving Article 86, dealers in the EEC may have acquired an important weapon with which to attack the distribution arrangements of their suppliers.[26] This has occurred at a time when, in the United States, various commentators have suggested that per se legality be granted to such arrangements. Time will tell whether competitors in the EEC will use the statute against one another.

V. What Is to Be Done?

There are no easy and costless remedies for the abuse of antitrust by those who use it for protection from competition. The difficulty is inherent in the problem, for anything that is done to make it harder for plaintiffs to use our antitrust institutions anticompetitively automatically also makes it easier for others to get away with acts of monopolization. This trade-off is apparently unavoidable, because anything that makes conviction of the defendant more likely necessarily makes suits more attractive to plaintiffs in pursuit of protection from effective competition. The Japanese, as we have seen, have largely solved the problem of protectionism, but only by virtual prohibition of initiatives by the victims of monopolistic behavior. In dealing with the shortcomings of our antitrust institutions that are the subject of this paper, we must be careful not to undermine the antitrust laws themselves.

The most obvious remedial change is a restriction of the sort of circumstances to which treble damages apply. One should consider both the use of a multiple smaller than three, at least in those types of cases, such as predatory pricing, in which rent-seeking protectionist activity seems to abound, and in some types of cases one might even consider restriction of the amount of the award to the magnitude of the damage actually shown to have been sustained.

Such proposals are not new, but we do have a new wrinkle to suggest. The choice of multiplicand in damages payments faces at least two conflicting goals. Given the possibly low probability of discovery of an antitrust violation and of conviction on the charge, optimal deterrence clearly calls for a multiplicand greater than unity, and on that score trebling of damages may perhaps not be too bad an approximation to the optimum.

[26] In the United Kingdom, such practices are also examined in the Restrictive Practices Court in which there is "a great deal of wasted time particularly with economists swearing against each other—canceling each other out!" As was observed extrajudicially by Advocate-General Warner of the Court of Justice of the European Communities, in Enterprise Law of the 80's 235 (F. M. Rowe, F. G. Jacobs, & M. R. Joelson eds. 1980).

On the other hand, if this encourages rent seeking we may want, on this score, a much smaller damages award.

Environmental economics has shown how an analogous problem can be dealt with. There, deterrence policy can use the polluter pays principle as an effective instrument. But if that payment is used to compensate the polluter's victims on the basis of the amount of damage they suffer, a moral hazard problem arises—for it undermines the incentive for potential victims to seek pollution-avoiding locations or to take other measures to protect themselves from damages. Indeed, it can be proved that *any* such compensation to utility-maximizing victims will reduce their pollution-deterrent resource outlays below the socially optimal level. The solution implicitly advocated by economists for pollution policy is simple. The polluter should indeed pay, but the payments should be collected by government, at least in part, and should not go to the victims. In that way the payment scheme is provided with two parameter values—the price the polluter is charged, and the amount that victims are compensated. These parameter values can then be chosen so as to elicit both the optimal reduction of polluter emissions and the optimal self-defensive effort by the victim.

In private antitrust suits a similar solution is at least worth considering. That is, the defendant who is found guilty might continue to pay three times (or some other multiple of) the estimated damages. But the plaintiff can be made eligible to a smaller multiple (and perhaps even a multiple less than unity) of that damages figure. The difference would then go into the public treasury as a tax on violators of the antitrust laws. Once again, this provides two distinct parameters (the defendant's multiple and the plaintiff's multiple) to the designers of public policy who can select their values separately so as to provide the proper incentive for deterrence of violations while at the same time offering an appropriate disincentive for rent-seeking protectionism.

One may want to take a further step in this direction. Mere accusation and trial subjects the defendant firm to enormous expenses and even greater ex ante risks of an expensive adverse decision, even if it transpires ex post on the basis of convincing evidence that it is completely innocent. The possibility of required compensation to the defendant for these damages caused by the plaintiff might well discourage frivolous and mischievous suits, including those undertaken in the hope that an out-of-court settlement will prevent the latter from having to reveal the weakness of his case. Thus, the third remedy we propose for consideration is liability of the plaintiff for costs incurred by the defendant in the event of acquittal.

A fourth line of defense against protectionism is the adoption of clearer criteria of unacceptable behavior, such as the predation tests proposed by Areeda and Turner or those we have suggested.[27] For reasons already discussed, vagueness in the standards of unacceptable behavior plays into the hands of those who would use the antitrust laws as anticompetitive weapons.

Fifth, one may well consider it desirable, for similar reasons, to inhibit, if not necessarily prohibit, the ability of the management of a company that is a takeover target to bring an antitrust suit against the unwanted acquirer.[28]

Here it should be emphasized that we do not want to immunize mergers or acquisitions from the antitrust laws. Rather, we suggest the possibility that (only) those most likely to misuse the process for protectionist purposes be limited in their ability to bring private suits against the transaction on antitrust grounds. Others, including the pertinent government agencies, should clearly remain free to do so.

All of these suggestions are offered very tentatively and with great hesitation. They are mostly untried, and our lack of competence in the law surely raises questions about their workability, their consistency with other legal rules, and perhaps even (in some cases) their constitutionality.

We end by repeating an earlier caveat. It is not by accident that every one of our very tentative proposals incurs some social cost in that it reduces to some degree the available deterrents to monopolistic behavior. This is unavoidable, because any measure that offers some promise of dealing effectively with the problem discussed in this paper must necessarily involve some reduction in the incentive to bring litigation and hence must weaken to a degree the position of the potential plaintiff. It seems clear to us that *some* move in this direction is urgent if antitrust and regulation are to be prevented from becoming major impediments to competitiveness, efficiency, and productivity growth in the U.S. economy. The question is not whether some such moves are justified. The issue, rather, is how substantial those moves should be—how great a modification constitutes a social optimum in the trade-off between the two competing perils to true competition—excessive weakening of the deterrents to monopolization and excessive facilitation of attempts to subvert effective competition through protectionist misuse of our antitrust institutions.

[27] William J. Baumol, Quasi Permanence of Price Reduction, 89 Yale L. J. 1 (1979); Janusz A. Ordover & Robert D. Willig, An Economic Definition of Predation: Pricing and Product Innovation, 91 Yale L. J. 8 (1981).

[28] In a recent case, the U.S. District Court for the Central District of California ruled that the target of a tender offer lacks standing to seek a preliminary injunction to halt the acquisition as a violation of the Clayton Act. Carter Hawley Hale Stores, Inc. v. The Limited, Inc., 587 F. Supp. 246 (C. D. Cal. 1984).

PART III

GENERALITIES ON THE ECONOMIC LITERATURE

[13]

THE
QUARTERLY JOURNAL
OF ECONOMICS

Vol. CXV February 2000 Issue 1

WHAT MARSHALL *DIDN'T* KNOW: ON THE TWENTIETH CENTURY'S CONTRIBUTIONS TO ECONOMICS*

WILLIAM J. BAUMOL

Some of this century's many valuable contributions to economics, like macroeconomics, econometrics, and game theory, are widely recognized. However, arguably equally important is the enhanced role of empirical study permitted by more abundant data and improved methods. Also insufficiently recognized are the increased rigor and use of applied economics in public finance, regulation, corporation finance, etc., employing abstract theory and sophisticated data analysis. The striking contrast with earlier intuitively based applied economics and empirical study is illustrated. Comparison with Marshall's *Principles* also indicates that, except for macroeconomics, remarkably little space in today's texts deals with some of the rich contributions of this century.

What has twentieth century economics accomplished? A great deal, as will be shown here. But the discussion needs an illuminating starting point. In 1946, after arriving at the London School of Economics as an entering graduate student,[1] I soon found that in

* Professor and Director, C. V. Starr Center for Applied Economics, New York University; and senior research economist and professor emeritus, Princeton University. I am deeply grateful to Jess Benhabib, Avinash Dixit, Claudia Goldin, Lawrence Katz, Andrei Shleifer, and Jerry Hausman for their extensive and valuable comments, many of which I have shamelessly incorporated into this article verbatim.

1. When I came in 1946, Keynes had recently died, and Marshall was, of course, long gone. But I did hear Pigou lecture and describe himself as an ancient squid who, purely by force of habit, still continued to eject squirts of ink. Dennis Robertson repeatedly told me how on passing Pigou's lair, the great man would regularly emerge, demanding "Robertson—tell me, what is the Pigou effect?" At the London School of Economics Lionel Robbins, Arthur Lewis, Friedrich Hayek, Nicholas Kaldor, and James Meade were on the faculty, and Frank Hahn and Ralph Turvey were fellow students. But enough of nostalgia. I promise to impose no more of it on this article. I must admit, however, with respect to the "It's all in Marshall" assertion, that I am considerably more sympathetic to the remark of logician-astronomer C. S. Peirce in an 1871 letter to astronomer-economist Simon

The Quarterly Journal of Economics, February 2000

the United Kingdom new ideas were frequently met with the Cambridge response: "But it's all in Marshall." Alfred Marshall's *Principles* [1890] was, at the inception of the twentieth century, already in the fourth [1898] of its eight [1920] editions, having first appeared ten years earlier. All of this patently invites use of the book, supplemented by his other writings, as the initial point—the standard, against which twentieth century contributions to our discipline can be measured. It is, indeed, the criterion proposed by the editors of this *Journal* when they graciously invited me to produce this piece. For all these reasons, in the pages that follow I will accept Marshall as the zero point of my measuring rod. But I will not do so without pointing out the shortcomings of that choice. For even in 1900 it was not all in his writings, and we can hardly credit to our century matters that, although apparently unrecognized by the professor at Cambridge, were known to others.

It should also be remarked that many of the twentieth century contributions that will be emphasized here were stimulated by historical developments that Marshall could hardly have foreseen. These include the Great Depression and its stimulus of macroeconomics, and the great outburst of innovation after the Second World War that no doubt played a substantial role in the return of economists' interest to growth analysis.

The scope of my assignment here is enormous, and much will have to be left out. Accordingly, although I will discuss them, only limited effort will be devoted to roundup of the usual suspects. Partly, this is because review of the obvious contributions will offer little of which readers are not fully aware, but also because I hold somewhat heterodox views on the century's most fruitful contributions. Much sophisticated theoretical analysis, sometimes using powerful mathematical tools, was already available, a good deal of it still being used in the literature, albeit in modified and (usually) improved variants. Rather, the major upheaval occurred in three arenas. The first is, of course, the formalization of macroeconomics. The second is the construction of powerful new tools of empirical study and their use to provide important insights on the workings of economic reality, as well as to investigate and add substance to the theory. The third, and least

---

Newcomb on profit maximization under perfect competition: "P. S. This is all in Cournot." This is, incidentally, particularly remarkable, as in 1871 Cournot had supposedly not yet been rediscovered (by Jevons) for the English and American adherents to our discipline.

widely recognized, is the widespread employment of theory and econometric analysis in *application*—the formulation of macro policy, the design of taxes, the analysis of portfolios of financial instruments, and the resolution of litigation on antitrust and other economic subjects before courts and regulatory agencies. Before the twentieth century there was nothing remotely similar to the frequent inquiry by learned judges into apparently esoteric mathematical theorems from the microeconomic literature, which they accept as a legitimate and important part of the basis for their decisions. The contention that the major departures of twentieth century economics are to be found in these three areas is the central conclusion of this paper. I will also suggest that a field about ready to burst forth is the *microeconomics* of innovation and entrepreneurship as a key to analysis of capitalistic growth, deriving from the Schumpeterian legacy. A substantial flow of rigorous and substantive contributions is already emerging, promising that the theory is about to take its appropriate place as a central element of microeconomic analysis, rather than a peripheral adjunct to the literature.

Throughout, I will resist the considerable temptation to refer to any of my own work, hoping it will manage to fend for itself.[2]

I. What the Century Contributed: The Textbook Test

Before embarking on the central part of my quest, I will undertake a preliminary inquiry that may, at first, be considered facetious. I will consider what portion of the materials in today's standard economics textbooks provided to beginning students in colleges and universities was unavailable before the arrival of the new (twentieth) century. Such a comparison is suggested by Marshall's *Principles* itself, which, after all, was intended "... as a general introduction to the study of economic science" [Preface to the eighth edition, p. xii]. But there is a reason that I find more persuasive. Today's textbooks, after all, are designed to be read preponderantly by students who will *not* become specialists in the field. The material selected for such a book can therefore be expected to focus on subjects deemed to shed light on the workings

2. Aside from sources of bibliography, there is only one insignificant exception that will go unidentified, and that is introduced only because it serves as a convenient illustration of the point being made. I may note that to save them embarrassment I have also avoided reference to any of the very valuable contributions of the editors of this *Journal*.

of the economy and the design of policy. They are intended to sum up the contributions of economics that really matter to others, and not just to those who labor at the frontiers of our discipline, sometimes perhaps, as Marshall put it, largely ". . . for the purpose of mathematical diversion" (see below for more of the quotation). It follows that the textbook criterion can indicate what economists believe others should glean from the work of our profession during the course of our century, that is, what *useful* pieces of analysis are known today that were not recognized one hundred years ago.

I believe that the results of the textbook test are mixed—in some fields there is a world of difference between the materials available at the century's end and those at its beginning. In other areas, however, the differences are disturbingly small.

The really big change in the contents of textbook volumes is, of course, to be found in the field of macroeconomics, a subject virtually excluded from or at least never given what may now be deemed a serious treatment in Marshall's book. In contrast, much of the textbook discussion of microeconomic subjects has shown much less change, other than in methods of exposition. This is true, for example, of the theory of the firm and industry under perfect competition, of the firm under pure monopoly, of market behavior under these regimes, and of the theory of income distribution. This is not meant to deny the very substantial and profuse new material in the specialist literature, but rather to claim that a relatively small part of these important contributions found their way into the elementary texts in the form of extended and integrated exposition.

So far as macroeconomics is concerned, it can reasonably be claimed that serious treatment of the subject had just had its inception with the completion of Wicksell's revolutionary work in 1898 (see the discussion in Blaug [1968, Chapters 14 and 15]). Of course, there had previously been a profusion of rather rudimentary models of the business cycle, the quantity theory, and other monetary issues. But it can surely not be claimed that any of these provided a systematic structure susceptible to extended analysis. Marshall himself constitutes a good example. Although he lived through several significant recessions, there is not in the *Principles* or in *Money, Credit and Commerce* [1923] or in the *Official Papers* [1926] anything that can lay claim to being a systematic discussion of unemployment. The following quotation is representative, and although it is just an excerpt, it is taken from the only two pages in the *Principles* in which the subject seems to be mentioned: "The chief cause of the evil [of unemployment] is a want of confidence. The greater part of it could be removed almost in an instant if confidence could return, touch all industries with her magic wand, and make them continue their production and their demand for the wares of others" [*Principles,* p. 711].

This is not meant to suggest that Marshall's views of the subject were uninformed or unhelpful. The point, rather, is that such a brief and intuitive discussion hardly provides the framework for a systematic and extensive analysis such as followed the work of Keynes.

Later, I will say more about the twentieth century contribution to, or perhaps more accurately, its creation of macroeconomic analysis. For now it need merely be emphasized that the fact that the field is not only included in today's standard text, but that it routinely takes up roughly half of its pages, constitutes a marked departure from the contents of Marshall's book—the quintessential textbook of 1900. Marshall did, of course, include some subjects that today fall in the macro sections of our texts—money, business cycles, and productivity growth. But these constituted no coherent and extensive part of the volume. There is no chapter on money in the *Principles,* and I have been able to find only three pages [709–11] on "trade fluctuations" (which are not even listed in the index of the eighth edition).

As already noted, matters are very different when it comes to today's core textbook chapters in microtheory. The demand chapters are almost entirely Marshallian, with their focus on elasticities (apparently Marshall's term but not his invention), and the grounding of the demand curves on utility, cardinal or ordinal. Even where ordinal utility is the focus, that need not be interpreted as a significant departure, since by the beginning of the twentieth century Edgeworth [1881] had introduced indifference maps in a book that was well-known to Marshall, and the discussion is cited in the *Principles.*

The textbook versions of the theory of the firm and the industry under perfect competition, it can be argued, are also unchanged in any essential, despite the major additions to the theory that pervade the literature. The exposition has, indeed, been modified and perhaps simplified by the introduction of the marginal cost and marginal revenue[3] curves and the $MC = MR$ requirement for profit maximization. But Marshall certainly used the concept of marginal cost, and his profit maximization requirement (that marginal profit be equal to zero) is surely a thinly reformulated variant of the necessary condition the textbooks use today since, obviously, marginal profit is identical with $MR - MC$.

It is also difficult to find a major change in formal theoretical structure in the chapters on income distribution and their reliance on marginal productivity theory, a theory well explored by 1900 by Walras, Wicksteed, J. B. Clark, and others. Even Euler's Theorem had been given its place by then [Flux 1894]. Marshall was thoroughly conversant with the theory, and even the institutional flavor of the discussion, with its use of what today would be called "casual empiricism," is paralleled in today's texts. He also took a general equilibrium view of the relation between the price of an input and its marginal productivity, e.g., "Marginal uses do not govern value, but are governed together with value by the general relations of demand and supply" [*Principles,* p. 521]. In sum, exposition aside, on the *formal theory* of distribution it can be argued that the textbooks of the end of the twentieth century have added little to the prime textbook of the century's inception. Descriptions of institutions and their implications have unavoidably changed. There have been relatively recent contributions such as human capital theory and the analysis of dual labor markets that modern textbooks do include. But the main formal theory, from the Ricardian rent model to marginal productivity theory, continues to be at the heart of the exposition.

No doubt, various bits and pieces have been added to other portions of the microeconomics sections of today's textbooks. But the startling fact is that there really seem to be only two sets of substantial changes in the microtheory that are found in all standard texts. The first relates to the role of externalities and public goods in the theory of welfare economics. The second is concentrated in what is often a single chapter in current texts: the chapter on oligopoly and monopolistic competition. And, even here, the novelties are not as novel as they may seem.

The absence from Marshall's *Principles* of the concept of externalities as a prime source of market failure entails a double

3. Indeed, it was apparently Marshall who contributed the term "marginal" to the literature of marginal analysis: "I got 'marginal' from von Thünen's *Grenze*" (letter by Marshall to J. B. Clark, 2 July 1900, cited by Guillebaud [1961, p. 8]).

irony. First, it was surely Marshall who invented the distinction between external and internal economies of scale and, apparently, introduced it in the *Principles,* no later than the second edition. But even in the final edition of the book the concept is given little space. Its main role is to point out that a small firm can sometimes reduce its costs not only through its own expansion, but also through benefits derived from "an increase in the aggregate volume of a national or a local industry" (see Guillebaud's notes in Volume 2 of the ninth edition [p. 347n]). The second irony is that it was left for Marshall's student and successor in the Chair, A. C. Pigou, to work out almost fully the theory of externalities in modern welfare theory (the term "welfare" also apparently introduced by Pigou in this connection—but see the note on Hadley, below). This new analysis appeared in 1912 (and more fully in 1920), nearly a decade before publication of the final edition of the *Principles.*

Yet, Marshall did contribute substantially to welfare theory. He had taken over the concept of consumers' surplus from Dupuit, and had shown its relation to producers' surplus, as well as the relation of the latter to rent, quasi rent, and profit. He also showed that the sum of the consumers' and producers' surplus is the proper measure of the contribution of an industry's output to the general well-being. The theory of quasi rents, to which Marshall devoted so much space, can itself be considered a major addition to the theory of welfare, as well as to the theory of distribution. The consequences of monopoly and perfect competition for welfare were also explored. Still, Marshall's discussion leaves an enormous gap, without the current understanding of the role of externalities, that now plays so critical a role in areas as diverse as environmental economics and the theory of innovation.

Clearly, in Marshall's day, game theory had not yet been invented, and Joan Robinson and E. H. Chamberlain had not yet written. But evidently there already was a good deal of material in the general area. The Cournot duopoly analysis remains a model of sophisticated reasoning, and its relation to game-theoretic concepts such as the Nash equilibrium as well as the frequent allusions to Cournot's work in the literature of game theory confirm this. Marshall knew Cournot's work well and admired it. He also was well acquainted with Edgeworth's work on duopoly [1897]. Moreover, Marshall himself recognized that pure monopoly was rare and that the more interesting case was something less extreme. Yet, it is clear that the modern textbook's discussion of oligopoly and monopolistic competition goes well beyond what Marshall said and, very probably, beyond what he knew. Certainly, one would not send a student to his book for a good grounding in either of these subjects.

Yet, it is easy to exaggerate the point that there is surprisingly little beyond Marshall in the micro sections of our textbooks apart from the theory of oligopoly and monopolistic competition. A number of texts do offer more new microeconomic material than this. Small amounts of human capital theory, the economics of discrimination, moral hazard, principal-agent problems, contract theory, and the Coase theorem are found in many principles texts. But these subjects do not normally constitute separate chapters, they are not usually discussed extensively, and are hardly near the heart of the microeconomic portions of modern texts.

The conclusion from all this must be that, macroeconomics apart, what the elementary textbook authors believe it is important for (nonspecializing) students in economics to learn differs surprisingly little from what Marshall already offered readers a century ago. One is tempted to argue from this that our century's microeconomics has contributed very little insight of importance for practice and application. But I will presently argue the contrary—that economics (both micro and macro) has progressed remarkably in what it offers for practice. Rather, there are at least two reasons other than paucity of progress in our discipline why much of this advance is not *substantially* reflected in our basic texts (although, as noted, items such as moral hazard, principal-agent theory, and Ramsey [1927] analysis are mentioned, often quite briefly). The first seems to me a legitimate reason for exclusion: the fact that these contributions are characteristically too technical and complicated to invite their teaching to beginning students. However, it is possible for much of this difficult material to be taught in elementary courses in a very simplified and intuitive way and, in fact, many instructors do so. The second, more questionable reason is the choice of subject matter by the authors of textbooks (including myself) that simply follows tradition in the teaching of these subjects and offers material calculated primarily to be attractive to the instructors. It may therefore not always focus upon the subjects that it would, arguably, be most useful for such students to learn.

II. WHAT THE CENTURY ADDED: ROUNDUP OF THE USUAL SUSPECTS

I have already mentioned a number of the areas of our discipline in which, most would surely agree, the past century brought substantial contributions to our discipline. The names of the major contributors are a good starting point, and they patently include (in more-or-less chronological order) Fisher [1892], Wicksell [1898, 1901], Veblen [1898, 1899], Pigou [1912], Keynes [1936], Hicks [1941, 1946], Samuelson [1947], Koopmans, Friedman, Neumann, and Morgenstern [1947], Tobin and Arrow [1951], and Solow [1956], among others, and their names readily suggest some of the fields in which significant breakthroughs have occurred. These obviously must include macroeconomics, encompassing recent growth analysis, the refounding of value theory, notably in the work of Samuelson and Hicks, game theory, general equilibrium, and its implications for trade theory and welfare economics. I will discuss some of these, but space limitations force me to omit a number of substantial contributions. Among others that come to mind I must mention, in no particular order, Arrow's analysis of social choice and his impossibility theorem, Tobin's contributions to monetary theory, Modigliani's work on corporate finance and his and Friedman's permanent income hypothesis, Lucas' [1987, 1988] creation of rational expectations theory, the work of Buchanan and Tullock [1962] on public choice and rent seeking, the advances in trade theory including the Heckscher-Ohlin model, the work of Stolper and Samuelson, of Dixit and Norman [1980], and of Rybezynski,[4] Patinkin's [1956] reformulation of the neoclassical monetary theory, the Anglo-Italian models, including work of Sraffa [1926], Robinson [1933], Kaldor and Passinetti, the theory of the second-best, with Viner's [1921, 1950] preliminary contribution and the analysis of Lancaster and Lipsey, work on moral hazard, principal-agent problems, and information costs, with contributors including Stiglitz and Akerlof, the work of the institutionalists, following Veblen's writings [1898, 1899]. This list omits major contributors such as Gary Becker, Oliver Williamson, Michael Spence, and William Vickrey, and new fields of study such as environmental economics (see Cropper and Oates [1992], behavioral economics (see Thaler

4. I also venture to predict that, although highly controversial, Gomory's recent work in international trade [1994] will eventually be recognized as a major contribution.

[1991], law and economics and cultural economics (see Towse [1997]—but one must stop somewhere).

I will conclude that these most obvious categories of research are not generally the ones that bring us most markedly beyond Marshall. Rather, my heterodox view is that advances in empirical work and application of theoretical concepts to concrete issues of reality are where one can find the most distinct advances beyond the state of knowledge at the beginning of our century.

Some Ruminations on Macroeconomics

I have already cited Marshall's views on unemployment as an indication of the rudimentary state of thought on macroeconomic issues in about 1900. And it will surely be admitted, even by those furthest removed from Keynes' positions, that his work, along with that of the Stockholm School, and that of several others, has injected a degree of depth and systematic thought into the field. Thus, the analysis of the monetarists, despite its conflict with that of the Keynesians, owes to the latter an enhancement of its structured investigations. It is arguable, for example, that without the macroeconomic literature that followed the *General Theory* the rational expectations analysis might never have been extensively explored. There is a clear link from Keynes to Friedman to Phelps and Lucas. Whatever the achievements of the Keynesian revolution may have been, it certainly succeeded in inaugurating a massive and extremely active field of specialization, as well as a more formal and more rigorous exploration of its relationships than we had ever possessed (on this, see Lucas and Sargent [1978], Lucas [1987], Blinder [1987], Gordon [1990], and "Symposium: Keynesian Economics Today" [1993]).

"Macroeconomics" can be taken to have two defining features. First, it deals with entire economies, rather than any of its constituent components. This, of course, is hardly new, as the title of Adam Smith's magnum opus reminds us. Second, the approach achieves analytic tractability through simplification by means of aggregation, discussing broad classes of agents as organic entities—consumers, investors, etc. But this, too, was previously done, as, for example, in the classical theory of distribution with its combining of all inputs into land, labor, and capital. It is the combination of these two attributes that makes the field different from others, and makes it, arguably, a creation of the twentieth century. For although early cycle theories dealt with related matters, it was not the underconsumption models alone that deserve to be called "naïve."

While I have argued that Wicksell [1898, 1901] was an exception, providing a sophisticated and coherent analysis of the process of inflation in a full-employment economy, one can conclude that his work, too, is essentially of the twentieth century. He did manage to get ahead of 1900 by a scant two years, but the revisions of this work and the subsequent publications by him on similar subjects are in the spirit of our own century, in which they in fact appeared. I conclude that the broad field of macroeconomics is in essence a twentieth century phenomenon, whose earlier predecessors are but feeble ancestors.

I end this discussion by disagreeing emphatically with the view, so often heard, that macroeconomics is in terrible trouble. I believe this opinion stems from a misunderstanding of what one can and cannot reasonably expect from it. The genius of macroeconomics consists of felicitous oversimplification, which is traded off for concrete conclusions that are much harder if not impossible to obtain from less simplified models. And macroeconomics has delivered on this promise, offering insight and understanding to economists and policy makers that were totally unavailable before. However, the very oversimplification that makes this possible means that the utmost caution is required in reliance upon and use of these conclusions. They must be labeled carefully to admonish the user to "handle with care" because, taken improperly, they can be dangerous to the economy's health. That is surely not a failure of macroeconomics, but one of its inherent features that was recognized from its beginnings. A second misunderstanding is the notion that it is desirable to impart great rigor to macroeconomic theory, perhaps even giving it strong microeconomic foundations. But such a move is likely to deprive the field of its very reason for being—the ease with which it can be used to derive concrete (if frequently controversial) conclusions such as results indicating public policies that promise to be useful in combating unemployment or inflation.

On Growth Analysis: Macro and Micro

In my view, it is a historical accident that, despite Schumpeter's [1912, 1942, 1954] emphasis on the role of the firm and the state of competition, growth theory does not reside primarily in the *microeconomics* literature, but instead became largely an offshoot of general macroeconomics in postwar contributions to the theory of growth. This is the literature flowing from the work of Solow and Lucas (for a survey of this subject, see, for example, "Symposium: New Growth Theory" [1994] and Jonathan Temple [1999]). This analysis provided enormous new opportunities for empirical investigation of the theoretical constructs. As will be described more fully later, the macroeconomic growth studies have, for example, yielded evidence on the magnitude of the contribution of innovation to growth and on the degree to which convergence among economies in productivity and GDP per capita (or its absence) has occurred. They have done more than that—for example, Romer and others have built on the convergence results to show the need for modification of the macroeconomic models, arguing that they relied too heavily on diminishing returns and failed to take sufficient account of the evidence that innovation is, at least partially, an endogenously determined activity. Thus, the macroanalysis of growth has very effectively brought together theory, empirical study, and it should be added, application to policy.

But looked at purely as theory, at least three observations can be offered about the novelty of the work and its explanatory power. First, it can easily be argued that today's growth models, *taken purely as theoretical constructs,* are not all that different from the classical model of Ricardo and his contemporaries. It is not difficult to translate the magnificent Ricardian growth model into mathematical terms. Indeed, one may well say of Ricardo what Edgeworth, perhaps with less justification, said of Marshall: that he bore ". . . under the garb of literature the armor of mathematics" (as cited by Guillebaud [*Principles,* ninth edition, Vol. II, p. 14]). In that well-known model, quantities of labor, capital, and land determine output, with diminishing returns to the first two inputs. The surplus of output over differential rent and the subsistence (but not actual) level of wages then determines both accumulation of capital and growth of population. This sequence easily translates itself into a formal dynamic model whose equilibrium point is the stationary state. And in the Ricardian discussion it is explicitly recognized that the production function can be shifted upward, thereby postponing the stationary state indefinitely.

An essential role in the mechanism is played by the production relationship, which one can write as $Y_t = A(t)f(L_t, C_t, R_t)$, with Y, L, C, and R, representing aggregate output, labor, capital, and employed land, respectively. $A(t)$ is productivity growth attributable to exogenous innovation. The point in all this is the close resemblance between this scenario and those offered in recent growth models. There are, of course, significant differences. For example, Ricardo did not use Cobb-Douglas functions, he did not deal with a separate $A_j(.)$ function for an individual industry, j, nor did he endogenize the innovation process by making A_j a function of total investment in human capital or total investment in innovation. But these are, arguably, modifications of a venerable construction and not theoretical breakthroughs of the twentieth century. The considerable achievement of that literature, in my view, lies elsewhere—particularly in its facilitation of empirical study, as will be argued presently.

Second, as is appropriate for a macroeconomic model, the new growth analysis is a deliberate and marked simplification of the pertinent relationships. For example, endogenization of the innovation process is represented by means such as the premise that innovation in a particular field depends on the size of the set of innovations in the entire economy (thus taking account of the spillovers created by the process—see, e.g., Arrow and Romer) or, alternatively, that it depends on the economy's investment in human capital. (For references, see "Symposium: New Growth Theory" [1994].) Now such assumptions are surely valid, but it is equally clear that they leave out much of what is entailed. It can even be suggested, with Schumpeter, that a theory that confines its description of the innovation process to these two phenomena and does not attempt to deal with the extraordinary growth record of capitalist economies amounts to a performance of *Hamlet* from which the Prince of Denmark is absent. Because the analysis is macroeconomic, it cannot easily take account of the market forces and fierce competition among firms for priority in new products and processes. Yet these, arguably, are among the key determinants of the magnitude of the resources the economy devotes to innovation and are at the heart of the explanation of the historically unmatched production and growth performance of free-enterprise economies.[5]

5. This is not meant to overlook or to denigrate the mass of valuable papers on the microeconomics of innovation that have appeared in recent years. And writers such as Grossman and Helpman [1995] and Aghion and Howitt [1998] have made major contributions to particular issues related to innovation and growth. Thus, the former have provided a profound analysis of the influence of international trade on these matters, while the latter have explored the detrimental externalities caused by the introduction of new products via obsolescence of older products. Thus, they have shown how spillovers can conceivably lead to socially excessive expenditure on R&D. But I have been unable to find any recent theoretical

It is, rather, to Schumpeter [1911, 1942] that we must look for insights closer to the core of the issue. It was he who described a competitive mechanism that spurs innovation and in which innovation is the critical source of profits that exceed the normal level. He also described how competitors' imitation erodes those profits and forces the profit-maximizing firm to leap once more unto the breach—to innovate further if the source of economic profits is not to dry up. In my view, as in that of the later Schumpeter, that is no longer the predominant scenario, since relative freedom of entry into the innovation process drives *expected* profits for the innovative industry toward zero. Nevertheless, it seems clear that only an explicit micro analysis of the process of competition that uses innovation as its most potent weapon, and in which firms are determined to be second to none, will bring the Prince of Denmark back to center stage. Thus, while, as I will argue, the macroeconomic investigation of growth constitutes a major twentieth-century contribution, its achievement is *not* primarily *as theory.*

Third, simplification, with its great payoff, forces these models to be ahistorical. They contain nothing that distinguishes *market* economies from Soviet or Roman or medieval Chinese economies. Thus, designed as they are to deal with other matters, these models are incapable of shedding any light on one of the most critical issues for growth analysis: the capitalist economy and its special accomplishment—its unprecedented growth performance.

I may add that in my view things are about to change in the theory of growth and innovation. Valuable theoretical work on this topic and on the related subject of entrepreneurship is pouring forth from an impressive multitude of sources. The contributions are many and extremely varied, including the invaluable earlier contributions of Griliches, Jorgenson, Mansfield, Nordhaus, Scherer and Shell [1973], and joined more recently by Nadiri, Richard Nelson, Kirzner [1973], Paul Romer [1986], and Bronwyn Hall [1993].[6] The theory is beginning to recognize that the amazing growth performance of the capitalist economies must be explained by the behavior of firms and such attributes of the competitive process as the use of R&D rather

---

exploration of what I believe to be the great gap in growth theory—explanation of the growth explosion in free market economies.

6. For references to all except those whose names are followed by a year, see the bibliography in Nelson [1996].

than price as a competitive weapon of choice. The result in at least some industries is an innovation arms race. In the process, innovation is co-opted into the set of routine business decisions, making it far easier to incorporate the analysis into the standard models of the theory of the firm and industry. This will, I believe, make it possible to bring innovation closer to the core of micro-theory, rather than keeping it on the outer fringes of the analysis. This development will, in my view, also enable us to deal with the anomalous conclusion of welfare theory that the market economy has a propensity to approximate *static* efficiency (and actually to achieve it in a perfectly competitive market without externalities), while market failure from sources such as spillovers seriously damage its *growth* performance, cutting its investment in R&D and other innovative activities well below their optima. This conclusion is an anomaly because it flies in the face of the casual observation that the economy's static performance, beset by market power, government intervention, and externalities in many ways falls far short of optimality, and the well-documented fact that its growth performance has been spectacular and totally unprecedented in recorded history.

Value and Welfare Theory: Buttressing the Foundations

Along with some sophisticated nineteenth century work on the theory of utility, new tools were introduced, including more powerful instruments for maximization and minimization, and new methods of comparative statics.[7] It soon became clear that these approaches to the study of the consumer could also be applied to the activities of the firm and other entities. This led directly to the momentous contributions of Samuelson [1947] and Hicks [1939] who laid out the entire structure of value theory once more, but at a level of sophistication and analytic power that had never before been achieved. This material is sufficiently well-known to require no recapitulation and little comment here. It would, of course, be foolish to surmise that the task was completed in these two works. No doubt a future generation will find much more that is yet to be said and along lines that we cannot now hope to predict. Yet the magnitude of the accomplishment is attested to by the absence of significant attempts to replace or improve upon the materials as a body in the half-century after their appearance.

7. The Appendix offers some descriptive materials on nineteenth century contributions to modern theory of utility and demand, leading up to the discovery of the Slutsky relationship and further pertinent insights.

As an entity they stand unchallenged as both a summing-up and a vast step forward. It is ironic that Hicks always considered his part in this work as among his minor contributions.

Along with value theory, the century inaugurated a systematic analysis of the implications of the theory for economic well-being. The founder of welfare economics was, surely, A. C. Pigou, [1912]. It is noteworthy that perhaps the primary insight to emerge from his book was not an investigation of the benign side of the market mechanism—its vaunted static efficiencies. Rather, Pigou offered us a crucial element for study of market *failure,* taking the concept of externalities from Marshall and expanding it into one of the most powerful concepts of welfare analysis. Monopoly and oligopoly, too, have long been recognized as sources of imperfect performance by the market. More recently other sources of market failure have been identified, among them imperfect and costly information, moral hazard, and principal-agent problems in the work of economists such as Akerlof, Spence, and Stiglitz.

The very legitimate analysis of market failure became a key theme of twentieth century economics. It led to calls for government intervention which, in retrospect, seem in many cases, but hardly always, to have been justified. But it overlooked government failure—the fact that the imperfections of governmental decisions are probably at least as serious as those of the market mechanism. The work of Buchanan and Tullock [1962] on rent-seeking, and the structure of political activity more generally, provided some balance to this line of discussion.

It was left for Arrow [1951] and Debreu [1958] to carry out the other side of the task—rigorous investigation of the venerable insight that perfect competition can, under appropriate circumstances, yield maximum static efficiency. In a sense, this work of those two authors *can* legitimately be deemed to be the end of the line. There seems to be little if anything more that needs to be said about the topic. This is so, in my view, because the subject is really of secondary importance for the real economic welfare of society. As already suggested, at least in the long run, the state of welfare depends on growth and productivity far more than on static efficiency, and this is the really crucial issue that I believe welfare analysis must face.[8]

8. Here it may well be tempting to ask whether it isn't "all in Adam Smith," who surely wrote about both static efficiency and growth. There is some truth in the observation, but not as much as seems widely to be supposed. Despite diligent

On General Equilibrium Theory in the Twentieth Century

The twentieth century addition to general equilibrium theory is, perhaps, clearer than that in any other area. This is because there is a sharp and protracted break between what had been achieved before 1900 and what was added after that. Despite a few primitive predecessors, it was clearly left to Walras [1874] to lay out the formal relationships that make up a full model of general equilibrium. Jaffé tells us, "... it was this book that directly inspired Vilfredo Pareto, Enrico Barone, Knut Wicksell, Irving Fisher, Henry Ludwell Moore and Joseph Schumpeter during Walras's own lifetime" [Walras 1874, 1954, p. 5] (Walras died in 1910). Thus, the basic general equilibrium model had been laid out and was widely recognized by the beginning of the new century. Walras' mathematical knowledge, however, was relatively elementary. As we know, he really never was able to deal with three critical issues: whether the solution to his system would always yield nonnegative prices and outputs, whether the solution existed, and whether it was unique. Walras struggled with these issues simply by counting equations and unknowns, and devised a way to show that their number was equal.

It was left to F. Zeuthen in Denmark and Karl Schlesinger in Vienna to show that it could not be legitimately assumed that the identity of the resources that would be used to capacity was known ex ante, so that in a fully legitimate general equilibrium model many of Walras' equations must be replaced by inequalities. They also provided what were probably the earliest expressions of some of the Kuhn-Tucker [1951] conditions, notably the transverse orthogonality requirement that either price or excess capacity of an input (or both) must be equal to zero. Then, Abraham Wald, in three short papers (one of which is lost) solved the problem of existence and uniqueness of equilibrium. In it he introduced what amounts to the concept of revealed preference,

---

effort I have only been able to find one or two passages in *The Wealth of Nations* (and none in *The Theory of Moral Sentiments*) that deal with the price mechanism and its role in the allocation of resources. The invisible hand passage deals with quite a different matter—the ineffectiveness of good intentions—of the wish (or the affectation) to "trade for the public good" as a means to promote the general welfare, and the far greater effectiveness of pursuit of self-interest here. Smith does comment on influences that promote growth (in Book III), notably division of labor (in the very first chapter of *Wealth of Nations*). But surely his growth analysis is quite primitive and ahistorical. After all, it is his "early and rude state of society. . . ." and similar constructs by other economists who followed him that led Marx to remark that to them ". . . there has been history but there is no longer any" [*The Poverty of Philosophy,* nd., 1846–1847, 1884, p. 102].

but his proof entailed some rather questionable assumptions that were needed to prove uniqueness. Then, Dorfman, Samuelson, and Solow [1958, pp. 366–375] provided a more straightforward and intuitive proof, using the Kakutani fixed-point theorem (for all the references in this paragraph, see Dorfman, Samuelson, and Solow [1958]).

From the point of view of the economics, one can remark that the path chosen by general equilibrium theorists then takes the direction opposite to that of macroeconomists. I describe the latter as "the simplifiers," meaning that their success rests on a willingness to trade off simplification of economic reality, for a marked increase in analytic tractability and enrichment of results. The general equilibrium theorists, in contrast, are "the complicators," who omit as little as possible from their models and, as a result, sacrifice tractability and the opportunity to derive conclusions that are directly applicable.[9] As Dorfman, Samuelson, and Solow put the matter:

> Before going on to formulate a simple general-equilibrium model . . . it is worth wondering what kinds of questions can usefully be asked of such a model . . . that cannot be answered by less ambitious models? It seems apparent that a system which leaves many supply and demand functions (or the utility and production functions which lie one step further back) almost completely unspecified as to shape can yield only incomplete results. If we ask the Walrasian equations what will happen to the price of Commodity A if the supply of Factor F shifts to the right, the answer we get is literally the disappointing "That depends"—depends on the shape of just about every schedule appearing in the equations of the system. . . . Actually, in connection with abstract Walrasian systems, the main question that seems to have been studied in the literature has to do with the *existence* of an equilibrium solution to the collection of equations and with the *uniqueness* of the equilibrium if it exists [p. 349].

More recently, there has been work indicating that, under plausible assumptions, not only is uniqueness likely to be violated, but the number of possible equilibria can be very large and unstable.[10]

9. It has been suggested by a reader of the manuscript of this paper that "generalizers" is perhaps a better description than "complicators" of the general equilibrium theorists. I will not quibble with this suggestion, although it strikes me that the models sometimes rely on rather drastic assumptions and so fall considerably short of generality.

10. Recent work by Sonnenschein, Debreu, Mantel, and others has shown just how serious the problem is. Given any finite set of n-dimensional vectors, and a corresponding set of n-by-n matrices satisfying only the basic requirements of demand response matrices, it is possible to specify an economy consisting of no more than n rational consumers, for which the specified vectors will be the equilibrium price vectors, and the specified matrices the responses of the excess

It may appear from all this that there is not much to be said for the achievements or promise of general equilibrium theory. But that, I believe, would be a great error. I am not seeking to praise the theory with faint damns by concluding that it is unreasonable to expect such a deliberately complex theory to provide general and rigorous results that offer substantial insights on the way the economy actually works. However, it can and often does prove that intuitively plausible conclusions of partial models do *not* always hold, so that they cannot be relied upon. It is claimed that an old Yiddish proverb asserts "for example is not a proof." But a general equilibrium counterexample can be a *disproof.* The theory thereby provides invaluable warnings that unqualified acceptance and promulgation of the results of plausible partial models can sometimes be little more than a leap of faith. For the general equilibrium analysis can demonstrate that very different alternatives are also possible and perhaps even likely. International trade analysis has provided a profusion of examples, showing, for instance, that it is not possible to predict the exact commodity composition of trade on the basis of comparative advantage information and autarky price ratios alone (see, for example, Dixit and Norman [1980, pp. 95–96]). Such negative results demonstrate the great value of general equilibrium theory, a product of the nineteenth century, to which much rigor has been added in the twentieth.

Imperfect Competition and Game Theory

Cournot's [1838] work, with its two chapters on the theory of monopoly, was well-known to Marshall, as was Edgeworth's pioneering article of 1897, at least by the time later editions of the *Principles* were published. Both these sources also dealt with duopoly and oligopoly. Edgeworth even arrives at and describes very clearly a saddle point solution (he calls it a "hog's back") and shows some of the game-theoretic properties of the solution when the participants do not adopt the strategies that are optimal only against the optimal strategies of their competitors. But Marshall chose to use little of this. Instead, he employed more rudimentary

---

demands to the prices at each equilibrium. There is no natural way to say which of these cases is more plausible than any other. Thus, the number of equilibria can be arbitrarily large. Moreover, since the local stability of an equilibrium depends on the matrix of price responses, and these matrices can also be specified almost completely arbitrarily, the stability properties of these equilibria are also almost completely indeterminate (on this see, e.g., McFadden, Mas-Colell, Mantel, and Richter [1974]).

graphic approaches, characteristically devoting the bulk of his discussion, instead, to wise intuitive observations and institutional material. His material on the monopolistic firm proceeds without even the concept of marginal revenue, and his basic diagram is not easy to read, so one can readily understand why it was avoided by later writers.

Yet, despite all this, Marshall is able to discern results now familiar but apparently new for the time. Thus, he notes that while monopolistic profit maximization obviously tends to call for an output lower than that which yields zero economic profits, it may still exceed the output of an otherwise similar competitive industry because amalgamation of production and distribution can shift the monopolist's cost curves downward. He also shows that a tax that is fixed either in total or as a percent of total profit will lead to no change in the profit-maximizing price and output.

He is, perhaps, most innovative in his comparative statics. Cournot had already introduced a comparative statics analysis of such matters as the effect of an excise tax on product price. But all of Cournot's analysis used differential calculus, so he could explore only very local movements resulting from very small changes in the parameter values. Marshall's diagrammatic method, in contrast, enables him to represent the entire range of possibilities, including multiple (local) maxima, where they exist. He is thereby able to show that where several local maxima are present, a small change in parameter value can make the global maximum jump from one such local maximum to another, even when the latter is located rather far from the first. And even if the two equilibrium points themselves are only slightly apart, the result can be a large modification in the payoff yielded by the global maximum. Thus, for example, he shows that a small rise in the cost curves produced by an excise tax can lead ". . . to a great diminution of production, a great rise in price and a great injury to the consumers" [*Principles,* pp. 483–484 fn]. Here, as he sometimes does elsewhere, Marshall shows that occasionally more can be learned using a rudimentary method than one that is more sophisticated.

Simply because it is so widely known even to beginners, there is not much to be said about the theory of monopolistic and imperfect competition, much of it stemming from debate over Marshall. The notion that there is something in between perfect competition and pure monopoly long antedated 1900. I know of no one who wrote analytically about pure monopoly who failed to recognize the existence of an intermediate state between that and perfect competition. Then, in the 1920s the subject came up in writings calling for modification of the standard model of perfect competition. For example, Viner [1921] pointed out the significance of product heterogeneity. Even earlier, discussions of price discrimination in railroad rates had injected doubts about the pertinence of the competitive model. In the United Kingdom there was debate on Marshall's attempt to use external economies to produce a downward-sloping average cost curve for a competitive industry whose firms had to have rising average costs for stability of equilibrium. In particular, Sraffa [1926] pointed out that an alternative way to reconcile stable equilibrium with scale economies is to abandon the assumption of perfect competition. These discussions led directly to the related but disparate work of Chamberlin [1933] and Robinson [1933], which hardly requires summation here. It is sufficient to say that the analysis provided some new tools that were not terribly complex but were helpful and rapidly attracted widespread use. It also offered some insights on firm behavior that are illuminating, if not universally accepted. Nevertheless, the initial popularity of the analysis has since waned, and even Joan Robinson herself later downplayed its significance.

Still, the framework continues to influence and complicate research. For example, in the significant recent work on international trade under scale economies a number of writers have devoted great ingenuity to incorporation of imperfect competition into their general equilibrium models (for references see Helpman and Krugman [1985]). The fact remains that it is far easier to deal with perfect competition in complex theoretical models, particularly those studying general equilibrium, primarily because for decision makers under monopolistic or imperfect competition prices are not exogenously given data. Thus, while the significance of these market forms in reality continues to be recognized, in recent years they have, with a few noteworthy exceptions, occupied a secondary place in purely theoretical analysis.

Matters are rather different when it comes to oligopoly theory. Game theory, invented by Neumann and Morgenstern, with rich contributions soon following from Kuhn, Nash, Shubik, and others, brought unity to the field, but only to a degree. (For references see Leonard [1995] and *The New Palgrave Dictionary of Economics and Law* [1998].) Game theory certainly contributed a powerful and revolutionary set of mathematical instruments, offering economists a route for escape from exclusive dependence upon the physicists' formal tools. The new approach is a flexible way to deal with a variety of special issues and situations in oligopoly markets. Add to that the demonstrated relationship of the mathematics of game theory to mathematical programming, duality theory, and other analytic developments of the twentieth century, and it is clear that the field of oligopoly analysis (as well as other areas interpretable in game-theoretic terms) has undergone a major and useful upheaval. Only one reservation may be appropriate here. The very substantial degree of generality of the concept of game theory means that its results can be expected to be tailored to the particular model, that is, the special case that happens to be under consideration. But then, as we know, heterogeneity of behavior is also characteristic of the real oligopoly markets. As in general equilibrium theory, the game theory results that are *general* are consequently likely to indicate what propositions *cannot* be assumed to have universal validity, rather than providing conclusions about oligopolistic behavior that are universally, or usually, valid.

Oligopoly theory and related analysis have also assumed great importance for application. The theoretical tools of imperfect competition and oligopoly analysis have contributed to practice in antitrust activities and in the regulation of firms designed to constrain the exercise of monopoly power (see below). At this point it should only be noted that, for application, various modifications of, and additions to, the theory were required. For example, it was necessary to focus on the multiproduct activities in which almost all firms in reality engage. For many of the competition issues that occupy the courts and the regulatory agencies are related to this attribute of the firm. For example, a common question is whether a firm under investigation has employed "cross subsidy," that is, whether the firm has used profits above competitive levels earned on products sold in markets in which it is suspected of possessing monopoly power to finance uncompensatory prices for other products. Later, I will cite Ramsey analysis as an example of the sort of theoretical development that is applied to such practical issues related to multiproduct firms.

Conclusions on the Usual Suspects

There is unlikely to be much controversy about the list of contributions reviewed here so far, although my conclusions to this point will, predictably, elicit some limited dissent. Before turning to the portions of the century's contributions that may not be quite so obvious, a few words should be said about its innovations in method, including formalization of comparative statics analysis, revealed preference theory, experimental economics, and duality theory, in the sense of correspondence between expenditure and demand functions. The advances continue, as in Dixit and Pindyck's [1994] new approach to analysis of irreversible investment decisions under uncertainty.

Clearly, the most radical change is the victory of mathematical economics. Of course, such work has a long and distinguished earlier history. But what the century brought was recognition and triumph where, previously, mathematical economics had been in the hinterlands. Far from the mainstream, it was an object of suspicion rather than admiration. It may be hard for younger economists to imagine, but nearly until midcentury it was not unusual for a theorist using mathematical techniques to begin with a substantial apology, explaining that this approach need not assume that humans are automatons deprived of free will.

A number of contributors, Fisher, Moore, Bowley, Hicks, and Allen, were among those who led the way, and it is undoubtedly Samuelson, with his magical powers, who secured the final triumph. Since then, the approach has gained strength from new methods such as linear, nonlinear, and integer programming, the work of analysts such as Danzig, Gomory, Kuhn, Koopmans, and Tucker. There are even some who are driven to argue, perhaps with some validity, that the takeover by mathematical methods has gone too far. That it is imposing too much uniformity on the training of our graduate students may be true to a degree. But the occasional claim that it has forced theory into pure abstraction and deprived it of all relevance to reality as well as applicability is emphatically not true, as will be shown presently.

I turn next, and finally, to the two types of contribution that I believe most sharply differentiate the century's termination from its beginning.

III. The Revolution in Application of Theory and Empirical Investigation

Econometrics and Empirical Analysis

I have already alluded to the elementary state of the empirical evidence cited by Marshall. It is easy to find other writings from the first decades of the century to illustrate this, without denying that the theory and practice of statistics was already making substantial advances. The interest in data and their analysis also affected economics. For example, in the United States the work under the leadership of Wesley Mitchell at the National Bureau of Economic Research on business cycles and other subjects added much to our knowledge of these matters. Kuznets is a heroic figure in the empirical fields, opening up major avenues to measurement in our subject.

Substantial activity applying measurement to policy and theoretical issues seems to have begun soon after the First World War. Solomon Fabricant [1984] tells of the origins of the National Bureau of Economic Research in the aftermath of conflicting testimony by conservative engineer-statistician Malcom Rorty of AT&T and Nahum Stone, an economist with Marxist associations, at the hearings of the famous 1915 New York State Factory Investigating Committee. Their difference was over the workability of a minimum wage, and both participants came to realize that they were arguing without benefit of the requisite information. No data were even available on the share of national income obtained by labor. Meanwhile, the war ". . . revealed an appalling lack of the quantitative information needed to cope with the urgent mobilization and reconstruction problems facing the nation [p. 7]." Rorty and Stone decided to take remedial action, and soon after the armistice Rorty succeeded in getting financial support from the business community. This was used to found the National Bureau of Economic Research as a nonpartisan organization dedicated to the collection of data that could be used to shed light on policy issues. With this, systematic economic-data collection and analysis was launched in the United States, with application as a primary incentive for the undertaking.

However, it is arguably with the work on econometric theory at the Cowles Commission and the inauguration of a journal, *Econometrica,* dedicated to the subject, that econometric research attained the status of an important subdiscipline of our subject. Koopmans' pioneering work on identification and estimation was followed by that of a number of noted contributors, including Frisch, Theil, Klein, Chow, Quandt, Goldfeld, Stone, McFadden, Hendry, and Deaton (for references, see *The New Palgrave Dictionary*'s [1998] entry on econometrics).

Empirical research has benefited not only from new and more powerful methods. The century has also provided invaluable new sources of data.[11] Government and international agencies such as the Bureau of Labor Statistics in the United States and various agencies associated with the United Nations have played key roles, along with the efforts of individual scholars such as Summers and Heston, Kravis, and Maddison. The data include the national income accounts inspired by the groundbreaking work of Kuznets, longitudinal data on households, firms and industries, extensive financial statistics, statistics on the state of the environment, productivity growth, and on and on. (For references to this work, see Baumol, Blackman, and Wolff [1989].) Today, it is hardly necessary to document the role of the study and analysis of data, its use to test theoretical models and hypotheses, and its place in the curriculum. Here, it is noteworthy that the first Nobel Prize in economics was awarded (to Tinbergen) for pioneering empirical work.

There is probably no significant economic issue that is untouched by investigation of pertinent data. For example, productivity growth and the hypothesis that the productivity levels of various economies are converging has been studied with the aid of the pertinent statistics by investigators such as Abramovitz, Wolff, Dowrick and Nguyen, Barro and Sala-i-Martin, and Quah. (For references see Baumol, Nelson, and Wolff [1994].) There are well-known studies of demand relationships, the behavior of firms and industries, and the fundamental relationships of macroeconomics. There are many commendable studies of behavior of the securities markets, of pricing in oligopoly markets, of the role of entrepreneurship, and so on. There are even empirical studies putting substance into welfare analysis (see Slesnick [1998]). At the same time, topics well outside mainstream theory are not

11. Of course, collection of economic data did not begin in the twentieth century. Indeed, since it is not just a century but a *millennium* that is being celebrated, it is appropriate to recall that early great database, the *Domesday Book,* whose principal investigator was, arguably, William the Conqueror. Lest it be argued that William was no economist, we need only recall that Ricardo was a stockbroker, Adam Smith was a professor, first of logic and then of moral philosophy, and that William Petty, generally taken as the founder of economic statistics, was a seaman, physician, surveyor, professor of anatomy, professor of music, land speculator, and jack of other trades. It should also be noted that in its survey of the King's new lands in southern England the book provided evidence of the degree of incursion of the prime instrument of the industrial revolution of the later middle ages—the water mill, that freed economic activity from dependence on human and animal power. The survey found nearly 6000 mills in southern England alone, estimated at about one for every 50 families. These mills did not just grind flour. They pitted olives, fulled (roughly, softened) wool, sawed lumber, ground mash for beer, crushed cloth to make paper, milled coins, hammered metal, and operated bellows for blast furnaces.

neglected. As just one significant illustration, only very recently a new and very illuminating empirical investigation of the effects of affirmative action on the lifetime performance of minority students by William Bowen and Derek Bok [1998] may for the first time have carried study of the subject beyond reliance on conjecture.

Empirical analysis has helped in a variety of other applications. For example, studies of the returns to education and the effects of education on income distribution have provided illumination for discussions of government spending on education. Studies of the incentive effects of taxation have contributed to rational examination of tax policy. The reader will undoubtedly find other illustrations.

The marriage of data study with systematic and rigorous methods of analysis has also led to new types of inquiry that themselves became specialized fields of study. Cliometrics is an illustration that brings out a significant point. By its very nature, economic history has from its beginnings emphasized facts rather than theory. Indeed, in the late nineteenth century the German historical school, notably Gustav Schmoller, had used its study of history as a weapon to attack economic theory (see Schumpeter [1954, pp. 814–820]). What is new about cliometrics is the sophistication with which it studies the facts and its propensity to act as a complement rather than a competitor to theoretical research. The field has progressed with the aid of contributors such as Fogel.

In some fields such as labor economics the new profusion of data has had revolutionary effects. It shifted from an arena that was heavily institutional to one that was primarily data-driven. Econometrics evolved along with labor economics, and great strength was added to the analysis of items such as limited dependent variable models, panel data, and selection bias. Moreover, the availability of household data sets shifted the focus of the field from labor demand and internal labor markets to labor supply and the returns to human capital. Thereafter, the recent emergence of matched establishment-employee data sets and the data files of the personnel of firms has returned the focus to labor demand and relationships within the firm.

But there is more than these observations to bring out the radical change during our century in the position of empirical research. For we have grown increasingly uncomfortable with theory that provides no instruments for analysis of the facts and no opportunity for empirical testing. Earlier, in the discussion of the recent macroeconomic models of growth and innovation, it was suggested that theoretical insights are not their only or even their most fruitful contribution. Rather, it is their role as the basis for statistical estimation and testing of theory that can perhaps be considered their primary accomplishment. From its inception in Solow's work, modern macroeconomic analysis of growth has featured empirical investigation as its most novel contribution, and one of profound significance. The growth analysis has permitted us to grapple with the difficult problem of estimation of the contribution of innovation to growth (see Temple [1999]). Thus, the theory has helped empirical research, and the favor has been returned. A good example is provided by studies of the convergence hypothesis, which have also led to modifications of growth theory. The various methods used by different investigators of convergence pretty much agree that there is a small group of wealthy nations whose productivity levels and per capita incomes have been converging toward approximately common levels. However, the poorer countries are falling further behind the members of that convergence club. Romer pointed out that these statistical results do not fit comfortably with the original Solow model in which diminishing returns to capital appear to call for universal convergence. This led to attempts to incorporate innovation as an endogenous variable in the growth macro models, as an alternative mechanism capable of creating convergence among more successful economies if technical progress stimulates more technical progress, but does not require that convergence be ubiquitous.

Interaction of theory and empirical research now pervades the literature. It is, for example, at the forefront of the writings seeking to account for growing income inequality in the United States and elsewhere, entailing an amalgam of international trade theory, theory of technical change, and extensive study of the data (for references see Burtless [1995]). Statistical investigations of income distribution in earlier decades of this century gave us the evidence that was claimed to have shown remarkable constancy of the share of GDP received by labor and led to much theoretical work designed to explain this observation. More than that, this work gave theorists the Cobb-Douglas function whose attractive and simple analytic properties have led to its invasion of various branches of economic theory, some very distant from the theory of distribution.

Here it should be noted that the emergence of data, the advance of theory, and the use of both in application have not proceeded in lockstep. In different fields sometimes data availability, sometimes theory, has lagged substantially behind the other, significantly impeding application.

One last example, input-output analysis, will move us toward my central conclusion that a major accomplishment of the century is the mutual support that theory, data *and application* have come to provide to one another. It has become a commonplace among those in the field, encouraged by Wassily Leontief himself, to assert that input-output analysis has emerged as the current end-product of a line of thought beginning with Quesnay. In outline, the usual story is that the *Tableau Économique* is the first general equilibrium model in the literature and that, minor figures such as Canard and Isnard apart, Marx was the direct successor of the physiocrats in the arena. Next, Marx having left his transformation problem unsolved, Bortkiewicz took up the implied challenge and built upon Marx's rudimentary general equilibrium model (the "simple reproduction model") to provide a viable solution to the transformation problem, one that is still widely relied upon. Then, when Leontief arrived in Berlin as a student, Bortkiewicz was assigned to him as dissertation adviser [conversation between Leontief and this author], thereby completing the chain that carried the interdependence analysis from Quesnay to Leontief.

But what a break there is between input-output and its presumed predecessors! The directly pertinent work of Quesnay, Marx, and Bortkiewicz in each case had its narrow circumscribed purpose, with no empirical connection. Quesnay used his table largely to support the view that manufacturing is a sterile activity and that only agriculture offers a surplus. Marx explicitly translated Quesnay's work into a static two-sector model, his "simple reproduction" concept. There the only immediate conclusion is that in a balanced and stationary economy divided into a sector that produces consumption goods and one that supplies producers' goods, the producer's goods used by the consumption sector must be equal in value to the consumption goods that go to the capital goods sector. Finally, Bortkiewicz used the Marxian reproduction scheme just to solve Marx's transformation problem. Marx had recognized that there must be some definable relationship between prices and the "values" of commodities, as he defined them, but he was unable to discover the precise character of that relationship. The solution was the last stage in the pre-Leontief story. Each step, it will be noted, pursued its author's immediate objective, *and was not designed to lead further.*

In contrast, input-output offers us a tool with a vast array of uses. The techniques have been applied to subjects as heterogeneous as international trade, economics of the environment, and productivity. It is not merely *capable* of using data; rather, it is designed for the purpose. Just to make the point—how such theory, a product of our century, permits both application and use of facts—I will provide a single illustration selected because it is so far afield from the topics to which input-output is commonly applied.

The topic is energy conservation, and various energy-saving projects such as public transportation by rail (subways), recycling of oil, and the use of solar energy and other new energy sources. As advocacy of such measures grew in intensity in the 1970s, dispassionate observers noted that these processes all *used up* energy resources, as well as providing or saving energy. For example, the agricultural products that are employed to produce biomass may be transported in trucks that use up gasoline, and the digging of subway tunnels also consumes enormous amounts of power. Seeking to analyze the issue systematically, engineers invented the concept of "net energy" in which the energy used up by a proposed activity is subtracted from the energy it is expected to contribute. But it soon became clear that the engineers' calculations had at least one major shortcoming. No account was taken of the fact that it requires inputs to make inputs—that the trucks carrying the biomass themselves had to be built and used energy in the process of their construction, and that the same was true of the assembly line used to build the trucks, and so on ad infinitum. Clearly, there was a Leontief process at work. In the usual notation, if we let D represent the vector of energy consumed per unit of output, and A is the Leontief matrix, then the proper measure of energy consumed is

$$D + DA + DA^2 + \cdots + DA^n + \cdots$$

But most of the engineers carrying out the net energy studies were considering only D as the measure of energy use. Some studies were more sophisticated and used $D + DA$ as their energy consumption measure. A *very* few studies even subtracted DA^2, but none went beyond that, thereby in effect assuming that $DA^3 + \cdots = 0$.

A full input-output calculation, using the standard data on the U. S. economy offered rather startling conclusions. The usual approach that takes into account only the energy of the directly used input overlooks, on average, over 60 percent of the true quantity of energy used. Even if a second round—the inputs used to make the direct inputs—is taken into account, some 28 percent of the total energy consumption is omitted. Thus, investments in what are deemed to be energy-saving measures that project, say, a 20 percent net energy yield were shown by the input-output calculation as more likely in fact to use up more energy than they provide.

Ménage à Trois: Marriage of Theory, Data Analysis, and Application

My central contention in this paper is that our century produced a new integration, or at least brought to a far higher level, the integration of theory, empirical investigation, and application. The preceding discussion of input-output analysis illustrates the sort of combination of these three strands that I have in mind. Marshall's *Official Papers* [1926] provides an illuminating contrast. Reading his extensive and impressive pieces of testimony, one comes away feeling that here is a well-informed man with considerable intuitive insight and common sense which, as is often true in our discipline, misleads him occasionally. But what is missing to a striking degree from that testimony is direct reliance on any theorems drawn from the formal analysis of economics, or any buttressing of his position with the aid of systematic statistical analysis. A few empirical data are occasionally cited, but they serve more as background, description, or illustration rather than anything that pretends to constitute analysis.

What led economists to turn to application based on more rigorous theory and analysis of data? Here it should be made clear that the focus on application is hardly a product of the twentieth century. Adam Smith, Ricardo, and their contemporaries did not study economic issues out of "idle curiosity" (as Veblen characterized the primary motive of academic research). What the century contributed was a new foundation for the discipline's applied work. Here it is difficult to provide any general explanation of this development, for its sources undoubtedly differed from one area to another. What is noteworthy is that in a number of cases it represents a response to external demand. For example, in industrial organization, at least some of the work grew out of consulting assignments, as attorneys for regulated firms seeking permission from the regulatory agencies for more flexible pricing rules heard that economic theory contained material called "marginal analysis" that could be used to help their cause. Economists (including this author) who were asked to provide help in their effort were not content simply to leave the story as the lawyers envisioned it. They were led to undertake further research, reinterpreting and applying older ideas (such as Ramsey pricing) and introducing new ones (see Schmalensee [1979]). I suspect that work on theory and data related to fields such as public finance and corporation finance was also stimulated by demand from outside our profession. But all this is conjecture about the mechanism driving the recent history of our field, conjectures themselves driven by neither data nor theory.

The Role of Government and Other Matters

Before continuing my discussion of applied work through the century, it is appropriate to comment on the role that economists have expected government to play. This is not to deny that applied economics has sometimes been oriented to bodies outside the public sector. Economists' writings on operations research and management science have addressed their advice primarily to business firms and other private organizations. Yet it is true that, even in these areas, research began in earnest during World War II, sought primarily to be helpful to the military services, and was heavily financed by them. However, work on topics such as inventory theory, transfer pricing, and transportation planning was not directed exclusively or even primarily to government operations.

Still, the applied economic analyses, on subjects such as inflation and unemployment, environmental policy, antitrust activity, taxation, and interest rates are surely aimed primarily at the public sector, and this immediately raises the general question whether the attitude of economists toward the role of the public sector has changed markedly since 1900. My impression is that there has never been a consensus on this role and that attitudes today are not radically different from what they were a century ago. There were, of course, economists who were passionately devoted to laissez-faire and some who believed that the market, left to itself, would cure most economic ills. But not many were disciples of Dr. Pangloss; few held that the ideal economic state of affairs was what has been described as "anarchy plus the constable" (on this, see Lionel Robbins [1952, 1978], especially Lecture II). After the creation of the Interstate Commerce Commission in 1887 in the United States, many economists, including Marshall (see below) discussed the regulatory role it was appropriate for the agency to play.[12] Similarly, following J. S. Mill, early twentieth century economists often examined the advantages and disadvantages of socialism dispassionately and did not simply reject it out of hand.

It is true that after the appearance of the *General Theory* many economists began to advocate a role to macroeconomic policy much more extensive than before. But this was merely a change in orientation; discussions of monetary and banking policy, including issues such as bimetalism and the gold standard, go back to the dawn of our discipline. The Great Depression also brought with it a school of market socialism led by Abba Lerner [1946] and Oskar Lange (see Lange and Taylor [1938]), but the same period witnessed the contrary positions of Hayek [1948] and von Mises [1949, 1966]. Not even the University of Chicago had a monolithic economics department. That department had a libertarian wing led by Milton Friedman, but it also contained more moderate voices such as those of Paul (later senator) Douglas, and Jacob Viner and produced Samuelson and Patinkin. In my view, then, the century displays no clear trend in the discipline favoring or rejecting government intervention markedly more than the past. Rather, the interesting and novel material is more systematic analysis of *what and how much* it is appropriate for the government to do and how it can best do these things.

And while in the macroeconomic arena many economists have advocated an enhanced role of government, in microeconomics the predominant trend seems to have gone in the other direction. Mainstream economics has generally applauded privatization and deregulation, and at the end of the century it surely contains few if any advocates of central planning. Most economists do favor intervention to protect the environment, to control monopoly power, to prevent fraud in financial markets, and so forth. Still, they recognize that all this incurs costs to society, and

12. Actually, some British regulatory measures were enacted before those in the United States. The early 1800s marked the beginning of British legislation intended to prevent railway companies from exploiting monopoly power. But only after the First World War, when the British government reprivatized the railways it had taken over as a wartime measure, was the Railway Act of 1921 adopted, which first imposed controls on rates and services.

that many types of intervention offer little benefit, or benefits that do not justify their costs.

Another noteworthy development related to application is the great expansion in the number of students completing graduate work in economics. This has been accompanied by a marked increase in the number of economists employed in government, the number of lawyers with degrees in economics, etc. This seems to have led to enhanced receptivity by government, including the courts, to the ideas of economists and that, in turn, has undoubtedly stimulated research activity designed to cast light on applied issues.

The enormous expansion in the number of undergraduates who have studied economics may have done even more to turn economists toward application, and to increase the interest of practitioners in the results. For example, the number of lawyers who studied economics as undergraduates surely far exceeds those who took graduate economics. The same is surely true of the politicians, judges, and ordinary citizens who studied economics as undergraduates and who demand the use of economic analysis in application.

The interest in application has also encouraged work in what can be called "the new institutional economics," encompassing a broad line of endeavor very different from that of Veblen and Wesley Mitchell. It has, for example, included work on law and economics by jurists such as Areeda and Posner and by economists such as Fisher, Joskow, Klevorick, Ordover and Willig, Peltzman, and Schmalensee. But the work is broader than that, and encompasses material on the workings of the firm (on matters such as corporate governance) and the household. It should be clear that there are significant arenas (such as the construction and working of contracts and the operation of markets with heavy sunk costs) in which traditional neoclassical economics needs to be supplemented by the sort of institutional material supplied by these writers. It is no denigration of their contribution to note that earlier economists recognized the need for such work. It seems clear to me that Marshall, in particular, was an institutionalist at heart, and that a hallmark of his writings is attention to such matters, with systematic discussions of theory judged by that author to be a matter of secondary importance. This differentiates his work from that of the new institutionalists, whose hallmark is analysis grounded, wherever possible, in systematic and extensively structured theory. (For references see Hodgson [1998] and the *New Palgrave* [1998].)

Contributions of Formal Macro Analysis to Policy Formulation

The century has witnessed a complete change from Marshall's circumstances in terms of the theoretical resources available to economists who are called upon for advice by policy makers. This has occurred both on the macro and micro levels. The macro story is so well-known that little need be said about it here. Soon after the Second World War the Council of Economic Advisers was established in the United States, by act of Congress. The Keynesian revolution had overcome all opposition, to the point where President Nixon was later moved to declare: "We are all Keynesians." The Council followed Keynesian formulas, and for a while they seemed to steer the macroeconomy with remarkable accuracy and predictability. Then, with the military spending of the Vietnam War, the economy began to misbehave in ways that had not been expected, and the Keynesian positions were assaulted by the monetarists, notably Milton Friedman and his colleagues, not without effect.

Today, there is much greater skepticism about the effectiveness of fiscal and monetary policy in steering the economy between unemployment and inflation, or in avoiding their simultaneous occurrence, except in the relatively short run. Still, policy designers surely feel that they understand their options much more clearly than their counterparts did at the beginning of the century. They also feel that there now exists a substantial body of analysis, both Keynesian and monetarist, which it is necessary for them to master to a degree, and from which they can expect illumination, if not a foolproof set of behavioral rules. Yet it is ironic that when faced with the prospect of an economic downturn we do still sometimes retreat to Marshall's suggestive dictum that the ". . . chief cause of the evil is want of confidence."

Microeconomic Policy Arenas

Though less widely publicized, contributions to policy from the microeconomic literature have been no less extensive or effective. The breakthrough came in 1927 with one of the great contributions of that young and tragically short-lived genius, Frank Ramsey. Expressed as a result about optimal taxation, it was only generally recognized as a rule for regulation of pricing by a firm with market power after Boiteux (along with many other noted contributors) rediscovered Ramsey's result independently, and recognized its other uses. The theorem tells us that where there are scale economies or diseconomies, so that marginal-cost pricing does not yield zero economic profits to the firm, second-best prices may be taken to be those that are Pareto-optimal subject to a profit constraint. The analysis then yields an explicit formula for determination of that second-best price. In the simplest case where all other activities are perfectly competitive and, for the products of the firm in question, cross elasticities of demand are all zero, the formula is particularly straightforward. It is what has come to be called "the inverse-elasticity rule:" that the percentage deviations of the prices of the firm's products from their respective marginal costs should all be equal to the same constant, multiplied by the inverse of the firm's elasticity of demand for that product. The intuitive explanation is simple—if to cover costs, prices must be raised above marginal costs, revenues can obviously be increased with minimal demand distortion by raising most the prices of the products with lowest demand elasticities.

To me it is astonishing that, in the many regulatory agencies with which I have dealt in the United States and a number of other countries since the mid-1970s, I have almost never met a regulator who was unaware of what now is called "Ramsey pricing," and who did not have strong views on its relevance. I can easily cite decisions of courts and regulatory agencies in which it plays a significant and explicit role. And this is but one example. Regulatory agencies routinely consider such matters as marginal costs, demand elasticities, and the other paraphernalia of elementary economics. Very recently, in the course of litigation before a panel of three judges, one of them asked me to explain the prisoners' dilemma, and the other two judges then used the concept repeatedly in their subsequent remarks.

Thus, the concepts used are often quite sophisticated, and microanalysis is often called upon to deal with new issues as they arise. For example, there is a debate under way throughout the industrial world on the appropriate pricing of access to "bottleneck" facilities owned by a monopolist, which the law requires the monopolist to rent to competitors in the final-product market. This plays a critical role, for example, in deregulation of electricity generation, where rival generators need access to the transmission facilities of the public utility that is itself also a generator. The same problem occurs under the Telecommunications Agreement of 1977 among 70 countries, in which each pledges to admit competitors from the other countries. For, given the high cost of plant replication, a rival from country X seeking to provide telephone service in country Y will need to rent facilities from a telephone company (often a monopoly) in Y. Economic theory has been used by Robert Willig [1976] to derive a formula for efficient pricing of such access, and the debate over the proposed formula occupies space not only in economic journals, but in a plethora of court and regulatory agency decisions throughout the world. Academic research on applied theory of industrial organization continues in profusion (see, e.g., Schmalensee [1979] and Laffont and Tirole [1999]).[13]

Fortunately, it is easy to compare this sophisticated analysis with its counterpart at the beginning of the century. Railroad rates had for some time been a subject of heated public debate. The Interstate Commerce Commission Act was only a bit more than a decade old, so that railroad regulation was an issue of great interest to economists and much was written on the subject. Arthur T. Hadley, the noted economist-president of Yale University, had devoted an entire book to the subject. In his *Principles of Economics* [1912] Frank Taussig of Harvard has two chapters, and in *Industry and Trade* Marshall includes four chapters on transportation, railroads, and rate setting. These discussions are marked by two attributes: remarkable intuitive insights and very primitive analysis. Marshall clearly is frustrated by the inadequate data available to regulators (and to economic analysts). Here is an illustrative passage:

> When the studies of the Commission have made considerable progress, it will probably be possible to arrive at an approximate judgment as to the relations between the total costs and the total charges of any particular railway that may fall under suspicion. Its original cost can be estimated roughly from the statistical history of the railway, and can be compared with similar estimates as to other railways: and its methods of administration can be noted; with special reference to the question whether fresh capital was raised to carry out simple improvements the cost of which should have been defrayed out of income. Also, a direct comparison can be made of its charges as a whole, with those of other railways which have about equal facilities for obtaining a dense and regular traffic, equal costs for materials, etc. Some of these railways are sure to be managed efficiently and honestly and they will serve as a touchstone for the rest [*Industry and Trade*, pp. 843–844].

The economists of the time were aware that there are two

13. For discussion of microeconomics and legal analysis more generally, see Cooter and Rubinfeld [1989].

main sources of the special problems in determining appropriate prices for different types of freight, different types of passenger traffic, etc. The first complication is the substantial share of common costs, notably rails and roadbed, that serve every type of traffic, and the second problem is the apparent presence of scale economies. To cover the common costs, the economists (not yet having the Ramsey solution) were prepared to approve, in principal, markups for each service proportionate to costs. "From a purely abstract point of view it might seem proper to assign to each service its own direct costs, together with a proportionate share of those which belong specially to services of a like kind with itself, and another proportionate share of those which are common to the whole railway" [*Industry and Trade,* p. 469]. But they recognized that the demands for the different services of the railroad may not permit such markups, so they were prepared to accept price discrimination of at least some degree. Thus, Hadley concluded in a discussion of rail regulation: "The principle of charging what the traffic will bear, adopted by our large corporations, is a good one; it is only when it is made a pretext for charging what the traffic will *not* bear, that it gives rise to abuses" [1902, p. 175].[14]

Taussig sums up the state of the analysis effectively:

> Railways have two marked economic characteristics . . . first, the great size of the plant; and, second, the fact that the operations are conducted largely at joint costs. Both have important consequences for the problems of public regulation. . . . Connected with the large plant is . . . a tendency to decreasing cost per unit of traffic . . . it follows . . . that concentration and monopoly promote the thriftiest way of laying out the railway net. . . . Many peculiarities in railway rates are explained by the principle of joint cost. It underlies the much-misconceived practice of "charging what the traffic will bear. . . ."
>
> [T]he great mass of joint expense . . . must be got back somehow, or else railways will not be built. Some items of traffic will "stand" a heavier charge than others; that is, they will continue to be offered even though the transportation charge be high. . . . The joint expense will be got back from the former set much more than from the latter. . . . That the principle of joint cost explains (in the main) the practice of charging what the traffic will bear does not prove the practice to be just. . . . To arrange [regulate] railway charges on a "just" basis . . . is a task of peculiar difficulty and complexity. . . . Rates as a whole should not be higher than will suffice to yield a normal return on the capital invested in railways. . . . Even though no absolutely precise settlement of such a rate of return be feasible, an approximation to it can be

14. Note, incidentally, that the book is subtitled "An Account of the Relations Between Private Property and the Public Welfare," thus bringing the term "welfare" into the literature nearly a decade before Pigou.

> reached—six per cent, or eight per cent, or something of the sort. But this helps very little as to any individual rate. Whether the individual rate is "reasonable" is a question of its right adjustment to traffic demand and to the best utilization of plant and equipment. It happens that this question of principle has not often been deliberately considered in the United States or in other countries [1913, Volume 2, pp. 366–376].

Application of sophisticated modern micro theory has also occurred in arenas other than rate regulation, such as securities markets, where portfolio theory and other sophisticated concepts have made a substantial mark. The work of Black and Scholes [1973] on real options can be considered one of the literature's great accomplishments since Marshall, and not just for finance theory. Tax policy, too, has felt the influence of microanalysis. The same is true of environmental economics. And much of this sort of application of microtheory *has* found its way into modern textbooks. Nor is this all. In short, application of formal economic analysis has achieved a substantial standing far beyond anything that could have been imagined at the beginning of the century.

IV. Concluding Comment

I am well aware that in attempting in so brief a space to select the main accomplishments of our discipline during the preceding century I have engaged in blatant chutzpah. Worse than that, I have undoubtedly overlooked some invaluable accomplishments whose authors will have good reason to take umbrage at my carelessness or ignorance to which such omissions must be attributed. Finally, in my efforts to avoid confining myself to the obvious, this review may well have gone off in odd directions. But this is all by way of apology for myself. It should not detract attention from what seems to me to be the main lesson of this discussion. In our discipline, the century has been full of accomplishments. New ideas, new directions, and powerful new tools have emerged in profusion. Evidently, our field of study is alive and well, and poised for a rapid start into the twenty-first century.

Appendix: On Nineteenth Century Precursors of Modern Utility and Demand Analysis

I will argue that the use of Marshall's work to indicate the state of the economic literature at the turn of the century is somewhat misleading. For this I will note some ideas that may be considered modern and that had already been explored before 1900 but were absent from the master's works, using utility and demand theory as my example. As a matter of fact, a considerable number of writers in the nineteenth century went well beyond Marshall in this area. Several of the writings were known to him, although he chose to mention their contributions only briefly, if at all.

Marshall's failure to build on these can be attributed to a considerable degree to his reservations about formal theory and the use of mathematics in economics. This was despite his having achieved the status of Second Wrangler in the Mathematical Tripos in 1861, and starting off in economics by translating ". . . as many as possible of Ricardo's reasonings into mathematics" [Keynes, 1951, pp. 131, 151]:

> In a stationary state . . . [e]ach effect would be attributable mainly to one cause; there would not be much complex action and reaction between cause and effect. . . . But nothing of this is true of the world in which we live. Here every economic force is constantly changing its action, under the influence of other forces which are acting around it. . . . In this world therefore every plain and simple doctrine as to the relation between cost of production, demand and value is necessarily false; and the greater appearance of lucidity which is given to it by skillful exposition, the more mischievous it is. A man is likely to be a better economist if he trusts to his common sense, and practical instincts, than if he professes to study the theory of value and is resolved to find it easy [*Principles,* pp. 367–368].[15]

And also:

> It is obvious that there is no room in economics for long trains of deductive reasoning. . . . It may indeed appear at first sight that the contrary is suggested by the frequent use of mathematical formulae in economics. But on investigation it will be found that this suggestion is illusory, except perhaps when a pure mathematician uses economic hypotheses for the purpose of mathematical diversion; for then his concern is to show the potentialities of mathematical methods on the supposition that material appropriate to their use has been supplied by economic study. He takes no technical responsibility for the material, and is often unaware how inade-

15. Note the similarity in spirit to Veblen's view: "the psychological and anthropological preconceptions of the economists [entail a] conception of man [as] that of a lightning calculator of pleasures and pains, who oscillates like a homogeneous globule of desire of happiness under the impulse of stimuli that shift him about the area, but leave him intact. He has neither antecedent nor consequent. He is an isolated, definitive human datum, in stable equilibrium except for the buffets of the impinging forces that displace him in one direction or another. Self-poised in elemental space, he spins symmetrically about his own spiritual axis until the parallelogram of forces bears down upon him, whereupon he follows the line of the resultant. When the force of the impact is spent, he comes to rest, a self-contained globule of desire as before" [1898, pp. 389–390].

quate the material is to bear the strains of his powerful machinery [*Principles*, p. 781].

Marshall knew and cited a number of the earlier writings on demand and utility that anticipated things likely to be credited to the twentieth century, but he often chose not to build on them. Thus, Marshall was aware of the indifference curve concept. He mentions it in notes xii [first edition, 1890] and xii bis [second edition, 1890] of the mathematical appendix to the *Principles*, attributing them, appropriately, to Edgeworth [1881]. In that note Marshall also reports on Edgeworth's concept of the contract curve and (implicitly) notes that it is the locus of points of tangency of the indifference curves of the two parties under consideration. Two decades before the new century Marshall had also constructed a rather elaborate model with many diagrams employing offer curves throughout, although he did not derive them from any indifference maps [1879, much of it reproduced as Appendix J of Marshall 1923]. Yet, he did not choose to use anything beyond simple demand curves in most of his analysis. He does discuss utility and its relation to demand, but prefers simplistic functions that are additively separable, so that complementarity and substitutability are essentially ruled out: "Prof. Edgeworth's plan of representing [utilities] as general functions of x and y [the quantities of different commodities consumed] has great attraction to the mathematician; but it seems less adapted to express the every-day facts of economic life than that of regarding, as Jevons did, the marginal utilities of apples as functions of [the quantities of apples] simply" [*Principles*, p. 845].

As a matter of fact, utility and demand theory had gone well beyond this by the beginning of the new century. Although nine years were still to pass before publication of Pareto's *Manual* and fifteen years before the appearance of Slutsky's now famous paper (but neglected for two decades outside of Italy), there had already appeared the relatively primitive work of Edgeworth [1881] and Fisher [1892, 1925] on the subject. But major steps of far greater sophistication had already been taken by G. B. Antonelli [1886] and W. E. Johnson and C. P. Sanger [1894], bringing them close to the noted contribution of Hicks and Allen [1934]. It is easy to understand why Marshall did not know about the former's work, since it was privately printed by an engineer who never wrote anything else on mathematical economics, and remained unknown until Wald called it to our attention more than a half century later. However, the Johnson-Sanger piece might have stood a better chance of eliciting Marshall's attention since both authors became members of the faculty at Cambridge (at King's and Trinity, respectively), both subsequently published in the *Economic Journal,* and their paper was presented to the Cambridge Economics Club in 1894. The Antonelli article provides one of the first examples of the use of determinants in economics, and studies the issue of integrability ahead of Fisher's and Pareto's [1911] consideration of the subject. Johnson and Sanger study the theory of utility maximization subject to a budget constraint, examine the role of variations in income, and investigate the interpretation of the marginal utility of money, as well as that of consumers' surplus, when the model contains an arbitrary number of interdependent commodities. In short, the theory of demand had advanced well beyond Marshall by the beginning of the twentieth century. The same is true of a number of the other subjects he treated.

NEW YORK UNIVERSITY AND
PRINCETON UNIVERSITY

REFERENCES

Aghion, Philippe, and Peter Howitt, *Endogenous Growth Theory* (Cambridge, MA: MIT Press, 1998).

Antonelli, G. B., *Sulla teoria matematica della economia politica* (Pisa: privately printed, 1886).

Arrow, Kenneth J., "An Extension of the Basic Theorems of Classical Welfare Economics," *Proceedings of the Second Berkeley Symposium on Mathematical Statistics and Probability* (Berkeley: University of California Press, 1951).

Baumol, William J., Sue Anne Batey Blackman, and Edward N. Wolff, *Productivity and American Leadership: The Long View* (Cambridge, MA: MIT Press, 1989).

Baumol, William J., Richard R. Nelson, and Edward N. Wolff, *Convergence of Productivity: Cross-National Studies and Historical Evidence* (New York: Oxford University Press, 1994).

Black, Fischer, and Myron Scholes, "The Pricing of Options and Corporate Liabilities," *Journal of Political Economy* LXXXI (May/June 1973), 637–654.

Blaug, Mark, *Economic Theory in Retrospect* (Homewood, IL: Richard D. Irwin, 1968).

Blinder, Alan S., "Keynes, Lucas and Scientific Progress," *American Economic Review, Papers and Proceedings,* LXXVII (May 1987), 130–136.

Bowen, William G., and Derek Bok, *The Shape of the River: Long-Term Consequences of Considering Race in College and University Admissions* (Princeton, NJ: Princeton University Press, 1998).

Buchanan, James, and Gordon Tullock, *The Calculus of Consent* (Ann Arbor, MI: University of Michigan Press, 1962).

Burtless, Gary, "International Trade and the Rise in Earnings Inequality," *Journal of Economic Literature,* XXXIII (June 1995), 800–816.

Chamberlin, E. H., *The Theory of Monopolistic Competition: A Reorientation of the Theory of Value,* eighth edition (Cambridge, MA: Harvard University Press, [1933] 1962).

Cooter, Robert D., and Daniel L. Rubinfeld, "Economic Analysis of Legal Disputes and their Resolution," *Journal of Economic Literature,* XXVII (September 1989), 1067–1097.

Cournot, A. A., *Researches into the Mathematical Principles of the Theory of Wealth,* Bacon translation (New York: [1838] 1897).
Cropper, Maureen L., and Wallace E. Oates, "Environmental Economics: A Survey," *Journal of Economic Literature* XXX (June 1992), 675–740.
Debreu, Gerard, *Theory of Value* (New York, NY: John Wiley, 1958).
Dixit, Avinash, and Victor Norman, *Theory of International Trade* (Cambridge: Cambridge University Press, 1980).
Dixit, Avinash, and Robert Pindyck, *Investment Under Uncertainty* (Princeton, NJ: Princeton University Press, 1994).
Dorfman, Robert, Paul A. Samuelson, and Robert M. Solow, *Linear Programming and Economic Analysis* (New York: McGraw-Hill, 1958).
Edgeworth, F. Y., *Mathematical Psychics: An Essay on the Application of Mathematics to the Moral Sciences* (London: C. Keegan Paul & Co., 1881).
——, "Teoria Pura del Monopolio," *Giornale degli Economisti,* 1897, translated and published in *Papers Relating to Political Economy,* Vol I (London: Macmillan and Co., 1925), 111–142.
Fabricant, Solomon, *Toward a Firmer Basis of Economic Policy: The Founding of the National Bureau of Economic Research* (Cambridge, MA: NBER, 1984).
Fisher, Irving, *Mathematical Investigations in the Theory of Value and Price* (New Haven, CT: Yale University Press, [1892], 1925).
Flux, Alfred W., review of P. H. Wicksteed, *Essay on the Co-ordination of the Laws of Distribution, Economic Journal,* IV (1894), 308–313.
Gomory, Ralph E., "A Ricardo Model with Economies of Scale," *Journal of Economic Theory,* LXII (1994), 394–419.
Gordon, Robert, "What Is New-Keynesian Economics?" *Journal of Economic Literature,* XXVIII (September 1990), 1115–1171.
Grossman, Gene M., and Elhanan Helpman, *Innovation and Growth in the Global Economy* (Cambridge, MA: MIT Press, 1995).
Guillebaud, C. W. See Marshall, *Principles of Economics.*
Hadley, Arthur Twining, *Economics: An Account of the Relations Between Private Property and Public Welfare* (New York: G. P. Putnam's Sons, 1896, 1902).
Hall, Bronwyn H., "Industrial Research during the 1980s: Did the Rate of Return Fall?" *Brookings Papers in Microeconomics* (1993), 1–50.
Hayek, Friedrich, A. von, *Individualism and Economic Order* (Chicago: University of Chicago Press, 1948).
Helpman, Elhanan, and Paul R. Krugman, *Market Structure and Foreign Trade* (Cambridge, MA: MIT Press, 1985).
Hicks, John R., *Value and Capital,* second edition (Oxford: Oxford University Press, 1946; first edition, 1939).
——, "The Rehabilitation of Consumers' Surplus," *Review of Economic Studies,* VIII (February 1941), 108–116.
Hicks, John R, and R. G. D. Allen, "A Reconsideration of the Theory of Value, Parts 1 and 2," *Economica,* N.S. No. 1 (February 1934), 52–76 and N.S. No. 2 (May 1934), 196–219.
Hodgson, Geoffrey M., "The Approach of Institutional Economics," *Journal of Economic Literature,* XXXVI (March 1998), 166–192.
Johnson, W. E., and C. P. Sanger, "On Certain Questions Connected with Demand," *Cambridge Economics Club,* Easter Term, 1894 (eight pages).
Keynes, John M., *Essays in Biography* [1933], expanded edition (New York: Horizon Press, 1951).
——, *The General Theory of Employment, Interest and Money* (New York: Harcourt, 1936).
Kirzner, Israel, *Competition and Entrepreneurship* (Chicago: University of Chicago Press, 1973).
Kuhn, Harold W., and A. W. Tucker, "Nonlinear Programming," in J. Neyman, ed., *Proceedings of the Second Berkeley Symposium on Mathematical Statistics and Probability* (Berkeley and Los Angeles: University of California Press, 1951).
Laffont, Jean-Jacques, and Jean Tirole, *Competition in Telecommunications* (Cambridge, MA: MIT Press, 1999).
Lange, Oskar, and Fred M. Taylor, *On the Economic Theory of Socialism* (New York: McGraw-Hill, 1938, 1964).

Leonard, Robert J., "From Parlor Games to Social Science: von Neumann, Morgenstern, and the Creation of Game Theory, 1928–1944," *Journal of Economic Literature,* XXXIII (June 1995), 730–761.

Lerner, Abba P., *The Economics of Control: Principles of Welfare Economics* (New York: Macmillan, 1946).

Lucas, Robert E., *Models of Business Cycles* (London: Basil Blackwell, 1987).

____, "On the Mechanics of Economic Development," *Journal of Monetary Economics,* XXII (July 1988), 3–42.

Lucas, Robert E., and T. Sargent, "After Keynesian Macroeconomics," in *After the Phillips Curve: Persistence of High Inflation and High Unemployment,* Conference Series No. 19, Federal Reserve Bank of Boston (Boston, MA: 1978).

Marshall, Alfred, *The Pure Theory of Foreign Trade; The Pure Theory of Domestic Values,* privately printed and circulated, 1879, reprinted 1935 as No. 1 in the Series of Reprints of Scarce Tracts in Economic and Political Science, London: the London School of Economics and Political Science.

____, *Principles of Economics* (London: Macmillan & Co., first edition 1890, fourth edition 1898, eighth (and final) edition 1920., ninth (Variorum) edition, edited, with a volume of notes, by C. W. Guillebaud, 1961.

____, *Industry and Trade* (London: Macmillan & Co., first edition, 1919, fourth edition 1923).

____, *Money, Credit and Commerce* (London: Macmillan & Co., 1923).

____, *Official Papers* (London: Macmillan & Co., 1926).

Marx, Karl, *The Poverty of Philosophy* (London: Martin Lawrence, nd., [1846–1847,1889]).

McFadden, Daniel, Andreu Mas-Colell, Rolf Mantel, and Marcel K. Richter, "A Characterization of Community Excess Demand Functions," *Journal of Economic Theory,* IX (December 1974), 361–374.

Nelson, Richard R., *The Sources of Economic Growth* (Cambridge, MA: Harvard University Press, 1996).

Neumann, John von, and Oskar Morgenstern, *Theory of Games and Economic Behavior* (Princeton, NJ: Princeton University Press, 1947).

New Palgrave Dictionary of Economics and the Law (three volumes), Peter Newman, ed (London: Macmillan Reference Ltd.; New York: Stockton Press, 1998).

Pareto, Vilfredo, *Manual of Political Economy* (A. S. Schwier, trans.) (New York: Augustus M. Kelley, [1909, 1971]).

____, "Economie Mathematique," *Encyclopedie des Sciences Mathematiques,* Tome I, Vol. IV, Fasc. 4 (Paris: Gauthier-Villars, 1911), pp. 591–640.

Patinkin, Don, *Money, Interest and Prices* [1956], Second edition (New York: Harper & Row, 1965).

Pigou, A. C., *Wealth and Welfare* (London: Macmillan and Co., 1912).

____, *The Economics of Welfare,* fourth edition (London: Macmillan, 1932; [first edition, 1920]).

Ramsey, Frank, "A Contribution to the Theory of Taxation," *Economic Journal,* XXXVII (March 1927), 47–61.

Robbins, Lionel, *The Theory of Economic Policy in English Classical Political Economy* (London: Macmillan, [1952] 1978).

Robinson, Joan, *The Economics of Imperfect Competition* (London: Macmillan, 1933).

Romer, Paul M., "Increasing Returns and Long-Run Growth," *Journal of Political Economy,* XCIV (October 1986), 1002–1037.

Samuelson, Paul A., *Foundations of Economic Analysis* (Cambridge, MA: Harvard University Press, 1947).

Schmalensee, Richard, *The Control of Natural Monopolies* (Washington, DC: Heath, 1979).

Schumpeter, J. A., *The Theory of Economic Development* (Cambridge, MA: Harvard University Press, [1912] 1934).

____, *Capitalism, Socialism and Democracy* (New York: Harper and Brothers, 1942).

____, *History of Economic Analysis* (New York: Oxford University Press, 1954).

Shell, Karl, "Inventive Activity, Industrial Organization and Economic Growth," in J. A. Mirrlees and N. Stern, eds., *Models of Economic Growth* (London: Macmillan, 1973), pp. 77–100.

Slesnick, Daniel T., "Empirical Approaches to the Measurement of Welfare," *Journal of Economic Literature,* XXXVI (December 1998), 2108–2165.

Solow, Robert M., "A Contribution to the Theory of Economic Growth," *Quarterly Journal of Economics,* LXX (February 1956), 65–94.

Sraffa, Piero, "The Laws of Returns under Competitive Conditions," *Economic Journal,* XXXVI (December 1926), 535–550.

"Symposium: Keynesian Economics Today," *Journal of Economic Perspectives,* VII (Winter 1993), 3–82.

"Symposium: New Growth Theory," *Journal of Economic Perspectives,* VIII (Winter 1994), 3–72.

Taussig, Frank, *Principles of Economics* (New York: Macmillan, 1912).

Temple, Jonathan, "The New Growth Evidence," *Journal of Economic Literature,* XXXVII (March 1999), 112–156.

Thaler, Richard H., *Quasi Rational Economics* (New York: Russell Sage, 1991).

Towse, Ruth, editor, *Cultural Economics: The Arts, the Heritage and the Media Industries* (Cheltenham, UK: Edward Elgar, 1997).

Veblen, Thorstein, "Why Is Economics not an Evolutionary Science?" *Quarterly Journal of Economics,* XII (July 1898), 373–397, reprinted in T. B. Veblen, *The Place of Science in Modern Civilization* (New York: Viking Press, 1942).

——, *The Theory of the Leisure Class* (New York: Macmillan Company, 1899).

Viner, Jacob, "Price Policies: The Determination of Market Price," in L. C. Marshall, ed., *Business Administration* (Chicago: University of Chicago Press, 1921), pp. 242–347.

——, *The Customs Union Issue* (New York: Carnegie Endowment for International Peace, 1950).

von Mises, Ludwig, *Human Action: A Treatise on Economics,* third edition (Chicago: Henry Regenery, [1949], 1966).

Walras, Léon, *Elements of Pure Economics* (William Jaffé, trans.) (Homewood, IL: Richard D. Irwin, [1774] 1954).

Wicksell, Knut, *Interest and Prices* (R. F. Kahn, trans.) (London: Macmillan & Co. [1898] 1936).

——, *Lectures on Political Economy,* Lionel Robbins, ed. (London: George Routledge, [1901, 1906] 1934).

Willig, Robert D., "Consumers Surplus without Apology," *American Economic Review,* LXV (1976), 589–597.

[14]

A Millennium of Economics in Twenty Minutes: In Pursuit of Useful Knowledge*

WILLIAM J. BAUMOL

Director, C.V. Starr Center for Applied Economics and Professor of Economics, New York University; and Senior Research Economist and Professor Emeritus, Princeton University.

The role of merchants in medieval and early renaissance society as instigators of economic, political and scientific innovations is seldom fully appreciated.... It is no mere coincidence that Fibonacci, one of the principal conveyors of the Hindu-Arabic numerical system to Europe, was also a merchant.

F.J. Swetz, Capitalism and Arithmetic: The New Math of the 15th Century, *La Salle, Ill.: Open Court, 1987, pp. 291–2.*

RECENTLY, IN anticipation of year 2000, I was invited to prepare a paper for a leading journal on major accomplishments in my discipline during the century past. But at the recent meeting of the American Philosophical Society the ante was raised. I was asked to comment on developments in my field during the entire millennium, and at a rate of two minutes per century. The reader will then understand the rather episodic character of my remarks.

I will seek, nevertheless, to incorporate several themes: first, the fact that, with some recent exceptions, economic thought has aimed to provide *useful* knowledge, such as the founders of this Society meant to promote. Second, until the eighteenth century, ideas in the field were contributed predominantly by persons who patently were not economists. Third, two variables that have provided the interstices of economic analysis are the de-

*Read 23 April 1999.

termination and role of price and the means to achieve economic growth. In this somewhat disorganized survey, with its unavoidable profusion of major gaps, I will also take note of two mysteries, one early in our period and one that emerges toward the end.

King William's Domesday Book and the Medieval Industrial Revolution

To save time, I will simply ignore most of the first century of the millennium, and start with the *end* of the eleventh century and its remarkable statistical compendium, the *Domesday Book* of (approximately) 1085. Arguably, it is the first great data banks available to economic historians, who have not neglected it. Its focus, certainly, is economic growth—not of the economy as a whole, a concept plainly incomprehensible at the time—but that of the only individual who mattered, William the Conqueror.[1] Some 19 years earlier he had multiplied his possessions, adding Britain to his vast holdings in northern France. For, as in ancient Rome and ancient China, pursuit of wealth was considered a respectable activity, provided it was done by respectable means such as aggressive warfare, bribery, and exaction of ransoms. Only productive or commercial transactions were considered reprehensible avenues to wealth.

Thus, the new wealth that William surveyed in the Domesday Book was not tainted by contribution to economic growth for the society. Yet Domesday reveals that somehow a major contribution to growth had managed to emerge—a profoundly revolutionary innovation. It was not like that other revolutionary innovation, the stirrup, whose primary contribution was military (indeed, it has been suggested that William's possession of the stirrup may have made the difference at Hastings). Rather the crucial innovation was the water mill, which, for the first time in history, freed producers from reliance on human or animal power. True, the Romans and others had pos-

1. It will understandably be objected that William of Normandy can hardly be deemed to have been a professional practitioner of the dismal science. But then, as will be noted later, neither were such noted contributors as Adam Smith, James Mill, or David Ricardo.

sessed the water mill, but the evidence suggests that it was used little, and used only for the most obvious tasks.

In contrast, in what historians have called the "medieval industrial revolution" (eleventh to thirteenth centuries), the water mill was put to a striking variety of uses: pitting olives, fulling wool, sawing lumber, grinding mash for beer, crushing cloth for paper making, milling coins, hammering metal, and operating the bellows of blast furnaces, all of these using a variety of sophisticated gear arrangements. These mills were widespread in southern France, were sufficiently numerous to impede shipping on the Seine at Paris and, the Domesday book tells us, they dotted the landscape in the south of England. Nearly 6,000 mills in this circumscribed area are recorded in the survey, which, it has been estimated, provided on average one mill for every 50 families.

Here, indeed, is a contribution to economic growth, and it facilitated the prosperity of the twelfth and thirteenth centuries when so many of the great cathedrals were built. But this is where my first mystery enters.

Unlike other growth episodes, this unprecedented industrial revolution, with its widespread and effective utilization of a great invention for productive purposes, was *not* introduced and operated primarily by private enterprise. Certainly the guilds in the growing towns did not take the lead—indeed, they were prone to resist change with determination. Rather, its entrepreneurs were predominantly monastic, and those predominantly from one order—the Cistercians. Why? I have some hypotheses, but so far I have found no medieval historian able to provide an answer.

A Word on Just Price and Practical Pricing

Modern economists, with their predisposition to focus on the analysis of pricing, generally turn to the theological discussions of just price as the central topic of medieval economic thinking. It is true that writers such as Saint Thomas in the thirteenth century did devote attention to the subject. Here I will merely note that while the modern reader may well doubt whether any useful knowledge emerged from these discussions, that is far from what the theologian of the time would have concluded. Surely to them there was no knowledge more useful than knowledge that could contribute to salvation of the soul.[2] Indeed, it was only in the late Middle Ages that avid opposition to the search for knowledge (on the ground that it constituted prying into God's secrets) began to recede. In the thirteenth century this view was still powerful, as that genius Roger Bacon found to his misfortune. Thus, knowledge of the paths to salvation was the most permissible form of useful knowledge, and discussions of just price were designed to contribute such knowledge.

Yet pressures of the growing commerce were forcing thinkers to turn to the search for ideas and information we would more readily consider practical today. An example is the application of mathematics to economic decisions. Here we must not forget that as late as the fifteenth century Europeans were still having trouble using the Arabic number system and decimal notation. A fourteenth-century example indicates how limitations of the available mathematical tools affected business. By this time merchants had devised various evasive procedures to overcome the prohibition of usury. We have records of a transaction in Siena, an example of repayment of a debt before its due date. The parties to the transaction recognize that the amount the borrower should consequently pay the lender was smaller than if payment had been delayed to the due date. But they could not figure out how the reduction should be calculated, and in fact, they got it wrong. This should not be surprising for an era in which multiplication and division were considered advanced and difficult calculations.

The type of calculation required for the Sienese lender's problem, now common in the economics literature, was not actually understood until the seventeenth or eighteenth centuries, and the mathematical relationships were worked out fully in a publication on forestry (!) in 1849.[3] By the beginning of our century, the concepts were well understood and written about by a number of economists. It is remarkable, then, that this type of analysis did not become commonplace in the business school curriculum or in business practice until after the Second World War.

---

2. It is noteworthy that religious considerations did not disappear from economic writings until the nineteenth century. For example, specialists recognize that the 1776 invisible hand of Adam Smith was no less than the hand of providence.

3. See Martin Faustmann, "Calculation of the Value Which Forest Land and Immature Stands Possess for Forestry," *Allgemaine forst-und jagt-zeitung,* (15 Dec. 1849), pp. 441–55.

A MILLENNIUM OF ECONOMICS IN TWENTY MINUTES

Useful Economic Knowledge and Employment of Mathematics

The noted writers who populate writings on the history of economic ideas first make their appearance in the seventeenth century. They did indeed write on economics, but they were not trained economists, nor would they have considered this their profession. William Petty was a seaman, physician, surveyor, professor of anatomy and of music, land speculator and jack of other trades; Cantillon was a merchant; Adam Smith a professor of logic and, then, of moral philosophy; and David Ricardo a stockbroker. Arguably, T.R. Malthus was the first professional economist. And all of them wrote on economics not in order to provide knowledge for its own sake, but because they believed it to be useful. Adam Smith, for example, emphasized the importance of economic growth, and a central purpose of the *Wealth of Nations* was to indicate what governments should *not* do, in order to avoid handicapping of the process. Ricardo was concerned with freedom of trade as a means to facilitate growth and as a way to benefit the members of the labor force and the nascent class of capitalists. Going all the way to Alfred Marshall, who can be considered the bridge between the nineteenth and twentieth centuries, I doubt whether one can find a major contributor to my discipline who would have admitted to being driven by what Veblen characterized as "idle curiosity," the motive, in his view, of most academic research.

It was only in our century that many economists began to devote themselves to what they considered pure research. Arguably, this work has provided deep and illuminating insights, though it has also encountered skeptics, notably Marshall, Keynes and Viner (who described some of the literature as illegitimate intercourse with beautiful models). It is ironic that, as will be described later, some of this "pure research" has constituted the basis of a new flowering of applied economics in which economists are not merely offering unsolicited advice, but rather, find their services heavily demanded.

The redirection of research and writing away from application was accompanied by another phenomenon: the emergence of formal mathematics as one of the economist's primary tools. When French mathematician A.A. Cournot published his great contribution to our discipline in 1838, there had already been a number of writings in the field that made use of algebra and a little more. But Cournot was the first to show what mathematics really could do for economic analysis. It took half a century and more for the lesson to take hold, and only in the 1950s was mathematical economics able to sweep all before it in the graduate schools and in the specialists' literature. Today, it is the nonmathematical article that is a curiosity, as a glance at any of the leading journals readily confirms. But mathematics has also emerged as a prime tool of applied economics, in widely disparate applications including work designed to help combat inflation and unemployment, in the analysis of government finance, in study of effective measures for regulation of industry and rules for antitrust activity.

On Useful Knowledge Related to Pricing

So we have leaped forward to the eighteenth century and beyond—to the era in which economics finally emerged as a distinct discipline with investigation and practice carried out by specialists. Economists have, of course, dealt with a vast range of topics, and time forces me to confine myself to two: pricing and growth, which pervade the literature and serve as interstices for the rest of the workings of the economy to a degree that nonspecialists are unlikely to recognize.

Price theory, in particular, has been a focus of writings in economics for at least three centuries. The theory seeks to explain both how the magnitudes of prices are determined by economic forces, and what effects they have upon economic behavior. Consumers obviously care about the magnitude of the prices they pay, and pricing decisions can seriously affect the financial condition of firms. But the importance of price goes well beyond this.

To see why else prices matter, it is suggestive to recall the propensity some decades ago for Marxists (basing themselves on nothing Marx had ever written) to say that chaos was a prime attribute of the capitalist economy. Millions of producers daily and *independently* make decisions about what and how much to produce and how to produce it. At the same time, millions of consumers *individually* decide how much of each good to demand, doing so without consultation or systematic guidance. Why are markets not flooded with unwanted goods and chronically short of things consumers urgently desire? As it turns out, for reasons now well understood, it is the planned economies that fell into the chaos that their central direction was intended to avoid, while the individualistic, uncoordinated free-market economies, though not immune from other serious problems, conducted their day-to-day activities in a manner whose orderliness must be astonishing when the matter is considered.

The secret of the synchronized behavior of the market economies is price. Its operation can be described in simple terms. If producers happen to err and produce fewer buttons than the market demands, their price will rise. That will induce button makers to expand their output and consumers to cut back on demand. If the price rise proves still insufficient to equate demand and supply, that price will rise even further. It will continue to do so until the button shortage is eliminated. Thus, without anyone having planned it, with no conscious intervention by anyone, with no deliberate coordination, the market *automatically* manages day after day, in every geographic area to bring supplies and demands together.

That is even more of a miracle than it may seem at first, because the demands and output needs of different commodities are mutually interdependent, characterized by implicit simultaneous solution of millions of equations with millions of variables. The production of energy for example, requires steel, copper, labor and a vast variety of other inputs. But none of those inputs can be supplied without obtaining adequate quantities of energy whose required amount depends on the size of the outputs of the user industries. The manufacture of transport vehicles to bring those inputs to the energy production facilities in turn requires energy and all the other inputs as well, in interdependent quantities. Thus the economy's production mechanism is a complex tangle of interdependencies and mutually determined requirements. It is the set of prices of all of these items that conveys the requisite information to all of the decision makers involved and automatically induces them to coordinate their decisions so that the entire mechanism works reasonably smoothly and rarely collapses into chaos.

If one accepts this standard piece of economic analysis, it must surely be recognized to be informative. But is it also *useful* knowledge? The answer is, emphatically, yes. It is proving vital in a variety of areas, in business decision making, in government policy and elsewhere. And it is the modern mathematical analysis of the workings of price that has played a crucial role here.

Let me give just one illustration, which happens to involve an issue that affects many industries in nations throughout the world. In particular, in telecommunications, after decades of operation as legal private monopolies or as nationalized monopoly firms, the world has begun to recognize that full competition offers great advantages in the form of improved service, new products, and lower prices. Accordingly, in 1997 some 70 nations signed an agreement permitting foreign suppliers of telephone service to invade their borders as competitors to each nation's former monopoly supplier.

The problem is that modern telecommunications networks have vast capacity and are extremely costly to construct. With the native supplier often already having much of the capacity that is likely to be needed, and with the cost of replication of the facilities by a new competitor prohibitive, entry with new facilities is unlikely to occur. To salvage competition in such circumstances, governments have turned to an alternative course of action. The entrant firms are encouraged to rent access to the facilities already in existence, and the incumbent firms are *required* by their government to rent the access to their prospective competitors.

However, unless a rental price is specified along with the rental requirement, the latter becomes an empty gesture. If the incumbent telecommunications monopolist is left free to charge prohibitive access prices to prospective entrants, that is patently tantamount to complete withdrawal of any rental offer. But the rental price can also be too low. If a government forces the incumbent firm to rent access to its facilities at a price that is not compensatory, that amounts to requiring that firm to subsidize its competitors. The result can well be destruction of the native telecommunications firm while handing over the business to foreign rivals, who then conquer the market not by superior performance but by virtue of the subsidy with which they have been provided.

Thus, either too low or too high a rental price can have disastrous consequences, and a method for determining the "right" price is clearly useful knowledge. And economics has indeed provided such a formula, one which, as the cliché goes, yields the only price that provides a "level playing field" for the incumbent and entrant firms. This pricing principle has already been adopted in a number of arenas and countries and is under (heated) discussion today before government regulators in virtually every industrialized nation of the world.

A MILLENNIUM OF ECONOMICS IN TWENTY MINUTES

Finally— On the Mystery of Capitalist Growth

Despite the importance of price, in many firms it is being replaced by *innovation* as the prime weapon of competition. Enterprises focus on improved products and increased productive efficiency as the most effective means to deal with their rivals.

This brings us to the issue of innovation and its role in the incredible growth record of capitalism. As Marx and Engels put the matter:

> The Bourgeoisie [i.e., capitalism] cannot exist without constantly revolutionizing the instruments of production. . . . Conservation of the old modes of production in unaltered form was, on the contrary, the first condition of existence for all earlier industrial classes. . . . The bourgeoisie, during its rule of scarce one hundred years has created more massive and more colossal productive forces than have all preceding generations together. . . . It has accomplished wonders far surpassing Egyptian pyramids, Roman aqueducts and Gothic cathedrals. . . . (Marx and Engels, *The Communist Manifesto*, 1847).

The growth of per-capita income and productivity in the free-market economies is so enormous that it is virtually impossible to comprehend. Since the beginnings of what we think of as *the* Industrial Revolution (which occurred around the time of George Washington), per-capita income and productivity have probably grown more than 2,000 percent in the U.S. In contrast, average growth rates of per-capita incomes were probably approximately *zero* for about one and a half thousand years before the Industrial Revolution. In 1776, even the wealthiest consumers in England, then the world's richest country, had only a half-dozen consumers' goods that had not been available in ancient Rome. These new products included (highly inaccurate) hunting guns, (highly inaccurate) clocks and watches, paper, window glass and very little else. Besides, Roman citizens enjoyed a number of amenities, such as hot baths and paved roads, that had long disappeared at the time of the American Revolution. In contrast, in the past century and a half, per-capita incomes in the typical capitalist economy have risen by amounts ranging from several hundred to several thousand percent. Recent decades have yielded an unmatched outpouring of new products and services, and the flood of new products continues. When a few years ago many of the world's communist regimes collapsed and when even the masters of China turned toward capitalist enterprise, surely part of the reason was their public's desire to participate in the growth miracle of the capitalist economies that Marx and Engels—those high priests of anticapitalist movements—were among the first economists to discern.

This leaves us with my parting mystery. Just what is it that is so different about the free-market system—the capitalist economy—that permits it to attain levels of prosperity and rates of growth unmatched at any time in human history under any other economic arrangements? The inventiveness of medieval China, the vast military construction of ancient Rome and the central planning of the recently defunct Soviet economies produced no such record. In the West, as recently as the seventeenth century, famines and mass starvation were common occurrences. But in today's industrialized countries, that is all incomprehensible ancient history.

Economists are increasingly devoting study to the explanation. And that, too, promises to provide useful knowledge, particularly to the more than two-thirds of the world's nations that are impoverished, and that continue to fall further behind the prosperous societies of which our nation continues to be a leader.

[15]

Journal of Economic Literature
Vol. XXVII (September 1989), pp. 1160–1162

Communication

The Optimal Cash Balance Proposition: Maurice Allais' Priority

By WILLIAM J. BAUMOL
Princeton University and New York University
and
JAMES TOBIN
Yale University

Maurice Allais' well-deserved Nobel Prize fortuitously brought to our attention an injustice inadvertently done him, to which we were unknowing accessories. For years the literature has ascribed to us the parentage of the transactions-cost model of optimal cash balances, with its notorious square-root formula derived from inventory theory.[1] *Recently, we found that its essence is contained in Allais' 1947* Economie et Intérêt *(pp. 238–41). As Jacob Viner used to say, no matter to what source the origin of an economic proposition is ascribed, someone is sure to come up with an earlier one.*

In any event, here is a translation of the pertinent passages. Allais describes the model in footnotes (11) and (12) to the following text (pp. 238–41):

One may note that the value of the benefits obtained from an additional [money] balance of 100 francs when the average balance is already 10,000 francs is much less than when that balance is zero. If, for example, a consumer carelessly invests all his funds he will almost certainly have trouble meeting his basic needs, of which some will perhaps be essential and for which he will not even have the time to have recourse to credit. Holding the mere sum of 100 francs will by itself avoid for him a thousand petty inconveniences by permitting him to have lunch, go home on the bus, buy a newspaper, give a tip, etc., and maintenance of this balance could provide him a yield of much higher value, say 500 francs, for example, representing a liquidity premium of 500 percent. In contrast, when his average balance is already high, say 10,000 francs, for example, an additional 100 francs would evidently have a very low value, of the order tenths or hundredths. (footnote 11)

It is then easy to see how the amount of the average balance held in equilibrium by an economic agent is determined. In effect, to the extent that the marginal liquidity premium ℓ_m of the average balance is higher than the pure interest rate, it in the agent's interest to keep his capital in the form of a money balance. This balance is only superficially "sterile," because in reality it brings, each time period, advantages equal in value to the liquidity premium. When, on the other hand, the liquidity premium becomes smaller than the pure interest rate, investment of disposable capital becomes more advantageous than keeping it in the form of money balance. *The optimal situation in equilibrium obtains when the size of the balance*

[1] The inventory-theoretic derivation goes back to 1925–27 when it was independently contributed by some half-dozen authors. This was described in Baumol (1952) on the basis of information obtained from Thomson Whitin who had first called the literature to Baumol's attention. On the early literature see Whitin (1953, chapter 2, esp. p. 32. footnote 4).

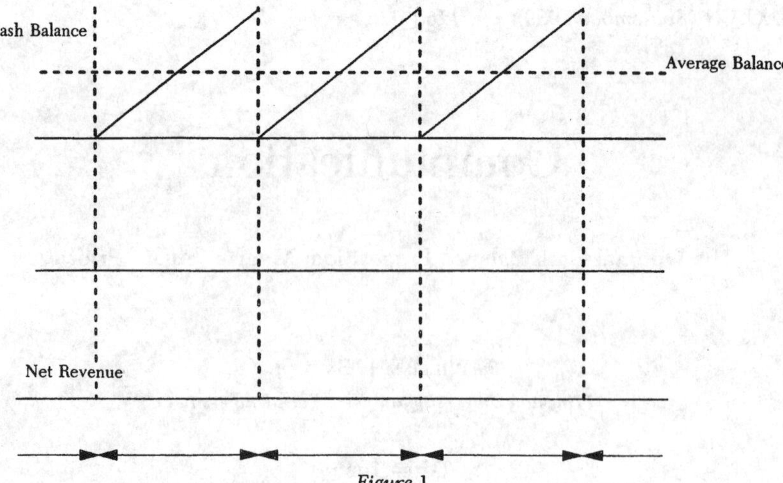

Figure 1

is such that its marginal liquidity premium is equal to the pure rate of interest [emphasis in original]. (footnote 12)

Thus, one sees that the service of money is advantageous but that no price is paid for it directly. Its cost comes *indirectly*, from gain forgone because of the loss of interest that would arise from investment of the money balance. Equilibrium occurs when the marginal value of liquidity, the service rendered by money, is precisely equal to the interest lost, and the money balance is increased or diminished as the marginal liquidity premium is higher or lower than the market interest rate.

The footnotes follow: We begin with Allais' footnote 11.

(11) It is in fact easy to make precise via a particular example these intuitive, but obviously rather fuzzy, ideas.

Consider, for example, an economic agent who has a continuous inflow of net receipts equal to R per unit of time (Figure 1) and suppose that he only invests the money received in this way at intervals of time of length T, when his balance reaches some certain value. In these circumstances the curve representing his balance as a function of time will be made up of a series of linear segments and will oscillate between zero and RT, so that its mean value will be

$$M = \frac{RT}{2}. \tag{1}$$

If one then used $F(V)$ to represent the [transactions] cost of investing an amount equal to V in value, the transactions cost per unit of time will be equal to $F(RT)/T$, that is, to $RF(2M)/2M$. If the average balance increases by ΔM, the cost saving per unit of time, which is equal to the marginal liquidity premium of the average balance, will equal the derivative of the quantity, so that one will have

$$\ell_m = -R\frac{d}{dM}\frac{F(2M)}{2M}. \tag{2}$$

If F is constant one then obtains

$$\ell_m = \frac{RF}{2M^2}, \tag{3}$$

a function decreasing in the average balance, M.

This extremely simple example has the advantage of making it easy to understand how things work out and of showing how a rigorous and general theory of liquidity can be constructed.

Here we proceed to Allais' footnote 12.

(12) In the example of note (11) the balance, M_E, held in equilibrium is determined naturally by the relation

$$-R\frac{d}{dM}\frac{F(2M)}{2M}=i. \quad (4)$$

It is, as a matter of fact, easy to derive this relationship directly. Let C be the amount of capital held by the agent under consideration. At the end of each period, T, one has

$$\Delta C = iTC_0 + RT - F(RT), \quad (5)$$

where C_0 represents the capital held at the beginning of period T. This relation yields

$$\frac{\Delta C}{T} = iC_0 + R - R\frac{F(2M)}{2M}. \quad (6)$$

One may be tempted to use the rate $\Delta C/T$ as a first approximation to the derivative dC/dT, but such an approximation amounts to the assumption that the income R is invested in a continuous manner, whereas in fact it is invested only discontinuously. This assumption would attribute to dC too high a figure for the amount of interest earned on the balance during each period, T, an excess approximately equal to the product, iM, of its average value, M, and the market rate of interest, i. In fact, it is clear that one should write

$$\frac{dC}{dt} = iC + R - R\frac{F(2M)}{2M} - iM. \quad (7)$$

The optimal balance is then attained when capital accumulates most rapidly, that is to say, when the sum

$$R\frac{F(2M)}{2M} + iM \quad (8)$$

attains its minimum, a result that is realized when one sets

$$\frac{d}{dM}\left(R\frac{F(2M)}{2M} + iM\right) = 0. \quad (9)$$

In the case where F is a constant, the size of the balance is determined by the relation

$$\frac{RF}{2M^2} = i.$$

Thus, if R = 100,000 frs, F = 200 frs and i = 5%, one obtains M = 14,000 frs. One sees in this way that even an investment transactions cost that is relatively modest can imply a substantial value for the average balance. Because

$$\frac{M}{R} = \sqrt{\frac{F}{2iR}}$$

one sees that in the case considered the relationship of the average balance to annual income is weaker the higher is this income. This result continues to hold if F increases with income R, but less rapidly than the latter. This is a state of affairs that seems to prevail quite generally.

References

ALLAIS, MAURICE. *Economie et intérêt.* Paris: Imprimerie Nationale, 1947.

BAUMOL, WILLIAM J. "The Transactions Demand for Cash: An Inventory Theoretic Approach," *Quart. J. Econ.*, Nov. 1952, *66*, pp. 545–56.

TOBIN, JAMES. "The Interest-Elasticity of Transactions Demand for Cash," *Rev. Econ. Statist.*, Aug. 1956, *38*, pp. 241–47.

WHITIN, THOMSON M. *The theory of inventory management.* Princeton: Princeton U. Press, 1953.

Name index